Politicians are not born.
They are excreted.
CICERO,
51 B.C.

Factory Guys

Factory Guys is a work of pure fiction. A resemblance of any characters to real persons living or dead is coincidental, excepting a few well-known public figures, who, in the interest of authenticity, appear briefly as themselves. Certain corporate entities and government agencies are named herein, again in the interest of authenticity. Nothing appearing in the novel is intended to reflect on the activities or performance of these entities or agencies.

ISBN 0-9702412-0-8
LOC 00-105949

$24.95 US, $32.95 Canada
Ramm Press
PO Box 637
Saddle River, NJ 07458

PREFACE

The car business, like any other, has its own unique *patois,* an example of which is the appellation "factory guy(s)."

A factory guy is anybody who works for any of the car manufacturers, in whatever capacity, whether in sales, distribution, marketing, advertising, or even actual manufacturing. In short, a factory guy needn't ever have set foot in a factory to be so designated. And in fact, many factory guys wouldn't know an assembly plant from a coal-fired electric power plant.

Car dealers and their employees generally consider factory guys a cross to be borne, people to whom they must be nice, or at least civil, unlike such types as cold-calling stock brokers or telemarketers, on whom one can rudely hang up. Car dealers think factory guys don't know anything about the retail business, advertising, styling, product planning, option packaging, leasing and incentive programs, or how to generate customer satisfaction. In fact, car dealers generally think factory guys don't know anything about the car business at all.

For their part, factory guys generally feel that car dealers are characterized by the most inverse relationship between earnings and IQ of any group in the world.

Both groups doubtless would agree with H. L. Mencken's observation that all stereotypes are basically true.

* * *

Chapter 1

Premier Wu Chen Lieh idly watched the heavy, wet snowflakes blanketing Beijing in the afternoon twilight. His joints ached, as they always did at the onset of a winter storm. He sighed audibly and turned his attention once again to the economic report for the fiscal year, which showed an astonishing eight percent growth rate in GNP for the People's Republic, slightly short of the ten percent rate confidently predicted at the Party Congress the previous year, but still remarkable by any standard. What was even more remarkable to Wu was that, unlike the reports generated in earlier times, this report was accurate, perhaps even understated, since the communist bureaucracy really did not yet understand the intricacies of accurately gauging or even keeping track of China's burgeoning free-market activity.

As with all the older party leadership Wu found China's economic changes largely incomprehensible, even frightening, representing, as they did by their very success, a stark repudiation of Marxist dogma. Like many old men, Wu found himself doubting his most cherished values and assumptions. On the other hand, not unlike a man who had long resisted learning to drive a car, ridiculing it as an inefficient and wasteful device, then finding himself reveling in its power and speed, Wu found himself secretly enraptured with sitting at the control panel of the surging Chinese economic engine. He found himself actively thinking constantly about economic opportunities, how to exploit new markets, ways to enhance the economic as well as military power of the People's Republic. The plan, in outline form before him, was Wu's latest and most ambitious initiative to date. Maybe I should get a top hat and a big cigar, he chuckled, briefly picturing himself as a caricature of a capitalist tycoon.

Wu glanced at the wall clock, which showed five minutes till his meeting with China's Minister of Finance, Chiang Shu Peng, whom he considered a malleable ally at best, a toadying, goat-molesting, dung-eating party hack at worst. Chiang, never one to take the lead in anything (a generally uninspired but wise approach to leadership in the People's Republic), now also reveled in the successes of China's still largely experimental economic reforms. Wu had noticed with growing annoyance Chiang's artfully subtle attempts to remind him and other potentially useful members of the party leadership of his support of all successful reforms, all the while ignoring or downplaying his always equally noted reservations. Wu wondered momentarily if he should be making his proposal to Chiang at all, knowing that Chiang's responses would be carefully measured, qualified, and ultimately meaningless in terms of soliciting any truly valuable input. He sat staring at the falling snowflakes for a long moment, shrugged almost imperceptibly, and pulled his scribbled notes closer.

* * *

Sheridan "Sherry" Maxwell wrestled painfully, as he did practically every morning, with the decision of whether to get up to empty his bladder, filled with the runoff from eleven gin-tonics. He feared that once he arose he'd be unable to get back to sleep. To piss or not to piss, that is the question, thought Maxwell, as he stared at the ceiling through half-lidded eyes.

After perhaps fifteen minutes of carefully weighing the pros and cons, he finally arrived at the conclusion that he'd be unable to get back to sleep with the discomfort of his painfully distended bladder anyway. Having thus met and conquered the first major dilemma of his day, he slowly sat up and swung his feet to the floor, then rose and walked a bit unsteadily to the bathroom. He urinated noisily and copiously, then sidestepped to examine himself in the fly-specked bathroom mirror. His eyes were bloodshot and he had two days' worth of salt and pepper stubble on his face, which seemed to have aged rapidly in the two years since his abrupt and forced early retirement from Mazda Motor of America at the age of fifty-five. Sherry was among the many forlorn and often hopeless victims of corporate downsizing. Jesus, I look like shit, thought Sherry Maxwell, scarcely noticing that he also felt like shit, having long since forgotten what it was like to wake up without a hangover.

Having thus confirmed to himself, as he did every morning, that his dissipation was proceeding apace, Sherry walked into the so-called living room of his little house trailer, sat heavily on the couch, then remembered that running out of cigarettes the previous evening had occasioned his decision to finally go to bed. With the vague hope that his recollection was somehow a bit faulty, he picked up the flattened Marlboro pack, completely tore off the top and peered inside, finally upending the pack and shaking out the few remaining tobacco crumbs. He grunted unhappily, crumpled the empty pack and threw it angrily against the wall, then began searching through the overfilled glass ashtray on the battered coffee table for a suitably long cigarette butt. He located one, examined it, then wiped the ash off the filter on his stained and sodden T-shirt. He was about to light the two inch stub but then abruptly thought to himself, Christ Almighty, I'm acting like a goddam Bowery bum. The thought so shocked and disgusted him that he threw down the cigarette butt and jumped to his feet, the sudden exertion sending a shock wave of pain through his head. He lurched toward the bathroom, violently stubbing his toe on a coffee table leg. He fell back on the couch, howling with pain and holding his toe tightly. I gotta get hold of myself, he muttered through clenched teeth, resolving once again to try for the shower.

Thirty minutes later Sherry Maxwell, showered and shaved, was applying a bit of toilet paper to the persistently bleeding cut on his chin. His still wet gray hair was plastered tightly against his scalp, but he was clean-shaven, and other than the damage done to his chin by his shaky right hand, he looked fairly presentable.

He pulled on shorts and a golf shirt, then inserted his feet into a pair of leather sandals. He started to make the bed, but then realized it hadn't been changed in at least four months. He tore off the sheets and pillow cases, stood indecisively for a moment, then stuffed them into the little hall closet. I'll deal with that later, he told himself. Christ, I can't keep letting myself go like this, Sherry thought. He reflected guiltily that he owed that much to Nancy, his wife of thirty years, who had died of a stroke three years earlier.

He put on his sunglasses and stepped into the bright Key West sunshine, squinting uncomfortably in spite of the dark glasses. He took a deep breath, straightened up, and began walking the fifty yards to the 7-Eleven across the highway.

Five minutes later Maxwell, a carton of Marlboros under his arm, was sifting through the mail as he stood in front of his rusted and faded mailbox. As he walked back toward his trailer he tossed all the mail but the *Automotive News* into the trash barrel beside the little gravel sidewalk.

Back inside, feeling a bit winded and thirsty from his exertions in the hot Florida sunshine, Sherry noted that it was nearly eleven o'clock, late enough in the day to render a nice cold beer respectable. He went to the refrigerator, took out a cold Stroh's, and sat down on his threadbare couch to read the *Automotive News*, the only publication, in fact, that he ever read.

Maxwell glanced at the front page of the industry trade publication, hoping to spot the name of someone he knew in one of the lead stories. Lately he seemed to recognize fewer and fewer of the names that appeared in the automotive publication. He also began noting that the ages given of all the executives of the various companies seemed lower than he had ever remembered men in such positions as being. True to recent form, Sherry recognized nobody on the front page.

With a weary sigh of acknowledgement that his estrangement from the car business was becoming ever more distant, Sherry Maxwell turned to the employment classifieds, more to see what was going on and who was hiring than in any hope that he could find further employment in the industry. He scanned the classified pages quickly, looking down through the usual ads for district service and parts managers for the various established importers and domestic automakers. What he was really looking for was a position as a district sales manager, one of the many jobs available in the industry that required little or no specialized knowledge. He worried that a service rep might actually have to know something about cars and their mysterious innards, or that a parts rep would have to be able to know what all those strange part numbers meant. Sherry was fundamentally opposed to any job in which he might need specialized knowledge, or worse, get his hands dirty. After all, he had managed to make it through a long if not altogether fulfilling and satisfactory career without ever having to compromise this principle.

He was about to set aside the paper and get himself another beer when his eye caught a small ad for some outfit he'd never heard of, one Red Tiger Motor Company, headquartered in Chino, California.

DISTRICT SALES MANAGER, SOUTHEASTERN USA

If you're a knowledgeable, energetic self starter with a broad grounding in automotive retail and wholesale operations, who wants to join the fastest growing, most dynamic automotive importer, representing the largest nation in the world, send resume with salary requirements to: Human Resources Department, Red Tiger Motor Company, PO Box 6209, Chino, CA 91710

Maxwell of course saw himself as one whose qualifications fit the requirements in the personnel ad perfectly. Why, he'd even been a district sales manager in the southeastern US for two other companies before coming to Mazda, his final (thus far) stop on the way to oblivion. Sherry could already see himself being feted, taken to three-martini lunches, and generally welcomed by wealthy and successful auto dealers, many of whom would be eager to sign up for the Red Tiger franchise, whatever it might prove to be.

He'd been around long enough to know that auto dealers in general were notoriously bad judges of the probable success of a new company and that nearly all were more than willing to take on a new franchise, at least as long as the investment requirements weren't too stringent. This could ensure him at least two or three years of employment before either he or the company was fully found out. Plus, he knew Chino wasn't too far from LA, which was the last known domicile of his thirty-two year old son, whom he had not seen nor heard from since his wife's funeral.

Now as he sat looking at the ad, he began to wonder about the product line and its country of origin. Red Tiger? What could that mean? And what was the biggest country in the world? He speculated briefly that maybe it was South America, but then wondered if South America was a country. It was big, he was pretty sure. Africa? Naw, hell, that ain't a country, either, concluded Maxwell. Plus, he figured, there wasn't much advanced manufacturing in Africa that he knew of. Must be Russia or China or someplace like that, he thought. They could do it. After all, they make ships, tanks, and missiles. A car can't be too hard for people like that. He'd have another beer and then work out a resumé with pencil and paper, take it up to the local Kinko's in Key West and have it done up nice and professionally, and shoot it out to this outfit in California. He walked back into the bathroom and examined himself in the mirror. Despite living in the perpetually sunny Florida Keys, he was pale and decidedly unhealthy-looking, not the sort of energetic, dynamic appearance one would want to present to a prospective employer.

Abruptly, as if there were no time to lose, he strode briskly from the bathroom, down the hallway, and into the second bedroom, which served as a sort of all-purpose junk and storage area. It was still piled high with cardboard boxes and unused furniture, left over from his move from Gainesville eighteen months earlier. He stepped over an old chair and box of dated suits and sports jackets to retrieve the corroded aluminum and plastic lawn chair, lifted it from a pile of debris, and carried it out the front door, after stopping at the refrigerator to get the remainder of the six-pack of Stroh's. He set the chair up facing the morning sun, stripped to the waist, and sat down in the chair to drink his beer and plan his resume. A couple days of this and I'll look twenty years younger, he told himself hopefully.

* * *

Sid Burnside, president and CEO of Red Tiger Motor Company of North America, sat behind his cheap woodgrain composite board desk, grimly surveying the bare walls of his still undecorated and unfinished corner office. Red Tiger was occupying a relatively small thirteen thousand square foot office building in a low rent office park just south of Chino, California, hardly, Burnside thought bitterly, a proper headquarters for the soon-to-be newest Asian giant among automakers. But the Chinese refused to go any higher than nine bucks a foot for office space, leaving Burnside no choice but to move further out from LA, with its myriad Japanese automotive and electronic industry corporate headquarters. How the hell did they expect to be a serious player in the market working out of a hovel in Chino, Burnside fumed. The Chinese had no idea of the importance of image. Nobody, not the automotive press, the dealers, or even the prospective employees would take Red Tiger seriously when they saw that they were headquartered in something that looked appropriate to a used furniture outlet.

Burnside, in the sixty days since he'd come on board the fledgling North American distribution arm for The Long March People's Automobile Cooperative Manufacturing Company (mercifully renamed Red Tiger Motor Company for the US affiliate), had come to regard his

Chinese masters as maddeningly overbearing micro-managers, clearly regarding him as little more than a bothersome lower life-form, an unfortunate but necessary cost of doing business in the US. All purchases, from furniture down to office supplies, required a minimum of five competitive bids, which had to be submitted to Beijing for approval.

Curiously, the one area in which the Chinese showed no interest in meddling was personnel selection, other than to insist that they could see no immediate need for him to have a personal secretary. They did ask to see the personnel ad he was running in the *Automotive News,* but beyond that seemed content to let Burnside make his own selections, at least so long as he didn't try to exceed the salary maximums they'd grudgingly approved.

Burnside sat pondering this strange contradiction in their behavior as he grimly surveyed the stack of envelopes on his desk, containing the responses to his personnel ad. Thus far the results had not been particularly encouraging. He could ascertain from the lengthy and varied career histories of the various respondents that most were aging has-beens, never-weres, and assorted ne'er-do-wells, the sort who bounced from start-up to start-up, to be discarded when the company either foundered or their shortcomings were clearly revealed.

Burnside sat staring indecisively at the stack of unopened envelopes for several seconds, grunted, then reached for the topmost letter in the pile, once again reflecting angrily that a CEO of his stature, by right, should have a secretary to open the mail and screen resumes. He ripped open the envelope with a pencil, skipped the cover letter, and briefly scanned Sherry Maxwell's resume. Hummph, he snorted disgustedly, noting that Maxwell's resume was entirely too typical of the chaff he'd been getting in his response to his ads. Started with a domestic, then jumped ship to join an upstart import in the early seventies, then back to AMC, then a stint with Volkswagen of America, then to Mazda in the late eighties. Burnside noted that Maxwell hadn't worked in two years, rightly assuming that he'd been retired early from Mazda, though as with all such resumes, it described the last two year's worth of activity as "consulting." Bullshit, he thought, figuring a more realistic description might be "sales consultant" in a Burger King. "Hi! Can I take your order?"

He was about to crumple the resumé and toss it into the trash basket (with no secretary Burnside wasn't about to take it upon himself to mail out acknowledgements of receiving the resumés), when he noticed that

Maxwell lived in Florida, and further, that he didn't have a Spanish sur-
name. He sat reflectively for a moment, considering that he'd eventually
need a district sales manager for the Southeast, and further that he'd probably not have to pay any relocation expense, and finally, that he didn't
need any grief from EEOC if some taco-chomper applied for the job and
then sued if he didn't get it. He could always point out that Maxwell had
applied first. Hell, this stiff might even protect me from an age discrimination suit, thought Burnside, raising his eyebrows and shrugging.

* * *

Wu Chen Lieh fumed as he read the report from the Ministry of Foreign
Trade and Economic Cooperation, describing the progress, or more correctly, the lack thereof, of Red Tiger Motor Company getting started in the
US market. In the eleven months since the decision had been reached to
invade the US market with China's doughty little Red Whippet four cylinder family sedan, there had been nothing but explanations, excuses really,
from MOFTEC on the difficulties of readying a car for export into the US.
The main obstacles dealt with modifying the cars to pass America's
exhaust emission and safety standards, both of which were merely, in Wu's
mind, political constructs to keep the Chinese from competing in the US
market.

Air pollution, snorted Wu. Here the Americans were riding around in
these huge so-called sport utility vehicles, consuming vast quantities of
fuel, and no doubt belching forth great clouds of deadly pollutants. Then
there were these ridiculous airbags! What sort of piss-guzzling idiots
could conceive of such a thing, thought Wu angrily. Things that blow up
in your face, tearing the heads off children and deafening the survivors!

As he sat seething indignantly he wondered for the hundredth time
how a people as lazy and stupid as the Americans could have gotten so
much money to throw around. Marxist dogma, of course, held that they
got it by exploiting other less fortunate peoples, though Wu could never
get it quite straight in his mind exactly how this process was supposed to
work. After all, here he was, literally begging to be exploited, proposing to
sell the Red Whippet—produced with the labor of political dissidents and
other wreckers—for the equivalent of a mere five thousand US dollars.
And the incomprehensible fools were throwing obstacles in his way!

Wu, used to the processes of a command economy, was not a man to be thwarted or even contradicted. What we need here, he thought, is a bit of publicity, as the capitalists would say. He buzzed his secretary, who immediately entered his office holding her steno pad before her expectantly.

* * *

Vice-President Nate Garmin looked up from the remaindered copy of his book, EARTH OUT OF BALANCE, which he was signing for admirer Ted Kaczynski. He finished, then tossed the book onto a huge stack of similarly remaindered and autographed copies, awaiting distribution to visiting dignitaries. His secretary stood in the doorway, patiently waiting to be acknowledged. "Uh, yes, Cassie?"

"Mr. Vice-President, Ms. Twombly is here to see you." Ms. Twombly, head of the EPA, was a thirty-six year old former sixth grade teacher with a PhD. in elementary education.

Garmin looked up, giving his half-lidded smile, mouth agape. "Uh, hi, Penny."

Penelope Twombly, as she did every time she looked at the vice-president, couldn't help reflecting on his dim-witted visage, which was compounded by his every utterance. Between his appearance and his southern drawl, Nate Garmin had always struck her as the likely offspring of Jed Clampett.

It wasn't just that Nate Garmin, a former representative from Alabama, *seemed* stupid. That was self-evident to anybody who'd ever watched him in person or on TV. No, rather it was that Nate Garmin *was* stupid, unbelievably, irredeemably, colossally stupid, a man who stumbled through his political career surrounded by speechwriters, ghostwriters, spinmeisters, elocution coaches, teleprompter technicians, and most recently, Alpha male image-makers. Plus, of course, a coterie of clinging sycophants, always willing to testify that Nate—a Harvard graduate, to the acute embarrassment of his alma mater—was the Sir Isaac Newton of Our Time.

The voters generally bought it, reasoning that anybody who seemed as stupid as Garmin couldn't succeed, even in politics, unless he were actually brilliant. This was not an altogether unreasonable assumption, since the average voter had to get through life on his own without the extraordinary level of support afforded Nate Garmin. Of course, a few unreconstructed cynics muttered among themselves and occasionally in op-ed columns that Garmin clearly was a slack-jawed dolt, despite the fabrication released by Garmin's handlers through the *Washington Post* that his IQ was a strong if not spectacular 134. These unkind observations, however, were normally dismissed by the mainstream press as politically motivated.

Penny Twombly, though a rabid supporter of the administration, fully realized that the veep was none too bright, though she regarded his motives and agenda, if he truly could be said to have any of his own, as pure. Purity of motive and agenda, without regard to intellect, skill, experience, or morality, was paramount to Penny, who was not exactly long on qualifications for her post, either.

Only the previous week she'd had to have it explained to her that the world wasn't running out of water, that the amount of water was a constant and could only change form. "But what about the water used in irrigation?" she'd demanded suspiciously. "And what about the water that ends up in the sewers? I suppose they expect us to drink *that!*" Nate Garmin, who'd been a party to the discussion, thought her points were extremely telling.

But now Penny was about to rush in to present the Vice-President with a truly exciting bit of news, one that she knew he'd respond to with energy and enthusiasm, for it proved beyond all doubt what she, Nate Garmin and all their supporters had claimed all along.

"Nate, have you heard the news from Beijing this morning?" she asked, clasping her hands to her chest. Before Garmin could respond she rushed on, "Oh, it's simply incredible, wonderful, it's what you've been claiming all along, all *along!* This could be the keystone we've been looking for for your industrial policy!"

Nate Garmin's mouth gaped further. "Huh?"

"It's about global warming, air pollution, *everything!*"

"Huh?"

"The Chinese have done it!"

"Huh? What'd they do?"

"They've invented a car that gets seventy miles to the gallon and creates only twenty percent of the pollution of today's cars. And it'll be available in the US market in a few months!"

"Why, that's fantastic, just amazing," said Nate Garmin. "Gosh, imagine that."

"Think of it, Nate. When all the other automakers have been complaining about not being able to meet higher standards, the Chinese have gone and done it. It just proves what's possible with a focused industrial policy, where the government shows the way."

"Gosh, that's right, Penny. I get so mad when I think of all the great things we've developed under government supervision. I mean, like your agency, for example, or the IRS, or OSHA, or EEOC, or any other things that make life better for Americans and protect them from each other. Not enough people appreciate this or understand what we've done for them. And I've always known we could make better cars if the government forced people to do it." He paused, frowning. "Uhh, Penny, how much does this car cost?"

"That's the best part, Nate. The Chinese say they can sell it for only five thousand dollars!"

"You're kidding. Does that include airconditioning and white-walls?"

"Well, I'm not sure what the price includes, but I think it proves that the automakers have been ripping off the American people and lying to us as well!"

"You're darn right, Penny! Boy, this really makes me mad." He paused again. "Hey, you don't mean those Chinese on Taiwan, do you?"

"Of course not. I said Beijing. That's on Mainland China."

"Oh, that's right. I was worried for a minute that we'd have to let the Chinese on Taiwan bring their cars in here. They're against everything we stand for. Like, somebody told me their tax rate's only like fifteen percent."

He paused again to organize his thoughts, such as they were. "And we're trying to be friends with the Chinese. I mean the *big* Chinese. I mean, uh, the Chinese in the big China. Oh, I'm so glad this is their car instead of those people on Taiwan."

"Oh, so am I," said Penny Twombly, her voice breaking. "Oh, this is such a great day!"

She clapped her hands and gave a little hop.

* * *

The cause of the Vice-President's and Penny Twombly's gleeful excitement was a press release issued jointly by the Chinese State Development

Planning Commission and the State Economic and Trade Commission. It was short, to the point, and read as follows:

May 22—

The People's Republic of China today announces the development of a new generation family-size car, which independent tests indicate can achieve over seventy miles per gallon of low octane gasoline and which emits only 20% of the pollutants currently allowed under U.S. Federal, California, and New York standards. The same tests also confirm that the vehicle offers fully competitive performance with contemporary American and Japanese designs.

The car, which would fall under the U.S. government classification of "compact," achieves these milestone performance standards while fully equipped with options most commonly selected by American consumers. While the vehicle continues to make use of the internal combustion engine, Chinese engineers, unrestrained and unindoctrinated with conventional technologies and approaches, have been able to refine this familiar and easily manufactured power source to bring it to altogether new standards of pollution-free performance and efficiency.

The engineers have also introduced new standards in process engineering, tooling, and production techniques, which will allow the vehicle to be brought to market at a cost of approximately five thousand U.S. dollars at time of introduction, which is expected to be within six to eight months.

END

The news was greeted with unrestrained enthusiasm by most of the mainstream media in the United States, who like Nate Garmin and Penny Twombly, felt certain that their deepest suspicions regarding American business leaders in general and automotive executives in particular were thus vindicated. Dan Rather reported grimly that, "The Chinese bombshell has rocked the other automakers of the world..." Tom Brokaw intoned, "US automakers are scrambling for explanations..." And finally, Bernard Shaw, choking with indignation, commented, "apparently, the Chinese, without billions invested in obsolete and inefficient technologies, have managed to do what auto industry executives claimed couldn't be done..."

Members of the established automotive press, who knew a thing or two about how a car works, were less enthusiastic. Brock Yates and Pat Bedard of *Car and Driver,* upon reading the press release, responded with identical comments. "Bullshit!"

Throughout the world, from Detroit to Hiroshima, the boardrooms of the auto industry resounded with groans, curses, and imprecations hurled at the Chinese for precipitating the inevitable calls for drastically tightened emission and fuel consumption regulations, congressional and parliamentary inquiries, and the coming flood of hostile sound bites directed at them from politicians whose technical acumen was limited to the workings of a swizzle stick.

* * *

Sid Burnside was just returning from his lunch hour, which in the past several weeks had gradually elongated from thirty minutes—which Burnside had hoped would impress his Chinese masters—to upwards of three hours recently, after Burnside had come to realize that the management of The Long March People's Cooperative Automobile Manufacturing Company didn't seem to pay any attention to his comings and goings. They seemed quite content to leave voice-mail messages and faxes and never seemed to wonder or inquire as to his whereabouts.

At first Burnside had been curious and inquisitive about the company's timetable in getting the Red Whippet certified through EPA and NHTSA for sale in the US. His queries of his Chinese masters were met with vague responses to the effect that "we're working on it," or "you'll be informed when the time comes." They didn't seem concerned that the task of pulling together the US distribution company was linked to the timing assumptions on getting the car ready for sale.

After a few weeks of growing de-sensitized by their apparent indifference, Burnside eventually came to share it and became content to do little more than collect his $120,000 annual salary and respond to occasional queries from Beijing.

As he walked into his office, just a bit unsteadily from the two outsize Manhattans he'd consumed during his health salad lunch, Burnside noticed that the fax machine had spit out a single page message of some sort. He almost ignored it, assuming it to be the menu he'd requested from a nearby Mexican restaurant that morning, but then finally walked over to the machinc, leaned heavily and a bit shakily on the desk for support, and began to read.

A moment later Burnside had finished the press release, his emotions going from rage that he hadn't been consulted or even advised, to elation at the substance of the announcement and all it might imply for the success of Red Tiger (and his future status), and finally to apprehension that his bosses probably were fabricating an absurd falsehood.

Burnside sat heavily in his swivel chair and re-read the fax. What the hell could the Chinks know about cars that the Japs don't, he wondered. He simply assumed, as did many people in the car business, that if the Japanese didn't know something about automotive technology, then nobody else did either, being completely convinced of their technical and manufacturing invincibility. He decided to send a return fax to Beijing to request confirmation and details.

Two hours later he was reading the answer to his query, tersely advising him that the announcement was correct in its entirety and that he'd be receiving further details shortly. Hummph, grunted Burnside, that's just peachy. His phone mail already had messages from *Automotive News, The Detroit News,* the *New York Times, Road and Track,* and several smaller publications. He decided merely to confirm what the press release indicated, embellishing it a bit with the addition of the highly confidential nature of the Chinese technological developments, which would at least make it appear that he might have known what was going on.

* * *

Sherry Maxwell lay sleeping on his threadbare couch, snoring loudly as he slept off his lunch, which had consisted of two small bananas, three Oreo cookies, and four sixteen ounce cans of Old Milwaukee, which had been on sale at the local package store. His nose was white, covered with Noxzema as an antidote to the sunburn he'd suffered after failing asleep in his old beach chair, while trying to get some color in preparation for his hoped for interview with Red Tiger Motor Company.

He was awakened by the insistent ringing of the wall phone in the little kitchenette. He cursed his lack of a portable phone as its insistent buzz raised him from unconsciousness, to semi-consciousness, to a fuzzy-tongued full awareness. He staggered to his feet and lurched unsteadily into the kitchenette, lunged for the phone, and caught it by the fifth ring.

"Hello?" croaked Sherry Maxwell, cleared his throat, then more distinctly announced, "This is Sherry Maxwell."

Jesus, thought Sid Burnside, sounds like I caught the bastard still in the sack, noting that it was two in the afternoon in Florida. But he managed to conceal his irritation and sound ebullient in his greeting to his distinctly heavily breathing applicant. "Mr. Maxwell, this is Sid Burnside from Red Tiger Motor Company in Chino. How ya doin' today?"

"Just fine, Mr. Burnside. You caught me looking through my mail out on the patio."

Sherry tried to take a deep breath as quietly as possible. "Everybody calls me Sherry, by the way."

"All right, Sherry it is," replied Burnside, not inviting Maxwell to use his first name. "I see you've been with other imports during your career. How much experience do you have in dealer development, would you say?" Burnside was referring to the process of selecting and signing up new dealers, which would occupy much of the field reps' time as the company moved toward product introduction.

"Oh, I've had a lot of experience in that area. I must've appointed close to a hundred dealers in my time, mostly for Subaru and Mazda. I had to do all the financial analysis, sales forecasts, facility requirements, all that stuff."

"Have you ever worked in the retail end of the business?" asked Burnside.

"I worked as a sales manager in a Ford store a few years back," lied Maxwell, knowing there was really no easy way for Burnside to check up on it. "I only did it for about six months. That's why it wasn't on my resumé."

Burnside grunted non-committally. He placed great stock in retail experience, having once worked as a salesman in a Chevrolet dealership shortly after graduating from college. He felt that it provided insight into "how dealers think," though in truth the average salesman didn't see enough of your typical dealership owner to know how, or even *if,* he thought. "Well, that's good. I always like people with retail experience, gives you a broader perspective."

The phone interview went on in like vein for another three minutes, with Burnside instructing Maxwell to come on out the following week for a personal interview. Suddenly realizing that he'd overlooked a vital point,

Sherry finally asked Burnside, "Uh, just what kind of cars does Red Tiger make?"

"Don't you read the papers? Go out and get a current copy of *Autoweek*, Sherry. They got a story on the whole thing. They get fantastic mileage, put out almost zero emissions, and cost five grand."

After they'd hung up, Maxwell found himself growing excited. Hey, this could be the break I've been waiting for all my life, he told himself. The claimed low emissions didn't register with Maxwell. He doubted that anybody, not the dealers, Red Tiger Motors, nor especially the customers gave a good rat's ass about the exhaust emissions. The price and the mileage, that's what mattered to everybody. Fantasies of being entertained, feted, and even bribed by dealer candidates for the Red Tiger franchise danced in his head.

This calls for a celebration, thought Maxwell. He decided to take a ride down to the local package store and splurge on a quart bottle of 101 proof Wild Turkey and a case of Heineken for chasers. I won't be drinking the cheap stuff any more!

* * *

As Sherry Maxwell was joyously contemplating a prosperous future, replete with quality liquors and beer, Premier Wu Chen Lieh was confronting, for the first time in his life, a clearly aroused and determined Chiang Shu Peng, his Minister of Finance.

"In the name of your father and mother, Wu, what were you thinking?" Chiang demanded angrily. "How are we to maintain any credibility at all with the trading nations, with you making such outlandish claims? The Red Whippet is inferior to the Japanese cars of thirty years ago, we all know that. We'll be a laughingstock. Nothing we say will ever be believed again. As Minister of Finance I am responsible for the success of our commercial endeavors."

Wu waved his had dismissively. "The Red Whippet is still a good value at five thousand dollars. Why, I'm told that in America the average car costs over twenty thousand dollars. Its other shortcomings will be overlooked when one considers the price."

"You do not understand, Comrade. Unless the Red Whippet can pass the American government standards, we cannot sell it in America. Even if the citizens of their country are clamoring for it, they cannot buy it if their government forbids it."

"Hah, and I thought America was supposed to be a democracy," retorted Wu. "Well, no matter, the Red Whippet will pass their standards easily enough, and then nobody will remember our claims for fuel mileage or low pollution."

"How can you be so sure? I'm told that we cannot even come close to meeting their exhaust emission standards with production vehicles. Our production processes are not yet good enough to create the quality controls we need to do it. It is only by accepting the help of the Japanese that we will have access to the technologies we need."

"Never! We will never accept the joint projects proposed by Toyota and Honda!" said Wu, his voice rising. "The Red Whippet must be all Chinese, designed by Chinese engineers, built by Chinese workers. We will not try to enter to the US market with something the Japanese designed and helped us make. To do so would signal a great failure for socialism. It would be a grave insult to the Revolution, to the Chinese people, who have sacrificed so much to come this far."

"We must be practical, Comrade," said Chiang in a more conciliatory tone. "We must face reality. One day China will be a technological and industrial power of the first rank. But until that day, we must learn to walk before running. If the Japanese are foolish enough to extend us help in competing with them, we would be very much greater fools not to accept their assistance."

"You are thinking too much like an unreconstructed capitalist, Chiang. But there is an element of truth in what you say. But do not worry. Whatever happens with their government tests, I am quite sure that their government will be most accommodating in allowing us to sell the Red Whippet in America." He smiled thinly and, Chiang thought, a bit mysteriously. Chiang was about to point out that the American government agencies allowed no special dispensation to American companies in meeting the standards, but in the end he decided that he'd perhaps risked enough political capital for one day. He nodded briefly, excused himself ritually, and left.

* * *

17

Sid Burnside was in a state of considerable agitation regarding the fax from the general manager of The Long March People's Cooperative Automotive Manufacturing Company, which he'd received less than a week after Wu's bombshell press release. For the past several days Burnside had been fielding calls from various publications, networks, and news agencies seeking to get some additional detail on the Chinese claims for the soon to be introduced Red Whippet sedan. The vehicle had yet to be furnished to either EPA or NHTSA for emission or crash testing. Nor had the Chinese submitted any preliminary supporting data for their claims, leaving Burnside to provide little more elaboration to the press than to say that, "our claims for vehicle performance are fully supportable, as U.S. government agency tests will confirm in the near future."

Now in the midst of all the hoopla, he'd been informed that a delegation of Chinese executives and officials, numbering some twenty-two men and women, would be arriving at LA International within two days, expecting a full briefing from him on his progress to date in getting the infrastructure established for the US affiliate company, Red Tiger Motors.

Burnside went from complacency, to irritation, to panic in the time it took him to read the unwelcome fax from the factory. Jesus H. Christ, thought Burnside, *what* progress? I haven't even got a secretary, let alone a management staff, or any plans. In a few minutes he began to calm down, as he remembered the marketing paper a consulting company had put together for him when he was in on the start-up of Hyundai in the U.S. market. He still had a copy of it at home. He could just get it out, dust it off, and. substitute the name Red Tiger for Hyundai throughout, change any dates to the present, and update any supporting industry sales data for use with all the requisite charts and graphs. He could get the whole thing done at Kinko's overnight! Just like in the commercials. What the hell, the Chinese have never done anything like this before, he told himself. He'd dazzle 'em with smoke, mirrors, and pure unadulterated bullshit (and see to it that the humorless commie bastards were well-fed and possibly well-laid in the process), and, hopefully, they'd go home all smiles. It was the American way!

Amid the preparations and attendant excitement, Burnside completely forgot about his appointment with Sherry Maxwell, scheduled for the same day as the arrival of the Chinese delegation.

* * *

Chief of Powertrain Engineering for The Long March People's Cooperative Automotive Manufacturing Company, Chen Wan Le, looked dispiritedly at the little 1500cc four cylinder engine spread out on the table before him. The engine had been disassembled and laid out precisely, as if for a photograph, the head and cylinder block at the head of the table, with all internal components, valves, pistons, rods, bearings, etc., spread out below. This particular Red Whippet engine had just been through a non-stop 75,000km durability run, the results of which had not been encouraging.

At 48,000km (roughly 35,000 miles) the engine had begun using oil. At 55,000 km the dynamometer tests showed it to be down on power, with excessive cylinder leakage. At 65,000km oil pressure began dropping from excessive bearing wear, and by the conclusion of the test sequence the engine, though still running, had several bearing knocks and, in general, sounded, as one candid but remarkably incautious test driver noted, like a clothes dryer full of walnuts. In addition, by the end of test the engine was emitting one hundred thirty times the U.S. Federal limits for unburned hydrocarbons (HC), seventy-four times the limit for carbon monoxide (CO), and eleven times the maximum allowable nitrous oxide (NOx) emissions.

All in all, as Chen noted unhappily, this was not very far along in the development cycle for a car supposed to go on sale in the U.S. export market in less than a year. Everything about the Red Whippet, under Chen's direction, had been designed for cost containment and ease of manufacture. The engine used only three main bearings, rather than the five more normally specified for modern four cylinder engines. The cylinder block was cast of a soft iron alloy to ease cylinder boring and prolong the life of the machine tools. The crankshaft was a poorly balanced and crude casting, with the bearing journals so haphazardly machined and finished that several different size bearing shells had to be available to the assemblers to ensure a reasonable fit. There was no safety glass in the car, and in fact no safety devices of any description, save front lap belts.

The Red Whippet, in its entirety, was designed for the home market, where its users were deemed lucky to have at their disposal a motor vehicle of any description. Complainers and malcontents simply had no alternatives. Besides, as Chen was fond of pointing out, and as was the slogan and focal point of the Red Whippet's promotional literature, the car was "easy to build, and easy to rebuild!"

19

Everything had been going very well, thought Chen bitterly. Then that fool of a fool Wu got the idea that he was going to conquer the U.S. market with the Red Whippet, sell it to people who were utterly helpless when something broke down or failed. Chen, like Wu, once again wondered how a people as helpless as the Americans wound up with so much money, and again like Wu, idly wondered how such a nation so successfully exploited more resourceful, harder working peoples.

Realizing that nothing productive would come of such idle ruminations, Chen pulled his mind back to the problem of somehow upgrading the Red Whippet, in very little time, to a point at which it would be saleable in the United States. While failure would no longer get him an appointment with the district firing squad, it would mean the end of the comfort and relative affluence accorded a high level industrial manager, and very likely his very own spot in the hottest, dirtiest place in The Long March People's Cooperative Automotive Manufacturing Company assembly plant.

* * *

While Chen was unhappily contemplating the improbability of readying the Red Whippet for sale in the U.S. anytime soon, Sherry Maxwell was once again confronting the nagging issue presented daily by his bladder, this time distended by his celebratory conduct of the previous evening. As he lay in bed he reflected dejectedly that a premium liquor hangover, all theories to the contrary notwithstanding, was no less wretched than one occasioned by his usual brands.

An hour, two cups of instant coffee, a shower and a shave later, Sherry was once again ready to confront the rigors of preparing for his interview with Red Tiger Motors. He planned to go to a nearby travel agency for his round trip ticket to LA, which, he'd been assured by Sid Burnside, would be reimbursed by Red Tiger. Then he'd take a couple of suits down to the cleaners, buy two new shirts, maybe a new tie, see the local hair stylist, and generally make himself presentable.

Maxwell, in truth, had always been a rather fastidious dresser and was capable of projecting a fairly impressive executive image, at least until he was drawn into any conversation that went beyond the bounds of small talk. He also had the good sense to neither drink nor smoke during the interview process and planned to "train" for this particular ordeal in the days ahead leading to his interview. I'll see how long I can make it today without a cigarette, he told himself, then decided to postpone the test and instead lit up and dragged deeply.

Next, he decided to go back through the last six months' issues of the *Automotive News,* which were scattered randomly throughout the little trailer, and see if he could pick up any useful knowledge of industry trends, hopefully to be displayed tellingly in his interview with Burnside.

And hour later, however, he hadn't seemed to assimilate any profound insights while perusing the back issues of *Automotive News,* other than to note that light trucks now comprised over half the total market. He decided to try to develop an original sounding theory as to why the market was ready for the Red Whippet, something beyond the patently obvious contention that *any* market would be interested in a car that cost five grand and got seventy miles to the gallon.

Sherry had been around the car business long enough to be vaguely aware that most marketing types won their spurs not by seizing on the obvious and developing strategies to capitalize on it. Rather, they showcased their savvy by devising approaches that only a highly trained marketing type could see and develop. This often led to such celebrated, award-winning disasters as Nissan's intriguing but weird and incomprehensible "Mr. K" campaign, featuring a mute Japanese octogenarian smiling inscrutably into the camera. The advertising campaign was, of course, not abandoned merely due to the resultant plummeting sales, but rather when it came to the unwelcome attention of Jay Leno and David Letterman.

Now Sherry sat concentrating on coming up with some sort of theme that would impress Mr. Burnside with his marketing acumen. "Drive a Red Whippet. The planet will love you for it!" Hmm. Not bad, he thought, maybe a bit too long. "The Red Whippet makes the dinosaurs last longer!" Or, "The Red Whippet, fossil-friendly and cute, too!" Yeah, thought Maxwell, something like that, that's the ticket. We got a cheap car people can feel good about buying. He got out a yellow legal pad to record his creative gems, lest they be forgotten.

* * *

Chapter 2

Vice President Nate Garmin was practically trembling with excitement. By God, this was *it!* The announcement of China's apparent Great Leap Forward in automotive technology had spurred his thinking toward the development of a comprehensive national industrial policy, where the government would show the way, in which farseeing thinkers would replace the random wastefulness of the markets. He sat looking at the sheet of paper on which he'd written the proposed names of the industrial committee, which he saw as a first step to national planning. Garmin saw the committee staffed by labor leaders, economists, ecological groups, and even a few corporate CEOs, providing, of course, that they'd been generous campaign contributors. He mentally added a few actors and rock stars to the proposed august body, reasoning that they'd give the concept appeal and credibility with the youth of America. Oh, God, this is gonna be great, thought Nate Garmin joyfully. Now what he needed was a catchy name that formed a good acronym, something that communicated the whole idea and that people could remember easily.

Committee for Industrial Planning and Review. CIPR? He mouthed the word. Kipper? Or is it sipper?

Policy Review Industrial Committee. PRIC. Not bad, thought Garmin.

American Industrial Development Studies. AIDS. Boy, this one's really good, Garmin told himself. He thought for a moment, then frowned. Aw, heck, somebody's already got that one. Gee, I hope all the good ones aren't taken, he thought, momentarily a little let down.

A few moments later, however, Garmin knew he'd finally hit on it. Diversified Industrial Liaison and Development Office. That's gotta be it, Nate Garmin told himself. It's about planning and development, it's about diversity, and liaison implies a partnership between industry and government! "Hey, Cassie," he shouted through the door to his secretary, "get Penny Twombly on the phone right away!"

* * *

While Nate Garmin was eagerly anticipating a return call from Penny Twombly, Sid Burnside was frenziedly ripping into old boxes of files in his basement, looking for the twelve year old Hyundai marketing study, which he hoped to update into a similar document for Red Tiger Motor Company for presentation to the visiting Chinese dignitaries. Jesus, thought Burnside, I know the stupid thing's here somewhere, ripping the masking tape from another packing box. He knew he hadn't discarded it, regarding it, as he did, the high point of his career. In truth, Burnside's involvement in the study was limited to commissioning it and signing the $58,000 check to the consulting company. To be fair, he had skimmed it briefly before making the elaborate slide presentation to the Koreans and the other members of the American management team, who congratulated him heartily on the caliber of the study and its keen insights.

Finally Burnside found what he was looking for. He still had several copies of the seventy-eight page handout, along with all the 35mm slides. He paused, suddenly frowning. The text would be easy enough to reproduce with a scanner, then edit and update, but the color slides could be a problem. He dropped the box, raced upstairs for a phone book, and began flipping through it looking for a video production company. Ten minutes later he'd been assured by a confident sounding young man that he could indeed have new slides made within eight hours, assuming he had all the material assembled and ready to go. "You'll have it tomorrow morning," Burnside said. "And there's another three hundred bucks in it for ya if it's done right and on-time." I'm gonna make it, he told himself happily.

That night Burnside went to work editing and updating the long-winded marketing study, carefully deleting the name Hyundai wherever it appeared and adjusting industry sales figures, dates, and other items that might have revealed a lack of originality in the presentation.

Had Burnside shown a keener interest in American politics he'd doubtless have noticed the reference to the Reagan administration's generally free trade policies in the introductory paragraphs of the study. But he was in a hurry and was specifically looking for numbers, dates, the name Hyundai and the like.

* * *

Lin Cho Hsin, the president of the Long March People's Cooperative Automotive Manufacturing Company, lit a Pall Mall (another of those wonderful American products to which the privileged elite in China had access), inhaled deeply, held it in, then exhaled loudly, enveloping Zhu Fei, general sales manager of Long March's newly formed export division, in a cloud of blue smoke. Zhu fanned the air pointedly with his hand, looked at Lin narrowly, and asked, "What is the purpose of this meeting, Comrade? I am very busy with our preparations for our visit to America to check on the progress of our American affiliate company. As you know, nothing is more important at this juncture than to have our organization ready to sell the Red Whippet in America."

Zhu smiled inwardly, assuming that it would be many months, perhaps several years, before the Red Whippet would be ready for sale in the United States. But like any manager of a Chinese state-owned industry, he knew that appearances, fantasies in many cases really, had to be upheld. All projects always had to be reported as on schedule, deadlines, on paper at least, met. For this reason he had not been particularly concerned about the specifics of what was going on in the United States with Red Tiger Motor Company or its sole employee and CEO, Sid Burnside.

Zhu only that morning had been shown a copy of the highly confidential report, procured by one of his sources in Product Engineering, of the Red Whippet's dismal performance in its durability test cycle. As with all such state-supervised enterprises, the ultimate failures would be explained away as due either to natural phenomena (earthquakes, floods, and droughts were always convenient explanations) or, should these prove too implausible a fit for the actual circumstances, by the actions of counterrevolutionaries and other "wreckers." In the latter instance the usual suspects were rounded up and executed or imprisoned.

In any event, Zhu figured he'd be able to maintain his position for quite a while before having to worry about producing any tangible results.

It was poor Chen in Engineering who walked the tightrope over the snakepit at this point.

Lin regarded him coldly, fully aware that Zhu felt totally secure in his assumption that there would be no Red Whippet fit for sale in the United States for the foreseeable future, all bombastic pronouncements to the contrary notwithstanding. "Well, I am glad that you take your responsibilities so seriously, comrade. Nothing would be more disastrous, and I might add, embarrassing, than to find the workers and the plant ready to turn out these fine products like so many rice balls, only to find that we don't have the infrastructure in place to service the market."

"I can assure you, Comrade Lin, that such an occurrence is impossible. Our organization will be ready to perform as needed, provided you can supply us with the requisite products."

"I am glad for your confidence, Zhu. I think you will find that we will be ready to proceed with the export of the Red Whippet, perhaps much sooner than you had anticipated, regardless of what rumors you might have heard to the contrary." He looked at Zhu pointedly. "You had best be ready."

"Of that you have my firm assurances, Comrade," said Zhu, suddenly a bit nonplussed by Lin's remarks. What does he know that I do not, he thought a little apprehensively. Was there a special, higher quality version of the Red Whippet for the export markets? Zhu resolved to re-read the report for any reference to a special export version. "Is that all you wished to see me about?"

"That is all. You may return to your preparations for your visit to America."

After leaving Lin's office, Zhu resolved to take his upcoming visit to the U.S. a bit more seriously. He hoped it wouldn't cut into the time available for shopping or his much-anticipated tour of the stars' homes in Beverly Hills.

* * *

Sid Burnside looked with satisfaction at the full tray of 35mm slides, all nicely reproduced from the original Hyundai color transparencies and updated appropriately with current industry data. Between the slide presentation and the twenty-five spiral-bound handouts, he'd have, he was quite sure, a highly impressive and glitzy little dog and pony show, sure to impress his Chinese visitors. He'd also made arrangements to have a Chinese restaurant of some local renown cater a lavish and hopefully authentic Chinese luncheon for his guests.

The only element of the visit about which Burnside felt uneasy was what the Chinese might want in terms of entertainment. He had visions of unsmiling communist bureaucrats in baggy Mao suits, studying their little red books at every opportunity, though he did have to concede that, given their population of 1.4 billion souls, they obviously found time in their busy Marxist schedules for the occasional dalliance.

He'd found an escort service in LA at the recommendation of a friend in the business who was knowledgeable about such matters, which provided ladies and gentlemen often willing to do, within reason, whatever the client was willing to pay for, though he did specify that rough sex and S&M were definitely frowned upon. Accordingly, Burnside had the service set aside a standby contingent (at full normal rates) of male and female escorts, ready to go on short notice should his visitors exhibit the slightest interest.

As he sat mentally reviewing his preparations for the visit, Burnside reflected unhappily that he really knew nothing at all about his Chinese masters. He didn't know what they liked, what they disliked, what they respected, what or whom they held in contempt, whether they could be trusted (this he doubted), or even whether they had any sense of humor.

Jesus, he fumed, all I know is the bastards racked up a hell of a body count over the years. Then he had a sudden inspiration, as a dim recollection of a Nikita Kruschev visit inserted itself vaguely in his ruminations. Disneyland! That's it! Everybody loves Disneyland, thought Burnside happily. Abruptly he picked up the phone and called LA information for Disneyland's number.

* * *

As Burnside sat finalizing his preparations for the briefing, entertaining, and (if all went well) debauching of his Chinese guests, Sherry Maxwell was becoming increasingly apprehensive about his interview with Red Tiger Motors. He had left two messages on Sid Burnside's voice mail system, advising him of his arrival time and flight number, but had heard nothing in return. He was debating whether to call again but was afraid that he'd either sound overeager or begin to annoy Burnside with the implication that the man was an inattentive dummy. Finally he told himself that he'd be better off not to badger his potential boss with further attempts at communication and decided to simply show up in LA and then make his way to Chino if Burnside had nobody there to meet him. What the hell, he reasoned, Burnside's paying my expenses, so it's no skin off my ass if I have to take a cab from LAX to Chino or stay an extra night in LA. It might even be fun!

With that Sherry decided to put on his shorts and work on his tan a bit more before packing his overnight bag. He went to the refrigerator, took out two cans of Old Milwaukee—might as well save a trip, he reasoned—and headed out for his corroded old aluminum beach chair in the little front yard.

During the past few days his nose had healed nicely and he'd actually picked up a rather healthy-looking tan, which contrasted quite strikingly with his silver hair. He stopped at the bathroom mirror, drew himself erect, and pulled in his midriff. He admired his steely-eyed gaze, which was enhanced by narrowing his eyes just enough to hide the bloodshot whites. Hell, he thought, they oughtta make me a vice-president o'this outfit. Well, why not? If this dumbshit Garmin's vice-president of the whole friggin' country, I should rate a shot like that.

Two hours and five more cans of Old Milwaukee later, the proposition sounded more reasonable than ever to Sherry Maxwell. He fell asleep and dozed happily as the sun fell below the roofline of the little trailer, dreaming of a rosewood-paneled corner office with "VP, Sales and Marketing" in raised gold letters on the door.

* * *

Jimmy Bimstein, head of the Commerce Department, wondered why Nate Garmin wanted to have lunch with him. The note from his secretary said only that the vice-president wanted to talk about Chinese automobile imports to the U.S. Bimstein assumed, correctly, that it had something to do with the Chinese claim of making some sort of car that got terrific gas mileage and ran super-clean. He sighed and rolled his eyes, both in response to the improbability of the Chinese announcement, but more at the thought of an excruciatingly boring lunch with Nate Garmin, whom he considered to be intellectually about on par with a beagle.

Whatever, Garmin's acquiescence to Bimstein's suggestion that they save time by having lunch sent into his office indicated to him that Garmin was quite excited about whatever it was he wanted to discuss, causing him to waive the normal protocol of having Bimstein come to *his* office. Jimmy Bimstein groaned inwardly as he thought of the last time Nate Garmin had come to his office, all a-twitter with his latest scheme to promote duty-free barter of Indian elephants on a one to one exchange basis for diesel powered Allis-Chalmers farm tractors. Garmin felt sure that the elephants could be sold to Amish farmers as an environmentally-friendly power source, capable of plowing a forty acre plot in jigtime, though he did express some reservations about the methane gas released by the heaps of elephant dung. "But it's the symbolism that counts, get it?" Garmin had said excitedly. "We'll show that you don't need the internal combustion engine to farm in this country!"

"Umm, yes, Nate, that's quite an idea you've got there, I must say," Jimmy had assured him. "But I think it's something you should take up with the Department of Agriculture first. If they give it the OK, you can count on my support." Garmin thanked him and rushed off. Jimmy Bimstein never heard from Garmin again on the elephant barter scheme but later heard that someone over in USDA had sidetracked Garmin with the claim that the Indian elephants were on some group's endangered species list. He chuckled as he thought of how easy it was to send the gullible Nate Garmin off on a wild goose chase and wondered into which hapless department he might have to bounce the VP this time.

His thoughts were interrupted by his secretary, who stuck her head in to announce that the vice-president had arrived and to ask whether he'd like lunch served immediately. "Oh, please send him right in, Joan, and yes, you can send in the lunch cart now, too." He hoped, rather evilly, to force Garmin into the demanding challenge of trying to eat and talk at the same time. What the hell, this might even provide a little entertainment, thought Bimstein.

"Jimmy, how are ya today?" asked Garmin loudly, grimacing slightly with the effort of trying to crush Bimstein's hand. Nate had been taught by his father that a firm handshake and prolonged eye contact were essential to success in politics. Once again Bimstein wondered why Garmin continued to stare fixedly at him as he backed uncertainly into his chair.

"Well, Nate," began Bimstein, "just what can I do for you today?"

"I'm glad you asked that, Jimmy, because I came to talk to you about something important." The lunch cart, pushed by Bimstein's secretary, bumped and rattled across the edges of the oriental carpets on the floor. Garmin was momentarily thrown off stride, his attention diverted from the conversation to the lunch cart. "Hey, what's for lunch?"

"Just some cold cuts and potato salad. Help yourself, Nate."

"Hey, that's great," said Nate Garmin, eyes widening happily with child-like surprise as he reached over and lifted the cover off the platter of coldcuts. "I really like to make my own sandwiches." He immediately set to work making a hugely thick sandwich of Swiss cheese, pastrami, a slice of tomato, and a quarter of a thick dill pickle balanced precariously on top. He slathered a piece of bread with mayonnaise, closed the sandwich, and gingerly lifted the rather shaky concoction to his gaping mouth.

Jimmy Bimstein watched with suddenly heightened interest as Garmin struggled to fit the edge of the sandwich between his teeth, then guffawed involuntarily as the mayonnaise-lubricated pickle, then the tomato slice, squirted from the sandwich, bounced off Nate Garmin's tie, and slid down into his lap.

"Aw, fudge!" exclaimed Nate Garmin, his face registering abject chagrin as he gazed at the mess in his lap, which was joined by three slices of pastrami several seconds later. Carefully, so as not to add to the growing deli-disaster in his lap, Garmin put the remnants of his sandwich back on the tray, picked up the tomato, the pickle, and the pastrami slices in his fingers, and dropped them into his upturned mouth.

Bimstein momentarily gaped in disbelief, then reached for a handkerchief with which to stifle his nearly uncontrollable sobs of hilarity, which he tried to disguise as a coughing fit. "Sorry, Nate," he gasped, "something musta gone down the wrong pipe." He continued alternately choking and laughing as Garmin hurriedly chewed the now breadless pastrami sandwich, which he finally swallowed with a highly audible gulp. With that, he turned to blotting up the mayonnaise and various briny vegetable juices on his tie, shirt, and trousers with a paper napkin.

"Darn," he said unhappily, "Bootsie's gonna have a fit. She gave me that tie for Christmas."

29

"What do you say we get started again, Nate," suggested Jimmy Bimstein, finally regaining his composure and making himself a sandwich. "I've got a meeting with Treasury at one."

Garmin looked longingly at the remnants of his sandwich but was afraid to risk another mishap by trying to finish it. "Ah, yes, Jimmy, that's what I came to see you about. That's exactly right."

"I'm listening, Nate."

"OK, that's good. Well, what I wanted to talk to you about is that new car the Chinese have invented, you know, the one that gets like seventy miles to the gallon."

"What about it, Nate?"

"Well, I think it represents a tremendous leap forward, especially the price. By the way, on the price, I don't know yet if that includes stuff like whitewalls and airconditioning, but even if it doesn't, it's still a great buy, don't you think?"

"What are you getting at, Nate?"

"Well, I think, I mean, this is a really great opportunity we have here, Jimmy. Think about it for a minute."

"OK, I've thought about it, Nate. What's this big opportunity?"

"Well, just think, it shows what industry can do if the government leads the way, you know, lays out the standards."

"I suppose that's a good point, Nate. But what's that got to do with Commerce?"

"Well, your people'd be involved. We have an interest in promoting trade with China to get these cars over here to set an example for the other automakers."

"How'd we do that, Nate?"

"Just think about it. We could help provide incentives to speed things up, like give the Chinese special low import duties for their cars, for example. And give people who buy them special tax credits."

Bimstein instantly saw the opening he'd been waiting for. "You know, Nate, I think you're on to something with this idea, I really do. But this sounds like something you'd have to take up with Treasury and maybe Customs first, and the whole thing'd have to go through the legislative process. But I think you oughtta get the ball rolling right away," saying it as if Garmin had no time to lose.

To Bimstein's immense relief, Garmin took the bait and jumped to his feet with some urgency. "You're right, Jimmy, I gotta get going on this." He started to leave, turned back and began to make himself another thick sandwich. "Hey, these coldcuts are really good," he said, piling a piece of pumpernickel high with sandwich makings. He carefully wrapped the completed sandwich in a napkin and strode purposefully out the door, stopping briefly to ask Bimstein's secretary if she happened to have a toothpick with which to pin together his sandwich.

Jimmy Bimstein shook his head. If the public only knew, he thought unhappily.

* * *

As Jimmy Bimstein sat watching Nate Garmin make his way out of his office, inserting a straightened paper clip through his sandwich, Sid Burnside was anxiously putting the finishing touches on his preparations for his Chinese visitors.

He planned to meet them at LAX with a Lincoln stretched limo for the highest-ranking members of the management group, with the others to follow in a fifteen passenger Ford Club Wagon. A third Econoline transport van would carry the luggage. He'd deliberated at some length on the transportation arrangements, finally deciding, wisely as it turned out, that despite their egalitarian ideology, the Chinese were in fact extremely status and privilege conscious. He'd let Zhu Fei select those who would ride in the limo.

Zsu had interviewed him for his job as CEO of Red Tiger Motor Company, reading, in his halting English, from a list of carefully prepared questions. Burnside had responded, he was sure, confidently and insightfully, though he'd been unable to gauge Zhu's reaction to his answers. The thin, ascetic looking Chinese executive seemed to weigh Burnside's answers carefully, nodding thoughtfully from time to time. At length, Zhu smiled warmly and stood, dismissing him with the assurance that, "You will hear from us shortly, Mr. LaBella," which was the name of the previous candidate.

In truth, Zhu had understood virtually nothing of what Burnside or any of the other candidates had said. His command of English was limited primarily to being able to read, with a reasonable level of pronunciation, prepared text. Nonetheless, Zhu selected Burnside, after the confusion regarding his name was cleared up, primarily on the basis that he thought he bore a passing resemblance to Ernest Borgnine (he did) as he'd appeared in THE WILD BUNCH, Zhu's all time favorite American movie. Zhu and his friends liked to bet on the number of killings in the screenplay, which was actually quite difficult to gauge accurately, what with perhaps the most lavish and chaotic expenditure of red dye, pyrotechnics, and blank cartridges in film history. Zhu and his friends all agreed that it was America's finest cinematic hour.

* * *

Jake Dougherty began flipping back to page thirty-seven of the *Automotive News* to continue reading the front page story on the Chinese press release of the previous week, containing the rather startling announcement on the now much-discussed Red Whippet family sedan. "Big Jake," as he liked to be called, was skeptical about the performance claims for the Chinese car, but he really couldn't imagine anybody who sought to be a serious player in the international automotive marketplace deliberately and totally falsifying such product reports. He considered calling Red Tiger Motors in Chino, California to inquire about introductory timing and franchise requirements but found that his initial interest was somewhat tempered by his experience with Hyundai, and much later, Kia.

He had learned, as had a few others with little or no anthropological interest or training, that all East Asians were not alike, merely Japanese clones who just happened to speak a somewhat different sounding language. His mood soured as he remembered the tidal wave of red ink that accompanied the disintegration of the early Hyundai products and which, in turn, occasioned the avalanche of repos that ended up on his used car lots, with balances owed pegged at several times the value of the cars. Christ, that fucking franchise cost me a ton of money, thought Big Jake. Then they *double*-fucked me, he fumed bitterly, recalling that he'd got rid of Hyundai after he'd weathered the worst of it, only to see it turn around while in the hands of the operator to whom he'd sold it. Goddammit, they finally figured out how to make good cars, and now I ain't got the franchise anymore.

Dougherty also owned a Honda, a Chevrolet, and a Ford store, which

rendered the Hyundai debacle at least survivable for him, though his recollections of the period caused him to mumble curses and racial epithets
whenever he heard or read any reference to Korea, in whatever context.
His thoughts were interrupted by a cigar ash landing on his ample belly,
causing him to jump to his feet and swat at the still burning coal with the
Automotive News. He dropped his cigar into an ashtray already filled with
well-chewed cigar butts and inspected his silk shirt, which now displayed
a burn hole and a brown spot at navel level. Jesus Christ, he thought, this
shirt cost me a hundred and twenty bucks. Abruptly he remembered that
reading the story about the Chinese car had led to his reminiscences,
which in turn caused him to ignore the growing ash on the cigar clamped
in his teeth. Goddammit, he thought, the bastards are already costing me
money, and I haven't even made the friggin' phone call yet!

Jake Dougherty angrily walked out of his office into the showroom of
his Sacramento, California Chevy store. "Hey, Billy, what's goin' on?" he
asked Billy Joe Sisson, his new car sales manager for the Chevy store.

"Ah, hell, Jake, GMAC's not buyin' shit lately," Billy Joe replied, referring to the two out of three deals the dealership had submitted to the GM
finance company that morning which had been turned down.
"Everybody's over-obligated," he continued, "and everybody wants a
twenty thousand dollar car for a hundred and a half a month with nothin'outta pocket." Sisson was describing the mathematical impossibility
encountered daily by dealership finance and insurance managers.
"Christ," he went on, "one o'these stiffs had eighteen grand in credit card
debt, and he only makes twenty-five grand a year."

Normally Big Jake turned a deaf ear to excuses of any sort, considering them little more than unproductive whining. But he knew that there
was nothing more exasperating and ultimately demoralizing to automotive sales personnel than beating one's brains out to get a prospect on
paper, only to find that the customer couldn't get financing on a lawn
mower. He knew there was nothing to be gained, and quite possibly much
to lose, by berating his sales manager. He put one hand on Sisson's shoulder and scratched his furry belly with the other, looking unhappily at his
holed shirt as he did so. "Ah, shit, Billy, don't let it get to ya. This shit
comes and goes. Ya gotta take 'em one at a time."

"Ah, hell, I know that, Jake, and I'm not gettin' down or anything like
that. I just wish we had some kinda car we could sell these people, that's all."

"Well, don't worry about it. Something'll turn up. It always does."

* * *

As the first flickerings of interest in Red Tiger Motor Company were just beginning to spark among the new car dealers of the United States, Sherry Maxwell was impatiently awaiting his boarding call at Miami International. His flight was due off at 8:30AM with an ETA of 11:10 in Los Angeles, which caused Maxwell to speculate that there must be some very fast airplanes in trans-continental service of late.

He wore a blue pinstriped suit, crisp white shirt, and nicely selected tie, looking for all the world like a successful senior level executive. The only thing wrong with the picture was the *Penthouse* magazine he'd picked up at the newsstand, which he hoped to read surreptitiously once aboard the waiting 757. For the moment he contented himself flipping through the pages while hiding behind the open lid of his briefcase. Damn, he thought, ogling an exceptionally furry pubic thatch and feeling the first real stirring in his groin in quite some time. His rapidly forming fantasies evaporated as a severe looking older woman sat down next to him, causing him to slap the magazine closed, thankfully on a rear cover that featured nothing more lascivious than a Camel Lights ad. Sherry Maxwell snapped his briefcase shut, stood up, and headed back toward the newsstand to pick up a Wall Street Journal, calculating that it might be a good idea to bring himself up to speed on current events during the flight to LA.

He still had not heard from Sid Burnside but figured that he had a confirmed appointment, with no information to the contrary. And if Burnside was simply out of town or in some other way unavailable, Maxwell felt that Red Tiger still had an obligation to pay for his trip. He had spent some time forming in his mind the little spiel he'd use on Burnside, with just the right measure of indignation and disappointment that they hadn't connected as planned. The more he thought about it, the more convinced he became that Burnside might actually feel a slight twinge of guilt, which hopefully would lead to a sense of obligation toward him. He began actually hoping that Burnside had forgotten all about the interview, thus giving him the edge he was seeking, plus putting off the tension and stress of the interview itself for a day or two, maybe more.

As Sherry would learn before the day was out, his calculations would be rendered moot.

* * *

As Sherry Maxwell was doing his best to figure all the angles regarding his employment prospects with Red Tiger, Sid Burnside was nervously awaiting the arrival of the Chinese delegation at LAX. Everything seemed to be in place. He planned to take the group, check them in at the airport Marriot, give them forty-five minutes to clean up, then take them out to Chino for the briefing, which itself would take about forty-five minutes. Following the briefing, he'd have the catered lunch served, after which he'd take them back to the Marriot to rest up for the evening's activities, which included a tour of various nightspots on Hollywood boulevard and a late dinner at a local seafood restaurant. Then, if his guests were paired off with members of the escort service, as he hoped would happen, he'd cut them loose for the rest of the evening, instructing the escorts to make sure they got safely back to the Marriot. Then the following day, Disneyland! And then they're outta here, on their way to Washington, thought Burnside happily.

He checked his watch nervously for the tenth time since his arrival at the airport, then looked at the little sign he'd hold at the exit to customs, neatly printed in bold red letters, Red Tiger Motor Company. The limo and the vans were waiting in the pickup area. Burnside had slipped the airport detail cop fifty bucks to ensure that they'd not be ordered to move and thus be ready and waiting to carry the visitors the short distance to the airport hotel. Everything's set, thought Burnside with satisfaction. He'd even arranged to give each member of the delegation two hundred dollars in spending money, with the advice that if they needed more they needed only to ask.

Burnside heard the flight arrival announced and involuntarily sucked in his ample paunch, then reached up to straighten his tie, though he knew it would be at least thirty minutes before his charges would be able to exit customs, perhaps more.

* * *

While Sid Burnside stood occasionally wiping his sweating palms on his trouser legs, Vera Hawkins, known to the clients of Starlight Escort Services as Mavis Belle, swore softly as she tried to scoop the tropical fish she was getting for a customer into the little plastic bag. She worked part-time, perhaps an average of thirty to thirty-five hours a week, in Paws and Claws, a Hollywood pet store, where she hoped to come to the attention of a talent agent or movie producer.

Vera, twenty-two years old and formerly a cocktail waitress from Memphis, had moved to Los Angeles six months earlier in hopes of being discovered, if not for the movies, then at least for some sort of interesting career, which she'd yet to define even vaguely. She was a natural blonde, very pretty, shapely, and unschooled, almost a real-life caricature of Daisy Mae Yokum, an assessment with which Al Capp himself doubtless would have agreed.

Unfortunately, Vera quickly learned that Hollywood and the surrounding territory was filled with leggy, blonde, and very pretty young aspirants. She also learned that these normally impressive attributes couldn't even guarantee her a job as a cocktail waitress. Hence, her seven dollar an hour job in Paws and Claws, which, she'd reflected, would be more appropriately named Scales and Fins, since scaly and finny things were generally more suitable for the self-absorbed lifestyle of Hollywood's denizens, and in fact comprised the majority of the pet store's volume.

A Paws and Claws co-worker had introduced her to Starlight Escort Services, which paid minimum wage but allowed her to keep all tips, which could sometimes be, depending on the level of "services" Vera provided, quite substantial, enough so that Vera kept her pet store job mainly to maintain her self image as just a typical working girl with a part-time evening job. Her pseudonym, Mavis Belle, she used mainly because she thought it sounded a bit more theatrical than Vera Hawkins, but also because she harbored a vague apprehension that she'd somehow end up in the papers in a less than flattering situation and, however improbable it seemed, didn't want her parents back home to be embarrassed. Or perhaps more to the point, she didn't want her father, Lucas Hawkins, a traditional Tennessee hill man, driving to Hollywood in his battered '69 Chevy pickup and dealing with the debauchers of his only daughter with a hail of buckshot from his ancient Model 1897 Winchester pump gun.

Now, as Vera, dressed in tight white short shorts and a pink halter top, rang up the $2.50 fish sale, she wondered what she'd be doing that evening. All she'd been told was that she was on a standby status, to possibly pair off with an Oriental gentleman, believed to be from China. If called, she was told she'd be part of a fairly large group, escorting both men and women. Though she wasn't excited at the thought of spending an evening out with a group of Chinese businessmen and women, she had been told that they were often big tippers, and also that the client would appreciate her doing whatever, within reason, was necessary to keep the visitors happy. This, particularly, didn't appeal to her, since she didn't find Oriental men in general very attractive (though she wouldn't have minded a shot at someone like Bruce Lee). On the other hand, she'd heard that they were usually very fastidious about personal hygiene.

She glanced at her watch and wondered what she should wear that evening.

* * *

Sherry Maxwell, having exhausted the visual possibilities of his *Penthouse Magazine* during the first ninety minutes of his flight, and not particularly caring about anything but the pictures, once again began worrying about whether Sid Burnside would be at the airport to meet him. Finally he decided that he'd make one more call to Red Tiger, using the flight phone. He signaled for the flight attendant, and less than two minutes later was actually talking to a human voice instead of Burnside's answering machine. He was so startled that he was momentarily speechless. "Ah, is Mr. Burnside there?" he asked the temp Burnside had brought in for the two day visit by the Chinese.

"I'm sorry, Mr. Burnside isn't available at the moment. Can I take a message?"

"Well, my name's Maxwell, and I'm supposed to have an interview with him today. Do you expect him back?"

"I do expect him back," she chirped, "but I don't know anything about an interview. I do expect him to be tied up most of the day."

Now Maxwell actually began to get angry. "Hey, look, I'm comin' all the way from Florida to see him, and now you're tellin' me he's gonna be too busy?" he asked, his voice rising.

"Well, I don't know, sir, he didn't tell me anything about an interview."

"Well, what the hell, I'm just gonna take a cab out to your place when I land. I guess I can just sit around and wait to see him."

"I guess you can always do that, Mr. Maxwell. If he comes back I'll tell him that you're on your way. Do you have any idea when you might arrive?"

"I should probably be there in about two hours," Maxwell said, still not factoring in the three hour time difference.

"Very good, Mr. Maxwell. I'll look forward to seeing you in a couple of hours."

* * *

Sid Burnside was by now in a state of considerable agitation, wondering if the little Chinese delegation was being held up in customs, an occurrence for which he was sure he'd be at least partially blamed. His agitation finally turned to relief as he spotted Zhu Fei striding down the corridor, wearing a gray suit and followed by a score of identically attired Chinese men and women, practically all of whom looked very young to Burnside.

Zhu recognized Burnside (or at least the sign he was holding) immediately, walked up to him, hand extended, and inquired, "Missa Bunsid, mewe go?"

Burnside took Zsui's hand, pumped it vigorously, and replied, "Very well, sir, and how are you?"

Zhu looked quizzically at a rather cold-looking but very attractive young woman next to him, who looked at Burnside and said, in perfect, almost unaccented English, "Mr. Zhu asked if we can go."

"Yes, of course," said Burnside, immensely relieved to have an accomplished English speaker among the group. "Follow me, and we'll go to the hotel for a short time and then to our headquarters for our briefing."

He watched as the woman translated rapidly, then listened to Zhu's response. She looked at him without expression. "Mr. Zhu wishes to know when we'll tour Beverly Hills to see the stars' homes."

"Oh, of course," said Burnside loudly, looking at Zhu and nodding vigorously. "We'll do that tomorrow afternoon, right after we're through with Disneyland."

She translated for Zhu, whose face lit up. Burnside thought he heard him say something that sounded like Disneyland, nodding approvingly.

"Mr. Zhu says he is very pleased. Lead the way, Mr. Burnside."

Ten minutes later, after a bit of a struggle to load all the luggage and assign the delegation members, based on rank, as either Lincoln or Econoline riders, they were on their way to the airport Marriot. During he short ride Zhu asked Burnside through his female interpreter how many of his staff would be on hand to participate in the discussions.

Burnside, with as much confidence as he could muster, replied, "Our people are all out in the field, interviewing dealers and doing market studies. I'll be handling the briefing by myself, but they all participated in the preparation for our meeting."

This was duly translated for Zhu, who looked at Burnside, eyebrows raised. He spoke in rapid-fire Chinese to the interpreter. "Mr. Zhu is very disappointed that your staff is not on hand for the meeting, Mr. Burnside. He wishes to know where they are at this moment."

"Well, they're in various places, Miss, ah..."

"Lin. My name is Lin, though you should address your answers to Mr. Zhu. Pretend I am not here."

"Ah, yes, I'll do that," said Burnside, just beginning to notice that Miss Lin was rather difficult to ignore, with classically beautiful Oriental features, unadorned with any makeup whatever, and every hint of a firm and shapely body under her dark gray suit. "To answer your question, Mr. Zhu," he said, looking directly at him, "they are in various locations throughout the United States at this time. America is a very large country, as you know, and it would not be practical or cost effective to bring them together for a two day meeting." There, I handled that one pretty well, he told himself.

Miss Lin quickly translated, got Zhu's response, then spoke to Burnside. "Mr. Zhu says that surely you must have somebody available on the west coast who could join us. He is most eager to meet members of your staff and make his own analysis of them."

The way the conversation was trending made it rather obvious to Burnside that it would be most unwise to inform Zhu that he had no staff, though he had given the Chinese no indication that he had actually hired anyone. What's this bullshit all about, he asked himself. "Let me see what I can arrange on short notice, Mr. Zhu," he said reaching for his pocket cell phone, entering a number and then pretending to press the SEND button. Moments later he had made a show of demanding to speak with somebody, leaving the instruction that he was to call back as soon as possible. "That should take care of it," he said to Zhu with a winning smile. Zhu merely nodded, then looked out the heavily tinted window at the looming Marriot hotel.

* * *

As Burnside was sweatily contemplating just how he was to assemble a staff sometime in the next hour, desperately wondering whether to call the local chapter of the Screen Actors Guild, Sherry Maxwell stood looking about tentatively in the arrival-departure lounge, hoping to see somebody from Red Tiger Motor Company. He gave the lounge a final look, then began walking slowly toward the main concourse, keeping alert for anybody bearing a sign indicating Red Tiger. Ten minutes later, however, he'd reached the passenger pickup area and still saw no one. Sherry, as he looked around, suddenly solved the mystery of the missing three hours. Holy shit, he thought, I'm three hours late! No, wait a minute, I'm early, thought the befuddled Sherry Maxwell. No, I'm late, he finally concluded once again. Burnside's probably already left. Gloomily, he reset his watch accordingly, wondering why it seemed like midday at five o'clock in the afternoon. He started to head for the Hertz desk to rent a car, but then figured he could save maybe thirty minutes by taking a cab. Not wanting to be any later than he already was, he gave one last look around and hailed a taxi.

* * *

As Sherry was issuing instructions to the swarthy, turban-topped cabbie, Burnside was anxiously pacing the lobby of the airport Marriott, desperately, but with fading hope, trying to think of a way to come up with a stand-in body on short notice. Suddenly he began to relax a bit as he thought of Zhu's obvious enthusiasm for the Disneyland and Hollywood tours. What the hell, there was no way anybody could make it from, say, San Francisco to LA in time for the meeting that afternoon, which if rescheduled for the following day, he would carefully explain to Zhu, would certainly interfere with Zhu's scheduled entertainment. Then if worse came to worst, he'd have another day to think of something. He thought of calling a friend over at American Honda to see if he'd be willing to come over and play VP of Finance, or whatever. What the hell, thought Burnside, I've done wackier things in my day

He chuckled as he thought of the time that the president of Hyundai, N.Y. Chang—known to the US affiliate employees as New York Chang— had demanded to visit a local Hyundai dealership which he'd picked at random from the US dealership directory. Burnside had realized that Chang specifically wanted to avoid the typical carefully staged dog and pony show occasioned by such visits, preferring to take his dose of reality straight and unadulterated. Unfortunately, the dealership that Chang picked was not exactly one which the US management was eager to showcase, being located in a ramshackle 1958 ex-VW facility in a rundown part of Burbank.

Fortunately, Burnside knew the local police chief, to whom he promised the free use of two new Hyundais for his teenage kids in return for blocking off all access to the dealership, advising Chang's driver that there was a gas main leak in the neighborhood and that they were evacuating. This caused a bizarre series of contradictory stories by the police and the gas utility company, which the local press never really did fully sort out. However, all ended happily. The chief got his two cars, the local network affiliate TV stations got a two minute filler episode on a slow night, and the unsuspecting but duly impressed New York Chang was whisked off to a palatial Hyundai store fifteen miles away, which went bankrupt four months later.

Burnside's thoughts were interrupted by the elevator door opening, revealing about half the group of Chinese visitors, now identically dressed in tan poplin suits. Miss Lin was again standing next to Zhu as they exited the elevator, this time in heels. A pair of what looked like Serengeti aviators now hid her large almond eyes. Wonder if old Zhu's gettin' any of that, Burnside wondered idly. She's really a fox.

"Are we ready to go, Mr. Burnside?" asked Miss Lin.

"The cars are standing by." The other elevator door opened, revealing the rest of the group. "It'll take us about an hour to get to the office, so we'd better get started. And I'm still checking to see if we can bring in some of our people on short notice for today. I'm pretty sure we can have some of the guys in here tomorrow, but then we'd have to cancel the Disneyland and Hollywood trip." He looked at Zhu pointedly as Lin began to translate.

Lin and Zhu conversed for a few moments, then she looked at him and said, "Mr. Zhu would be very disappointed if you had to change your plans for tomorrow, but he still wishes to see members of your staff."

Well, what the hell's that supposed to mean, thought Burnside. But he shrugged and replied, "I'll see what I can do to make the arrangements," which seemed to satisfy Zhu for the moment.

As they were riding in the Lincoln limo to Red Tiger's rather spartan Chino offices, Zhu began to question Burnside about the potential sales volume for the Red Whippet sedan in the US market.

Burnside replied that it depended on a great number of factors, including price, specification, and quality. "You may be assured that the specification and the quality will be first rate," said Zhu through Miss Lin, who seemed to look at Burnside with a certain level of contempt. "As to the price, you already have been told that it is $5000. Now, how many of these fine cars will America buy per year?"

"Well," said Burnside, beginning to grow annoyed, knowing as he did that the quality and specification were likely to be anything but first rate, "if the car is comparable to the Honda Civic, the Toyota Corolla, or the Mazda Protege, we should be able to double their volume in perhaps two years."

"You may assume that the quality will be far superior to these Japanese cars. Now, how many will you be able to sell in the first year?" Miss Lin now had a definite edge to her voice.

To hell with it, Burnside decided. The quality'll be for shit, the styling'll be straight out of the sixties, and these guys probably think an automatic transmission's a luxury item. "Oh, I can confidently predict sales of at least two million units the first year, given those assumptions. Of course, you'll have to able to supply them in those sorts of quantities." He looked at Zhu pointedly.

Miss Lin translated, Zhu nodded, then replied. "That is very good. Of course, we will be able to supply any quantity you will be able to sell. I give you my personal assurance." Lin finished translating, then Zhu added, "You must be ready to sell these cars when they arrive. That is why I am anxious to see about your progress in building your organization."

Oh, shit, there it is again, thought Burnside. Hoping to change the subject slightly, he asked, "When will you submit the car to the government for emission and safety testing? This takes several months to complete. Only then can we begin appointing dealers to sell and service the cars. I need a timetable on which to operate."

"You need not concern yourself with these government tests. All this is being attended to as we speak. The Red Whippet will be ready to go on sale in no more than six months!"

Burnside thought about objecting to Zhu's obviously ridiculous timetable, but then figured, what the hell, it ain't gonna happen and I can't get blamed. Screw it, I'll humor this asshole. "That's very good, Mr. Zhu. Now I can get going on picking an ad agency, selecting dealers, and hiring all our field people."

"Why do you need an advertising agency?" asked Zhu. "You should not have to advertise such a fine product, sold at such an attractive price."

Burnside had to keep from rolling his eyes. "Perhaps you are right. We needn't make a decision on advertising until later."

The inane conversation went on in like vein until their arrival at their Chino facility. For the first time Zhu seemed to register approval, congratulating Burnside on doing a fine job in facility selection. "But where will you park the cars?" he asked. "Surely you will need room for at least one hundred thousand, perhaps more."

"That area is in the ports of entry in San Francisco, Los Angeles, Jacksonville, and Newark," Burnside replied, beginning to realize that Zhu knew nothing whatever about the import car business or probably any business at all, for that matter. "We will ship directly from the ports to the dealers. That's how it's done."

"Ah, well, perhaps it's time for a bold new approach," retorted Zhu. "That is one reason I wanted to meet your staff," he continued through Miss Lin, "to see if they were receptive to bold new ideas." Zhu, like many outsiders to the car business, as is often the case with outsiders new to any business, didn't appreciate that certain methodologies had evolved over a long period of time for good and valid reasons.

"For example," he went on, "why can't the customers come to the ports and pick up their cars there? Why do we need dealers if the Red Whippet is such a value? We would save on the shipping charges and we would cut out the dealers' profit, which is completely unnecessary. That is the kind of bold thinking I am speaking of." He looked triumphantly at Burnside, who was momentarily thrown off-balance by the sheer enormity of Zhu's ignorance, but who also began to realize that the man was little more than a posturing bureaucrat whose ideas would be utterly irrelevant, at least in the short term. Burnside figured there was no way the Red Whippet or anything else made by the Long March People's Cooperative

Automotive Manufacturing Company was going on sale in the US market anytime soon. I might as well humor this dickhead, he told himself.

"That's a brilliant idea, Mr. Zhu," he replied. "We have saying in this country that sometimes one can't see the forest for the trees." He waited expectantly for Miss Lin to translate this bit of Occidental wisdom.

Zhu listened, then looked at Burnside a little doubtfully, wondering about Burnside's strange reference to the logging industry, assuming it to be some sort of American allegory or perhaps a reference to one of America's weird and, to him, incomprehensible environmental concerns. "Yes," he replied, "the Red Whippet will be good for the trees and forests, of that you can be sure."

* * *

As Burnside and Zhu continued feeling each other out with a series of mindless observations and banalities, Sherry sat, with growing agitation, looking at the back of the cabbie's turban-swathed head. "How much longer?" he demanded for the third time in thirty minutes.

"Teminit," replied the driver, not turning around.

"Goddammit, you said that half an hour ago," shouted Maxwell, by now truly exasperated. Christ, the opportunity of a lifetime, my last chance, is being pissed away by a goddam camel-jockey who can't even speak English, he told himself angrily.

"Teminit," the man repeated, unperturbed.

Maxwell sat back in his seat, arms folded, and ground his molars. Remarkably, exactly ten minutes later they were pulling up in front of a non-descript stucco-covered office building, with a small sign out front that announced the tenant as one Red Tiger Motor Company, Inc. Maxwell noted that the employee parking lot was empty, save for Burnside's Olds Cutlass, the temporary secretary's car, the Lincoln limo, and the Club Wagon. Maybe they're all out to lunch, he speculated. Between the empty parking lot, the ratty shrubbery in front of the building, and the total lack of activity in or around the headquarters, Sherry was not encouraged. He got out, settled up with the cabbie, and walked slowly toward the front door. A blast of refrigerated air hit him as he walked inside, taking off his sunglasses as he peered down the empty corridor.

A young woman looked up at him from a small office on his right. "Can I help you?" she asked.

"Ah, yes, my name's Maxwell, Sherry Maxwell. I'm here to see Mr. Burnside."

"You know, I haven't had the chance to ask him about your appointment, Mr. Maxwell. He's in a meeting with a bunch of people from China right now, but I'll try to let him know you're here as soon as I can."

"Ah, that'd be fine, miss. Is there any place I can wait without being in the way?

"The next office is empty. Why don't you just wait in there?"

"Hey, that's great," said Maxwell, actually glad for the opportunity to collect his thoughts. He went into the empty office, at the desk, and took out his *Wall Street Journal,* hoping to appear aware and erudite if Burnside unexpectedly appeared in the doorway.

While Sherry was cooling his heels in the empty and bare little office, Burnside was lowering the lighting in preparation for his slide show. The Chinese sat leafing through their handouts with apparent interest, though only four of their number could speak any English, and only one, Miss Lin, was fluent. The group quieted as the lights fell.

Thirty minutes later Burnside concluded the presentation to a smattering of tentative applause, which startled six of the group out of the jet-lag induced slumber into which they'd fallen. One of them was Zhu, who abruptly straightened up, turned to Miss Lin, on whose shoulder he'd been lolling, mouth agape, and spoke loudly and rapidly.

She and Zhu turned to Burnside while she translated. "Very good, very informative, Mr. Burnside." Burnside nodded and smiled modestly. "Now," she continued briskly, "Mr. Zhu would like to meet your staff."

Burnside's mouth dropped open in surprise and dismay, but he recovered quickly. "Very good, Mr. Zhu, let me check and see how they're doing in getting some of our people together. In the meantime, lunch will be served in the conference room at the end of the hall. Please follow me."

Three minutes later Burnside had deposited the Chinese in the conference room and was hurrying worriedly down the long hallway toward his office. He bolted right on by the office in which Sherry Maxwell, having straightened up and smoothed back his hair as he heard Burnside's footsteps, sat fixedly studying the editorial page of the *Wall Street Journal.* Burnside walked into the office and ordered the temp to get him American Honda over in Torrance on the line. God, I hope Pisano's there, he thought, planning to get his friend to come over and play-act for some sort of executive position for his visitors.

"I've got his voicemail," the temp reported. "Do you want to leave a message?

Burnside snatched up his phone. At the beep he barked into the handset, "Hey, Lou, call me back right away. It's urgent. My life's in danger."

He stood up and paced momentarily, then punched the palm of his hand with his fist. Now what do I do, he thought.

The temp looked at him a little worriedly. "Uh, Mr. Burnside, there's a Mr. Maxwell here to see you. He says you're scheduled to interview him this afternoon."

"Jesus Christ, I haven't got the time today. Tell him to come back tomorrow. Look, if Pisano calls back, come get me immediately, I mean immediately, got it?"

She nodded, wondering just what kind of totally disorganized nitwit she was working for.

With that, Burnside dashed out the door and began striding rapidly down the hall, stealing a glance at Maxwell as he rushed by. Maxwell didn't look up but remained staring fixedly at his paper. Burnside had gotten perhaps ten feet past the little office, looking determinedly at the floor, when his eyes suddenly popped wide open and he stopped so abruptly that he skidded nearly three feet on the polished tile floor. He spun about and saw the temp about to disappear into Maxwell's office. "Hold it!" he practically shouted, "I'll handle this!"

"Maxwell, isn't it?" he boomed as he marched through the door, practically elbowing the temp aside. He held out his hand. "Sid Burnside, pleased tameetcha."

Maxwell, who'd almost fallen asleep staring at Al Hunt's column, jumped to his feet and snatched Burnside's hand and pumped it. "Sherry Maxwell, Sid, I'm glad to be here. I hope I'm not too late. The cabbie got lost on the way over."

"No harm done, Sherry, I was tied up anyway, got a bunch of Chinese visitors in here for a coupla days. Hey, tell ya what, wait here for a few more minutes while I get 'em settled for lunch and I'll be right back."

"Great, I'll be right here."

Jesus, thought Burnside, talk about luck! This guy even looks halfway respectable, and he's older. Burnside vaguely remembered hearing something about the Chinese (or was it the Nips, he wondered) having great respect for their elders.

He marched back into the conference room confidently, located Zhu and Miss Lin, and announced, "Well, we're in luck. Our new Vice President for sales and marketing is just getting in from Miami. I hadn't expected him until this evening, but he's on his way from the airport right now."

Miss Lin translated, listened to Zhu's response, and said to Burnside, "That is very good news, Mr. Burnside. Please have him join us when he arrives."

While Burnside sat surrounded by noisily slurping and lip-smacking Chinese, Sherry stood making small talk with the temp. "Gee, Mr. Burnside seems like a nice guy," he said to the girl, who merely smiled and went back to her issue of *Cosmopolitan*.

Nice guy, right, she thought, he's a lunatic. Other than that he's just swell. She'd entertained hopes of a permanent job with Red Tiger, but after two days of watching Burnside's frenzied, almost comical efforts to prepare for the meeting, she decided she needed employment with Red Tiger Motors about like she needed a melanoma on her upper lip.

"Yeah, he seems like a real decisive, ah, decision maker, you know, a guy who makes real decisive, uh, decisions," Sherry blundered on.

"Umm," the girl replied noncommittally, glancing up briefly from her magazine.

"Nice guy, too," Sherry continued on, "and he, ah, looks pretty young, doncha think?" hoping to suck up to whom he assumed to be Burnside's personal secretary.

Yeah, young compared to Mick Jagger, thought the twenty-one year old temp. But she merely looked up and said, "Yeah, I guess so."

Meanwhile, Burnside watched squeamishly as Zhu deftly plucked the eye from a steamed carp with his chopsticks and ate it with gusto. "Ah, why don't I check and see if our man's arrived from the airport," he said to Miss Lin, who nodded by way of acknowledgement and continued shoveling in rice and vegetables with her chopsticks. He made his way hurriedly from the room and headed quickly for the office where he'd left Sherry Maxwell.

Maxwell had just reseated himself in the little office when Burnside reappeared in the door. "Sherry," he boomed, "I like the way you handle yourself." He clapped his hands and rubbed them together. "Yeah, I got a good feeling about you, Maxwell. You got presence, an executive look."

Sherry looked at him blankly. Throughout his career, though he had in fact suspected that he possessed these elusive attributes, he had to acknowledge that nobody else appeared to have noted them. In fact, Maxwell had spent most of his career consciously attempting to remain as invisible as possible. "Well, I'm glad to hear that," was all he could think to reply. Burnside was making him uneasy.

"Well, Sherry, I don't see any point in beating around the bush. I want you for my VP of sales and marketing, starting right now."

Sherry's mouth hung open in a Nate Garmin-esque look of rictal stupefaction. "No shit?" he asked.

"Ah, no kidding, Sherry, you're the man I want. Now, I've told the Chinese that you've been on the payroll for a while, so you gotta support me on that. They wanna meet you pretty quick, so I want you to tell 'em you've been checking out port facilities in Jacksonville, looking over proposals from port handlers to get the best deal. They'll buy it. They don't know what questions to ask. And we'll tell 'em you've been with the domestics and, ah, just Mazda. I don't want 'em askin' any questions about why you been so many places. Just try to smile a lot and laugh when they laugh. It's easy. And watch what you say around that surly-lookin' interpreter, Lin's her name. She speaks perfect English. In fact, maybe some more of 'em maybe can, too, so watch your ass around 'em."

Events were moving too quickly for total and ordered assimilation by Sherry Maxwell's alcohol-diminished brain. "Oh, so you don't want me to speak English around 'em, is that it?" he asked.

Burnside looked at him narrowly. "Ah, no, not exactly, Sherry, just watch what you *say* in English, and try to use a lotta buzzwords, like market penetration, exclusivity, residuals, CSI, you know, the usual bullshit. They won't know what the hell you're talkin' about, anyway. You're gonna do fine. Now, follow me, and I'll bring you down into our lunch meeting."

Burnside felt an almost palpable sense of relief in having Maxwell show up on his doorstep. His buddy Lou Pisano could still come in handy if he needed a further show of executive strength. Later, he could always have Maxwell retire for health reasons.

Two minutes later Maxwell was being introduced as Red Tiger's VP of Sales and Marketing, just returned from a vital mission to the southeast, where he'd been reviewing port operations for suitability in handling the expected vast numbers of Red Whippets soon to be flooding the US market. Burnside hoped Maxwell, whom he quickly judged to be a bit slow of wit, would be able to get the story straight.

Zhu looked at Maxwell, thinking he looked wise and experienced, though he was a bit disappointed that he couldn't seem to relate his appearance to that of any known Hollywood personality. They shook hands firmly, with Miss Lin saying that he appeared to be a man of great experience in the car business.

"Ah, yes, that's certainly true, Miss, I guess I've seen and done it all in my career," replied Maxwell, thinking it remarkable that for the first time in his life he'd be working for people who truly appreciated him.

"Please join us, Mr. Maxwell," Miss Lin said, gesturing to a seat next to Zhu. "The food is excellent."

Maxwell looked a little desperately at the bottles of Chinese beer and rice wine being enjoyed by the guests. What the hell, he started to think, I'm already hired, why not? He looked up and noticed Burnside watching him. With a supreme display of self-discipline, Sherry reached for the porcelain teapot and poured himself a cup, hand shaking only slightly.

Fifteen minutes later Burnside began to relax, then actually began feeling rather upbeat. He had watched Maxwell closely, noting with relief that he abstained from any alcohol. He speculated that Maxwell's apparent bourbon blush was merely due to sun exposure in Florida. He also noted that Maxwell's answers to Zhu's questions were vague and noncommittal, which Burnside considered a good sign. As he looked around at the tables throughout the room, Burnside noted that the food, wine, beer, and jet lag were all having their effects on the gathering. Several of his visitors, including Zhu, were clearly having difficulty staying awake. He looked at Miss Lin and Zhu and said, smiling, "I believe everybody could use a little nap before we go out again this evening. Why don't I take you back to the hotel where everybody can relax?"

Miss Lin didn't even bother translating the proposal to Zhu, but merely answered, "I believe that's an excellent idea, Mr. Burnside," leaving Burnside to wonder briefly who was really in charge of the Chinese delegation.

Forty-five minutes later he and Miss Lin were finalizing the plan to meet them in the lobby at 7:30 that evening, with a group of American escorts who would "help them enjoy their stay in Los Angeles," as Burnside put it. Miss Lin smiled faintly at Burnside's comment, saying, "Yes, I am sure they will be very helpful."

* * *

Vera Hawkins, aka Mavis Belle, lay flat on the floor, struggling to wriggle into the much stretched and abused denim of her freshly laundered designer jeans. Finally, with a supreme effort, she buttoned them, zipped them up, and slipped into her black heels. A frilly white middie blouse completed the outfit. She brushed her long blond hair one last time, dropped the brush into her shoulder bag, inspected herself in the mirror with satisfaction, and left her apartment.

An hour later she and seventeen other young women and four young men were being deposited at the curb of the airport Marriot. As they stepped from the two Club Wagons, Sid Burnside greeted them. "OK, gals pair off with guys, guys pair off with the women. At least that's what I hope they want." There were smiles from the escorts but no laughter. Burnside wondered briefly if he'd committed some sort of gross faux pas of political incorrectness, then noticed Sherry Maxwell ogling Vera Hawkins. "Hey, they're for the guests, Maxwell," he whispered. "We're just here to make sure everything goes smoothly. Keep that in mind, and I think it'd be a good idea if you just drank coke or iced tea tonight."

"Don't you think they might be insulted, I mean if we don't offer to drink with them?" asked Maxwell hopefully. "I mean, they might think they're losing face, or something like that, doncha think?" Maxwell continued, dredging up something about "the Oriental mind" from the dim recesses of his memory.

Burnside looked at him narrowly. "Umm, no Sherry, I think it'd be better if you stay completely off the sauce tonight. I mean that," he said with emphasis.

Within ten minutes the visitors and their escorts had paired off, to the apparent satisfaction and even delight of the Chinese. Zhu had immediately demanded to make the acquaintance of "Mavis Belle," to the acute disappointment of every other male member of the delegation. Miss Lin, perfunctorily reviewing then dismissing the potential male "dates" available (to *their* acute disappointment), quickly latched onto one of the escort service limo drivers, a six foot two inch, blond, Muscle Beach type named Zack Johnson, who wasted no time in taking note of her ample physical attributes. Within two minutes they were looking soulfully into each other's eyes. Jesus Christ, thought Sid Burnside, I hope the commie bitch can keep her pants on till we finish dinner. Christ knows what'll happen with this group if she takes off with Arnold, Jr. and I gotta try to talk to Zhu without her.

Five hours later the group had finished dinner and was being brought back to the airport Marriot in Burnside's rented little caravan. Maxwell had sulked unhappily throughout the evening, miffed that not only was he not allowed to have a few snorts, but that he didn't have a date either. Goddammit, he thought angrily, what the hell kind of company is this. The friggin' Chinks get all the perks, and I get shit. He decided to call room service and have them send up a bottle of scotch just as soon as he could break loose. In truth, Maxwell was far more agitated about the dry evening than he was about the lack of an escort.

The group parted with much hugging, shaking of hands, forced smiles, and loudly and slowly enunciated good-byes in Chinese and English, for other than Miss Lin, none spoke English with any real facility, and of course none of the escorts spoke Chinese. Zhu did manage to communicate to Mavis Belle that he wanted her to come to his room for a drink, to which she assented, having noted that he appeared to be the leader of the group and, therefore, she presumed, well-heeled.

Miss Lin simply handed Zack Johnson her room key surreptitiously and told him to give her about ten minutes, then come on up.

Finally, when the last of them disappeared either out the lobby doors or into the elevators, Burnside sighed with relief and headed home. Less than eighteen hours later and they'll be gone, he told himself. Then I can kick back, relax, and decide what I'm gonna to do with this character Maxwell.

* * *

Three hours later Mavis Belle, sleeping quite soundly, became aware that Zhu had slipped out of bed and disappeared into the bathroom. She saw the light come on from under the closed door, then a bit of rattling, followed by a couple of metallic clicks. She wondered sleepily what he was doing, then turned over and started to drift off once again.

Zhu had been neither a very demanding nor energetic sex partner, to her surprise and vague ego disappointment. He had coupled with her quickly and unimaginatively, rolled over panting, and gone to sleep. She was just falling asleep once again when she became aware of Zhu beside her. She stiffened slightly, then rolled over on her back, expecting to feel him pressing against her. Instead, he slowly began sliding down toward the foot of the bed, his head forming a ghostly white dome under the sheet. Mavis covered her eyes with her forearm, assuming that Zhu was about to engage in a bit of oral sex. Her assumption was seemingly confirmed when he elbowed his way between her legs.

She could feel his hot breath on her inner thighs. Despite herself, she felt a slight stirring of desire in the near darkness, imagining Zhu to be her ex-boyfriend from Memphis. She thought she felt something hard and cold against her left thigh, then a metallic click. Mavis looked up and saw only the dim white dome of Zhu's head under the sheet. She was about to reach down and caress his head when the world exploded with a brilliant, blinding white light through the sheet. She gasped in shock and surprise, seeing only brilliant colored orbs in the near total darkness of the hotel room. She sat for a moment, mouth open in surprise, when a second brilliant flash illuminated the room. With that, she tore off the sheet, still blinded, and reached around behind her for the light switch over the headboard. When the lights clicked on, she saw Zhu grinning toothily over his strobe-equipped Canon F-1. He nodded and continued grinning. "Very good, very good," he repeated to the gaping child-woman from Tennessee.

Mavis Belle screamed in horror and revulsion. "Aaaauuugh! You disgustin', filthy, li'l ol', you li'l ol' *pervert*," she shrieked. "You gimme that camera, raht now, you li'l creep, or Ah'm gonna cut off yore li'l cricket-dick!" She grabbed for the camera and succeeded in catching it by the lens barrel with her left hand. Zhu still had hold of it with both hands, and a brief but furious tug of war ensued. "Gimme that, you li'l shit," she screamed, then threw a pretty fair right cross that caught Zhu squarely on the nose. He fell back, blood gushing from his nose, and momentarily lost his grip on the camera, which she yanked away from him.

As Zhu moaned and made little owwing noises, she tried to open the back of the camera to extract the film, but didn't realize that she had to depress the rewind button in order to open it. While she struggled furiously with it, breaking two nails in the process, Zhu recovered sufficiently to grab the Canon's neck strap, and the tug of war resumed.

But Mavis Belle still possessed the strength and tenacity she'd gained growing up and often fighting with two older brothers, and soon tore the neck strap from Zhu's desperate but increasingly feeble grasp. As he fell off the foot of the bed, she swung the heavy camera by the neck strap in a lethal arc, intending to slam it against the wall, just as Zhu was regaining his feet. He stood up just in time for his head to intercept the sharp corner of the Canon's baseplate with a loud, percussive *crack*. He cried out hoarsely and collapsed on the bed, now with a deep, inch long cut in his scalp.

Between Zhu's nosebleed and his now profusely bleeding scalp wound the bed quickly looked took on the appearance of an axe-murder scene. Mavis forgot all about the camera and began frantically pulling on her clothes, intent only in getting away before hotel security showed up in response to the ruckus.

She was just closing the door, still pulling on one shoe in the hall, when Miss Lin and Zack Johnson emerged from the next room in bathrobes, staring at her wide-eyed. "Hey, what's goin' on, Mavis?" he asked. "What's all the racket about in there?"

Mavis was still far more enraged than she was fearful about the consequences of possibly having fractured Zhu's skull with the camera. "Ah sweah, Ah'm through with this business, Zack. That disgustin' li'l creep, that *pervert*, he was a'tryin' to take pitchers o' mah *thang* under the covers, thass whut he done! Why, Ah kin jus' see mah pussy in ever' magazine an' newspaper in China!"

"What happened, Miss, ah," Lin began.

"Hawkins, mah name's Vera Hawkins, and Ah'm through with this disgustin' business, an' as to what happened, I think Ah busted the li'l creep's head." And with that she brushed by Lin and Zack Johnson, summoned the elevator, and left.

Miss Lin went to Zhu's door, knocked softly, and asked in Chinese if he was OK. She heard a low moan, a rustling sound, then a loud thud. There was more moaning. She turned to Zack. "I think he is all right. As you Americans say, don't get involved. Now, please take me back to bed and fuck me some more."

As Zack Johnson was pantingly assenting to Miss Lin's demand, Zhu was struggling, in his battered and groggy state, to try and figure out how to summon help without having to explain why his head needed to be sewn up and why his room looked like the Manson family had just left.

He finally managed to stagger into the bathroom, then stood dizzily at the sink for a few moments trying to loosen the blood on his face and chest by splashing water on himself. Presently he gave up, turned on the shower, adjusted the temperature of the water, then clumsily lowered himself into a sitting position in the tub. The spray stung Zhu's scalp wound and even hurt where it pelted against his badly bruised nose. He sat unhappily in the tub and watched the water turn pink as it washed the crusted blood off his head and chest. He sat there for the next half-hour trying to think of a plausible and honorable explanation for his rather undignified condition. Presently, the blood loss, coupled with his exhaustion and dejected state, caused him to fall asleep under the tepid shower.

* * *

The following morning Sid Burnside was enroute to the airport Marriot, anticipating an untaxing day of squiring the Chinese around on the scheduled tour of Beverly Hills to view the stars' homes, then spending the afternoon and as much of the evening as they wanted at Disneyland. He picked up his cell phone to call Miss Lin, who was at that moment trying to get Zhu out of the tub, dried, and dressed.

"In the name of Chairman Mao, how could you let this happen, Zhu?" she demanded, examining the deep gash on his scalp, which had stopped bleeding but which would clearly require stitches to close.

"I was attacked by hooligans," replied Zhu. "They were waiting in my room when I got in last night. These Americans are barbarians, uncivilized. I thought surely we would be safe in this fine hotel. This country is even worse than we'd been told. Nobody is safe! We should report this outrage to the consulate!"

Miss Lin struggled to keep from smiling as she gently toweled Zhu's head. "Tell me, Comrade, just what did this assailant look like? Was he tall? What color hair did he have? Are you sure it was a man?" unable to resist the last.

"Of course it was a man, perhaps two or three of them in fact. Do you think I could be bested by a woman?"

"Do not be offended, Comrade, I just wanted to be sure," she replied. "We must gather all the facts before we go to the police."

"The police?" he asked, a little alarmed. "Why go to the police? Clearly, they cannot even provide security in this hotel. How would you expect them to catch the hooligans? I would not be surprised to learn that their police even cooperate with the criminals in this country. No, nothing can be gained by going to the police, of that I am sure."

"What will you tell the doctor who attends you, then?" Miss Lin asked, by now thoroughly enjoying herself and secretly admiring the blond American girl who'd given Zhu such a sound thrashing. She'd gathered from Vera Hawkins' outburst that Zhu had attempted to take some sort of pictures of her *thang,* as she'd put it, which in turn caused the wild brawl that left him in his present condition.

"Perhaps it would be best if you claimed to have fallen down the stairs," she said. "You could say you were trying to get ice from the ice maker in the stair-well and tripped and fell down the stairs."

Zhu appeared to be thinking about this for a moment. While the story would avoid any complications with the police, it made him seem, in his mind, a bit ridiculous, a senior manager of a huge state-owned enterprise, falling down a stair well after a night of (presumably drunken) revelry. Miss Lin watched him expectantly, smirking, he thought irritably. "No, never," he announced, "we must tell the truth in this matter, whomever is offended. If the Americans invite violent hooligans to prey on their guests right in their hotels, the truth must be known! Had there not been so many of them, I am sure this would not have happened. I am a martial arts expert, you know!"

Miss Lin shrugged. "Whatever you think is best. Shall I summon the police?"

"No, I believe that this should be reported to our colleague, Mr. Burnside. Doubtless he is experienced in these matters and will know what to do."

"Perhaps you are right, Zhu. I'll call him right away and report the incident," Miss Lin replied, struggling to appear grave, and also wondering how this latest development might interfere with her plans to see Zack Johnson later that day. "In the meantime you should lie down and apply pressure to your head wound with this wet towel."

Zhu was actually beginning to work himself into a state of righteous indignation over the thumping he'd suffered at the hands of Vera

Hawkins, whom he rationalized was herself some sort of Amazonian female hooligan who specialized in rolling innocent and credulous dates. I am sure she has a long history of arrests and convictions for assault, robbery, and probably prostitution, he thought with satisfaction. His head throbbed, and his nose jolted him with pain every time he became careless and touched it.

Miss Lin entered Burnside's home phone number from Zhu's room, got only the answering machine, and hung up without leaving a message. She then called the office but was told by Burnside's temp that "Mr. Burnside said he was going straight over to the hotel. I expect he'll be there any minute." Miss Lin thanked the girl, then informed Zhu that she was going down to the lobby to meet Burnside. She grew apprehensive, then a bit angry, at how this unforeseen development, amusing though it was to her, might throw a monkey wrench in her plans to see Zack Johnson that evening. She was still pleasantly glowing, though a bit sore, from the night of joyous and wild abandon she'd enjoyed with the Muscle Beach stud.

Abruptly she decided to go to her room and call Zack to ensure that he'd be available later that day. Actually, she needn't have worried, since Johnson was at that moment contemplating an almost painfully throbbing erection as he lay in his own bed, occasioned by his recollections of his night with Miss Lin, whom he'd taken to calling Suzy, after the fictional Suzy Wong. "Suzy" Lin, he'd decided, was the most fascinating and exciting woman he'd had in his twenty-eight years on this earth. Jesus, I gotta see her again, he thought.

Just as he was coming to this almost desperate conclusion, the phone rang. He tore his eyes and hand away from his throbbing member and reached for the phone with more than a little irritation. "Yeah?" he almost snarled.

"Zack, this is Suzy. How are you feeling this morning?"

"Suzy? Is that you? I was just thinking about you, no kidding. Am I gonna see you again? I mean, I really enjoyed last night."

"Yes, I had fun, too, Zack. I wanted to thank you for a very nice time. I'm sure we could see each other again if you'd like."

"Really? How about later today, or maybe tonight?"

Miss Lin almost had to bite her tongue to keep from asking "what time," but managed to show a bit of modest restraint and replied instead, "Well, I don't know, Zack. I'm not sure what our schedule will be today and tonight. Will you be available later today or this evening?" Actually,

"Suzy" Lin was disgusted enough with Zhu and infatuated enough with Zack to have managed to meet him anytime or anywhere he might have suggested.

"Really?" said Zack Johnson, sounding, in spite of himself, painfully disappointed. "I'm free all day today and tonight, too. I'm either off or on standby for the next four days." Zack was, when he wasn't driving for Starlight Escort Services, an MD-80 co-pilot for Continental Airlines, and thus had plenty of time off.

"Why don't I call you in a little while, when I know what's going on later today. I am afraid your colleague, the one called Mavis, had a disagreement with my boss last night. It, umm, would appear that he lost the argument rather badly and may have to go to the hospital, so all our plans are a little unsettled at the moment. I'll call you as soon as I can."

"Yeah, do that. I really want to see you again. I really mean that, Suzy."

"That's very nice, Zack. I'll see you soon."

After they'd hung up Zack lay wondering what had happened to Suzy's boss. He'd gathered that Zhu apparently had tried to take some pictures of Mavis Belle, pictures to which the girl had obviously objected. He chuckled as he thought of Mavis's sense of outrage and her reference to breaking Zhu's head. He also hoped, a little uneasily, that whatever damage Mavis had done to Zhu wouldn't interfere with his hoped-for meeting with Miss Lin. Jesus Christ, he reflected, I don't believe this. I got the serious hots for a commie Chink. For just an instant a frightening image played in his head, that of a comfortable domestic scene, Suzy meeting him at the door, surrounded by a bunch of little Chinklets in red-starred T-shirts.

* * *

While Zack lay uneasily fast-forwarding his life into what seemed an unusual and rather improbable scenario, the object of his fantasies was waiting in the coffee shop of the hotel for Sid Burnside to make his appearance, wondering how much to tell him about how Zhu suffered his broken nose and split scalp. She sat tapping her fingertips in time to a Wynonna Judd tune, which was playing softly on the coffee shop sound system, and trying to plan some sort of opportunity to break away from the group and join Zack Johnson for a pleasant little tryst later in the day.

She wondered how well the group would get along without her, even in a guided tour environment, for none spoke English well enough to communicate anything more complex than the need to find a toilet. She felt angry at herself at not having insisted on having at least one more interpreter for the little delegation. But then, she reflected, the one thing she hadn't foreseen was having a liaison with an American, of all things. Especially one who moonlighted as a limo driver for an escort service, though she had to concede that Zack's primary job as an airline pilot seemed respectable enough.

Miss Lin's thoughts were interrupted by the sight of Sid Burnside making his way through the lobby toward the coffee shop. She smiled and waved at him to get his attention. Burnside veered off to make his way toward her table. "Morning, Miss Lin," he said, extending his hand for her to take.

"Good morning, Mr. Burnside," she responded. "Why don't you call me Suzy. That's what my American friends call me." She wondered why she had invited him to call her by the name that Zack Johnson had assigned her.

"Well, that's a nice American name, Suzy. My friends call me Sid," he said, suddenly smiling at this first real display of warmth he'd felt from any of the Chinese, especially from this beautiful Chinese girl he'd taken to thinking of as the Dragon Lady. "Well, is Mr. Zhu all set to enjoy his tour of Beverly Hills and Disneyland?"

"Ah, well, Sid, we may have a complication with that." Burnside raised his eyebrows quizzically. "It seems that last night Mr. Zhu had a slight altercation with persons unknown, well, actually I think he had a dispute with the girl from the escort service, the one they call Mavis. I don't know all the details, but he appears to have a broken nose and a bad cut on his scalp. I believe he will need professional medical attention before he is ready to enjoy his outing today."

Burnside managed to look grave upon hearing this news but needed to call upon all his reserves of self-control to keep from grinning, then laughing uproariously. He wondered what sort of kinky behavior Zhu had displayed toward the girl, whom he remembered well as the lissome blond in the tight jeans. "Well, this should be attended to at once," said Burnside, jumping to his feet as though Zhu were in a life-threatening situation, perhaps minutes from death. Actually, he couldn't wait to see the Chinese factory boss and hear his explanation of his condition.

Five minutes later he was examining the gash on Zhu's head and inspecting his clearly broken nose. "My God, Mr. Zhu, this is an extremely serious matter! What happened here? Please tell me so I can summon the police!"

Miss Lin translated Burnside's request, also stifling a smile. Zhu replied in rapid-fire indignant Chinese. "He says he was attacked by hooligans, several of them," said Miss Lin, actually winking at Burnside.

"Did they take anything of value?" asked Burnside. As he asked the question his eye fell on Zhu's camera, which now sported a badly dented body. He picked it up and noted that the back was bent so that it wouldn't close.

"Did they strike you with this?" he asked.

"No, I am sure that they struck me with a large and heavy pistol, I'm sure of it! How can you allow people to have such weapons in this country? It's uncivilized!"

After Miss Lin had translated this Burnside looked horrified. "My God, a pistol? This is a very serious crime! We must notify the police at once! There is no time to lose if we are to catch the hooligans!"

"The police? The police?"repeated Zhu. "What possible good would that do? The hooligans are doubtless long gone by now."

"Perhaps, Mr. Zhu, but the police will want to interview you in order to gather clues. They will want to know whom you talked to last night, who knew of your whereabouts, who knew when you arrived back at the hotel. For example, I am sure they will want to talk to the girl who escorted you last night! Perhaps she noticed suspicious characters in our midst! Perhaps, God forbid, she was an accomplice in this terrible crime!"

As Miss Lin translated Burnside's emphatically delivered comments, Zhu's face clearly showed his chagrin and alarm. "The girl?" he asked. "They would want to talk with the girl? I refuse to believe that such an innocent young lady could be involved in anything like this! I cannot allow the police to interrogate this young lady. It would not be fair to her. I have heard all about your police brutality!"

"Well, I don't know," said Burnside doubtfully. "There are procedures to be followed in these things."

"What if we simply do not report this incident?" asked Zhu.

Burnside looked thoughtful, then distressed as he apparently wrestled with the grave legal and moral implications of not reporting a serious felony, involving assault with a deadly weapon. "I don't know. I simply don't know what could happen," he replied. He held his chin, seemingly lost in thought. "Do only the three of us know about this terrible crime?" he asked.

Zhu looked from Miss Lin to Burnside. "It would appear that we are the only ones, Mr. Zhu," said Miss Lin. "Certainly, I have told no one. And Mr. Burnside just learned of it this moment."

"In that case, perhaps it is best that knowledge of this heinous crime be kept between the three of us," said Zhu, seeming to regain some small measure of command presence for the first time.

Miss Lin translated for Burnside, who seemed to take a long moment to consider Zhu's proposal. Finally he nodded hesitantly, then more decisively. "All right, that's what we'll do," he said. "We'll keep this a secret between the three of us. But we must get you to the hospital at once, Mr. Zhu. Perhaps it would be best if you told them at the emergency room that you fell in the bathroom and hit your head. It is a common enough accident in our country, what with all these slippery tile bathrooms.

Zhu sagged with relief, then regained a surprisingly aggressive demeanor. "It is agreed! It disgusts me that I must lie to protect the honor and well-being of an innocent young woman in this country! This would never happen in the People's Republic!"

"I am sure, Mr. Zhu. There the police know how to deal with criminals! (and everyone else, thought Burnside) But we must be practical. I will call a cab to take us to the nearest hospital for treatment."

* * *

An hour and half later Miss Lin, Burnside, and a newly sutured and bandaged Zhu were leaving the hospital. At Miss Lin's suggestion they had simply canceled the Beverly Hills tour, giving the delegation the morning free to lounge around the hotel, sleep in, or read. She had also used the time to locate an interpreter through the yellow pages, who would spend the rest of the day with Burnside and the Chinese, accompanying them to Disneyland. The girl she'd found was a student from China, eager to earn the two hundred dollars "Suzy" Lin had promised for the day at Disneyland.

When they arrived back at the hotel, she suggested to Zhu that he would be well advised to return to his room for the day, which in fact was what the intern who'd sewn him up had said. He didn't argue. "Yes, perhaps you're right," he muttered, by now thoroughly dejected, embarrassed, and disappointed that he'd miss both his visit to the stars' homes and Disneyland.

"And Zhu?" she said. "I'll be taking the rest of the day off to see a friend. I should be back tonight some time."

"What? What if I need your help in making myself understood to the personnel in the hotel? You can't just take off and leave me here alone."

"I'm sure you'll be able to take care of your basic needs. Perhaps you'd like me to call the girl to keep you company, the one they call Mavis?" She stared at him for a long moment, eyebrows raised and smiling faintly.

Suzy Lin tossed her handbag over her shoulder, turned, and walked out the door, leaving Zhu fuming and wondering what, if anything, ultimately would come of their little conspiracy of silence.

* * *

Two hours later, as Sherry Maxwell and Sid Burnside were waiting impatiently for the Disneyland tour departure, Maxwell almost desperately wishing for a vodka on the rocks to steady his scotch-induced shakes, Miss Lin and Zack Johnson were relaxing, naked, in his hot tub, drinking a mixture of orange juice and ginger ale. Suzy Lin speculated that all the stories she'd heard about American sybaritic decadence must be true. He had greeted her at the door, immediately picked her up and carried her to the bedroom, where they'd taken up exactly where they'd left off the night before. They were practically dozing off when Zack reached over and ran his hand along her thigh. "Hey, Suzy, you know what'd be fun today?"

"This is fun, Zack. What could be better?"

"Let's go to Vegas for the day."

"What's there?"

"You know, Las Vegas, where they do all the gambling. I'll bet you've never seen anything like it."

"Can we go there in just the afternoon?"

"Sure, I got a friend who'll lend me his plane. I give him free instrument instruction once in a while and he lets me use it sometimes.

And so an hour later Zack Johnson and his Chinese communist female companion, who was beginning to rather enjoy the freedom and material abundance of the West, were winging their way to Las Vegas in the swift twin engine Acrostar Zack had borrowed from his friend at John Wayne Airport.

* * *

Chapter 3

Just about the time Zack and "Suzy" were entering the Terminal Control Area for the Las Vegas airport, Vice President Nate Garmin was going over in his mind what he'd say to the Chinese visitors and the ambassador the following evening when he'd meet the executives and engineering people of The Long March People's Cooperative Auto Manufacturing Company. He was having difficulty coming up with a short address that had just the right measure of lavish praise for Chinese engineering expertise brought to bear on socially desirable enterprises, but without degenerating into full-blown, fulsome obsequiousness. He also wanted to incorporate some sort of remark on the social limitations of unfettered capitalism and how it could dangerously compromise the security of the environment. He would show the Chinese that he was no mere capitalist tool, while at the same time dropping a passing reference to the gigantic Yangzte River dam project and how the Chinese should study all the possible environmental implications of such a vast enterprise. He was sure his hosts would not be offended by his suggestion, that they had already given full consideration to these issues and would therefore be in complete agreement with his remarks. Garmin imagined the Chinese interrupting his comments to applaud at that point, sure that they'd feel the same sense of east-west socialist solidarity with which he was suffused. We're all just passengers on Spaceship Earth, thought Garmin happily, suddenly resolving to incorporate this thought verbatim in his remarks. Why, maybe I could even expand on that, he told himself. I mean, like, the only thing that separates us is that we're in first class, and you're in coach! Hey, that's a great analogy, thought Garmin, stopping to scribble the thought on a notepad. He briefly considered calling Penny Twombly to run the Spaceship Earth comment by her, anticipating her agreement and flattery with pleasure. He was about to pick up the phone and call, then stopped, his brow furrowed in concentration.

Maybe it'd be better if she heard it tomorrow night for the first time, he thought. She could even lead the applause. Boy, this is gonna be great!

* * *

While Nate Garmin continued to work on his little speech, tongue protruding from the corner of his mouth in a perfect caricature of child-like concentration, Miss Lin and Zack Johnson were finishing lunch in a pleasant little Mexican restaurant a block off the strip. As the waitress finished clearing the table and took their order for coffee, Zack reached across and took Suzy's hand in what, for him, was an unusual display of affection. "Suzy, do you think you'll be assigned to the office here in California? I mean, they're gonna need someone as an interpreter, don't you think?"

"No, I don't think that could happen. I'm too high a pay grade to work for an affiliate company as an interpreter, plus they don't really need someone with my language skills for a job like that here in America. No, I'm afraid that when this little trip is over I'm on my way back home." She sighed a little wistfully.

"You mean, you don't know when we'll see each other again?" asked Zack, clearly showing his chagrin and not caring.

"Well, no, I don't, Zack. I'll probably be back in some capacity or another at some point, at least for a few days, but I don't know when, if ever."

"Well, why can't you just move over here? I know you could get a good job here in five minutes. I mean, how many people speak perfect Chinese and perfect English?"

She smiled and squeezed his hand. "Probably more than you think. But in any case, I can't walk out of China and go just anywhere I want. China's not quite like America, Zack. I wouldn't even be here if they didn't consider me politically reliable."

"Jesus, how can you live in a place like that?"

"It's easy. I was born there. They put me through school, educated me. Everything I have I owe to the party. It's not bad, really. I'm quite happy. That's probably hard for you to understand, or probably for any American to understand."

"Yeah, I guess it is. So you can't just leave and come here?"

"Zack, it's not just China that's the problem. It's your immigration officials, too. Not just anybody can pick up and come to America. If they could there'd be nobody living in Mexico."

Zack chuckled. "No, I guess there wouldn't be. I guess I never thought of these things before," he said a little sadly. "So what would you have to do to qualify to come with our immigration people?"

"I'm not really sure, but think it has to do with something like getting a student visa or having an employer show that he can't fill a job with an American. I'd have to have a unique skill. Or be married to an American. Then I guess even the Chinese government would let me go without conditions."

"All you have to do is marry an American to come here?"

"I'm pretty sure that's the way it works." Suddenly she smiled. "But I'm sure your parents wouldn't approve in any event."

"Who cares? Here in America we ignore our parents."

"Yes, so I've heard."

Zack called for the check, thinking how his fascination with this beautiful, intelligent, and mysterious Chinese girl was all rather unnerving. He was used to feeling in complete control with women. Now, though Suzy Lin did nothing to be overtly assertive, he had the uneasy feeling that she was the one in complete control.

Five minutes later they were walking toward the strip, holding hands. Suddenly Suzy stopped and looked across the street. She dropped Zack's hand and stood holding onto a parking meter with both hands, swaying like a child. "What's that pink building?"

"What, that place over there? That's a kind of Las Vegas institution. They call it a marriage chapel."

* * *

It was nearly seven o'clock when Burnside, Maxwell, and the Chinese delegation arrived back in the hotel, sunburned, tired, but happy. The day, in Burnside's estimation, had been a total success. The Chinese student Suzy Lin had found had proved to be an excellent interpreter, with a sense of humor that kept the little delegation laughing and in good spirits for the entire day. Once again Burnside found himself cursing the ridiculous

Chino office location. He would have liked to have had the student available for part time employment at Red Tiger, reasoning that the factory would much appreciate receiving their communications in Chinese.

As Burnside called up to Zhu's room to check on him, Maxwell disappeared into the cocktail lounge, intent on quickly reaching a blood-alcohol level which would re-establish a reasonable psychological equilibrium for him.

Burnside was told by Zhu, haltingly and with great difficulty, that he'd be taking dinner in his room but wished to see Burnside and Maxwell the following morning before their planned departure at nine-thirty in the morning. At least that's what Burnside thought Zhu had said. He wondered where Miss Lin was at the moment, a little concerned that he hadn't fully understood Zhu. A few minutes later Burnside joined Sherry at the bar. Unknown to Burnside, Maxwell was already into his third vodka martini, hoping to get his BA level up as high as possible before Burnside's arrival intervened.

"Well, Sherry, how'd you think it went?" he asked as he arranged himself on the barstool next to Maxwell.

"Pretty good, I guess," Maxwell mumbled. "They musta shot up a hundred rolls of film."

"Yeah, I guess. Hey, you ain't seen our interpreter, that girl Lin, have ya?" He had already tried reaching her in her room without success and had dismissed the student, giving her two hundred dollars in cash for her services.

"Not since this morning," Sherry replied.

"Hell, I hope she's around. We should probably have the rest of 'em to dinner here in the hotel, but I don't know what we're gonna do if she's not around here to translate." Burnside was mentally reviewing how he might translate a menu in sounds and sign language, briefly considering making moo sounds for beef, a couple of oinks for pork, and swimming motions for fish.

Maxwell ordered his fourth vodka martini as the bartender arrived with Burnside's beer. "Hey, take it easy on that stuff, Sherry," said Burnside, thinking that Sherry was ordering his second drink a little early.

"Two's my limit, Sid."

* * *

While Sherry Maxwell was reassuring Sid Burnside that he had no drinking problem with which to compound his present difficulties, Mr. and Mrs. Zack Johnson were on their way back to Los Angeles in Zack's borrowed Aerostar, each lost in private thoughts which centered mostly on the question of their sanity. Zack stole a glance at Suzy, who was staring fixedly out into the blackness of the desert. The panel lights reflected in her shining black hair. He engaged the autopilot, took her chin in his hand and turned her head to face him. He leaned over and kissed her gently, then drew back and looked into her eyes. "I do love you, you know."

"Do you really mean that, Zack? I think maybe we're both just a little crazy." Tears were welling up in her eyes.

"Yeah, I do mean it, and you're probably right. We *are* both crazy." In truth, Zack wasn't really sure exactly *what* he felt for the former Miss Lin. What he *was* sure about was that he didn't want to risk never seeing her again. Their precipitous decision seemed to the only certain way of foreclosing that possibility.

She threw her arms around his neck, whispering in his ear. "I'll try to make you happy, Zack. I promise."

The Johnson's hasty marriage, unremarkable though it may have seemed, at least by Las Vegas standards, would have remarkably far-reaching consequences.

* * *

Sid Burnside and Sherry Maxwell finally had hit on the simple solution of what to do with the Chinese delegation when Sherry made the observation that most employees of Chinese restaurants seemed to speak limited English and that it therefore seemed reasonable that their native tongue was...*Chinese!* "Why don't we just take 'em to a good Chinese restaurant, boss?" he had suggested. "Then they can order what they want."

Burnside noted that perhaps he might want to retain Maxwell, showing as he did such keen resourcefulness. Accordingly, the little group, less Zhu and the former Miss Lin, was herded into the Econoline van for the trip to an upscale Chinese restaurant less than four miles away. While the group was thus gorging noisily and happily, the Johnsons were arriving back at the hotel. Zack put his arm around his bride and pulled her close as she tried to call Zhu from the hotel phone in the lobby. He nuzzled her neck as Zhu came on the line. She pushed him away with look of good-natured exasperation, announcing to Zhu that she wished to come up and see him right away. Presently, she hung up, drew a deep breath, raised her eyebrows at Zack and announced, "Well, I guess I'd better tell Zhu that his interpreter is now a legal resident alien of the United States."

"I think you mean we'd better tell him."

"That's what I meant."

Two minutes later they were standing in Zhu's hotel room, noting that Zhu now sported two rather black eyes from the right hand shot he'd absorbed from Vera Hawkins eighteen hours earlier. "What's he doing here?" Zhu demanded, not looking at or otherwise acknowledging Zack Johnson. "And where have you been? I've been unable to get any work done or participate in any of Mr. Burnside's activities without your assistance. This will not look good on your record, Miss Lin." His tone left no doubt in Zack Johnson's mind that his new bride was being admonished.

"Hey, tell this little weasel that if he talks to you that way again I'll rip his head off."

"I'll handle this, Zack," she said, smiling faintly. "Zhu, I'd like to you to meet my husband, Zack Johnson. We were married this afternoon in Las Vegas, a city which apparently does not frown on brief courtships. Zack is an airline pilot here in America." She turned to Zack. "Please offer him your hand, my husband."

Zack held out his hand, which Zhu took tentatively, looking from Zack to Suzy in bewilderment. "But how could you do this without official permission, Miss Lin? Our government will never sanction this marriage, never! You must return to China when we leave. How could I ever explain this to my boss?" He looked at her beseechingly.

"I don't know what our, or I should say *your,* government can do about it. I'm a legal resident of the United States of America now." She glanced at Zack. "I have no family in China, save one old aunt. But I will stay with you for the duration of your stay in America and perform my duties as your interpreter." She explained to Zack in English what she had told Zhu.

"Of course, that will be necessary," Zhu nodded vigorously. He was already forming the thought in his mind that if Burnside hadn't arranged the evening out with the American escort service that he'd not be meeting the Chinese embassy staff in Washington looking like he'd tangled with a Thai foot-boxer. Nor would his interpreter, Luscious Lubricious Lin, have run off and married this blond muscle-headed lout. This whole debacle was Burnside's fault, he told himself angrily. Then his natural Chinese civility asserted itself. He turned to Zack and extended his hand once again. "I wish you both a long and prosperous marriage."

Suzy translated for him. "Why, thank you for the thought," replied Zack, who then turned to his wife and asked, "Are you going to Washington tomorrow, then?"

"Well, I think I'd better. It wouldn't be right to just leave the group at this point."

"Yeah, I guess," said Zack. "Hey, I'll join you. I'm not flying for another two days. I can fly standby to Washington, probably on the same plane with you. What airline are you taking?"

Zack's suggestion, innocent though it was, would set in motion a series of turbulent domestic and geo-political events.

* * *

Li Wan Le, the Chinese ambassador to the United States, sighed a bit unhappily as he thought of the dinner that night he had to host for the staff from the Long March People's Cooperative Automotive Manufacturing Company. It wasn't that he minded having the little get-together for the Chinese visitors, which, ordinarily, he would have enjoyed. He always looked forward to informal meetings with the young Chinese engineers, technicians, and managers on whom the prosperity and success of the new China depended. In such a setting he could talk to them without the obligatory political and "glory of the party" references (accompanied by much toasting) that he found so tiresome. No, what was bothering Li was the thought of having to endure an evening with Vice-President Nate Garmin, who in addition to being the most exasperatingly boring man Li had ever known, always made such an embarrassing effort to ingratiate himself with the Chinese. He remembered Garmin's observation that Chinese seemed a very difficult language, followed by the question, "I mean, like, how long did it take you to learn it?" Garmin embarrassed him, causing him once again to wonder at the workings of American democracy. It always seemed to Li that some of the most incredibly stupid people ended up as high elected officials in America.

69

And now he'd been told that the president himself might stop by later in the evening. He groaned inwardly as he thought of the last time he had met President Bob Carruthers, which had been at a White House function. Carruthers had ended up talking, not through, but *to* an extremely attractive female interpreter whom Li had brought along to work with members of his staff. Toward the end of the evening Carruthers had cornered him and rather artlessly asked him whether the interpreter might be available to help with a few basic Chinese words and phrases for his upcoming trip to the People's Republic. Li had informed him that the woman was due to return home the following week but that they had a very bright young man on staff who was very good at matching American and Chinese colloquialisms and who'd be happy to help him. He never heard from the White House again on the matter.

* * *

After they'd said their goodnights to Zhu, the Johnsons stood talking in the hallway. "Well, Suzy, I think we should go home and let me carry you across the threshold. It's an old American matrimonial tradition."

She giggled. "That sounds like fun. Let's go to my room for my things and then we can get going."

"Yes, we really should consummate this marriage properly so the authorities won't say this was just a scam to get you citizen's status."

"What's a scam?"

He looked at her in surprise. It was the first word she'd asked him about. "Oh, it's slang for a trick or confidence game. Something like that." He stopped walking and looked at her. "Hey, this isn't a scam like that, is it?"

She started to laugh, but then saw he was serious. "No, Zack. This isn't a scam. I'm not sure what it is, maybe insanity, but it isn't a scam. I never even thought about living in America before this afternoon. I think maybe you're just some kind of fantasy from my subconscious."

"Yeah, maybe that's what it is with me, too. I think I always wanted a beautiful Oriental mistress."

"Well, you've got more than just a mistress now."

Fifteen minutes later they were pulling up in front of a supermarket. "Why are we stopping here?" Suzy asked.

"We gotta get some stuff for the kitchen." He led her inside, where she followed him up and down the isles while he grabbed a variety of food-stuffs, toiletries, and a couple of magazines and a paperback from the book section. She found herself gaping at the incredible profusion of produce, meats, poultry products, and the endless variety of prepared foods, to say nothing of the literally thousands of non-food products. She watched, fascinated, as Zack paid for it all with a Master Card, which he swiped through some kind of device which registered the sale. In her two previous visits to America she had confined her shopping to a couple of clothing stores, which while interesting, was not particularly startling. The supermarket was like nothing she had ever seen before.

She took Zack's arm while they walked back to the car. "America's an interesting country," she said. "I think I'm going to like it."

When they arrived home, Zack, true to his word, picked her up and carried her through the front door. He put her down in the kitchen, then on an impulse, practically sprinted to the phone and erased all the messages. He didn't want to explain to his new bride who Cheryl, Tina, or Lisa were, at least not on their wedding night. As he stood by the phone he kept waiting for some sort of delayed reaction to their precipitous action of that afternoon to set in. But nothing seemed to be happening. God Almighty, he thought. I just got married. *Married!* To a Chinese girl from Communist China I just met yesterday! Maybe she's a spy! On reflection, however, he couldn't imagine what use he'd be to the Chinese. All he knew how to do was fly an MD-80. He shook his head to clear it. He heard her call from the kitchen. "Ah, coming, honey. I was just looking for something." He went back into the kitchen, put his arms around her and pulled her close, finding himself immediately aroused. Zack Johnson was an uncomplicated man. His concerns evaporated as he led her back to the bedroom.

* * *

Sherry Maxwell and Sid Burnside were just leaving LAX, having seen off the Chinese delegation from The People's Long March Cooperative Automotive Manufacturing Company on their trip to Washington, DC. Burnside was feeling better than he had since joining the company. He now had no doubt whatever that it would be years before he'd be required to do anything substantive, being convinced that the parent corporation for Red Tiger Motors wouldn't be ready to exploit even the Sumatran market within the decade. Plus, as long as he was reporting to Zhu, he figured that the man wouldn't be too demanding, knowing that Burnside was privy to at least some of the embarrassing details regarding the alleged attack by "hooligans." He was slightly concerned about Zhu's future, however, what with his highly trained and no doubt valued interpreter running off with a guy from a dating service. He didn't doubt that Zhu would be blamed, at least in part, for the girl's defection, both from the Chinese government and her race. He chuckled, then looked over at Maxwell, who was struggling to extricate a Marlboro from a fresh pack. "Hey, Sherry, whaddya make of that Lin girl running off with that guy from the escort service?"

"I dunno. I s'pose he's got a bigger dick than your average Chinese guy. By the way, what happened to their leader, that guy Zhu?"

"I think he tried somethin' weird with that blonde he was with and she beat the crap outta him."

"No shit? Whaddya think happened.?"

"I think she hit him in the head with his camera. I was up in his room and it was all busted. Jesus, this is a strange bunch we got here." Burnside was trying to decide what to do with Maxwell. On the one hand, he wasn't exactly anybody he would have hired as a lowly district sales manager, let alone a vice-president of sales and marketing. On the other, it seemed highly unlikely that either of them would be doing anything that required any talent for quite some time. And letting Maxwell go might raise questions that he'd have to answer. Even answering simple and reasonable questions required a level of effort which Burnside was loath to put forth if it could be avoided. Plus, he'd have to continue to cull resumes. Hell, he could fob off any additional personnel screening and hiring duties on Maxwell. Abruptly, Burnside made his decision.

"Sherry," he said, "we never got into your pay plan. How's seventy-five grand a year sound?"

Maxwell almost choked on the lungful of smoke he was holding. After he composed himself he hesitated, gulped, then thought that it would be unseemly for him to jump at the offer. After all, negotiation was part of the protocol. Lowering his voice an octave, he replied, with great apparent deliberation, "Well, I don't know, Sid. That job has a lot of responsibility with it. I think it's worth more than that."

"Oh, c'mon, knock this shit off, willya Maxwell. D' ya want it or not?"

"I'll take it," Maxwell squeaked hastily.

"Good. Now, I want you to hang around out here for a few days, Sherry. I got some odd jobs around the office that need doing."

"Sure. I can stay as long you need me."

Burnside had just decided to take off the next few days, during which he could have Maxwell hang around and man the phone and fax machine. This Red Tiger Motors deal is turning out OK, he told himself.

* * *

Suzy and Zack arrived at the airport rather late, though it didn't matter, since Zack was able to park in the Continental Airlines employee lot and then make it to the United gates in plenty of time for the flight. He also managed to get himself a seat on standby. Suzy, to his surprise, seemed sheepish, almost embarrassed, in the presence of the other Chinese, though they seemed to think the idea of Zack and Suzy getting married was OK, even a bit novel. They chattered happily and shook Zack's hand while he grinned rather foolishly, evidently making the occasional ribald remark, which caused Suzy to redden, and which brought forth further cackles and giggles.

Once they were airborne and hunkered down in their seats, Zack asked, "Well, what do they think of us getting married?"

"I'm not sure. I think they're a little shocked, but they don't know what to think of American customs or traditions. They may think Americans do this sort of thing all the time, and since they're in America right now, it's perhaps a little easier to accept. Plus, the girls all think you look like a blond god."

"Well, I do. You better remember that and take good care of me so I don't stray."

"You better not if you want to stay a rooster. We Chinese girls are very jealous, and we're prone to drastic solutions. Genital maimings are a common practice in China."

Suddenly Zack laughed. He loved this girl for her looks, her brains, and her sense of humor. Suddenly he knew, just *knew*, that everything would turn out all right. He was already planning how he'd tell his parents in Kansas about her and how they got married, deciding to tell the truth about being afraid to let her go back to China, but stretching the time-frame of their acquaintance to a more respectable three weeks or a month. He sighed contentedly, reached over, and took her hand.

Just under five hours later they were landing at Washington National, only two hours from their scheduled evening at the Chinese Embassy. After they'd landed Zhu was running about, trying to get everybody organized and on their way to the hotel so they'd not be late for the reception and dinner. Forty-five minutes after touchdown they were all jammed into five cabs and on their way to the Marriot in Crystal City. Unknown to Zhu, one of the finance people in his little group was a member of the Chinese Secret Police, who had already informed the embassy that one of their number had married an American, and that her husband was accompanying the group to Washington. When the ambassador had been informed of this development, he shrugged, muttered something about youthful hormones being out of control, and decided to call Zhu and have him bring the new bride and groom along to the embassy dinner. It would be just the sort of sentimental nonsense the Americans would love, he told himself. He could just see Nate Garmin reading all manner of idiotic symbolism into the actions of a couple of oversexed young people. Li snorted, partly in disgust and partly in bemusement.

Ninety minutes later Zack was fastening a necklace on Suzy as she got ready to meet the group downstairs, preparatory to taking the bus over to the Chinese embassy. The phone rang and Suzy Johnson stopped brushing her hair, went over and picked it up. Zack watched with interest as she spoke in rapid-fire Chinese, intrigued at her ability to slip effortlessly from one tongue into another. She put down the phone and looked at him. "That was Zhu. He says you've been invited to attend the dinner with us."

"Huh? They want me to go along?"

"That's what he said." She shrugged. "Maybe they just thought it was the hospitable thing to do."

"All I've got to wear is a blue blazer and some tan slacks."

"I'm sure that'll be all right. I'm not exactly formally dressed," she said, referring to the dark blue pinstriped pantsuit with the lowcut beige cashmere sweater she was wearing underneath.

"Yeah, I can see that," Zack replied, ogling her inviting cleavage lasciviously. The pantsuit, despite its modest cut, also managed to reveal subtly that underneath its fabric was a nicely formed and shapely woman. He walked over and put his arms around her, looking down into her eyes.

"You know, I've always been good at quick decisions."
"Good. I've always preferred decisive men."

* * *

Three hours later Zack and Suzy Johnson, happily full from an excellent dinner of Peking Duck, were listening to a carefully prepared speech by Nate Garmin, which was being translated simultaneously into Chinese by a male interpreter at his side. True to form with Garmin, the oration was degenerating into something bordering on toadying to the Chinese, sounding almost like a tribute to the technological triumphs of socialism. Zack Johnson had to stifle a snort of disgust. Then why are they buying their jumbo jets from Boeing, he thought. What an asshole.

There was a stir among the Chinese hosts when Garmin admonished them to adequately consider the environmental impact of the Yantgze River dam project. The ambassador glanced at his wife then looked a bit narrowly at Garmin. There was no applause, as Garmin had hoped. He paused expectantly at this point, appearing to have lost his train of thought, then cleared his throat and stumbled on. Penny Twombly, seated at one of the tables nearest the podium, beamed her happy and vacuous Betty Boop smile.

Garmin came to his most telling remark of the evening, the observation that they were all just passengers on Spaceship Earth. The interpreter seemed to have a momentary difficulty in translating this properly. Garmin paused and looked around the room trying to gauge the reaction to his deeply profound remark. There seemed to be none. He then completed the thought with his characterization of the American passengers as being in first class and the Chinese in tourist. But the comment came out in translation as the Chinese colloquialism for coach seating as *ja ching lei,* or "livestock." Garmin paused and looked around, greeted by stony silence, broken only by Suzy Johnson's involuntary giggle, which provoked other titters from those few communist hosts with a sense of humor regarding their apparent status in the eyes of the Americans. The more predominant reaction, however, was one of anger at the perceived insult. Two minutes later Nate Garmin completed his speech to the tiniest smattering of applause. He sat down, hoping that the speech had been so profoundly moving that his hosts were at a loss for words or adequate emotional response.

Ambassador Li thanked him and invited the guests to mingle, enjoy the open bar, and dance to the seven piece swing band playing for their enjoyment. As the guests were noisily sliding back chairs, beginning to talk and move around, Zack looked at his bride and asked, "What was so funny back there?"

His wife chuckled and explained Garmin's gaffe, though she added that the interpreter should have been a bit quicker-thinking than to use the Chinese vernacular. "I wouldn't say it was a brilliant comment in any event," she concluded. Zack snorted in disgust. Like most people with technical skills, he regarded the Vice-President as a rather dim bulb.

"Hey, would you dance with me?" he asked, looking down at her. The band, predictably enough, was playing Blue Moon.

"I'll try. I don't think I'm very good at it. This wasn't part of my education."

He escorted her out to the little three hundred square foot dance floor. As she'd said, Suzy Johnson wasn't an accomplished dancer, getting her and Zack's feet tangled up, much to his amusement. "Hey, I finally found something you're not good at. I feel better." She was just getting the hang of following his steps when the band trailed off, as Ambassador Li took the microphone and announced to the guests in quite passable English that they were privileged to have the President of the United States join them. There was an excited chatter throughout the crowded room as people strained to catch a glimpse of President Bob Carruthers striding confidently through the broad double-doored entrance to the banquet hall. An impromptu reception line began to form almost instantly, with the guests drifting over to queue up for the chance to meet the president.

Suzy stood on her tiptoes, agog at the sight of Bob Carruthers. "Zack, let's get in the line," she said excitedly.

Her husband rolled his eyes. Though he had no desire to meet the president, he surmised that it would thrill his bride. He took her hand and led her to the line, trying to smile enthusiastically. He noted that Nate Garmin would precede the president in the line of dignitaries waiting to receive them. Unknown to Suzy or Zack, they had been pointed out to Ambassador Li as the couple so precipitously married only the day before. Li looked at them with interest. He had somehow imagined the girl to be a rather frumpy-looking, studious, bespectacled little mouse, her groom small and unimpressive. Instead they looked to him to be a near story-book couple, a tall rugged-looking Nordic type, taking a beautiful Chinese bride in an almost too-perfect melding of the races.

The couple entered the line and moved slowly up to where the ambassador, Nate Garmin and the president stood chatting, shaking hands, and smiling. Zack Johnson noted that the ambassador was the only one of the three who seemed to give a normal handshake. Both Carruthers and Garmin seemed to grasp the guests' hands for as long as the greeting and small talk continued. Johnson hated people who did that and was already thinking of how to quickly extricate his hand from theirs. When he and Suzy reached the dignitaries he was surprised to hear Ambassador Li offer what sounded like sincere congratulations on their marriage, then turn to Nate Garmin and explain that one of the employees of the Long March People's Cooperative Automotive Manufacturing Company had married an American during their visit to the United States.

Garmin's eyes opened wide in surprise. "Wow!" he exclaimed, looking back and forth between them. "That's really neat! Are you going to live in China or the United States?"

Suzy answered for them. "We'll be living in Los Angeles, Mr. Vice-President," giving him a sparkling smile.

Garmin seemed momentarily confused. "Oh, I get it! I thought you were the Chinese one, not him."

Suzy cocked her head and looked at Nate Garmin, wondering if she'd heard right. "Ah, I *am* the Chinese one, as you put it, Mr. Vice-President. I'm an interpreter. My husband, Zack here, is from Los Angeles."

"Oh, I get it," said Garmin, nodding vigorously. "So you speak Chinese, too, right?"

Suzy Lin Johnson's eyes briefly met those of Ambassador Li, who was unable to stop himself from giving his head a brief little shake.

"Yes, I speak Chinese, Mr. Vice-President."

"Boy, that's really great," gushed Nate Garmin. "I hope you two'll speak it at home so the kids pick it up."

"Yes, we plan to do that," replied Zack Johnson, obviously not wanting to further confuse the vice-president by informing him that *he* didn't speak Chinese, and further, that it took two Chinese speakers to converse. He inched down the line to indicate that the small talk was at an end.

A moment later Suzy Johnson was shaking hands with the president of the United States, who was none-too-subtly inspecting her cleavage.

"This is a very great honor Mr. President," she said

"My, you speak good English, Miss...?"

"Mrs. Johnson. Many years of study and practice."

"Ah, yes, well, perhaps we'll have a chance to chat later."

Zack Johnson shook the president's hand perfunctorily, smiling rather tightly as he did so. He let his hand go completely limp in the president's grasp. Carruthers took the hint and released his hand. Well, I shook the president's hand, he thought. Big deal. He took Suzy by the waist and steered her away from the receiving line and back toward the dance floor. "Let's dance."

"You didn't seem very enthusiastic about meeting the president, Zack. Don't you like him?"

"Let's just say I didn't vote for him." They danced one more number then drifted over to a small group, which included Penny Twombly, Nate Garmin, Zhu Fei, and the young male interpreter who had carelessly translated Garmin's reference to the Chinese being in tourist seating.

As they reached the group Penny Twombly was enthusiastically congratulating Zhu on the Chinese technological triumph in producing such an economical and environmentally friendly car. Zhu puffed himself up to his full five feet eight inches and replied, "Yes, the Red Whippet is a true technological triumph, an example of what can happen when the desires of the people are placed before greed and the quest for profits." Nate Garmin mentally repeated Zhu's statement, hoping to remember it long enough to be able to write it down on a napkin or piece of scratch paper. "We intend to begin importing the Red Whippet within six months and expect it to sell far in excess of any other cars in the American market."

"What does the price of $5000 include, Mr. Zhu?" asked Nate Garmin.

"Why, of course it includes the same things as any other car," replied Zhu dismissively.

"You mean, like whitewalls?" Garmin persisted.

"White walls?" Zhu asked, looking puzzled. "No, we will have a variety of colors. Some will be white, others red. Perhaps some will be green or blue as well. The buyers will have many choices."

"Ah, what happened to your face, Mr. Zhu?" asked Peggy Twombly, deciding to change the subject in the long and somewhat embarrassing silence that followed Zsui's explanation of color selection. "Did you have an accident?"

Zhu, loosened up a bit from the three scotches he'd had prior to dinner and the two glasses of white wine during the meal, replied, "No, it was no accident. I was set upon by hooligans while in Los Angeles, right in my hotel! They tried to rob me, but I managed to subdue them and set them to flight. Fortunately, I have had training in karate and was not easily victimized."

Nate Garmin looked aghast. "My God, Mr. Zhu, did the police catch the muggers?"

"Hah! The police! They were able to do nothing. There was really no point in calling them."

Penny Twombly looked equally shocked, hearing of the brutal assault on the representative of a progressive and environmentally concerned country. "Let me apologize for our government, Mr. Zhu," she exclaimed passionately. "I promise you that this will be investigated vigorously. We in the federal government will not tolerate state visitors being attacked. I'll send someone around tomorrow morning to get the details from you. I have friends in the Justice Department." Suzy Lin Johnson looked at Zack and smiled faintly.

"I can be there in the morning to interpret for your people if necessary," she said to Penny Twombly. "We are staying in the hotel also." Zhu looked up sharply, wondering what she'd said. Suzy briefly translated for Zhu, enjoying the thought of his discomfiture and anxiety at the thought of the morning meeting.

Abruptly, Zhu replied to Suzy. "Wait, I will not be available tomorrow morning! I have an important business meeting." The former Miss Lin duly translated this for the eagerly indignant Penny Twombly, who pledged the full cooperation of American law enforcement in finding and punishing the miscreant(s) responsible for Zhu's condition.

Suzy and Zack drifted off to join another group. Zack chuckled and looked admiringly at his bride, of whom he was beginning to feel inordinately proud and very much in love with at that moment. "Why'd you do that to poor old Zhu? He was just enjoying making himself a hero for an evening."

"Oh, I know that. He's just too full of himself all the time. He's just like so many other party officials and company managers. Now that I'm not going back with him I feel like having some fun."

"I see you can be wicked at times."

They joined a small group of company managers who stood talking quietly with Ambassador Li and his wife, a plump and cheerful looking woman of about fifty. As before, the Chinese seemed to find the idea of Zack and Suzy's marriage certainly newsworthy, greeting their arrival at the little group with much sibilant chatter and giggling. Ambassador Li smiled and shook Zack's hand once again. "Mr. Johnson, you are taking one of China's most beautiful treasures. I hope you will take good care of her."

"Yes, I am, Mr. Ambassador, and I promise to take very good care of her. I hope we will be able to visit China together someday."

"But you must, both of you together," Li said with emphasis.

At that exact moment Bob Carruthers came over and joined the group, standing on Suzy Johnson's left. Her husband stood to her right. "I'd like to tell all of you how glad I am that I could be here tonight." He paused and looked at Suzy. "Can you translate for me?" She smiled, nodded, and repeated Carruther's statement in Chinese. "I believe that what you're doing will prove the beginning of a new trading and diplomatic relationship between our two great countries." Suzy began translating, then felt Zack surreptitiously fondle her left buttock. She managed to finish the sentence without the slightest change in inflection, then glanced neutrally at Zack, surprised and somewhat annoyed at his rather shocking lack of decorum and maturity. His face was relaxed, betraying nothing. "I believe the entire world automobile industry will benefit from the technology you've developed, and with it, the people of the world as well." Suzy began to translate for Carruthers, then in mid-sentence reached down unobtrusively to take Zack's hand in her own to stop his groping. She found his hand and took it, then started when she realized that there was still a hand gently kneading her buttocks. She stole a look at Zack, who simply glanced down at her and smiled. Suzy Lin Johnson continued with her translation, fumbling briefly, then finished as the hand kneaded her buttock more firmly. Carruthers began speaking again. "Your efforts will result in the saving of precious resources and keeping the air pure for our children." He stopped, but Suzy had heard only the drone of his voice, not his words. She was too shocked to think clearly. She started to speak haltingly, glancing at Carruthers, who maintained an expression of serene innocence. Suddenly his fingers dug hard into her buttock. She gasped and reached down to grab his wrist, but he had moved closer, thigh to thigh with her. She couldn't reach his wrist. The hand dug harder still into her flesh. Abruptly, Suzy Johnson let out a short cry, turned and slapped Carruthers hard across the face. The onlookers let out an explosive gasp of shock and disbelief, then instantly fell silent. Carruthers' face registered surprise, shock, then an expression of almost berserk rage. He clumsily leaned back and took a wild swing at Suzy Johnson. She saw it coming, leaned back and let his fist fly by a safe distance from her chin, then countered with a lightning blow to the president's rather bulbous nose with the heel of her hand. Unlike Zhu, Suzy Johnson had in fact had a great deal of training in martial arts. The crack of Bob Carruthers' breaking nose could be heard all throughout the ballroom. He let out a squalling cry and fell to the floor, holding his hand over his nose, which began bleeding immediately and profusely.

Zack Johnson stood rooted to the spot, watching the whole scene unfold in slow motion, Carruthers trying to punch Suzy, his wife's hand connecting perfectly with the president's nose, the president thudding to the floor, then two Secret Service agents piling on Suzy and half dragging, half knocking her to the floor, one of them getting her elbow in the eye in the process.

Zack's temporary stupefaction lasted about three tenths of a second, then he exploded into action. "You bastards," he screamed, "get away from her!" He dove into the melee, abruptly sending one of the agents flying through the air to crash on top of the bar six feet away, hurling shards of glass, orange slices, olives, ice cubes, and cocktail onions in all directions. He got his arms around the other Secret Service agent, who was struggling with the furiously resisting Suzy Johnson, and heaved him off, breaking two of the man's ribs in the process. Another Secret Service man shoved his way through, drawing his pistol and making ready to shoot the president's assailant as soon as a clear shot presented itself, but then a People's Liberation Army plainclothes security man, seeing the drawn gun, smashed his truncheon down on the agent's wrist, breaking it. With that, abruptly, the brief but wild melee, which had caused two broken ribs, a broken vertebra, a fractured wrist, a broken nose, a black eye, and eleven shattered bottles of premium liquor, ended. Zack Johnson was helping his wife to her feet. Ambassador Li looked impassively at President Carruthers, who was whimpering and repeating, "She broke my nose, the bitch broke my nose!"

When she finally recovered her feet and stood holding Zack tightly, Suzy Johnson screamed in Chinese, then English, "The pig grabbed me. He grabbed me and was feeling me! The pig!" Her suit jacket was torn completely down the back. "He's a pig!" she repeated with an almost frightening venom.

Everybody present at that moment, from the president, the ambassador, Zhu Fei, the Secret Service men, to the kitchen help, muttered a heartfelt, collective, "Oh, shit!"

* * *

It took several hours for the events precipitated by the mini-riot at the Chinese embassy to begin taking shape. Suzy and Zack were hustled off to the receptionist's office, where there were kept under the watchful eye of the truncheon-wielding PLA security man, while the ambassador and the Secret Service personnel tried to figure out what to do with them. After a few minutes of stony silence the guard finally asked Suzy in low tones what had happened. When she related the sequence of events leading up to the resounding slap she'd delivered to Carruthers' surprised face, the security man could scarcely contain himself. The president's frequent peccadillos were well known to the Chinese and followed by them with considerable interest, plus bafflement that the president was able to get away with them. In fact, in keeping with the well known Chinese propensity for assigning uncomplimentary nicknames to foreigners, especially westerners, Carruthers was known to the embassy staff as The Great One-Eyed Pink Python. Chortling merrily at he thought of how The One-Eyed Pink Python had been rendered instantly flaccid at the hands of Suzy Lin Johnson, the security man excused himself and went out to the remaining bar setup to fetch them a bottle of champagne, two glasses, and a small tray of canape's.

President Carruthers was led into the ambassador's private office, muttering and whining as he was led away, "The bitch broke my nose. She was trying to kill me. She was trying to kill the president of the United States. She coulda pushed my nosebone into my brain," he moaned, recalling the hoary ju-jitsu myth from his childhood.

"Now, Mr. President, I'm sure even *you're* your nose is not quite long enough to reach into your brain," said Li soothingly, as he continued to lead Carruthers to his office, struggling all the while to appear grave. He had no doubt whatever that Carruthers had groped Suzy Johnson. Nor had he missed the president's clear attempt to punch her with a closed fist. In his mind it was an altogether perfect exclamation point for generations of Asian women serving as compliant concubines for Caucasian men. And best of all, he knew that the entire episode had been captured on tape by one or more of the surveillance cameras mounted throughout the ballroom. Try as he might, he couldn't even begin to imagine all the wonderful uses to which the tape could be put. What *joss,* he thought, what incredible, unbelievable *joss!*

For his part, Carruthers was blubbering and actually crying, trying to console himself with the thought that Suzy Johnson would be tried for attempted murder of the president. The bitch! To do *that!* To hit *me! * I'll see her in a maximum security federal prison for the rest of her life, getting gang-raped by a bunch of bull dykes with broom sticks! The thought temporarily distracted him from the throbbing pain of his well and truly broken nose. He allowed himself to be led into the ambassador's office and deposited supine on a long leather-covered couch. "I need a doctor," he sobbed. "I've got to have immediate medical attention. Jesus Christ, get Benson (the White House doctor) here right now. And tell him to bring me something for the pain. I need a shot."

Li watched him with growing contempt, thinking that the likes of Carruthers wouldn't have been of much use on Mao's Long March, or anywhere else where courage, toughness or stoicism might be required for that matter. "Try to relax, Mr. President. We are all feeling your pain," unable resist the little shot at this most "sensitive" of all American presidents. "Yes, you can be sure we feel your pain." Carruthers turned his head to the ambassador appreciatively, thinking it was most considerate of him to use one of his own most oft-used expressions of sympathy.

"Have they taken the bitch and that guy she was with away, yet?" Carruthers asked. "This is a federal matter, an assault with intent to kill on the president. I want both those people arrested immediately!"

"To be sure, Mr. President. It will be attended to shortly, I'm sure. But you will want to think about the public reaction. After all, you *were* fondling the girl, were you not? And when she slapped you, you tried to hit her with your fist, did you not?"

Carruthers looked momentarily as though he'd been slapped yet again. After a long moment, during which he stared at Li hatefully, he said, "Really now. Who says so? I certainly don't remember trying to hit her. Who says otherwise?"

Li shrugged. "I believe there were several witnesses to the incident, Mr. President"

"I doubt that anybody would believe them, Mr. Ambassador."

"Perhaps not. But the videotapes, recorded by a our security surveillance cameras, would be believed, I am sure."

"Videotapes?" the president croaked. "You were videotaping me?"

"It is purely routine, Mr. President," Li replied. "A simple security matter." Li was a little apprehensive that he, on his own authority, had reminded the president that there were many witnesses to the incident, and further, that the whole thing had been videotaped. But he found himself wanting to help the girl get out of the potentially ugly situation, regarding her as a minor heroine. Personally, he would have liked nothing better than to have the videotape play on every television station in the world. He sighed. Perhaps it might in due course, should the president not cooperate. Li sighed again. He knew that this president would cooperate. He had certainly made good on all his campaign promises to the Chinese government, given in return for cash contributions to the campaign. "If I may suggest, Mr. President, I do not think it would a good idea to publicize the events of this evening. I believe it would be better to let the girl and her husband go back home without further interference."

At that moment Carruthers' chief of staff arrived with the White House doctor. Li excused himself and left, going to the receptionist's office to check on the Johnsons. He smiled warmly as he entered the room, noting with approval that they already had both champagne and something to snack on. The security guard leapt to his feet. "I thought it polite to offer them something to eat and drink while they were waiting, Mr. Ambassador. I hope I have not incurred your disapproval."

"Not at all, Mr. Pei," said Li with a smile. "We must be hospitable to our guests at all times."

Suzy looked between the two men during the exchange, clearly apprehensive. Zack just stared straight ahead. He had no fear for himself, only the vague concern that his bride might be somehow snatched away and sent back to China. It had dawned on him that the incident had occurred, technically, in Chinese territory.

"I apologize for all the trouble I have caused, Mr. Ambassador. I am deeply ashamed of my conduct," Suzy said finally.

"Nonsense, child. You did only what any self-respecting woman would have done in your place." Li almost sounded rather pleased about the incident, she thought. "I believe we will be able to release both of you shortly. I do not believe your president will want this unfortunate episode publicized."

Zack and Suzy Johnson looked at one another. "I appreciate your kindness, Mr. Ambassador," said Zack. "I think we'd both just like to forget about what happened tonight."

"Yes, of that I'm sure," said Li, smiling faintly. "I'm going to check on the president. His doctor has arrived. I will stop in and see you again shortly, I believe."

At that moment Carruthers was explaining what had happened to a clearly agitated Timothy McGurn, his White House chief of staff. "The bastards set me up, Mac," Carruthers moaned. "They sent in this gook bitch to fuck up my mind. Jesus, that bitch had a peachy ass. And great jugs, too! I couldn't help myself. It wasn't my fault, I'm tellin' you, I was set up."

McGurn had heard this lament repeatedly from Carruthers in the four years he had served as his chief of staff. "Where are these two right now?"

"I think the embassy's got 'em under guard or something," replied Carruthers. "They're gonna pay for this, believe me."

"Well, I don't know, Mr. President. It might be better to just let this thing die a quick and quiet death. There must have been a lot of witnesses."

"Yeah, plus the ambassador says the whole thing was caught by their security cameras. They got the whole thing on tape."

"Oh, God, tell me you're not serious." McGurn rolled his eyes. "I'd say you better just let these two go and hope to hell they don't have any friends in the press." At that moment Li knocked, then entered.

"Mr. President, Mr. McGurn, I would recommend that you let the young bride and groom simply return home. I am sure that would just like to go on their honeymoon." McGurn wondered briefly if Li had been listening in on their conversation.

Then he looked at Carruthers accusingly. "On their honeymoon, for Christ's sake? You're trying to feel this broad up on her *honeymoon?*" He shook his head in disgust. He turned to Li. "Mr. Ambassador, I would appreciate it if you would let the two young people leave the embassy. We intend to press no charges against them."

"As you wish, Mr. McGurn," Li replied. "I will go and tell them."

After he'd left McGurn looked at Carruthers and shook his head. "How long will it take before his nose looks normal again, Doc?" asked McGurn of the White House doctor.

"A couple of weeks, I suppose," said the doctor. "I guess we could always hustle him off to a private clinic again, like with the old twisted knee story, unless you can come up with something better."

"Hell, I can't keep him under lock and key for the next two weeks."

"Well, we could say that, ah, we could say that he, ah, had to have a benign growth removed from a nostril, or something like that. It'd explain why his nose is all swollen up and red."

"Hey, that's it! We won't have to hide him that way. It might even make him look vulnerable, human. Hey, this could turn out to be positive." And perhaps in the short term, it was.

Fifteen minutes later the Johnson newlyweds were on the way back to their hotel in Crystal City in a Mercedes limo generously contributed by the Ambassador, along with a fresh bottle of Brut. "Do you think that will be the last of it, Zack?" asked Suzy. "I was so afraid of what might happen."

"I think so. I don't think they would have let us go at all if they were going to do anything about it. Plus they're probably afraid of the publicity if anything happened to you. There were a lot of witnesses who saw him try to hit you. By the way, you never told me you were an expert in karate, or whatever you call it. Where'd you learn it?"

"Well, up until I was about twelve I loved gymnastics, but then I got a little too big to be really competitive. So my gym instructors suggested I study martial arts instead. I've been doing it ever since." She shrugged. "Besides, you never asked me about it. I think men are happiest with a woman who's a mystery, full of surprises."

Zack laughed. "Well, I'm glad I didn't find out about this when *we* were having a fight. Now I'll have to think twice about spanking you when you need it."

She looked at him, one eyebrow arched suggestively. "You can *always* spank me, Zack, as long as you're gentle."

"Well, ah, that's good to know," he said thickly, shifting in his seat to more comfortably arrange his instantaneous, painfully constricted erection.

* * *

While the Johnson's were happily and strenuously re-consummating their marriage in their Crystal City hotel room, Zhu Fei was tossing sleeplessly two floors above them. Until the incident involving the president and the former Miss Lin, he had been quite confident that the Red Whippet was some years from introduction into the US market, if only because it couldn't possibly pass the 50,000 mile EPA emission test cycle. Nor did it have the federally required airbag system, though he expected that these items could be procured from the Japanese and installed without too much difficulty. But now, with the president practically assaulting a newly married woman in front of dozens of witnesses and getting a broken nose for his trouble, who knew what strings could be pulled on behalf of the Long March People's Cooperative Automotive Manufacturing Company? Zhu briefly wondered what strange pathologies afflicted the women of America. First, Mavis Belle broke his nose then nearly fractured his skull with his prized Canon F-1, and now the former Miss Lin, only two days before a respectful and proper Chinese woman, broke the *president's* nose and started a minor riot in the Chinese embassy. These people are all crazy, he told himself. And half of them have guns around the house! And worse, their government, apparently comprised of their worst and most verminous elements, controls nuclear weapons!

These speculations alone would not have caused Zhu great distress, but for the fact that Ambassador Li Wan Le had called him aside as he was leaving, and smiling broadly, whispered in confidential tones that the government of China anticipated no difficulty in procuring the full cooperation of the relevant US government officials in smoothing the way for the Red Whippet to take the market by storm. Zhu correctly interpreted Li's remarks to mean that the present administration would do whatever was necessary to avoid exposure of the incident.

As he lay in bed staring at the ceiling his thoughts turned once again to Sid Burnside, clearly the one responsible for his present woes. He was the one who arranged for the "dates" who accompanied them on their evening out. It was *his* fault that the blond harlot had broken his nose. It was *his* fault that Miss Lin, previously a valued employee and (so far as he knew) a dedicated communist, had run off with the Aryan baboon and then assaulted the president of the United States! He wanted nothing more than to fire Burnside, but then feared that he'd not get anybody to replace him on a timely basis. And timely it would have to be, since the Red Whippet was now clearly aimed in the direction of the American heartland and its hapless consumers.

Zhu finally fell asleep thinking of Burnside as Ernest Borgnine, dying deservedly and bloodily in THE WILD BUNCH.

* * *

President Bob Carruthers stood examining himself in the bathroom mirror, looking rather anxiously at the slight welt on his forehead, just below his hairline. This particular injury had come not at the hands of Suzy Lin Johnson, but some four hours later, after his return to the White House, when the First Lady confronted him. After listening for no more than perhaps ten seconds to his stammered and quavering explanation of his broken nose, Heather Carruthers (who'd already gotten the whole story out of Timothy McGurn) wordlessly flung one of her shoes at him, luckily catching him only with the back of the heel. Carruthers wisely bolted for the bathroom and locked himself inside while she raged for a good ten minutes and did a fair amount of damage to the presidential marital chambers. The two Secret Service agents outside the door looked at one another. One rolled his eyes, the other gave a little shake of his head.

Jesus Christ, thought Carruthers, I hope this thing doesn't bruise. We can get by with the growth thing story, but a bruise on my head, shit, I don't know. The occasional thumping and banging from the other side of the door had subsided and been replaced by an ominous silence. Carruthers was tempted to call out to her but was afraid of setting her off again. He was sure she was still out there, since he hadn't heard the slam of the bedroom door. Plus, once a few months earlier she'd tricked him into coming out by slamming the door, then waiting with a large and heavy vase, which she hurled at him as soon as he stuck his head out. Fortunately, he was able to get the bathroom door shut again before the vase crashed against it and shattered. Cunning bitch, he thought bitterly. Where's she get off with this shit? She knew what I was when she married me.

His anger at her intolerance momentarily supplanted the sheer terror he felt when she was in one of her rages. He stood fuming. What *is* this bullshit? Here I am, the most powerful man in the whole goddam *world*, and tonight some gook kung-fu bitch breaks my nose and then skates! And now some flabby, fat-assed old broad who thinks she's still a fucking sophomore at Vassar is holding me prisoner in my own fucking bathroom! I don't have to take any more of this!

With that, Carruthers turned and flung open the door and took one stride into the bedroom. "OK, I've have enough of this sh…" he started to shout, but was stopped cold by the portable phone glancing off the side of his head. The president let out a girlish little yelp and fell back through the door, slamming and re-locking it as he went. Jesus Christ, he thought, checking his head for blood, why doesn't the fucking Secret Service *do* something? They're supposed to protect me. He stood breathing heavily for a few moments, then unhappily sat down on the toilet seat. Dispiritedly, he picked up the only reading material in evidence, a recent copy of *Vanity Fair,* and began to read the letters to the editor. Fuckin' A, he thought as he scanned the correspondence page, that Chink broad had a perfect ass. It felt perfect, round and nice and firm. Wonder what her tits would have felt like. He began fantasizing about somehow seeing Suzy Lin Johnson again, when had they time to get to know each other a little better. She'd see I'm not such a bad guy, he told himself. It's just that men like me, powerful men, don't have the time to play games. His rapidly developing fantasies evaporated with the sound of her rasping, menacing voice. "You gonna stay in there all night, you *worm?* Well, you fucking well *better* stay in there, you *TURD,* 'cause when I get my hands on your sorry ass a broken nose'll be the least of your worries." Then silence.

Grimly Carruthers resigned himself to spending the night in the bathroom. Jesus Christ, he thought, held prisoner in my own bathroom by a middle-aged old broad, cellulite, saggy tits and all. And all because that fucking nincompoop Garmin thinks the icecaps are gonna melt.

The most powerful man in the world hung his head self-pityingly.

* * *

Chapter 4

The following morning Sid Burnside, knowing nothing of the events of the previous evening in Washington, and believing he'd heard the last of Zsu and his entourage for the time being, was giving Sherry Maxwell a short orientation around the office, preparatory to taking off for a few days up to Lake Tahoe for a bit of R&R. What the hell, Burnside told himself, I deserve a little rest, overlooking the fact that except for the last five days he'd been resting comfortably ever since joining Red Tiger Motors.

"OK, Sherry," he said to the slightly befuddled and still hung-over Maxwell, "all ya gotta do is man the fax machine and the phones. If anybody calls about when Red Tiger's gonna start operating here in the US market, just tell 'em that all the government testing is going ahead and that we expect certification shortly. Tell 'em you'll keep 'em informed. And if any dealer prospects call or write in, tell 'em to send us a short proposal with some photos of their proposed facilities for the franchise. Tell 'em we'll send 'em a full franchise application package after we get their proposal. Ya got all that?" Maxwell nodded a little uncertainly. "OK, good. Now, if anything comes up I should know about or something lands in your lap you can't handle, here's the number where I'll be stayin' for the next few days." He handed Sherry Maxwell the phone number for his brother's little cottage near the lake. "Oh, by the way, Sherry, you're on payroll as of three days ago. I already called Paychex, so you'll get your first paycheck the end of this week. You need an advance till then?"

"Naw, I'm covered till then, Sid." Burnside was a little relieved that Maxwell at least wasn't such a hopeless derelict that he needed a daily infusion of cash to support his daily infusion of vodka. He'd already begun to notice that Maxwell became visibly agitated if he to had to make it beyond six o'clock without a drink (or three or four), and that he arrived in the morning looking a bit rough around the edges. At least, though, he hasn't tried to get half-bagged during the afternoon, he told himself. Burnside wondered a little apprehensively how he'd behave when left unsupervised.

"Well, Sherry, I'm gonna hit the road then," he said, slapping Maxwell on the back ebulliently.

"You can count on me, Sid. I'll hold down the fort, and I know where to get ahold of you if I have to. And, ah, Sid, I'm gonna have to go home this weekend to get some more clothes and stuff."

"Fine, Sherry, go ahead and plan on that. OK, I'm outta here. He strode briskly out the door, leaving Maxwell alone in the empty thirteen thousand square foot office building. Sherry looked at his watch, noting unhappily that even an early lunch was still nearly three hours away. At that moment the fax machine began chattering.

* * *

Jake Dougherty finished sending the fax to Red Tiger Motor Company, asking for information on their vehicle lineup and franchise availability. He remained standing by the fax machine out in the showroom of his Chevy store, wondering how much effort would be involved in going through the franchise application process, and following that, just what franchise requirements Red Tiger would have. He was sure that they, like most manufacturers, would demand dedicated and exclusive facilities. Dougherty, like most dealers, wanted to give them a corner in an existing showroom in which to display their lineup, preferably a corner of the Chevy showroom. That way, if things didn't work out, he could always broom Red Tiger and its cars out the door without having made a major commitment in facilities, personnel, and capital.

Dougherty's mood soured as he thought of the new facility he'd built for Hyundai back in 1987, just before Hyundai's fortunes in the US crashed and burned, along with Dougherty's investment in the franchise. He had ended up selling the franchise to a used car operator, who located the dealership in a former gas station facility. His own ex-Hyundai facility ended up as a central used car lot for his Ford, Chevy, and Honda franchises. Actually, it had done rather well for Dougherty as a strictly used car outlet, though Dougherty had already decided to tell the Red Tiger reps to go shit in their collective hats if they demanded exclusive, stand-alone facilities for their still unproven franchise. He had to admit, however, that the idea of a five thousand dollar car was powerfully appealing, especially on that particular morning, since his finance and insurance manager had just failed to get four deals done through GMAC because of either bad credit or insufficient income on the part of prospective customers. Hell, any stiff can get bought on a five grand new car, he told himself. Jake Dougherty had forgotten that the initial price on the Hyundai Excel was $4,995, and that he had applied exactly the same rationale in acquiring the Hyundai franchise over a decade ago.

He left the fax machine and went back into his office, feeling cautiously optimistic about Red Tiger Motors. As Malcolm Bricklin and John DeLorean had amply proved, car dealers can be persuaded to take a flyer on just about anything. He picked up the Wall Street Journal and noted that the dollar had fallen by 2.16 yen that morning. Ya gotta diversify to protect yourself, Jake Dougherty thought.

* * *

As big Jake Dougherty was thinking how to best prop up the profitability of his Sacramento Chevrolet store, Suzy and Zack Johnson were arriving back at his pleasant little three bedroom stucco ranch in Pasadena. Both had been a little quiet on the drive back from LAX, seemingly lost in thought. Perhaps for the first time the reality of what they'd done in Las Vegas was asserting itself, not unhappily, for they still shared a powerful infatuation with one another, but with the sobering realization that Suzy had effectively uprooted herself from the land of all her ancestors, perhaps never to return, with only the clothes on her back and those in her single flightbag. And that now she'd have to be assimilated into an alien culture, albeit with the ability to speak the language with greater fluency than the average native-born American. Zack looked over at her as he pulled into the driveway, sensing exactly what she was thinking. "You know, I can't wait to go to China with you. That'd be a great trip, with you being able to translate everything for me. We can go next year, practically free, with my passes from Continental. Whaddya think?"

She looked over at him, tears welling up in her eyes. "Oh, Zack, that would be so wonderful. Would you really want to go?"

"You better believe I would. But first we gotta get all the formalities about your citizenship straightened out and find you a job, so you won't go crazy sitting around the house." He'd stopped the engine and they sat talking in the car.

"What kind of a job do you think I could get?"

"Well, you could get a job at the escort service. We could go in together to save gas."

She stared at him, her mind taking a long moment to realize for certain that he was joking.

"Your escort driving career is finished, husband. Doubtless you have many fond memories, but that is all that is left of that episode in your life. Now be serious, what do you think I should look for?"

"Well, we could check the classified employment ads this weekend. I'll bet you'll find a lot of stuff for people with fluent Chinese language skills. I bet you could even apply to this Red Tiger Motors company here in the United States. They've gotta have a need for someone over here who knows Chinese and something about the company. And I'll bet they'd pay a lot better than the parent company would."

She appeared to be thinking about what he'd said. She shrugged. "That's an idea, Zack," she said slowly. "I guess I should look into that."

"You know what else you'd better do? You gotta get some clothes, you're gonna need a driver's license, a whole lotta little things like that, practical things you'll need to live here. I gotta get you a couple of credit cards, and we gotta get a joint checking account so you have some money when you need it." Strangely, though Zack had always feared that any wife he might take would be a reckless spendthrift, he held no such apprehensions about his new bride. He vaguely assumed that coming from an austere society like China that she'd be thrifty and practical. Luckily, he was to be proven exactly right. "In fact, let's drop our stuff off and go out shopping for some new clothes for you. It's only three o'clock our time."

"I guess we could do that. Could we go to the supermarket again? I'd like to get some food and cook for you tonight."

"Sure. You're sure you don't want to go out for dinner?"

"I want to cook for my husband tonight."

"Suzy, I think I'm going to like this arrangement of ours." He pulled her to him and kissed her lightly on the lips

She pulled back and looked at him closely. "Zack, would you do something for me?" She asked it a little hesitantly.

"Well, sure. What is it?"

"When we're alone, would you call me by my real name. My name is Lin Shan, which I'm sure you forgot as soon as I told you the night we met. Would you call me Shan?"

"Well, of course, Shan, I've been wondering about this Suzy business. I started it as kind of a joke and it just stuck."

"I like it, Zack, and when we're with others I want you to call me Suzy. But when we're alone I want to be Shan. Shan and Zack."

"I like that, too, having my own special name for you." She picked up his hand and kissed it.

An hour later they were in a local Gap, outfitting Suzy Lin Johnson with an assortment of slacks, jeans (which she filled out very nicely), blouses, and an LA Dodgers sweatshirt. When they'd finished making their selections, she noted that certainly with such a large purchase they should at least bargain over the price. "We don't do that here," said Zack, "except when we buy a house or car or something big like that."

"Why not? In China everything can be negotiated."

"Hey, let's get you some nice shoes and sneakers and maybe some underwear and some things to sleep in."

"I already have pajamas."

"Yeah, they look like something Mao himself would wear to bed. I mean let's get some nice things to sleep in."

"You mean play or sleep?"

"Both." She looked up at him and chuckled.

By six o'clock they had managed to spend over six hundred dollars on what seemed to Zack to be very little merchandise. "Really, Zack, this should be enough for a while. I don't want to spend any more of your money until I have a job and a salary."

"Don't worry about that. We have plenty of money. I want you to have the things you need. Now let's go get some stuff at the supermarket and see what kind of cook you are. And then after dinner we can relax in the hot tub, then go to bed."

By ten o'clock there were in Zack's hot tub, naked once again. For the moment he was too bloated on Shan's quite extraordinary cuisine to even think about sex. "God, that was good. I can't believe you can cook like that.

I could have that same meal every night of the week." She had whipped up a sensational shrimp, sea bass, and assorted vegetable stir-fry dish, which she served up with a huge quantity of perfectly done snowy rice. The meal convinced Zack, as perhaps nothing else had, that he'd made a phenomenally lucky choice with Suzy Johnson. He sat mentally reviewing what else he could possibly want in a woman. *Jesus, she's beautiful, smart, knows how to cook, she's great in the sack, and doesn't act like she wants to piss away all my money. There has to be another shoe out there somewhere about to drop,* he told himself a little uneasily.

"Really, Shan, where'd you learn to cook like that?"

"I guess it's what you would call a hobby. It's the only really creative thing I know how to do."

"Well, that may be, but it's a hell of a lot better than doing ugly pottery or lousy paintings." He reached down and took her hand. "Hey, c'mere and give daddy a kiss." His stomach was settling a bit

* * *

Sherry Maxwell had been sitting at his desk staring indecisively at the fax machine, which had stopped its chattering and dropped a single sheet into the catch basket. He eyed the machine uneasily. It seemed to him to exude a certain malevolence, as did all bearers of electronic messages in Maxwell's mind. *Good news never came by fax, telex, or E-mail,* he reminded himself. He decided to ignore it for the time being, went back to pour himself another cup of coffee, and turned to the sports page of the LA Times.

Presently he sighed, put down the paper and went over to the fax machine to retrieve the message. He stood by the machine and glanced at the letterhead, then briefly scanned the letter from Jake Dougherty. He remembered Burnside's instructions regarding franchise queries and decided to put together a form letter with which to answer all such incoming correspondence. He allocated, quite reasonably he thought, two days for the composition of the simple one paragraph missive. Then he could actually get his response off to this Chevy dealer Jack Dougherty at least a day after that, using the mails as opposed to the fax machine, thus avoiding having to deal in any way with the dealer aspirant for at least another week. Don't want to seem too eager, rationalized Maxwell, makes it harder to get serious commitments from 'em. Sherry was already fantasizing about palatial Lexus and Mercedes caliber facilities for the Red Tiger franchise, replete with gala grand openings at which he'd be feted and toasted with nothing but the finest liquors and cordials. Jesus, a five grand car! How can it miss, thought Maxwell gleefully, forgetting, as had Jake Dougherty, that the intro price for the Hyundai Excel had been $4,995. Nor did Maxwell realize that the Koreans had at least a reasonably robust competitive economy in which, unlike China, consumers could punish indifferent producers of low quality products by taking their business elsewhere.

* * *

As Sherry Maxwell, feet on his desk with hands clasped behind his head, sat thinking about how adroitly he'd handled Jake Dougherty's query, the president of The Long March People's Cooperative Automotive Manufacturing Company, Lin Cho Hsin, was unhappily digesting both his lunch and the phone call he'd just received from no less a personage than Chiang Shu Peng. Chiang, China's minister of finance, seemed almost gleeful as he informed Lin that he had to be ready to move with all dispatch to begin exporting the Red Whippet to the United States. "After all, Comrade Lin," he'd pointed out, "China has some of the most advanced technology in the world. I need not mention our space program, or the fact that American companies use our rockets to launch their satellites. We are long overdue in the automotive business. We must show the common people of the world that they can look to our country to fulfill their everyday needs if we are to become the foremost economic giant of the 21st century."

Lin had started to protest that the Americans kept changing their exhaust emission and safety standards—no doubt as a means of keeping worthy competitors such as the Chinese from exploiting the US market—and that they were having some difficulty meeting the newest standards on a production level basis. "The technology is well within our means, Comrade," he said, "but it is difficult to meet these ever-changing standards with actual production parts, at least on a cost effective basis."

Chiang seemed to ponder this momentarily. Actually, he was grinning broadly, but he managed to keep his tone rather imperious. "It is your responsibility to see that all obstacles are overcome, Comrade Lin." He seemed to pause. "I would not be too concerned, however. As long as the Red Whippet cars run satisfactorily, I am quite sure that the American government will make whatever accommodations are necessary to see that it can be sold without regulatory problems."

"Are you sure, Comrade?" asked Lin. "I am told they make no special dispensations for their own automakers. Why would they be willing to give us special consideration to help us compete in their market?"

"Let us just say that certain very strong and influential people in their government are very appreciative of help we have provided them. Doubtless they will want to reciprocate in helping us in our endeavors, which will benefit not just them, but all of mankind. I am quite sure that they would not want us to be disappointed in their efforts on our behalf."

Lin wondered what Chiang meant. What help had his government provided the American administration? And what could they do if the Americans "disappointed" them, as Chiang had put it? Though he couldn't fathom what Chiang was talking about, Lin thought it unwise to question him further. "Yes, I am sure of your arrangements, Comrade. You may rest assured that we will be ready to begin shipping the Red Whippet to the American market within the year!"

"You must be ready to sell them in America within six months, Lin. Are you saying that this timetable is unrealistic?"

Lin felt himself beginning to sweat. Six months? Was Chiang mad? At no time had he given the assurance, which would have been ridiculously optimistic in any event, that he could begin exporting the Red Whippet within six months! But all he said was, "You may rely on it, Comrade," his mind briefly flirting with the idea of defection. He wondered momentarily about Lin Shan's circumstances, imagining himself in a hot tub with her, smoking a big cigar. And now some large, blond, American muscle-headed lout was ravishing this magnificently ripe example of Chinese womanhood, he thought bitterly. No doubt *she* is safely in a hot tub, but with that oaf, and I'm going to end up working down in the engine foundry as a common laborer six months from now. He grimaced and reached for the phone to call his chief of powertrain engineering, Chen Wan Le. Chen's was the critical area in getting the Red Whippet through the EPA test cycle and certified for sale in the US. Though he knew nothing could have changed since the previous month in which the Red Whippet had made such a pitiful showing in the durability testing, he hoped to find at least some solace in berating the hapless Chen. After all, that's what underlings are for, thought Lin.

* * *

Lin was not the only member of the Long March People's Cooperative Automotive Manufacturing Company to be feeling a bit uneasy at that moment. Zhu Fei, enroute from Washington, DC back to Beijing, was finding that he had plenty of time to contemplate his probable future should the Red Whippet founder in the US market. Long flights such as the one he was on always gave Zhu the opportunity to fixate on potentially calamitous events, which as long as he was in the isolation of the long aluminum cylinder at 35,000 feet, far from reassuring news or ideas, always seemed to grow exponentially in their gravity and scope. His thoughts had begun with the notion of a minor demotion and the loss of his corner office. However, after an hour of letting all conceivable permutations of events run their respective courses in his mind, Zhu was seeing himself kneeling in front of a jeering crowd, as his crimes against the people were read off by a pistol-wielding People's Liberation Army officer, preparatory to being executed by a single bullet in the back of the neck. Abruptly, he summoned the flight attendant and ordered two beers, which he drank down as quickly as possible to enhance their effect in improving his outlook.

Ten minutes later, his courage slightly bolstered, he assured himself that such things no longer happened in the People's Republic, and that in any event, whatever market failures he would suffer with the Red Whippet would be purely a function of its abysmal quality levels and therefore somebody else's responsibility. Zhu checked his watch, trying to calculate just how many more beers would be required for the remaining seven hours of the flight to maintain his present level of cautious optimism. Perhaps one per hour would do it, he estimated with satisfaction. Grumpily, he turned his thoughts once again to Sid Burnside, whom he held primarily responsible for his present precarious position. After all, had Burnside not arranged the night out with the escort service, the former Miss Lin would not have married the Arnold Schwartzenegger look-alike and then broken the president's nose, though he had to concede that Carruthers might well have tried to grope Miss Lin in any event (the thought had occurred to Zhu himself on numerous occasions), with what ultimate result he couldn't say. But now the American president had left himself open to the blackmail of Zhu's superiors and that of the Chinese government at the highest levels, with the probable result that the Red Whippet would not be delayed for several more years, which Zhu had counted on to situate himself safely out of the line of fire.

Like any member of a communist system, the military, or the American Bar Association, Zhu couldn't relate to the American truism, "Shit happens." In his mind, if something untoward occurred, under whatever circumstances, then, by God, somebody was responsible and somebody was going to pay. As far as Zhu was concerned, Burnside had precipitated the possible downfall of The Long March People's Cooperative Automotive Manufacturing Company, its affiliate corporation Red Tiger Motors, and very likely the current administration in Washington, all because of his ill-considered evening out with a band of American male and female prostitutes and violent criminals! He fingered his nose gently at the last thought, wondering if it would be permanently misshapen when it healed.

* * *

Nearly seven thousand miles away from where Zhu was nervously contemplating his probable future difficulties, all occasioned by the negligent miscreant Sid Burnside, Zack Johnson was contemplating a few of the so-far minor difficulties and inconveniences involved in getting his new bride situated and functioning normally in her new environment. That morning he belatedly realized that for the moment she couldn't very well go anywhere at all without his help and participation. As was typical throughout the southern California area, there was really no effective public transportation system throughout the various urban and suburban sprawls. And as he'd also learned when he suggested that they get her a California driver's license, Suzy Johnson had never driven a car. "I'm sorry, Zack," she'd said with embarrassment, "hardly anybody in China has a car, and I, well, I just never had any reason to apply for a driver's license. I always wanted to learn," she added hastily, "but without a need for one, you really can't get a license to drive in China."

Strangely, up to that point Zack had difficulty in thinking of Suzy as anything but a Chinese-American. Her perfect teeth, all-American cheerleader shape, and perfect command of colloquial American English were so at odds with the stereotypical image of an east Asian struggling haltingly in English that Zack found it hard to accept that she had lived in the United States for a total of only a few days. But the fact that she didn't have a driver's license, a *driver's license*, for Christ sake, now *that* registered loud and clear with Zack. How can anybody live without a driver's license, he thought.

"I'm really sorry, Zack, I didn't mean to upset you," she said, looking stricken by Zack's unconcealed look of disbelief.

Suddenly, he laughed. "Hey, it's nothing to be sorry about. I guess it just took me by surprise. I mean, in America, everybody has a driver's license, or at least they're supposed to. Well, I think we should take you out for a driving lesson."

"You mean out on the streets?"

"No, it's Saturday, so we'll find an empty high school parking lot and let you practice without anything around to run into."

"Really? You mean you'll let me drive your car?" He nodded. "Oh, Zack, that sounds like so much fun. Can we leave right away? Oh, I've never done anything like this, I'm so excited!"

Zack was taken aback by her show of child-like enthusiasm. "Hey, it's no big deal. Every kid in the country does it. Lemme shave real quick and we'll go."

An hour later Suzy Johnson, grinning from ear to ear, was sitting at the wheel of Zack's Firebird convertible, almost afraid to touch anything. They were in the middle of a nine acre parking lot at the local high school. Zack spent several minutes explaining the various controls and their functions. As a pilot, he had absorbed a certain level of instructional ability, going through a brief impromptu syllabus logically and clearly. Finally, he said, "OK, make sure your right foot's on the brake pedal, and pull the transmission into Drive." She complied nervously. "OK, honey, now I want you to just take your foot off the brake, don't touch the gas pedal, just take your foot off the brake, and the car'll creep forward slowly. We'll just let it go at about a walking pace. You practice steering for the moment, OK?" She nodded and released the brake. The car began rolling at about ten miles per hour.

"We're moving!" she exclaimed. "I'm driving a car!"

"OK, just turn the wheel to the left and make the car turn left. Just make a big circle." After a minute of this he had her turn right and describe a figure eight.

"I'm really driving your car," she squealed happily. "I'm really doing it!"

"Yeah, you're doin' great. Tell you what, go over that way and then stop. Just step on the brake pedal gently." A moment later the Firebird screeched violently to a stop. He started to tell her, "gently!" but then chuckled, reached over and put the transmission in Park, and kissed her.

She broke away briefly. "I stepped on it too hard. I'll do better next time." They were about to start off again when a local patrol car pulled up next to them. The young cop got out and walked over to the side of the car. "What're you folks doin' here?" he asked.

"Oh, hi," said Zack. "My wife here just arrived from China. She's never driven a car before, so I figured I'd start her out in an empty parking lot." Suzy looked at the cop a little apprehensively.

The cop smiled. "Well, let me welcome you to America." He nodded to Suzy. "You know, technically, she's not supposed to be out driving anywhere without her learner's permit. I dunno, it doesn't look to me like you two are much of a menace to public safety. Tell you what, I'm on this shift for another two hours, and I don't mind you drivin' around this parking lot as long as you take it slow and easy. The guy who comes on after me can be a hard-ass, though, so I'd be gone by the time he comes on."

"Hey, I really appreciate this," said Zack, smiling. "We won't be here too much longer."

The cop tipped his hat and smiled at Suzy once again. "Have a nice day," he said and returned to his cruiser.

Suzy looked at Jack. "Why didn't you give him anything?"

"What do you mean? Why would I give him anything?"

"You should have given him some money. What if he reports us?"

Zack looked at her curiously. "He's not gonna report us, honey. He's just a nice guy doing us a little favor. You don't have to give the police money in this country."

She looked at Zack doubtfully. "When a policeman stops you in China you should always give him some money, or he can create all sorts of difficulty for you. It's expected."

"Well, it's not expected here. In fact, you can get into all sorts of trouble by trying to bribe a cop in America. I'm sorta glad this little episode happened this way. I'd hate to see you out on your own one day and getting thrown in jail for trying to bribe a cop. I mean, I guess it happens, they got bad cops, too, but it's not normal."

"You mean in America people with authority don't try to take money from the people they control?"

"Well, like I said, it happens, but it's the exception, not the rule. For instance, if I tried to bribe an FAA inspector on a check ride, I'd never fly in this country again. You just don't do things like that."

She seemed to ponder this. "America is very strange in some ways. But I like it. Let's practice driving some more before the mean policeman comes on duty."

* * *

As Zack was continuing the driving lesson with his bride, wondering a little uneasily how the newly granted mobility and freedom of a driver's license might affect their relationship, Jake Dougherty was deciding to pay a personal visit to the Red Tiger Motor Company in Chino. He knew from long experience that mere correspondence was no substitute for face to face, press the flesh, liquor and food-lubricated persuasion. His sense of urgency regarding the Red Tiger franchise was currently being heightened by the frustration of losing three more deals from the weekend in his Sacramento Chevy store, all for credit problems. Hell, anybody can get bought on a five thousand dollar car, Jake reminded himself for the third time that morning. And by the time we bump these stiffs five points on the financing, sell 'em rustproofing, paint sealant, fabric protector, and a service contract, we can make a decent hit on the little shitboxes! Dougherty was quickly talking himself into the assumption that the Red Whippet represented a veritable windfall of profit opportunity for his Chevy store, which had been muddling along on a marginal basis at best for the past eighteen months. He ground out his cigar in the ashtray, opened the *Automotive News* to find the Red Tiger personnel ad he'd noticed, and dialed.

The phone rang twice, then Jake found himself listening to the voice mail recording, taking him through the menu for parts, service, sales, distribution, and customer service. Sid Burnside believed in keeping up appearances, even though there no were yet no such departments or personnel to man them. Dougherty shrugged, then hit four for sales, getting "you have reached the office of (pause and deep male voice) SID BURNSIDE," and so forth.

"Hello, this is Jake Dougherty of Sacramento Sales Companies. I'm following up on a letter I sent a few days ago, asking about the availability of the Red Tiger franchise in the Sacramento market. I'd like to come out and see you and discuss the possibilities as soon as possible." He left his number with the request that a representative call him, then hung up feeling the satisfaction of having placed the ball in the other court. He decided to reward himself with another of the twelve dollar Haitian cigars he favored.

As Dougherty was lighting up his second eight inch stogie of the day, Sherry Maxwell was standing in the men's room of the Red Tiger office, examining his tongue in the mirror and confirming (as he often did) that it was not covered with fur. His eyes were bloodshot and his head still ached from the excesses of the night before, the effects of which were enhanced somewhat by the several days of relative sobriety imposed on him by Burnside's presence. He popped another peppermint lifesaver in his mouth in the hope of banishing the maddening urge to give his tongue the once over with his electric shaver. Jesus, I gotta knock this shit off, Maxwell told himself, then quickly rationalized that when Red Tiger began operating normally he'd have a modicum of discipline imposed on him by Burnside and others. What the hell, it'll take care of itself, he thought, momentarily buoyed by the thought. Yeah, I just need to get back into the routine and I'll be fine.

Sherry's ruminations were interrupted by the phone. He left the men's room and walked back down into Burnside's office, just in time to hear Jake Dougherty hang up. He played the message back, writing down Dougherty's name and phone number. Hmm, a meeting, thought Maxwell. He considered putting off a return call, but then, even in his hung over condition, considered that if he waited to contact Dougherty, Burnside would be the likely recipient of any lunch or dinnertime largess lavished by the eager dealer candidate. The fuzz on his tongue seemed to disappear as he thought of the icy warmth of a dry Finlandia martini. He cleared his throat and reached for the phone decisively.

*　*　*

Chen Wan Le, chief of powertrain development for the Long March People's Cooperative Automotive Manufacturing Company, angrily tossed the confidential report into the in-box on his desk, then stood up and walked over to his office window. Grimly he surveyed the belching smokestack of the engine foundry plant, where Red Whippet cylinder blocks and heads were being cast prior to final machining. He was still struggling with the 40% rejection rate for these components, due to porosity and inclusions in the iron castings. While this was bad, at least the rejected pieces could simply be tossed back into the smelter for re-casting. Reforming them involved a bit of labor, which was always in plentiful supply, but little more. What had angered Chen was the report on the emission control engineering for the Red Whippet, which had thus far failed to develop an engine and related hardware that had any hope of completing the US EPA 50,000 mile test cycle. The latest effort, involving a three way catalytic converter furnished by Toyota, had ended in failure when the engine ran so rich that the converter simply burned itself up in less than ten thousand miles. It had been standard practice to run very rich air-fuel ratios through the Red Whippet's single throat carburetor in the interest of satisfactory starting and driveability, plus the resultant cool burning gave the Red Whippet's exhaust valves at least a fighting chance for survival. Clearly, low exhaust emissions and satisfactory fuel economy were not high priorities in the powertrain engineering department.

Chen stared unhappily out the window, trying to think of how to explain to a bunch of communist bureaucrats, who knew nothing about cars, their components, their manufacturing, or their development, how China could build jet fighters but not a simple and serviceable car. The answer, of course, was that the military hardware was built on a cost-no-object basis, using whatever technology was needed to achieve the desired result.

A consumer product, whether a car or a refrigerator, had to be built to a price. And while a car itself was hardly a high-tech product, to be made successfully to a competitive price it needed to employ quite sophisticated manufacturing technologies and processes. The Chinese had no experience in developing these processes, never having had to cater to a demanding and responsive market. And now they were planning to enter the American market, the most demanding in the world, where consumers forgave no oversight or quality lapses, where the failure of a climate control unit was likely to be viewed as a life-threatening tragedy, to be discussed indignantly at cocktail parties and in the offices of slavering plaintiff's attorneys. Chen was acutely aware of this, well remembering the caterwauling that accompanied the occasional failure of the keyless entry system on the Mercedes M320 sport-utility. He idly wondered once again what would happen if the typical American actually had to cope with a real hardship. Keyless entry, he mused. Inserting a key and turning it is too trying for these people.

He dismissed his thoughts as irrelevant, however much he enjoyed contemplating the helplessness of the Americans. For without being able to pass the emission standards of the American government, or more ridiculous in his mind, the passive restraint requirements for airbags, all the Red Whippet's other shortcomings would be rendered moot. The cars simply couldn't be sold in the US without EPA and NHTSA certification, which clearly would not be forthcoming. Chen wondered again about the report that the timetable for the Red Whippet's introduction in the US was to be moved up, despite the dismal fact that vital component development was lagging way behind schedule. While this sort of absurd posturing was routine in the People's Republic, Chen was becoming a little concerned. Normally, at this stage of development great energy was being expended in devising suitable excuses for the impending disaster, scapegoats being sought and set up. Yet nothing of the sort had been set in motion. He couldn't understand it, especially since he hadn't exactly been reticent to Lin Cho Hsin, the president of the company.

Strangely, Lin had been airily dismissive in his last discussion with Chen. "I'm sure you will handle it with your usual expertise, Chen," he had said with a wave of his hand. "Yes, these things have a way of working themselves out. I suggest you devote your energies to ensuring that your department can supply sufficient numbers of engines and transmissions to meet demand in the US market. These regulations that the Americans devise to torment their competitors, well, I am sure that we can apply diplomatic pressures to ease the way. Besides, the American public will be clamoring for the Red Whippet! Henry Ford put America on wheels with a five hundred dollar car. Adjusting for inflation, that would be as much as ten or twenty thousand dollars today. And we are proposing to sell the Red Whippet for a paltry five thousand dollars! There will be a stampede of eager buyers. Surely the Red Whippet is better than a Model T, is it not?"

Chen had been so taken aback by Lin's sanguine prognostications that he hadn't been able to formulate an appropriate response. He left wondering whether Lin knew something he did not or was simply ridiculously uninformed.

Assuming that Lin's reference to "diplomatic pressures" had a basis in reality, Chen realized that he'd have to do something about the casting problems if he was to have any hope of building enough engines to supply anticipated demand, which that ninny Zhu had estimated at upwards of two million cars a year, based on his conversations with his American management team. These figures Chen dismissed as little more than fevered ravings, realizing that it was absurd to project sales of two million Red Whippets in a total market of sixteen million new cars and light trucks. Why, two million was as many as Honda and Toyota sold combined in the US market, with all their many models and American factories!

* * *

While Chen was puzzling over why his boss seemed so unconcerned about the coming launch of the Red Whippet in America, Suzy and Zack Johnson once again found themselves in their hot tub, discussing Suzy's driving lesson of that morning. Both were drinking strawberry daiquiries, which Suzy seemed to particularly enjoy, as long as Zack didn't make them too strong. "Oh, Zack, that was so much fun," she sighed. "I never dreamed that I'd be able to do anything like that, I mean drive a nice car like yours."

They'd stayed nearly two hours in the parking lot, time enough for Suzy to have gained a surprising level of proficiency in maneuvering Zack's Firebird, even learning the rudiments of parallel parking. "Yeah," Zack said, "We're gonna have to get you a learner's permit, so we can go out on the road and get you some real experience. I'll bet it won't take more than a couple of weeks before you can take the driver's test."

"Oh, do you really think so, Zack? Can I buy an older car then, one of my own?"

"Yeah, we can get you one I guess," he replied a bit uneasily. He was surprised at his depth of concern that his new bride might suddenly be able to fully exploit her newfound independence. His present situation seemed almost too perfect, a beautiful, desirable, compliant, and totally dependent wife, who was also a great cook, as well as being an exciting and totally satisfying lover. What am I going to do if she starts running amok on her own, he thought worriedly.

His fearful thoughts were interrupted by the phone. He quickly dried his hand on a towel and reached for the phone. "Hello?"

"Durn it all, I had a turrible time gettin' your number, Zack. This is Vera Hawkins."

"Who?" he asked, puzzled. Jesus, is this somebody I knocked up, he wondered.

"Sorry, Mavis Belle, Zack. Starlight didn't want to give out your number, but I told 'em it was urgent."

"Oh, hi, Mavis, how're you doin? You really quit the escort business?"

"Ah shore did, Zack, Ah'm through with that disgustin' business. An' call me Vera, that's mah real name, like I tol' you that night that li'l pervert tried to take pitchers o' me in a *compro*-misin' situation." She said it indignantly, as though Zsu's attempt to get a spectacular close-up of her snatch was truly beyond the pale.

"So what can I do for you, Vera?" He held his hand over the mouthpiece and whispered "It's that girl, Mavis Belle." Suzy gasped and held her hand over her mouth, giggling wide-eyed.

"Well, Zack, I think I need a new career, I truly do. I know you're an airline pilot and I was hopin' you could tell me how to git a job as a stewardess."

He chuckled. "Well, first they call 'em flight attendants now, Vera, so's not to offend all the boys. But if you're really serious about wanting to check it out, I can get some employment applications for you. I think they're mostly looking for college graduates now, but if you can get an interview I think you'd have a good shot at the job."

"That sounds really good, Zack. Are you still drivin' for the escort service?"

"Well, no, I'm sorta retired at this point."

"Well hell, whyn't ya'll come on over tonight? Us old retirees could have us a party."

"Well, I'm not sure my wife would approve." Suzy looked at him curiously.

"Your wife? I didn't know you was married. When'd you do that?"

"Last week, to the Chinese girl I was with the night you busted that guy's head."

"Oh, no, Zack, you're puttin' me on. You done married a Chinese girl when some pore li'l ol' American gal needs you? Tell me it ain't so."

"Yeah, it's true. She's great." He looked at Suzy. "I'm in love." He reached over and took her hand, which she placed on her breast, looking at him with raised eyebrows.

"Damn, Zack, I always knowed you work too fast for your own good."

"Hey, can you get a date tonight?"

"Sure, I guess."

"Why don't you come over for dinner. Suzy's a fantastic cook."

"Why sure, Zack, jus' give me a coupla hours to see who I can rustle up and I'll be over. Gimme directions."

After he explained how to get to his house, he hung up, then abruptly reached over grabbed Suzy, maneuvering her into a passionate clinch. She broke away briefly. "I have to go to the store and get some food."

"You'll go when I'm through with you, not before."

"You better make it quick. But not *too* quick."

* * *

Sherry Maxwell's attention span, none too long to begin with, was being further abbreviated by the lengthening afternoon shadows, which indicated to his subconscious the onset of the cocktail hour. He had been listening to Jake Dougherty's at first ebullient, but then droning, presentation of how he would take the Sacramento market by storm with the Red Whippet. Maxwell had looked perfunctorily at Dougherty's financial statements for the Chevy store into which he hoped to install the Red Tiger franchise, noting that the dealership was well capitalized but only marginally profitable in recent years. He had riffled through the eight by ten photos that Dougherty had included in his little package, correctly dating the construction of the Chevrolet facility at sometime in the early sixties. Maxwell was trying to balance an appearance of cautious enthusiasm for

Dougherty's proposal with the proper measure of reasoned reluctance, so as not to unduly endanger the lavish dinner he was anticipating that Dougherty would provide.

Sherry cleared his throat importantly and looked at Dougherty as though he were about to deliver an edict of monumental importance. "I don't know, Jake. We haven't really had a chance to look at the Sacramento market in detail yet. And frankly, we're looking for exclusive, stand-alone facilities for our franchise, especially in a big market like Sacramento."

Dougherty looked at Maxwell neutrally. He had fully expected that Red Tiger would propose that its dealers should provide exclusive, dedicated facilities in which to sell and service their products. He also believed, no *knew*, that such requirements, however firmly stated, were always negotiable, that the factory could always be held at bay by promises to provide exclusive representation within a certain time frame, promises that could always be re-negotiated as the deadline approached. And, of course, should the franchise prove to be a real home run, he'd need the extra space for sales and service anyway. As with practically all car dealers, Jake Dougherty believed firmly in the principle that one realizes the return first and invests second. And in truth, as Jake knew from bitter experience with Hyundai, this reversal of investment and reward was based less on cynicism than on a healthy skepticism regarding new market entries' prognostications regarding their future success. And finally, as an ace in the hole, Jake could always take out and dust off the old architectural drawings of the Hyundai facility and present these to Red Tiger as proof of his good intentions and earnest desire to provide them with nothing but the most elegant sales and service facilities. Just as soon, of course, as the requisite zoning variances and environmental impact studies could be completed. Such obstacles, irksome to businessmen as they might have been, were in fact their best allies in their attempts to stall the factories and get them to extend deadlines.

"Well, hell Sherry, I wouldn't want any franchise that didn't demand exclusive facilities," boomed Jake, thumping his fist on Maxwell's desk for emphasis. "In fact, I've already got the plans drawn up! I can Fed-Ex 'em to you next week."

"Oh, I thought you wanted to put it in with your Chevy store."

"Jesus, Sherry, that's just a temporary situation, till we can get our new place for Red Tiger built." He looked at Maxwell as though he couldn't believe that Sherry could have made such an outlandish assumption. "I already got an option on four acres in the best part of town."

"Oh, OK," said Maxwell a little uncertainly. "Yeah, that puts a different light on it. That's what we're lookin' for."

"Obviously, we'd get started in the Chevy store, but as soon as we had the new place up we'd move everything over."

"Yeah, that sounds a lot better," said Maxwell, nodding affirmatively.

"Hey, Sherry," said Dougherty abruptly, "you up for dinner someplace?"

Maxwell made a show of looking at his watch. "Yeah, that's not a bad idea. Just lemme make a couple o' calls and we can get going."

Dougherty excused himself from Sherry's office. "Take your time, Sherry. I gotta call home myself." He went into the little reception area down the hall, wondering how many people worked for the fledgling distribution company. Maxwell was the only one in the building as far as he could tell. Sherry had assured him that the field managers were out on the road, doing market surveys and signing up port handlers. Dougherty had no way of knowing that Maxwell and Burnside were the only two permanent employees of Red Tiger Motors. Nor did he have an inkling that both assumed that it would be quite some time before Red Tiger would be ready to import anything resembling sale-ready cars from China. He called home briefly and then estimated that it would take perhaps twenty minutes to get to the steak house he'd scouted prior to arriving at Red Tiger's Chino facility.

Two hours later Dougherty was watching Sherry Maxwell curiously as he started on his fifth Finlandia vodka martini. Thus far he had shown no signs at all of intoxication, looking for all the world as though he were just starting on his first. Maxwell lifted the freshly re-filled cocktail glass to his lips, made a perfunctory show of sipping, then abruptly gulped down a good two ounces of the drink. Unknown to Dougherty, Maxwell was already feeling loose and expansive. "Yeah, Jake," he said, "I think we're pretty close to an agreement with you. I like what you're offering, and I can see you're a man who makes good on his commitments." Dougherty nodded modestly, not wanting to interrupt Maxwell in the process of mentally approving Jake's yet-to-be submitted franchise application package. He looked over his shoulder and signaled the waitress to indicate another round. "Yeah," continued Sherry, noting that his cocktail glass, rather mysteriously he thought, was already half empty, "I think we got all the elements of a successful relationship put together here." He had started slurring his words ever-so-slightly in the past couple of minutes.

"So, Sherry, d'ya think we can do a deal, then?" asked Dougherty. "Like you were sayin', I think we got all the elements of an agreement. I mean, there's always details we gotta finalize, but it looks to me like we're a good match. You got the products and I got the money, the market, the facilities, and the track record."

"Umm," grunted Maxwell, trying to calculate how much of his drink was actually left. It's halfway down, he told himself, but the glass is cone-shaped. It's probably three quarters gone. At the moment Maxwell was devoting his full attention to the level of his glass.

Dougherty took Sherry's non-committal grunt as a lack of certainty or perhaps a partial retraction of his expression of interest of a few moments earlier. "Sherry, look, what ya gotta do is come on out to Sacramento and see what the market's got to offer first hand. I mean, everybody thinks Sacramento's just a nice little town in the middle o' nowhere, but I'm tellin' ya, we got first rate shopping, a million good restaurants, and some of the best lookin' chicks in the world." Dougherty figured he'd covered most of the essentials in what he hoped was Maxwell's likely range of interests. "Yeah, the women there are something else, and they like older guys with a little class and manners." Maxwell grunted non-committally again, which left Dougherty speculating as to the location of his hot button. "Hey, they even got some real good wineries," he said hopefully.

The mention of wineries didn't register with Maxwell, who ordinarily resorted to wine of any sort, vintage or vile, only in an emergency. "Ummm," he grunted, then finished his martini and reached up for the fresh drink on the cocktail waitress's tray, which had just intruded on his peripheral vision. He pulled out the skewered olive and ate it, remarking to Dougherty, "You should always eat when you drink," then took a healthy slug of the chilled martini.

"Yeah," said Maxwell, "it's not good to drink on an empty stomach." He turned to Jake Dougherty, who was now watching him a bit curiously. "Well, Jack, it sounds like we should be able to do a deal. But Mazda's like any other franchise. Ya gotta make a commitment for us, you know, put your money where your mouth is." He was now definitely slurring his words.

Jake Dougherty didn't bother to correct being called Jack, nor did he draw attention to the fact that Sherry no longer worked for Mazda. He was beginning to realize that Maxwell wasn't going to last too much longer at his present rate of consumption, nor was he likely to remember much of the conversation the following morning. He sat reviewing how he might best exploit this knowledge of Maxwell's weakness

An hour and a half later Jake Dougherty was signaling for the check impatiently. Across from him a glassy-eyed Sherry Maxwell was making a brave effort to maintain at least some semblance of business discussion by way of helping Dougherty justify paying for the dinner. "Yeah, Jack, at long as ya meet our shtandards I don' see why Mazda wouldn't go 'long with it." Sherry wasn't at all sure just what "it" was at that point, but he'd learned over the years to make innocuous and pointless conversation by way of appearing at least semi-conscious. "Gotta hit the head," he announced abruptly, lurching to his feet and marching resolutely, with great deliberation, toward the men's room. He thumped through the door, braced himself against the wall, fumbled with his fly, and finally stood before the urinal, swaying perilously as he relieved himself for the third time that evening. He walked unsteadily back to the table where Jake Dougherty waited for the check, tried to ease himself down, but then crashed heavily into his chair and fell over on the floor.

Dougherty looked down at him as he struggled to regain his feet, rolled his eyes, then extended his hand for Maxwell to grasp. "Up ya go, Sherry," he said, hoisting Maxwell off the floor and into his chair. "Hey, why don't I drive ya back to your hotel. You look a little sleepy." But Sherry had fallen asleep for the moment.

Five minutes later Jake Dougherty had managed to half carry and half steer Maxwell to the parking lot, where they fell into Dougherty's Acura TL. He drove him back to the office and offered once again to drive Maxwell to his hotel, but Sherry insisted that he was OK and that he'd drive himself. Dougherty thought about it a minute, then shrugged, reasoning that Maxwell was a fairly experienced drunk who'd learned to somewhat compensate for his frequently inebriated condition behind the wheel. "OK, Sherry, suit yourself," he said loudly as they pulled up next to Maxwell's rented Chevy Lumina. "Hey, it's been a great evening. I think we got a lot accomplished."

"Yeah, it was great, Jack. I'll be seein' ya." He staggered out of Dougherty's Acura, managed to get up to the Chevy, struggled with the lock for a bit, then finally opened the door and fell in. In less than ten seconds he was sound asleep.

Sherry awoke at first light, his mind taking a few moments to sort out how it was that he came to be sitting in a car in the bleak and colorless surroundings of what looked like an office park in the early dawn. His throat was sore from snoring and his head throbbed. Maxwell looked around to see that nobody was watching him, started his car, and drove slowly back to the hotel. Once inside his room, he tore off his suit, fell straight into bed, and slept until noon.

* * *

While Sherry Maxwell was getting a few hours of sobriety inducing sleep, sprawled across the front seat of the Lumina, the Johnsons, Vera Hawkins, and her date Billy Espinoza were relaxing in Zack's hot tub and watching an east coast hockey game on his forty-eight inch TV set, which was situated under the awning on his little patio. They'd enjoyed another of Suzy's remarkable dinners, this time a spicy beef and vegetable dish that caused Billy Espinoza to ask whether she did Mexican as well.

Zack reached into the cooler next to the tub and passed Vera another Coors. She smiled as she took the proffered can. He smiled back, noticing that he'd taken a clinical interest in Vera in her skimpy and revealing two-piece, but nothing more. I *must* be in love, he thought contentedly, finding it a little hard to believe that he wasn't fantasizing about ravishing the leggy and shapely blond from Tennessee. He reached down and took Suzy's hand.

"High sticking?" Billy yelled abruptly. "He never touched him! That guy's blind. Hey, don't give up your day job just yet, y'asshole," he shouted, as though he were at the game and the referee could actually hear him.

Suzy'd been trying to follow the action, wondering what it was about hockey that seemed to get the fans so upset. "Why are they stopping the game again?" she asked Zack.

"They called another penalty, honey, for high sticking. That's hitting the guy too high up with the stick, like in the head."

"Oh," she said a little uncertainly. It seemed to her that they seemed to spend most of their time skating aimlessly around or getting in or out of the penalty box. She looked at her watch, noting that the game had been in progress for nearly two hours, yet they were only in the beginning of the third period. Neither of the girls had any interest in the hockey game and soon began talking to one another. Suzy found Vera's Tennessee drawl and speech patterns strange but generally comprehensible.

"So what kind o' job you lookin' to get, Suzy?" asked Vera. "I know they always lookin' fer help in the pet store."

"I should keep that in mind," Suzy replied. "But I think I'd like to look for something where I can use my language skills. I've been studying all my life to perfect my command of English, so I'd like to be able to use my training."

"Yeah, that makes sense. Hey, you know, Ah took Spanish in high school. Hey, Billy, Como estah oostaid. How's that, you cute li'l ol' wetback?"

Billy Espinoza looked at Vera askance. "Hey, bebe, that pretty good. Joo stick w' me, I make joo beeg star in Tijuana," he replied, though in fact he spoke better English than Spanish.

"What's wetback mean?" asked Suzy.

"It means I'm from Mexico," said Billy. "The call us wetbacks 'cause our backs are wet from swimmin' the river to get here."

Suzy looked at Billy, sensing some sort of joke, but wasn't quite sure. "Did you really swim a river to get here?" she asked.

Zack was growing bored with the inane conversation. Before Billy could elaborate on the alleged border crossing (he'd actually been born in East LA of second generation Mexican American parents), Zack suggested going down to the local video store to rent a movie. After much discussion, he persuaded the others, largely in deference to Suzy's national origins, to agree on THE LAST EMPEROR.

They watched the film for a time from the hot tub until Billy and Vera, not normally appreciative of anything more cerebral than an Ace Ventura movie, excused themselves, ostensibly to watch television in Zack's little den. Perhaps fifteen minutes later Zack and Suzy heard a variety of grunts and squeals coming faintly from the den area of the house. Zack looked at his wife. "Hmm, sounds like a good idea, huh?"

To his surprise, she looked at him quite seriously. "I don't want to do that with other people in our house, Zack. This should be a private thing, between just us alone."

To his surprise, he found himself agreeing with her. Jesus, this is my *wife,* not some bimbo I picked up in a local gin mill. "Yeah, you're right, honey." He took her hand and kissed it gently, finding himself more than a little annoyed with Billy and Vera and their panting rutting sounds. "Let's just watch the movie for now."

* * *

Chapter 5

While the Johnson's were sorting out the nuances of being married as opposed to being "involved," Chen Wan Le sat staring at the directive from Lin Cho Hsin, the company president, which informed Chen that he must be ready to submit eighteen Red Whippet sedans for USA emission and crash testing within three weeks. The cars were to be airfreighted to the EPA test facility in Lansing, Michigan, with four more units to be sent to California and New York for further compliance testing by those states, which had stricter emission limits still.

The chief of powertrain engineering for the Long March People's Cooperative Automotive Manufacturing Company was sweating uncomfortably. Three weeks? Was Lin stark, raving mad? The Red Whippet lacked even the most rudimentary safety devices, let alone the mandatory airbags, side-impact barriers, and minimum collision damage bumpers demanded by the American government and its whining constituents. Nor could it hope to meet the absurdly stringent emission standards required by the empire-building bureaucrats within the EPA. Indeed, only last week one of the durability test drivers required treatment for acute carbon monoxide poisoning from an exhaust system leak in one of the test cars. Chen fumed as he thought of the U.S. specification Toyota his engineers had recently tested, which did not emit *any* really dangerous levels of CO, even if one breathed directly from the tailpipe. And here *his* people, a hopeless collection of cretins, he told himself, were building a poisonous gas trap that only the mad Doctor Kevorkian could love.

Chen was close to panic. He could not imagine being able to assemble the requisite number of prototype engines capable of passing the American standards within three weeks, let alone being able to provide them in production quantities for export within a few months thereafter. The requirement was simply impossible to meet. Utterly, hopelessly impossible. He thought briefly of Josef Stalin's well known propensity for simply executing scientists and managers who failed to meet deadlines or standards that he himself had arbitrarily established, with no knowledge of the technical or scientific difficulties involved. While Chen had never heard of such measures being applied in the People's Republic, he had no doubt that his failure to meet the impossible objective would have extremely unpleasant consequences. He had to play for time. Abruptly, he reached for the phone to confirm with Lin that the program had been moved up yet again, hoping that Lin would assure him that they knew that the requirement was unrealistic but to simply do his best.

But less than ten minutes later Chen had received no such assurance. The requirement would be met, Lin assured him. The cars would be ready for air shipment within three weeks. "But as for meeting the American government standards, do not concern yourself with this problem unduly, Chen," Lin had said. "I am quite certain that the Americans will be willing to grant certain dispensations to help us in this great cooperative enterprise between our two nations. I believe the important thing will be to provide engines that are the best that we can provide on such short notice. If they do not quite meet the standards, well, that is unfortunate and will require perhaps some strenuous diplomacy, but I am sure it will all turn out all right."

Lin's remarks left Chen more nonplussed than ever. Baffled, he shook his head and summoned his chief emissions engineer in the hope of cobbling up some sort of combination of three-way catalysts, exhaust gas recirculation, lean burning, and low compression that would at least get reasonably close to the American emission limits. He thanked his ancestors that at least he wasn't responsible for engineering the safety features, of which there was currently none, on the Red Whippet.

* * *

Sherry Maxwell had just received perhaps the greatest gift which could have been bestowed on him. With near trembling hands he tore open the top of the box on his desk, revealing, to his immense satisfaction, that the Finlandia vodka case indeed contained its normal full complement of twelve fifths. Secondarily, he looked at the little card taped to the top of the box. "Best regards, Jake," it said, nothing more.

Sherry was certainly aware that the case of vodka was little more than a bribe from Jake Dougherty and that he really ought not to have accepted it. However, during his long but uneventful career, Maxwell had become quite accustomed to accepting such gifts from dealers or dealer candidates, which as long as they were neither too large or in the form of cash, he rationalized as being little more than a simple business courtesy. He preferred consumables of the liquid variety, since they could be enjoyed privately and, once consumed, left no possibility of a raised eyebrow from his superiors. Burnside was due back that afternoon, causing Sherry to carry the case out to his car and deposit it in the trunk. He slammed the lid down on his treasure, then stood briefly wondering if the heat of the trunk might cause his vodka to spoil, as might beer under the same circumstances. He stood contemplating this dreadful possibility, then shook his head. Nah, he told himself, I never heard of spoiled vodka before. It'll be OK, he thought, though he resolved to leave early that afternoon to get his booty into the cool and safer airconditioned environment of his hotel room.

He went back inside and began sorting through the mail, tossing what looked like letters and resumes from employment aspirants into one pile to be reviewed by Burnside, and dealership envelopes, which he assumed to be franchise queries, into another. The latter he would open personally in the hope of availing himself of additional contraband. He went over to the fax machine and was pleased to find an additional four communications from potential dealer applicants.

He collected all of them, then went over to the office PC to generate the form letter he'd put together. Thirty minutes later he had all the responses nicely printed and ready to be faxed to the eager dealer candidates, notifying them that he, Sherry Maxwell, Vice President of Sales and Marketing for Red Tiger Motor Company, would personally review their qualifications and market data to determine their eligibility to be granted the coveted Red Tiger franchise. And, of course, implicit in all this was the critical importance of making a good first impression on such an exalted personage as the Vice President of Sales and Marketing for The Red Tiger Motor Company, a man who represented no less than the manufacturing might, economic power, and vast human resources of the People's Republic of China! Sherry's chest actually swelled slightly as he contemplated his position. It's like I'm the point man here, he told himself. I got a coupla billion Chinks behind me!

Ten minutes later he stood feeding the letters one by one into the fax machine. Shit, you'd think the friggin' Chinks'd at least give the point man a secretary, he thought angrily.

* * *

Vice-President Nate Garmin, temporarily chastened by the unfortunate events at the Chinese embassy the previous week, wondered once again what it was about the president that caused women to come on to him so strongly and then charge *him* with improper advances. It was all part, he was sure, of a great conspiracy to embarrass the president and his administration, a conspiracy that apparently had been operating for many years. And now even Chinese women were involved! I knew there was something funny about that girl, he told himself. I bet she's been to one of their spy schools, or something like that. And that guy she said she was married to. He's probably a Chinese with American parents! Garmin was worried that the strange altercation would somehow endanger his plans to use Chinese industrial and technological prowess as a shining example of government planning at its social, and hence, commercial best.

He looked at his watch, noting that Chinese Ambassador Li had asked if he would be so kind as to return his call before the end of the day. He wondered what Li wanted, but was really hoping for affirmation from him that his speech at the embassy dinner had been well, even reverently, received, and was even now being quoted in its entirety in Chinese newspapers. He'd not yet gotten over his considerable disappointment that nobody, Chinese or American, had commented on his insightful and profound remarks. He sat pondering this puzzling and disappointing lack of reaction to what, in his mind, was one of his best and most memorable speeches. Finally, he looked at his watch again, then called through the door. "Hey, Cassie, get Ambassador Li on the phone, willya?

Two minutes later Nate Garmin was speaking with Ambassador Li of the People's Republic of China. "Hi, Mr. Ambassador," he said. "Hey, that was really too bad about that little ruckus the other night. I don't know what got into that girl, but I guess this sort of stuff happens to Bob Carruthers all the time. Women just can't keep their hands off him. I don't know why."

David White

"Yes, I too am most sorry about the episode, Mr. Vice-President. You are certainly correct about women and your president. It is very strange, how all these women are always making these terrible and baseless allegations against him."

"Yeah, I just know there's a conspiracy to get him. Boy, someday we're gonna catch those people, and then they'll be sorry."

"Of that there is no doubt, Mr. Vice-President. There must be tens of thousands, perhaps millions of people involved. It has always amazed me that they've been able to maintain such total security with so many people in on it. But you are right, I am sure, eventually somebody will crack, and then the whole conspiracy will be revealed."

"That's what I figure, Mr. Ambassador, then we'll start getting things done around here." He paused. "Uh, Mr. Ambassador, what did you think of my speech the other night, you know, the one where I said we're all just passengers on Spaceship Earth," selecting what he felt was the most eloquently telling passage in his address.

"Ah, it was, ah, how can I put it, very moving, Mr. Vice-President, a powerful and important speech, one which doubtless will be studied for generations. I especially liked your comment about how you Americans are in the first class section, while we, temporarily of course, are in the, umm, tourist area, I believe you said. Very good, very good indeed. You have a great gift for communicating your thoughts," said Li, thinking how the embassy staff's sobriquet for Garmin, The Wooden Carp, was wonderfully appropriate.

"Gee, I'm really glad you liked it. I put a lot of work into it."

"Ah, yes, Mr. Vice-President, that was obvious, very obvious. Now, as to the reason for my call, I have a matter of greatest importance to discuss with you and possibly even with President Carruthers. It relates to the coming introduction of our wonderful new low pollution car, which will also, as you know, greatly reduce America's dependence on foreign oil."

Garmin's face lit up in an expression of delight. "Why, that's great, Mr. Ambassador. That's something I want to talk to you guys about, too. I think your new car will set a great example for American industry, where the government sets the priorities and industry, ah, produces the goods. I wouldn't mind those guys if someone else made the decisions about what kind of stuff they make. That shouldn't be left in their hands."

"Ah, quite so, Mr. Vice-President. I couldn't agree with you more."

Garmin fished in his breast pocket for a small slip of paper, which he unfolded, grinning a bit conspiratorially as he did so. "In fact, I shouldn't be telling anybody about this yet, since it's just in the planning stage, but I want to use your example to help me set up an American industrial policy. And I'm going to form a kind of think tank I want to call the Diversified Industrial Liaison and Development Office," he added, reading carefully from the scrap of paper. "Whaddya think?"

"A brilliant and necessary stroke, Mr. Vice-President," cried Li. "I am glad we are in complete agreement and that our efforts will be able to provide you much needed impetus for your, ah, industrial policy. And it is precisely these matters that I wish to discuss with you in detail, at your earliest convenience. Though perhaps you were not aware of it, we are submitting a number of pre-production cars to your EPA and NHTSA for testing in less than three weeks. I should like to discuss with you how we might best ensure that these testing procedures and other administrative details proceed smoothly and without delay, so that we may begin selling the Red Whippet in the US market very soon. It will be of great benefit to both our great nations, as you clearly agree, Mr. Vice-President."

"Well, you can count on my full cooperation, plus I'm good friends with the head of EPA. I know she's very excited about your new car and everything it'll do for the environment. She'll be a big help, I promise you."

"That is excellent. I had scarcely hoped for such a level of cooperation, Mr. Vice-President. May we meet in the next few days for our discussion?"

"Sure. I'm in town all the rest of this week. You wanna come over here?"

When they'd finished making arrangements for their meeting, Li sat looking at the pad on which he'd been doodling. Diversified Industrial Liaison and Development Office, he mused, unconsciously forming the acronym. DILDO? Li shrugged, thinking it a bit strange, then wadded up the paper and tossed it in the waste basket beside his desk.

* * *

As Li was quietly musing about the potential pressures the Chinese government might bring to bear on the Carruthers administration to allow special dispensations from their government regulatory agencies, Sid Burnside was sitting in his office looking through the stack of resumes

Maxwell had handed him on his return. He was moderately pleased that Maxwell had handled all the dealer application queries with the form letter, though he would have preferred some input from him on the resumes. Burnside was totally unaware, as were all Americans, save those present for the occasion, of the little melee at the Chinese embassy the week before and all that it might imply in terms of the Red Whippet's introduction. He still blissfully assumed that nothing would come of the company's efforts to ready their product for the US market, the introduction of which was, according to his best estimates, several years away, if ever. Thus, Burnside saw his job as little more than going through the motions of developing a retail distribution channel, which until an introduction date could be finalized, would consist of little more than maintaining a correspondence file with the interested dealer candidates. And, of course, he'd have to arrange for the occasional visits from Zhu and his people, which he calculated shouldn't be too trying, at least as long as he avoided the services of Starlight Escort Services and their unpredictable "dates."

Sherry Maxwell walked through the door as he was skimming a resume from an employment prospect named Edward White Feather, whom he correctly assumed to be a native American. Burnside briefly noted that White Feather had been employed as a distribution clerk by American Honda for six months, then as a district sales manager by Mitsubishi for four months, then as a parts retail counter man in a NAPA parts store in east LA for the past year. Hey, this guy might be a good move, Burnside told himself, tossing the resume into another pile for further consideration.

He looked up at Maxwell, who'd been standing for a few seconds waiting for acknowledgement. "Ah, Sid," he began, "there's this guy up in Sacramento I been talkin' to about the franchise. He sounds like a good prospect. If you can spare me around here, I'd like to take a ride up there and check him out, and maybe look around for some other dealer candidates while I'm at it. Whaddya think?"

Sherry, of course, was merely seeking an excuse for getting out of the office for a few days, plus hoping for a few more nice lunches and dinners from Jake Dougherty and some others like him. Burnside seemed to ponder this for a moment. "Yeah, that might be a good idea, Sherry. We gotta start gettin' together some files on some good prospects for when we're gettin' ready to get started. Yeah, why don't ya do that? I can hold down the fort around here while you're gone." Actually, Burnside was just as happy not to have anybody hanging around, for whom he'd have to set a reasonably respectable example. "Yeah, why don't you head on up that way and see what you turn up."

Fifteen minutes later Maxwell had made a hasty exit from the headquarters office, wanting to make his escape before Burnside thought of something for him to do. He had no idea that Burnside was relieved to see him go.

As Sherry was heading directly for the freeway, having already packed that morning in anticipation of his escape, Burnside was reaching to answer the phone, which was ringing annoyingly. "Red Tiger Motor Company," he said. "How may I direct your call?"

"Ah, Mr. Burnside, is that you?"

"Yes, it is," he replied, trying to make out the slight but unidentifiable accent.

"This is Suzy Johnson." Burnside said nothing, not making the association. "Ah, I'm sure you remember me, Mr. Zhu's interpreter."

"Oh, Suzy, sure, of course, how are you? Are you all settled in yet?" Burnside's first reaction was one of apprehension, since he knew nothing of her status beyond the fact that she'd precipitously married an Arnold Schwartzenegger look-alike named Johnson, who'd apparently screwed her into a state of befuddled euphoria. He momentarily felt a twinge of envy, first for Johnson's apparent sexual vigor, and second because he would have liked nothing better than to have screwed Suzy Johnson into a state of euphoric befuddlement himself.

"Well, actually, Sid, that's what I'm calling you about. I'm no longer employed by the parent company, you know, The Long March People's Cooperative Automotive Manufacturing Company. And my husband, Zack, suggested that I might be valuable to you as an employee of the affiliate here in the United States. I could function as interpreter when you need one, and I'm good at handling administration and things like that."

As she was speaking Burnside was hurriedly speculating that she could be an almost invaluable asset to him, what with her knowledge of the various personalities with whom he'd have to deal. Plus, he assumed her to have access to a vast apparatus of informants and rumor-mongers, which could help keep him advised on the internal thinking within the parent company, and thus out of trouble. His mind was also developing a parallel thought to the effect that she could be an elaborately placed spy in his midst, though just as quickly he dismissed the notion as absurdly

David White

improbable. After all, it was he who'd arranged the liaison between her and Zack Johnson, not the Chinese.

"You know, Suzy, that could be quite an idea you've got there. And you might even be able to work out of your house a lot of the time. It'd be great if I could send my communications in Chinese, you know, avoid misunderstandings and stuff like that." As he talked, Burnside was actually growing quite enthusiastic about the idea. Suddenly, another thought occurred to him. "Uh, Suzy, what do you think your former bosses would think of me hiring you? I mean, I imagine some of them were a little upset about your leaving so quickly."

"That's probably a good point, Sid. If they actually knew who I was, there might be some bad feelings. But if you just list me as an employee named Susan Johnson, I don't think any of them would make the association. They'd find out eventually, during one of their visits, but by then if I'd been doing a good job for you, I don't think they'd be too upset." She correctly assumed that Burnside knew nothing of the groping and broken nose incident in the Chinese embassy and didn't plan to enlighten him.

"Well, hey, why don't you come out here in the next couple of days and we can talk about it."

"Wonderful, how's tomorrow for lunch sound?"

"Perfect."

"Ah, Sid, do you mind if I bring Zack along? You see, I don't have my driver's license yet, and he'll have to drive me."

"Nah, that's fine. I"ll seeya both tomorrow around noon."

After he'd hung up Burnside found himself growing fairly excited at the prospect of hiring Suzy Lin Johnson. *Maybe I could even use her as a zone sales manager or something like that,* he speculated. Burnside assumed that anybody who could speak both perfect English and Chinese *had* to be a genius of some sort.

After Mrs. Johnson hung up, her husband, who'd just returned from flying a two day trip, largely spent fantasizing about his new bride, pulled her back into bed. "C'mon, honey, we gotta tune you up so you'll be sharp for your interview."

"Yes, husband, I believe I may need another little tune-up."

Zack reflected that he seemed to enjoy this arrangement more every day.

* * *

124

Chen Wan Le angrily threw the latest exhaust emission progress report against the wall. His technicians had hurriedly grafted a Honda three-way catalyst into the exhaust system of six Red Whippet test cars in the hope of getting the emissions into at least striking distance of the US federal standards. But because the engine did not operate with electronic engine controls, which regulated air-fuel mixtures and spark advance, the emission levels from the engine were simply too much for the catalytic converters to cope with. All had burned up within two thousand kilometers.

Strangely, nobody above Chen's level seemed to be overly concerned that he was about to submit for testing by the American federal government a sampling of products that had no hope whatever of passing even the initial tests, let alone the mandatory 50,000 mile durability tests. He wondered what pressures might be brought to bear on the American administration to get them to agree to a waiver of their standards on behalf of the Chinese. This, to Chen, seemed the only plausible explanation for continuing the plans to send the cars to the US for testing at this point. Either that, or the Chinese government, for reasons he could not fathom, was simply trying to provoke a trade confrontation with the United States. Chen, as with most higher level officials or managers in the People's Republic, was aware in general terms if not precise detail, how the Carruthers administration had given major concessions in the form of technology transfers and trade preferences to the People's Republic in return for campaign cash contributions. He thusly hoped that some sort of similar accommodation could be reached regarding the export of the Red Whippet, which could not, and never would, meet US safety and emission standards.

* * *

While Chen was glumly contemplating the emissions progress report and all it might imply for his future with the Long March People's Cooperative Automotive Manufacturing Company, Nate Garmin, practically trembling with anticipation, was waiting for Penny Twombly and Ambassador Li of the People's Republic of China to arrive at his office. Thinking about how much he'd enjoyed his lunch with Jimmy Bimstein, Garmin had arranged to have a sandwich platter of coldcuts and assorted breads delivered to his office. In deference to Ambassador Li, Garmin requested that a set of chopsticks be sent up with the tray. The kitchen staff, realizing that Garmin personally had made the chopstick request, complied without comment, though they exchanged a couple of quizzical looks. Garmin also arranged to have a dated and signed version of his speech printed, featuring the White House seal, on parchment, for personal delivery to Ambassador Li.

Presently Penny Twombly arrived. She greeted Nate Garmin with a peck on the cheek, then pulled off her trenchcoat, revealing a daringly short skirt over quite ordinary legs. She moved back a couple of steps. "Do you like my dress, Nate?"

"Ah, yes, I do, Penny," answered Nate Garmin. "It's very stylish, and you really have the legs for it."

"Oh, do you really think so?" she asked, beaming. "It's made from hand-picked cotton that's spun on a hand-powered loom. It doesn't use any electricity or anything! Isn't that wonderful! I feel so good when I can set an example like this, and I'm probably providing a job for some poor African-American or other minority."

"I think it's really great when people in your position live by their words, Penny, and set the example for the people. Just think, if all cotton materials were made that way we'd save a lot of energy, I mean a *lot*, and a lot more Negroes'd have jobs, too. I mean African-Americans'd have jobs," he added hastily. "That's what I meant to say."

Penny Twombly seemed not to notice Garmin's appalling gaffe of political incorrectness. "Really, Nate, I just don't see why people think they have to have all this technology to live well. Here I am, living proof that it's just not necessary."

"Well, you know my feelings on this stuff. Like I've been saying all along, it we just took all the people who think their livelihoods depend on high tech, wasteful industries and put them to work for the government cleaning up the environment at high salaries, we'd eliminate unemployment in this country overnight, and the American standard of living would shoot up right away! I just don't see why people can't understand that." This was indeed one of Garmin's favorite themes, one which, to the fearful exasperation of Bob Carruthers, he made repeatedly during their first presidential campaign. Fortunately, due either to the willing support the press granted Garmin and Carruthers, or the sheer economic ignorance of the reporters themselves, Garmin's strange theories never seemed to gain wide circulation.

"Nate, what do you think this meeting's about today with the Chinese ambassador?"

"Oh, I already know. He told me the other day. He wants us to cooperate with the emission and safety testing of their new car. Like, they've never tried to export a car into the United States before and they want to make sure they don't make any mistakes. I think he's just asking for help with the paperwork or something like that."

"Well, we'll certainly give them all the assistance they need. We want them to succeed and set an example. You know, Nate, it's really neat to work with people who don't see us as adversaries. They know the federal government is here to help them, not make things difficult. I wish more people in Detroit knew that."

"Yeah, well if they felt that way they'd have been the first to develop a car like the Chinese, one that's friendly to the environment and the world's resources. But, no, all they want to do is whine and complain. That's the big reason I want to help the Chinese. You know, Penny, I shouldn't say this, but sometimes I feel that we have more in common with the Chinese than we do with the people in Detroit, or in any American industry or business for that matter."

"Maybe we do, Nate. And maybe it's because we just want people to do the right thing, whether they want to or not. Can you imagine what kind of world we'd have if everybody just got to do what they wanted?" She shook her head. And at that moment Ambassador Li appeared in the doorway with Garmin's secretary.

"Mr. Vice-President! How are you today?" he boomed with an almost western ebullience.

"Oh, hi, Mr. Ambassador, how ya doin'?" Garmin strode over to take his hand and pump it vigorously. "And Mr. Ambassador, this here's Penny Twombly. She's head of our Environmental Protection Agency. Penny, meet Ambassador Li."

"Oh, I'm so pleased to meet you," she gushed. "I'm the one who brought Nate the news about your new car. We're both so excited about this development, a revolutionary new car brought out under government supervision. It makes a point we've been trying to make for years!"

"Ah, well, I am very pleased that you share our enthusiasm for the Red Whippet, as it is called. Yes, I believe we have common interests in showing what can be done with enlightened government not only setting the standards but actually doing the product development and manufacturing."

David White

"Gosh, you took the words right out of my mouth, " exclaimed Garmin, trying hard to remember Li's exact verbiage so he could commit it to paper before the day was out. He turned to Penny Twombly. "Hey, you know, Penny, what we should be doing here is try to set up a government owned corporation to design and manufacture cars. That's what we need to do long term."

Li could scarcely believe his ears. He'd hardly been in the room for a full minute and the fools were already falling all over themselves to ingratiate themselves with him! He didn't doubt that Garmin and Twombly could be persuaded to waive the standards for the Chinese with the most sophistic of arguments, and he knew that President Carruthers dared not publicly oppose the suggestion that the Chinese be granted special dispensation by the American regulatory agencies. The lovely former Miss Lin, loyal and dedicated former Chinese citizen that she'd been, had seen to that, however unintentionally.`

Li pursed his lips and thought of how to begin. The hardly concealed enthusiasm of both Garmin and Ms. Twombly for the Chinese market entry caused him to abandon, for the moment at least, an approach using any implicit threats. "Ah, well, I am greatly pleased that you both understand the benefits that accrue to all of us by expediting the Red Whippet through your certification tests. In fact, as we speak, tens of thousands of these remarkable vehicles are being readied for shipment to the US, ready to establish altogether new standards, both in operation and by example, for environmental awareness and benefit!"

Penny Twombly clasped her hands in front of her. "Oh, I'm so happy about this, Mr. Ambassador. This will prove a great day for the people of our two great nations and all mankind. And I'm so glad it was the Chinese government that made it happen."

"Then we are in total agreement, Ms. Twombly, that it is to everybody's benefit to begin the sale of the Red Whippet to American consumers without further delay."

"That's for sure, Mr. Ambassador," interjected Garmin. "Then I can get started on drawing up my industrial policy initiative and forming my committee."

"Of course, the DILDO, as you call it," replied Li, hoping to impress Twombly and Garmin with his command and mastery of American acronyms.

"Yeah, that's it," exclaimed Garmin happily. Penny Twombly looked at

128

both Garmin and Li curiously but said nothing.

"Very good," replied Li. "Then, on to the main topic of this meeting. I have been in close contact with both the Premier and the president of The Long March People's Cooperative Automotive Manufacturing Company, and both, of course, are eager to begin selling this new product in the US, and both wish that all potential obstacles be dealt with swiftly and effectively."

"They will be, Mr. Ambassador, you can count on that," said Nate Garmin, his face a mask of grim determination, as though he were preparing to personally lead the armed assault on a redoubt held by counter-revolutionaries, wreckers, and Detroit automotive executives.

"Excellent! For we do have one small obstacle to be overcome in readying the Red Whippet for sale in the US." Li paused, staring alternately at Garmin and Twombly, as though gauging whether their commitment was worthy of the great cause. "Yes," he continued, "a small matter, indeed. As you certainly can appreciate, Chinese technology is some of the most advanced in the industrialized world. Our satellite launches, our ICBMs, our submarines, our electronics industry certainly speak for themselves, do they not?"

Garmin and Twombly nodded in the affirmative.

"However, certain of our manufacturing processes for consumer products are not quite as developed as they will be shortly, certainly within a few months. Of course, the Red Whippet in prototype form is able to deliver on all its fuel consumption and low exhaust emission promises. However, we have encountered certain difficulties with a small percentage of the production vehicles, a few of which may not meet the high standards we have set for them. This is a simple matter of refining our process engineering to enable us to consistently meet our seemingly impossibly high standards with all production units."

"That doesn't seem like too big a problem, Mr. Ambassador," said Penny Twombly. "I'm sure my agency can persuade some of the other automakers to share some of their manufacturing techniques with you in order that you may achieve your goals." She said this with a slight smile, imagining the joy of coercing domestic automakers into sharing confidential engineering data with a competitor.

"That is very generous of you, Ms. Twombly, very generous, but there is a strong consensus within the government and manufacturing sector of China that the Red Whippet be the result solely of Chinese efforts. This is a consensus with which I agree, incidentally, both for political and psychological reasons."

"I think I understand," said Penny. "It's a self-esteem thing, right?" she said, drawing on her experience in elementary education and the utter necessity to promote self-esteem, even to the exclusion of actual learning, among her students.

"Well, I suppose you could put it that way," said Li, suddenly realizing he'd inadvertently made a telling point with Ms. Twombly. "Yes, we agree that, ah, self-esteem is very important to the further development of the Chinese nation. Therefore, I must regrettably refuse your generous offer to help us share in the process engineering techniques of the other automakers. It would compromise our self-*esteem*. We must go it alone or not at all, though in any event, within a few months we shall have met and conquered all problems related to meeting all standards with production vehicles."

"Oh, I fully understand," said Penny Twombly, her brow furrowing in an expression of sympathetic concern. "But if most of the cars meet your new standards, surely the rest will pass our Federal standards, and the California Air Resources Board (CARB) tests. After all, these standards are so much lower than those you've set for yourselves, aren't they?"

"Yes, of course, but it is important that all our new cars be sold under the auspices of meeting our new standards, not just that *some* of them meet the standards. The self-esteem of the Chinese people is at stake!"

"But, if, ah, you're not sure all of the cars will pass, how can you sell them with that representation?" asked Penny Twombly.

"Of course, they all would pass in due course, since our plan is to ship and sell them in their current condition, then retro-fit them with the necessary new components to bring them into compliance with our high, self-imposed standards."

Nate Garmin looked at Penny Twombly. "Hey, that'd work, wouldn't it, Penny? I mean, they could get started, then bring 'em back and have 'em fitted with the new parts when they get here."

"That is precisely what we are proposing to do, Mr. Vice-President," said Li, beaming, pleased but rather surprised that Garmin had grasped the idea without further repetition or elaboration.

Penny Twombly looked uncertain. She didn't know how the EPA test procedure was conducted but felt vaguely that the Chinese proposal fell well outside the normal procedure. "I don't know, Mr. Ambassador, I'm not sure we can do it that way," she said apologetically. "Are you suggesting that EPA forego the tests until some later date, after the cars have gone on sale?"

"Exactly, Ms. Twombly. After all, we intend to provide our own documentary evidence and our own sworn affidavits that the vehicles meet the standards, or certainly will, as soon as the requisite parts, which are under development as we speak, are available."

This was all moving a bit too fast for the EPA chief, who despite her near passionate desire to put the Red Whippet on display as an object lesson in successful government market intervention, still possessed some sense of equitable rule application within her agency. "Ah, you're now saying we should waive the tests altogether?"

"Only until the cars are retro-fitted, then you may test away to everybody's satisfaction." As though he were adding an afterthought of no great importance, Li waved his hand dismissively and said, "And, of course, certain items of mandatory safety equipment will be retro-fitted after sale also. But, as your government well knows, airbags are at best a mixed blessing, certainly killing nearly as many as they save, perhaps more!"

"Ah, Mr. Li, I'm not sure our government will be able to waive certain of these test procedures," said Penny. "I mean, there are certain steps that have to be completed, I mean, if we did it for you, we'd have to extend the same sort of thing to everybody who wanted special treatment."

Li actually managed to look a bit surprised, even shocked. "Are you saying that the assurances of the People's Republic are inadequate, that we cannot be trusted to fulfill our commitment to this great endeavor? I am not sure how to explain this to the Premier." He shook his head, brow furrowing. "I don't how he would react to such news. While he is certainly one of the great men of our time, his self-esteem is very fragile!"

Nate Garmin watched the ambassador's change of demeanor with growing alarm. He could see his national industrial policy and its planning committee deflating, even disappearing altogther. "Ah, Penny, I don't think we want to upset our friends in China, do we?" he said hastily. "I mean, if you can't trust the Chinese, who can you trust, right?" He looked at Li for affirmation, but Li only looked away, seemingly pouting for the moment. "Hey, I'll tell you what, Penny. Me and the president'll take the heat off you on this one. He can just do it by executive order, I think. We can waive the requirements to help them get started, then do all the tests just like Ambassador Li said, only a little later."

"I don't know, Nate," said Penny slowly, "I'm not sure it sets a healthy example." Actually, she rather liked the idea of having the president, by executive order, waive the emission and safety requirements for the Chinese. Just as long as she wasn't in a position to be blamed.

"Well, I don't know, Penny, we just won't do it for anybody else, that'll fix that. If anybody else comes in here looking for us to cut 'em a little slack, we'll just tell 'em tough cookies, it was a one time thing."

"Well," huffed Li, "perhaps we would be better served exporting the Red Whippet to Germany or perhaps Canada first. I'm sure that they will see the environmental and energy conservation benefits more clearly than the government of the United States." He looked at the door as if planning to leave.

"Wait!" said Garmin, almost shouting. "Those people don't even have an EPA! How smart can they be? I know we care a lot more about the environment than they do." He turned toward Penny. "I wanna make this happen for us, Penny, and I think the president'll agree with me."

"Please forgive me, Mr. Vice-President," said Li. "Perhaps I spoke in anger without thinking first. Of course we wish the United States to be the first power to be blessed with the Red Whippet, and, again, I ask only your help in seeing that certain of your regulatory rules can be waived, only until we can have the necessary parts on hand to make the required modifications. After all, we above all want the Red Whippet to be all that we have promised and more, much more."

"See, Penny," said Garmin, "isn't it great dealing with a government that wants to give people more than they bargained for."

"Well, I'm all for that," said Penny, "but we'll have to take up the issue of waiving the requirements with the president, if we're looking to him to do this by executive order. Understand, I'm not basically opposed to temporarily suspending our testing requirements as long as we get the assurances from the People's Republic that the cars will be retro-fitted with all the latest emission hardware. And I guess you'd have to get NHTSA to sign off on the safety equipment and maybe change or suspend their crash tests."

"I'm sure we can work out all the details, Ambassador Li," said Garmin with far more assurance that he felt.

"That is truly excellent, then Mr. Vice-President," said Li, smiling broadly for the first time in several minutes. "And Mr. Vice-President, there is something I would like you to deliver to President Carruthers personally, if you would be so kind." He bent down to unsnap the briefcase he'd laid on Garmin's desk, lifted the lid, and pulled out an unmarked

VHS tape. "We would prefer that the president only see this. Can you give your absolute assurance that you can deliver it personally?"

"Oh, sure, nobody's better at delivering stuff than me," replied Garmin as he reached for the tape.

"Splendid. Then perhaps we could meet in a couple of days to discuss the reaction of President Carruthers to your proposal, yes? I am sorry to appear anxious to reach a resolution of these problems, but we have set in motion our plans to begin exporting our cars to the US market within three months. Every day is crucial to our success."

"Of course we can do that," said Garmin. "I'll call you for a meeting within two or three days."

Penny Twombly smiled and said nothing. She was becoming vaguely uneasy about the Chinese proposal, though she felt that the whole problem had been dumped in Carruthers' lap, to what final effect she did not know.

Li picked up his briefcase and headed for the door after shaking hands perfunctorily with Penny and Garmin. The platter of coldcuts had remained untouched. "Hey, how 'bout a bite to eat, Penny," Garmin exclaimed happily. He immediately went to work fashioning another of his Dagwood sandwiches. Halfway through the process he noticed the chopsticks, shrugged, picked them up and dropped them in his breast pocket.

Li smiled as he left the building and nodded to his driver. He was glad that Garmin and not he had suggested the alternative of an executive order in order to bypass the rest of the US government. He was a little surprised that Garmin even knew that such an option might be available to the president. The self-esteem of the Chinese people is at stake! He snorted to himself and chuckled.

* * *

Two hours after Garmin had finished his meeting with the Ambassador, President Bob Carruthers sat looking at the VHS tape in his hand, suspecting the nature of its contents, especially after Garmin told him where he'd gotten it. He looked at the VCR and TV set in the corner, went over and shut the door, then went over to the VCR. He stood for a moment wondering what to do, then went back to the door, opened it, and called to the uniformed Secret Service agent in the hall. "Hey, you (he could never remember their names), c'mere and show me how to work this thing, willya."

The man followed him into the office, turned on the set and VCR, then popped in the tape, looking pointedly at Carruthers with a stare that as much as said "You dumb shit!"

"OK, you can leave now," said Carruthers rather unpleasantly, then stepped back to watch the tape. Oh, Christ! As he'd feared, there he was, standing next to the foxy kung-fu lady, their backs to the camera. His profile was, from time to time, completely identifiable on the black and white videotape. Within perhaps ten seconds of commencing, the tape clearly showed his hand reaching up to fondle the girl's left buttock. In spite of himself Carruthers felt a stirring in his groin. Damn, what a peachy ass! The girl then looked at the man on her right, her husband, then reached down to take his hand, clearly believing it was his hand on her lovely behind. Carruthers chuckled, then saw himself step closer to the girl, keeping her from reaching his wrist. He watched with interest as his fingers dug into her buttock, then dug harder still. He stopped smiling as he saw her turn to face him and slap his face. The bitch, he thought angrily, as he could practically feel the slap that had made his ears ring.

Abruptly, he was watching from another angle. Obviously, they had spliced another tape onto the first. Now he could see his own face, contorted with rage, as he reared back to hit the girl with his fist. He watched his clumsy swing, then the lightning movement of her hand breaking his nose. Christ, that was quick, thought Carruthers, once again feeling the stunning pain of his breaking nose. Goddam, this tape proves it, the bitch is a fucking professional kung-fu assassin! She was trying to kill me. The rest of the tape was given over to a wild confusion of flying bodies, the collapsing bar, pieces of glass and various bits of debris arcing through the air. At the last second Carruthers just caught an upraised arm with what looked like a nightstick in its hand.

Carruthers stood fuming, then turned off the VCR. Jesus H. Christ, he told himself, if it's not one thing it's another. Shit, with my stand on women's rights, with all I've done for these bitches, you'd think they wouldn't mind me coppin' a little feel once in a while. They oughtta be lining up to come across with a knob-job at least, or maybe some quality sheath time for the old sword!

Jesus, this bullshit all started with that big-hair bimbo telling everybody I'm a goddam wienie-wagger. Now this! All right, so I *am* a goddam wienie-wagger, he reminded himself. So what the hell's that got to do with my ability to *lead*, huh?

Christ, what the hell do these fucking Chinks want now, he wondered a bit fearfully. Last time it was the goddam missile booster technology, next the bastards are gonna want me to deliver our latest missile submarine with the fucking owner's manual printed in Chinese! All because these bimbos got no sense of humor.

Well, he consoled himself, long term it ain't gonna mean shit. Nothing can happen to me as long as Garmin's next in line. Even my own party wouldn't allow that dolt in the oval office, as he remembered once again the original strategy which had caused his wife to pick Garmin in the first place.

* * *

Sid Burnside strolled languidly into his office at ten thirty. Since the Chinese had left, and especially since Maxwell had gone off in search of additional dealer candidates and, hopefully, more free liquor and food two days earlier, he had grown even more relaxed, having moved a TV set into his office and ordering a satellite hookup so he could select from some two hundred channels as the mood struck him. His assumption that he would have little to do for the foreseeable future made the page dribbling out of the fax machine all the more alarming. He let it fall into the catch basket, picked it up with a flourish, and began to read. In a near-perfect caricature of Jackie Gleason's Ralph Kramden, his eyes abruptly bulged out in shock and disbelief. Above Zhu's name was the following communication:

Please to be advised that Long March People's Cooperative Automotive Manufacturing Company will be shipping 22,000 cars to US market in less than four months. Please to be telling us your distribution arrangements and where you wish cars be shipped. Also, Burnside please to advise undersignatured how customers pay for car when come port to buy.

Zhu Fei

Desperately Burnside searched the fax for some indication that the message was the product of some prankster's twisted mind, but the sending number was that of the Long March People's Cooperative Automotive Manufacturing Company, and certainly the final query had come from Zhu's perhaps untwisted but abysmally ignorant mind. Burnside had a momentary vision of rows of card tables set up on a wharf, with long lines of eager buyers standing before furiously writing sales clerks, all amid a cacophony of credit card printers. He smiled faintly at the image, then forced his mind back to the contents of the message. Abruptly Burnside concluded that Zhu had somehow confused years and months in his little missive. Yeah, that's it, he told himself as he sat down to compose a request for confirmation of Zsu's absurd timetable. He finished typing it on his computer, printed it, then sent it to Zhu via return fax.

Burnside watched the sheet being pulled through the fax machine, then went over to his TV set and turned on CNN. As the picture brightened he saw President Carruthers' head and shoulders filling the screen, wearing a broad white bandage across his nose. "...and I think I can now relate to people who've experienced the anxiety of waiting for the biopsy results," he was saying. "And I'd like to thank all the American people for their prayers and support during the past several days." Burnside wondered what was wrong with Carruthers' nose. Looks like someone gave him a chop across the old schnoz, he thought. He shrugged and began scrolling through the selections, stopping briefly to watch a German panzer column charging across the Russian steppes on the History Channel, then on to ESPN, where he was informed that Mike Tyson was back in jail. He had just begun channel surfing again when the fax machine resumed its chatter. Burnside walked over to it and waited patiently for the message to fall into the basket. He reached down and picked it up, noting it was from Zhu, and, further, that it was unusually terse. "What not understand about message?" it asked. It was signed by Zhu Fei again.

Burnside now definitely experienced a sinking feeling. Zhu actually intended to begin shipping these funny little cars in no more than four months. He as yet had heard nothing about certification testing for either emissions or safety and assumed that it was all being handled by the home company, as in fact it usually was by most importers. But now he had the additional problem of dissuading Zhu from his harebrained scheme of having the buyers pick up their cars in the ports of entry. Suddenly he found himself looking forward to his lunch appointment with the former

Miss Lin and her husband. Perhaps she'd be able to help him sort out what was happening back with the home company.

As Burnside was speculating what Suzy Lin Johnson might know about the peculiar goings on in China, Mrs. Johnson and her husband were getting ready to leave their little stucco ranch for the Red Tiger Motors office, forty-five minutes away in Chino. "Zack, I'm starting to feel a little funny about joining Red Tiger, especially if the people at home don't know about it," said Suzy to her husband. "I know it seemed like a good idea a couple of days ago, but now I'm not sure."

"Well, if it makes you feel uncomfortable, you don't have to do it. There's no reason you have to find something right away. We don't need the money, in fact, having you around to cook is cheaper than just me goin' out to eat every night. And a whole lot better. I think if you just want to take your time to find what it is you want to do then that's just fine." In truth, Zack was becoming a bit insecure at the idea of his bride suddenly running around freely in a world filled with no end of good-looking and often wealthy men. Jesus, he thought, I'm already getting jealous, and there's not even anybody to be jealous *of* yet. Suddenly he reached down, took her hand, and held it to his lips. "You still glad we did this, Shan?"

"I'll *always* be glad we did this, Zack, just as long as you are."

"That's my plan, honey." He looked and her and smiled. "I think we ought to at least hear what this guy Burnside wants to say. Who knows, it might be a good opportunity."

Within the hour they were meeting Sid Burnside in his office, from which Burnside had carried the TV set, fearing that Suzy Johnson might still have as yet undefined ties with the factory. She looked around as they stood in Burnside's office. "Ah, Sid, where is everybody? Still out in the field?" she asked.

Suddenly Burnside decided to roll the dice with Suzy Johnson and simply tell the truth. He smiled a bit wanly. "Actually, Maxwell and I are it right now, and Sherry's up around Sacramento talkin' to some dealers up there. There is no other staff."

Suzy Johnson smiled faintly, then laughed. "That's what I thought. I'd noticed that yours was the only salary being drawn off your payroll account. Don't worry, Zhu doesn't know what's going on. He never gets involved in the details."

Burnside shook his head. "Well, it looks like he's about to." He went over to his desk and handed her the faxes from Zhu. "Do you have any idea what's going on ."

She read both of them, then shrugged. "I really don't know. How can they move up the timetable on this?"

"That's what I can't figure out, Suzy. Are these cars already through the certification tests with the EPA and the safety administration? I mean, they're not supposed to even bring them onto US soil without that being accomplished."

"I don't think so," she replied. "I don't see how that could have been done. It wasn't being handled when I came over here a couple of weeks ago." She paused. "In fact, maybe I shouldn't tell you this, Sid, but that whole press release about the car being so advanced and getting such high mileage is totally untrue. From what I hear within the company, it could never pass the current US standards, let alone meet the claims we made for it."

Burnside looked at her in disbelief. "You've got to be kidding. How do you know this?"

"Well, for one thing, I helped edit the thing and did the translation. The orders came straight from Premier Wu himself. I guess he thought it would be a good idea to start stirring up some demand for it in advance.

"God, Suzy, you can't do something like that in this country, I mean going around making false claims. They'll hang us all when the whole thing gets exposed."

"Well, I didn't think it was legal, but I never really thought we'd be able to bring the cars in anyway for several years, so what harm was it. And in China, when you get a directive from the premier himself, it's not wise to question it. But I, and everybody, including Zhu, just thought nothing would come of it, since nothing was going to happen anyway."

Zack finally spoke. "Jesus, what kind of company makes plans it knows it can't go through with." He looked back and forth between Suzy and Burnside quizzically.

Suzy smiled. "Basically, any state-owned enterprise in China, Zack. Everything's just political posturing, grandiose plans and objectives that are never fulfilled, just like government plans and political promises made here in this country. That's what I and everybody else thought of this plan to send the Red Whippet to this country. I mean, we figured that eventually we'd get something going over here, but not for a long time. I really don't know what this means," she added, holding up the faxes.

Burnside sat down at his desk, gesturing for them to be seated. "To tell you the truth, I'd made pretty much the same assumptions. I figured that whatever Zhu said, nothing was gonna happen for several years. These things usually go off schedule anyway, and nobody in this company seemed to have any idea what was really involved in entering the US market with a new product. Plus, I wasn't aware that they were doing any of the EPA testing."

"As far as I know, they weren't. And from what I heard, the cars couldn't meet the standards from twenty years ago, let alone today."

"Well, then I still don't see how they're going to bring these cars in until they do, unless they could get some sort of waiver, which I can't imagine anybody granting. I mean, the government wouldn't think of granting a waiver for emissions or safety for an *American* company, let alone a foreign government."

"Ah, Sid, you must know more about American politics than I do," said Suzy, "umm, can you think of any reason your government would grant a waiver for these things."

Burnside thought for a moment, then shrugged. "I don't know, unless there was some big foreign policy thing involved. Or we wanted something badly from the Chinese."

"Well, I would think that either the waiver's been granted already or that the People's Republic is assuming that it will be shortly. Otherwise, I can't see why they'd be making shipping arrangements. I wonder what the US government could want from China that would cause them to create a possible big domestic problem for themselves." She looked at Zack as she spoke.

Zack returned the look, knowing that they were both thinking the same thing. "Oh, God, no, it can't be that," said Zack, who began chuckling, then laughing, then finally hooting uncontrollably. "Oh, God, it can't be," he choked. Suzy watched him for a moment, then began laughing herself, until the two of them were convulsed, holding on to one another for support as Burnside looked at them, utterly baffled by their outburst.

"What is this?" Burnside demanded. "You two are acting like the Chinese got pictures of Carruthers in a compromising situation with a goat or something."

With that their laughter redoubled, and Zack managed, between gasps, to get out, "You're close, but not quite."

When they finally quieted down, Suzy looked at her husband and said, "Really, Zack, we don't know if that's what's happening here."

"Maybe not, but it's as likely as any other possibility, don't you think? Did you see him on TV this morning, with that nose tumor story?" He started laughing again.

"Yeah, I did, as a matter of fact," said Burnside. "I don't get any of this. What're you two talking about?"

"Ah, Sid," said Suzy, now finally fully composed, "this is a matter best left undiscussed, for reasons that would be obvious if you knew all the details. Ah, why don't we talk about whether I might be able to help you in getting ready to import these cars, which right now certainly looks to be an imminent development."

"Well, yeah, I could sure use somebody with your skills and knowledge, Suzy, especially in this situation. With your knowledge of the company and its people you'd be a godsend right now." In truth, Burnside had no idea exactly what the former Miss Lin might be able to contribute, but she was obviously very bright and knowledgeable about the home company, plus she was totally bi-lingual. That all *has* to worth something, he reasoned. Abruptly, Burnside made his decision. "OK, I'll tell you what, Suzy, how about I make you Director of Human Resources, starting at four thousand dollars a month?"

Her mouth gaped in surprise, as Zack and she looked at each other. "But, what would I do? I mean, what would be my job description?"

"That's a good question, Suzy, yeah, I'm glad you asked that. You'd be responsible for, ah, recruiting, personnel, communications with the factory, and, uh, administrative functions here in the office. How about it?"

"I'm overwhelmed, I think is the word. Can I think about for a couple of days?"

"Sure, take all the time you want. I think you should even look around a little if you want. How about we go to lunch, huh?" Burnside was thinking that he'd got himself an invaluable asset. "We can work out the details there."

* * *

President Carruthers was highly pleased with his performance of that morning, especially with the clever reference to being able to relate to anybody who'd been awaiting a biopsy report. He could hardly wait to see the job approval ratings reflected in the coming polls. He glanced at his watch impatiently, dreading the appointment with his Vice-President, reflecting once again that the most complex thought Garmin had ever had, properly expressed, should have taken no more than thirty seconds to get across. He wondered a bit fearfully what Garmin wanted to see him about. As he understood Garmin's request for the meeting, it appeared that Garmin was functioning as some sort of emissary for Ambassador Li. Carruthers got up and paced in front of his desk nervously. Jesus Christ, he thought, what do the bastards want now? A tour through the Lockheed Skunk Works, or clear title to Pearl Harbor? Eglin Air Force Base? Hah, I should name Heather as ambassador to the People's Republic, that'd fix the bastards! He visualized his wife holding forth at a women's rights rally in downtown Beijing. "You're letting yourselves be ruled by a bunch of dead Oriental males!" he could hear her say. His musings were interrupted by his secretary. "Mr. President, the Vice-President is here to see you."

"Ah, yeah, send him in," said Carruthers wearily.

Garmin walked through the door briskly, then grasped Carruthers' hand in one of his vise-like handshakes. "How ya doin', Bob," he asked loudly.

"Great, Nate, you're lookin' good."

"Hey, do you really think so?" asked Garmin.

"Ah, yes, Nate, that's why I said it, right?"

Garmin seated himself. "Bob, I've gotta pass on a request from Ambassador Li, who's speaking for the People's Republic on this. I mean this isn't a personal request from him or anything like that, ya understand."

Carruthers sighed wearily. "OK, what's he want? Make it quick, I got a meeting with McGurn in a coupla minutes." This was untrue, but Carruthers would resort to any falsehood in order to get rid of Garmin.

"Well, ah, yes, it's about that neat new car the Chinese are bringing in, you know, the one that gets seventy miles to the gallon and is totally clean for the environment." He went on to explain, rather circuitously, the ambassador's request for a waiver of the emission and safety testing until the cars could be retro-fitted.

Carruthers had been having a bit of trouble following Garmin's explanation of the proposal and finally interrupted him. "OK, you're saying that some of the cars may not meet the claims they've made, so they want to sell them anyway, then when the new parts get here put them on the cars they've already sold?"

"That's it!" cried Garmin. "Boy, I love the way you can explain things so fast!"

"That's it, then?" Carruthers asked. "That's all?" His first reaction was one of immense relief. It suddenly occurred to Carruthers that Li's request might well just be the first installment on an ongoing blackmail scheme. "Ah, Nate, I'd like to have a meeting with Li myself, you know, just to make sure there's no misunderstanding of what we're trying to do. But you can report to him that my reaction is generally positive."

After Garmin had left, amid profuse expressions of gratitude, Carruthers sat thinking, a waiver? That's it? Shit yes, I'll give them a fucking waiver! I don't care if every one of their little shitbox cars is a rolling, smoking, deathtrap! Christ, I can't believe that's all they want. Suddenly Carruthers resolved to demand a return favor from Li. I want the name and address of Kung-Fu Kitty and her Incredible Hulk hubby, he told himself. One way or another, they're gonna pay for this! He fingered his still painful nose angrily. That'll be our little *quid pro quo,* he told himself. They want their waiver, they're gonna to have come across with every copy of that fucking tape and the whereabouts of that cock-teasing gookess. All at once, the most powerful man in the world felt more upbeat than he had since his altercation with Kung-Fu Kitty.

* * *

Sherry Maxwell appeared to be staring intently at the architect's rendering of the proposed Red Tiger dealership, which was spread out on the conference table in Jake Dougherty's office. The picture showed a Spanish-style but nonetheless modern dealership building that appeared to be at least 15,000 square feet. The rendering was, in fact, that of Dougherty's former Hyundai store, built over a decade earlier, which had been brought out, dusted off, and re-copied with fresh dates and graphics.

While Maxwell was indeed impressed by Dougherty's apparent commitment and sincerity, he was having difficulty in concentrating on the topic at hand, being as it was approaching the noon hour and therefore the appropriate time for somebody (Maxwell was, of course, hoping that Dougherty would rise to the occasion) to broach the topic of cocktails and lunch. "Ah, that's very nice, Jake, just about what we're lookin' for," said Maxwell approvingly. Almost as an afterthought he added, "Ah, I suppose you got the land to put it on, right?"

"It's all in progress, Sherry, I already got an option on over four acres, like I told ya." Then, to Maxwell's immense relief, Dougherty announced,

"Well, whaddya say we go out and get a bite to eat, Sherry?" slapping his ample belly.

Maxwell tried to maintain at least some level of decorum by continuing to stare at the rendering on the table. "Umm, ah, yeah, Jake, why don't we do that?" he said slowly, appearing to tear himself away from the drawings with effort. His mouth was watering at the thought of an icy Finlandia martini.

"Yeah," continued Dougherty, "we can have a nice lunch and then play a few holes up at the club. They got a great dining room and clubhouse up there."

"Hey, that sounds great, Jake, just gimme a minute to check in with the office." Dougherty left the office to let Maxwell use his phone in privacy. Sherry dialed the Red Tiger office, hoping that Burnside had already gone to lunch and was therefore not available for the issuance of further instructions or assignments. The phone rang twice before Burnside picked up. "Hey, Sid, it's Sherry, how ya doin'? Great, hey, ya got anything for me?"

"Well, I guess I maybe I do," said Burnside. "The shit hit the fan here yesterday. Zhu sent me a fax tellin' me they're gonna be shipping like 22,000 cars in the next ninety days. Like, we gotta get ready and start takin' this thing seriously."

"What, how're they gonna do that," asked Maxwell, clearly showing his alarm at this potentially disastrous turn of events. "I mean, they haven't got the cars certified yet, have they? Shit, we've never even *seen* one, Sid. What're we supposed to do?"

"Well, I haven't been able to get anything confirmed with Zhu in detail yet, but I'd say we'd better get started issuing letters of intent to potential dealers so we got somewhere to ship the cars when they get here. Whaddya got goin' with that guy you're seein' out there in Sacramento today?"

"Jake Dougherty? He says he wants the franchise, and he's got plans for a building and an option on some property already. I guess we could get him a letter pretty quick to get him started." Maxwell was unhappily contemplating the end of his honeymoon with Dougherty, once he got the letter of intent from Red Tiger Motors, which in turn would likely signal a cut-off of the lavish food and drink for Maxwell. Sherry decided at that moment to say nothing to Dougherty for the time being, thus extending the courtship as long as possible.

"Well, ya better get crackin' with him and start shakin' the trees for some more prospects right about now."

"OK, I'll get him nailed down this afternoon, Sid. Anything else for me?"

"Yeah, ya better get back down here tomorrow so we can start plannin' how we're gonna go about this."

"Yeah, OK Sid, I'll be back by mid-afternoon. Seeya then."

Maxwell was completely disoriented by this sudden change in his fortunes. He had, as had Burnside, simply assumed that he'd have perhaps years of relative inactivity, riding around the countryside being fed and watered by dealer candidates and preparing meaningless market reports for consumption by the home company.

Thirty minutes later Maxwell and Dougherty were sitting down to lunch at Jake's country club dining room, overlooking a pleasant view of the golf course, under the crests of the Sierra Nevada range in the distance. Dougherty ordered a gin-tonic, Maxwell his usual pre-prandial fix, a dry vodka martini. "Whatsamatter, Sherry, you seem a little quiet," said Jake. He was concerned that his presentation of the architectural plans was not having the desired effect.

"Oh, nothing, Jake. I was just thinking about the plans you showed me. I gotta admit they look good. Say, how many of these cars do you think you could sell in the first year?"

"Jesus, Sherry, at that price, what the hell, if I was the only dealer in town, we'd do maybe three thousand the first year." Maxwell was dividing twenty-two thousand by three thousand, silently arriving at the conclusion that with luck he'd need only seven or eight dealers in place to deal with the initial shipment from the Long March People's Cooperative Automotive Manufacturing Company. He began perk to up.

"You really think so, Jake? That seems like a pretty ambitious first year target."

"Well, hell, Sherry, do the math! Last year I sold almost twelve hundred new Ford cars and trucks. The average one listed for maybe twenty or twenty-five grand. Your car is only five grand. I figure I should sell three or four times as many, at least!"

"Yeah, what you're saying makes a lot of sense, I gotta admit," said Maxwell, nodding sagely. "How many d'ya think ya'd want in the initial allocation?"

"You know me, Sherry, like I always say, ya' can't sell off an empty shelf! I'll take maybe five hundred or a thousand right up front, have a huge week-long sell-a-thon to introduce the car to California!" Maxwell's mind was racing, his state of impending well-being helped along by several swallows of his Finlandia martini. Hell, a few more guys like Dougherty and my troubles'll be over, he told himself with cautious optimism.

"Well, I'm glad you're so bullish (or is it *bearish*, he wondered momentarily) on the franchise, Jake. Understand, I think you're absolutely right, maybe even a little conservative, but a lot of guys can't see an opportunity when it's starin' 'em in the face. That's one o' the things I like about you."

"So, we got a deal, then, Sherry? I wanna get started, be ready when the cars hit. Ah, like, when is that, by the way, Sherry?"

"Well, all indications are that the cars are gonna arrive sooner than a lot of people think, Jake. But I don't want to jump the gun with you. We still gotta have a look at the market and talk to some o' the other players in the area."

Jake managed to look hurt and a bit surprised. "Gee, Sherry, I thought we were ready to do a deal," he said. "What's it gonna take?" He was mentally reviewing what Maxwell might try to shake down him for and would have been surprised to learn that Maxwell was corruptible mainly to the extent of being entertained, fed and watered. He had never taken money nor expensive gifts, beyond consumables, and never would. "I mean, what do *you* want Sherry? Like, what do you want *personally?*"

"Huh? All I want is you to make good on your commitments, if we can come to a deal. That's all I want from any dealer," Sherry said with a just a hint of indignation. He had picked up on a Jake's implication.

Dougherty immediately realized that he'd made a tactical blunder. "Hey, Sherry, don't misunderstand, what I meant was what's your personal opinion of what we oughtta do for Red Tiger, not the official company line, that's all. I mean, you got a lotta time in the business, I value your opinion. That's what I'm tryin' to find out, your opinion. I mean, I know you speak for the company and all, but they gotta respect your opinions, just like I do." He looked at Maxwell almost imploringly.

Sherry was completely mollified by Dougherty's rejoinder and a bit flattered. "Well, if you're just lookin' for a personal opinion, I think what you're proposing is just what we're lookin' for, and I think your estimates of what you'll be able to do are in the ballpark, too. So I don't have a problem, Jake, it's just that I gotta go through the motions of checkin' out the market and the other dealers."

"Hey, that's great, Sherry, and I understand perfectly, like ya don't get married right away, even if it's love at first sight, am I right?" He motioned to the cocktail waitress for another round.

Three hours later Maxwell and Dougherty, weaving treacherously in their golf cart, were working their way to the eleventh hole of the golf course. Dougherty had arranged to have a cooler filled with assorted pre-mixed cocktails, gin, limes, ice, and tonic water put in the golf cart, and for the past hour and a half Maxwell, initially representing a fair level of men-ace to other golfers with his wild slices and hooks, had finally been rendered harmless by his complete inability to connect with the ball off the tee. He sat blearily in the cart and watched Dougherty, also going rapidly down hill, as he continued to slash away futilely. "It's these fucking rented clubs, Jake. They're too goddam short. They don't reach to the ground all the way."

"Ah, fuck it, you're right, Sherry, the goddam clubs are no good," said Dougherty as he launched a huge divot far downrange with his three-iron. "Let's go back to the club for a little snort." He watched disgustedly as the divot outdistanced the ball by perhaps ten yards.

"Yeah, that's what we need, Jake, another li'l snort," said Maxwell.

Christ, thought Dougherty, I gotta get this goddam franchise nailed down with this character before I get cirrhosis of the goddam liver. Jesus, I hate dealin' with these factory guys. He turned to get in the cart, just as Sherry reached in back to get himself another drink. He was rummaging around in the cooler, looking for a canned daiquiri, when his foot stepped on the accelerator and sent the cart, the cooler, and Maxwell himself careening down a fifteen foot embankment into the nearby water hazard.

Forty-five minutes later, following the long staggering walk back to the locker room, Jake had managed to get Maxwell showered, dressed, and sober enough to deliver him back his hotel room. Jesus Christ, thought Dougherty fearfully, wonder what they're gonna charge me for the friggin' golf cart. I already got a substantial investment in this goddam thing. This franchise better be worth it.

* * *

Ambassador Li hung up the phone and wondered why President Carruthers wanted a face to face private meeting with him. He assumed that the American president wanted something in return for the waiver he was seeking, else why wouldn't he simply have granted the request without further comment? Li decided to report this development directly to the office of Premier Wu. He expected that the response from Beijing would firmly instruct him to make it clear that there would be no concessions or negotiations on the question of the waiver. He further expected them to make it clear that the Chinese position on the issue was such that if he resisted their demand for a waiver, he could expect that the People's Republic would formally and publicly express its condemnation of his boorish and felonious conduct while on Chinese soil, under the jurisdiction of Chinese law. And that certain witnesses to his campaign funding sources might suddenly make themselves available or experience a remarkable recovery from their previous amnesia. The leadership of the People's Republic did not believe in making concessions when they held all the cards. The ridiculous incident in the embassy, precipitated entirely by the cartoonish American president, was just so much icing on the cake, as the Americans would put it, thought Li. What the next act of crass buffoonery by The Great One-Eyed Pink Python might be he could scarcely imagine. He knew only that there would be another, then another. And so forth. He chuckled, then shook his head in disbelief.

* * *

As Li was reflecting on the increasingly bizarre nature of American electoral politics, Suzy and Zack Johnson were just taking delivery of a two year old Mazda Miata, equipped with an automatic transmission in deference to Suzy's brand new California driver's license. She could hardly contain herself as the salesman went over the car and its controls. "Oh, Zack, I think this whole thing is a crazy dream and I'm going to wake up any minute in my little apartment in Beijing, and you'll be gone," she said, hugging him hard and looking up at him with tears in her eyes.

"Don't worry, honey, next time you wake up in Beijing I'll be right next to you." They finished the paperwork, shook hands with the salesman, who was eyeing Suzy surreptitiously but lustfully, then got in their respective cars to head back home. "Just stay right behind me. If we get separated at a light or something I'll pull over and wait for you," said

Zack. "Now just calm down and take it easy. And remember, that thing steers a lot quicker than my Firebird." She nodded, and with a look of grim determination, hands grasping the wheel firmly, followed him out into traffic.

When they arrived back at their little ranch house, Suzy immediately set to work getting out the garden hose, a bucket, and a sponge. "I want to wash and wax it," she explained.

"They just did that, honey. It's spotless."

"I know. It'll feel more like its really mine if I wash it, though." With that she disappeared into the house, emerging two minutes later in a skimpy yellow two-piece. A few moments after that Zack was watching her bending over the hood, intently scrubbing away as various bits of her anatomy shook and jiggled fetchingly. Hmm, can't say as I completely blame that dirtbag Carruthers, he thought.

"Ah, honey, when you're done, come on in and get me and I'll show you how to wax it right, OK?" He watched her nod without looking up, then went inside, going straight to the bedroom, undressing, and getting into bed to wait for his bride to summon him. Heh, heh, Hubby deserves a little payback for the car, he told himself.

Two hours later she was snuggling sleepily against him. "Zack, did you marry me just for my body?"

"Of course not. I married you because you know what to *do* with your body, that's why."

"You are truly a single-minded pig, husband."

"Well, you can cook, too, and you know how to wash the car, and you can speak Chinese, and you're funny, and you know what to *do* with your body…"

"Ummm, Zack," she purred languidly, "you were going to show me how to wax my new car." She rolled over and moved her rump against him.

"Uh, yeah, in a little while, ah, hey, ah, keep doing that."

And hour later they lay on their backs, holding hands. "Hey, babe," Zack finally said, "we gotta talk about that offer from Red Tiger. I mean, we told Sid we'd get back to him today."

"I suppose. But I think maybe I'd rather just stay home all day and fuck my husband. That way he'll be too exhausted all the time to think about other women."

"Well, I can't say I mind that, but I wish you wouldn't call it that. Why don't you say making love to your husband?"

"Why, is it wrong to say that I like to fuck you? That's what everybody else in America calls it, don't they? They even say it all the time in the movies."

"Some people do, I guess. But I make love to my wife. I fuck other women."

She seemed to ponder this for a moment. "Zack, I think I take your point, and I'm very glad you make the distinction between your wife and other women. But if I catch you fucking any other women, it won't matter, because you won't have anything left to fuck them *or* me with."

"You know, I think you mean it."

"I told you, we Chinese girls are very jealous. Now, let's call Sid and tell him I'll take the job, then we can wax my car."

"Can I at least look at other women?"

"All you want. Just come home to me when you want your fantasies fulfilled."

"That sounds reasonable. Do you think you might be up to fulfilling some more by tonight?"

"I don't know. I think I may have a headache by then." He laughed, flipped her over, and bit her gently on the behind.

The Johnsons' sweetly idyllic lives were about to enter a stormy period.

* * *

Sherry Maxwell turned into the little office park complex that contained Red Tiger Motor's corporate headquarters, such as it was. He actually felt rather good, simply going to bed and sleeping straight through after Jake Dougherty had dropped him off at his hotel. He'd lamely tried to explain that the golf cart had suffered a "sudden acceleration" malfunction, remembering something about allegedly runaway Audis back in the mid-eighties and figuring that a golf cart should, by all rights, be able to do the same thing. "Hell, we coulda been killed, Jake. Someone oughtta sue their asses!" Dougherty had merely looked at him and said something about calling his lawyer about it the following day.

Sherry glanced at this watch, noting that it was two in the afternoon, reasonably close to the time he'd told Burnside to expect him. He'd vaguely expected, after Burnside's call of the previous morning, to find the headquarters a beehive of activity, with people coming and going, trucks pulling up and offloading computers, Red Whippet parts, and office supplies. But as he walked through the front door he saw nothing, not even a secretary or receptionist. He marched directly down to Burnside's office, found it empty, and walked over to the fax machine. There was nothing in it, and Maxwell concluded correctly that Burnside was on his lunch break. Maxwell felt a huge sense of relief that nothing seemed to have changed since his departure, and especially since the disturbing news of the previous day. Probably a false alarm of some kind, he told himself. Hell, things are bound to get fucked up between here and China. Zhu probably meant to get ready in three years, not three months. Yeah, that's gotta be it. Abruptly, Maxwell made the decision to go to lunch himself, before Burnside could return and confirm the grim tidings of yesterday. He was halfway down the hallway when he saw Burnside coming down the walk. Dispiritedly, he returned to the office and sat at his desk.

"Hey, Sherry," said Burnside as he came through the door, "how ya doin'? I thought that was your car in the lot. You just get in?"

"Yeah, just this minute, Sid. What goin' on? You hear any more from Zhu?"

"Nothin' more than a confirmation that we somehow gotta be ready to sell these friggin' cars in the next three or four months."

"Huh? How're we gonna do that. They're not even certified, are they? And we don't have any dealers yet."

"Yeah, well, Zhu's got this crazy idea that people'll just come to the port to pick 'em up and drive home, like we don't need any dealers. I guess he thinks we'll just take Master Card or VISA for the five grand and send 'em on their way."

"Hey, you know what, that's a hell of an idea, Sid. Then we wouldn't need any dealers. I wonder why nobody ever thought of that approach before." Maxwell was momentarily caught between the desire to avoid the work of recruiting and signing an entire dealer network and his desire to avail himself of the goodies that they, like Jake Dougherty, might provide.

Burnside looked at Maxwell strangely. "Ah, you think this is a good idea, Sherry?"

Maxwell surmised from Burnside's tone that his boss might have certain reservations about the plan. "Well, I guess it might have some drawbacks, Sid, now that I think about it. Like, it's probably illegal in most states anyway, I mean ya can't have factory stores with a lot o' the state franchise laws, and I guess if we sold 'em in the ports, that'd be a factory store, right?" Maxwell trailed off uncertainly.

Burnside stared at him for a long moment. "Hey, you know, I think you're right, Sherry, a lot of the states got it in their state franchise laws that a manufacturer can't have factory stores. Hey, that's how I can get Zhu off my back on this stupid idea! I knew I did the right thing when I hired you, Maxwell," he said, grinning. Shit, I shoulda thought of that myself, he told himself, but what the hell, I gotta give credit where it's due.

"Jesus, Sid, that means we gotta sign up a bunch of dealers quick, and get the floorplan commitment letters, put together a parts package, special tools, all that stuff. I mean, shit, I don't how we're gonna do that all in less than three months."

"You know, Sherry, I think what we oughtta do is make a pitch to test market the car in California first. I mean, some other companies did that first, you know, tested the waters over here. That'd make our jobs a lot easier. I bet we could sell off the entire first shipment of twenty-five thousand right here in California alone, doncha think?"

"Yeah, I guess. This guy Jake Dougherty up in Sacramento said he'd take a thousand in the initial allocation. All we'd need is a few guys like that and we're home free," said Maxwell, obviously taking Dougherty at his word and conveniently overlooking the ongoing retail sales rate required to keep dealers like Dougherty taking cars at such a pace.

"You really think he'd take a thousand up front?" asked Burnside, eyebrows raised. "That's gotta be four to five million in inventory at the first go-around. And that reminds me, they're saying the car's five grand. I assume they mean at retail. What're we gonna price it at dealer net? I mean, none of this shit's been worked out." Everywhere he turned, Burnside was becoming aware that practically *nothing* had been worked out, including certification, so far as he knew. Abruptly, he decided to compose a lengthy and detailed letter to Zhu, making him aware of all the tasks needing completion before the Red Whippet could be imported, to include dealer appointments, his proposed California test marketing scheme, floorplan commitments from the dealers' banks, putting together a standard dealer sales and service agreement, hiring a field force, setting up at least two parts warehouses, technicians' training centers, doing individual market studies, and establishing wholesale and retail prices for parts and vehicles. He also had to make a convincing pitch that due to statutory restrictions in most states, Red Tiger would have to operate conventionally, through franchised dealers. With any luck, Burnside calculated, he'd be able to get The Long March People's Cooperative Automotive Manufacturing Company to put back its timetable at least a year. They gotta realize that nobody can operate this quick, he told himself.

His ruminations were interrupted by the phone, which Maxwell answered. After giving the standard Red Tiger operator's spiel, he looked at Burnside and said, "Hey, Sid, it's for you, some chick named Suzy Johnson."

"Hey, yeah, I got it," said Burnside, brightening considerably as he picked up the handset. "Suzy, this is Sid, how are you today? Getting settled in?"

"Very settled, Sid. Well, Zack and I thought about your offer, and we'd like to accept it."

"Hey, that's great, I'm really pleased. When can you start?"

"I guess I can start tomorrow, if that's OK with you."

"Boy, that'd be great, Suzy. Things seem to be heating up here real fast, and I'm about to send a long letter to Zhu about all the things we gotta do to get ready. I could really use your help putting it together, I mean how to put things best to the people in China."

"Well, I hope I can be useful to you, Sid. I'll certainly do my best. Should I come in at nine-o'clock tomorrow?"

"That'd be perfect," said Burnside, suddenly realizing that hiring Suzy Lin Johnson had imposed a certain level of not altogether welcome discipline on him.

After he'd hung up he looked at Maxwell and said, "Well, Sherry, we got our third employee. You remember that foxy interpreter, Lin? I just hired her."

"No shit? That'll dress the place up a little."

"Yeah, just don't get any funny ideas. That guy she married looks like he could crush our skulls, one in each hand."

Back in the Johnson's little Pasadena ranch house, Suzy looked at Zack and said, "OK, let's wax my car, then we can drive out to the Red Tiger office in Chino so I can practice driving my new car and learn the way to work and back."

"Sounds good to me. You wanna eat Mexican for lunch? Remember, that's where I got the idea for us to get married, in that little Mexican restaurant in Vegas. I just didn't realize it at that moment. Maybe Mexican food makes us both crazy. We could have a kind of two week anniversary celebration."

* * *

While the Johnsons were planning their day, Ambassador Li Wan Le of the People's Republic of China was heading toward the White House in the back of his Mercedes limousine, puzzling over why President Carruthers wanted to see him personally and alone. He had simply assumed that once he'd made his demand of the Vice-President and the former grade school teacher Penny Twombly, plus supplying Carruthers with his own copy of the tape, that Carruthers would simply make whatever arrangements were necessary to ensure that the Red Whippet would encounter no obstacles in the effort to import and sell it in the United States. He hadn't expected to hear from him at all and had merely been awaiting Carruthers' executive order or whatever other mechanism he might use to waive the government requirements. Li was reasonably certain that Carruthers wanted something from the People's Republic in return for his intervention. He suspected that it likely involved the lovely Chinese girl, the former Lin Shan, to whom he owed the benign nose tumor story, which seemingly had boosted his approval rating by at least five points. Li snorted, partly in disgust and partly in astonishment, at Carruthers' extraordinary ability to turn practically any disaster to his political advantage. Li would not have been surprised to see him go on Oprah and announce that he was HIV positive in response to his next personal debacle, whatever that might prove to be.

Whatever Carruthers' motivations in requesting a meeting with him, Li had already received the firm instruction from Beijing that under no circumstances would any concessions be made to Carruthers in regard to the embassy incident, and that this was to be made clear to Carruthers in the strongest possible terms. Li smiled grimly at being able to firmly hold his ground with Carruthers, holding forth no hope for any slack whatever.

Meanwhile, Carruthers (having mastered the VCR in his office) was once again watching the tape in which he was groping Mrs. Johnson. He'd taken to watching the tape surreptitiously in the past few days, causing his trysting fantasies about Suzy Johnson to grow more insistent and compelling. He watched his hand fondle her shapely behind and thought, Jesus, I should have grabbed a tit when I had the chance, conveniently overlooking the fact that such a move likely would have precipitated a fractured skull from her husband. Damn, I'd like the chance to meet her again, thought the president.

Carruthers' erotic fantasies, which somehow had Suzy Johnson prancing naked under a Chinese coolie hat, were interrupted by the phone. It was his secretary, informing him that the Chinese ambassador had arrived to see him. Carruthers abruptly walked over to the VCR, ejected the tape, then turned it off. He returned to his desk and pretended to be busy with a DOD military readiness report. He looked up as the ambassador was led into the office, smiling pleasantly but unenthusiastically. "Mr. President, how good to see you again. How is your nose?"

"My nose is nearly healed, Mr. Ambassador," replied Carruthers a bit coolly, then got right to the point of the meeting. "Mr. Garmin has come to me with your request that we waive certain government requirements in order to clear the way for you to sell your cars here in our country."

"Only temporarily, Mr. President," Li interjected, "until we have the parts on hand to retro-fit them in order to meet our high, self-imposed standards, which I need not point out, are much higher than those of the US government. In any event, this process should not take more than a few months at most, after which we will all benefit from the environmental and political impact of the Red Whippet cars. But it is critical that its introduction go smoothly and without difficulty, for much has been set in motion that cannot easily be pulled back." Li started to say something about Chinese self-esteem being at stake, but then thought the better of it, realizing that Carruthers might not share the views of the elementary school teacher who was his EPA chief.

"Umm," said Carruthers non-committally, "that's a pretty tall order, Mr. Ambassador. We don't grant such favors to our own automakers. It may be politically difficult for me to grant such dispensation to a foreign manufacturer."

"But Mr. President, think of the environmental and social benefits. And certainly you will want to consider the question of Mr. Garmin's DILDO, as well." Li was once again pleased to be able to demonstrate his mastery of the acronym.

"Huh?" said Carruthers, suddenly alarmed. Christ, what's this, he thought. Don't tell me that stiff Garmin's got some weird kinks of his own. I thought *I* was the only pervert in the White House! But he managed to conceal his surprise. "Ah, yes, that, of course," he mumbled. "Well, we can probably work something out, Mr. Ambassador, but I'm gonna need a favor from you in the process."

"Yes, Mr. President?" asked Li, eyebrows raised.

"Yeah, well, I can do what you want, but your people gotta give me all the copies of that tape. And I want the whereabouts of that girl who attacked me. I can't allow an assault on the president to go unpunished. We have to deal with her under the law."

"Really, Mr. President, an assault on the president? I would have thought it was self-defense, as would anybody viewing the tape of your behavior that evening." Carruthers stared at him balefully. "I'm afraid that my government will not accede to any demands in regard to this unfortunate affair, not the return of the tapes, nor revealing the whereabouts of the girl, in whom we still have perhaps a sentimental interest, though she is no longer one of our citizens. In any event, we have no knowledge of her whereabouts ourselves. If you have nothing further, Mr. President, I should like to say good day. Should I report to my government that the requirements will shortly be waived, certainly within a few days? If not, well," he shrugged with an almost Gallic gesture, "who knows what might happen?" He stood up to leave.

"Ah, Mr. Ambassador, just one more thing. What's this about the vice-president and his, ah, dildo?"

Li shrugged again. "I really don't know all the details. I suggest you ask him." With that, he left.

Jesus Christ, thought Carruthers, I always knew Garmin was a moron, but at least I always thought he was squeaky clean. He's too goddam dumb to be a successful pervert. Now I find out the fucking Chinks got something kinky on him, too.

After Li had left, Carruthers sat fuming at the ambassador's less than respectful tone toward the president of the United States. Won't accede to any demands, huh, Carruthers snorted. Well, fuck 'em. I can find the gookess without 'em. Hell, I got the whole Justice Department working for me, and the fucking CIA if I need it. He called out to his secretary through the open door. "Hey, Stacy, get me the attorney general right now, and tell him it's important."

Two minutes later the attorney general of the United States, plucked from obscurity as a two-bit county attorney in Georgia, and who held the current record for appellate reversals in that state, came on the line. "Yes, Mr. President?" asked Jack Landry breathlessly. "I was in the men's room, sir, that's the truth. I've had the runs this morning."

"God, Landry, spare me the details, please," said Carruthers. "I have an assignment for you that *must* be handled in complete confidence. It basically involves locating a known felon and keeping her under surveillance until I notify you otherwise. I can supply you with enough details on this matter to enable you to track her down. Can you come over here in, say, about thirty minutes?"

"Yes, sir, of course."

"Good. I'll give you the information you need in person. And Landry?"

"Sir?"

"Do you like your job, Landry?"

"Yes, sir! It's the best job I ever had. And the money's great, too."

"No shit, you pissant little bird-brain. You better remember that or I'll have you back prosecuting jaywalkers in Macon again." Carruthers had learned long ago that the surest way to guarantee absolute loyalty from subordinates was to promote inexperienced or incompetent lightweights many levels above what they ever could have achieved under normal circumstances and then remind them of this fact from time to time. Landry was simply one of many such individuals in key positions throughout Carruthers' administration.

As Jack Landry was dutifully rushing over to the White House to receive his instructions directly from the president, Ambassador Li was staring thoughtfully out the darkened rear window of his Mercedes limousine. He knew Carruthers to be a viciously vindictive man, despite his carefully cultivated public persona as a sensitive, kind, and thoughtful gentleman. He was worried about the beautiful Chinese girl, whom he was fairly certain Carruthers would try to locate. He had no doubt that he'd succeed, for tracking her down wouldn't be a problem for even a small town police force, let alone the FBI. Li had been speaking for himself and not the People's Republic when he'd told Carruthers that his government still had at least a sentimental interest in the girl's welfare. In truth, he imagined that had the demand for her whereabouts been formally communicated to Beijing, she'd have been sacrificed instantly. Abruptly, Li made the decision to have her located himself for purposes of sending her a copy of the security camera tape. It would be her only insurance, but it would be, he was quite sure, sufficient.

* * *

Chapter 6

As Li was making plans to ensure at least some level of protection for the Johnsons, the primary object of his concerns was assembling the ingredients for a sumptuous dinner. Suzy Johnson was about to pour a bit of peanut oil into her wok when the kitchen phone rang. Zack was outside cutting their little front lawn, so she picked up and announced, "Johnson residence."

Some thirteen hundred miles away in Liberal, Kansas Zack's father was a bit surprised by the formal nature of the response from his son's house, causing him to speculate, briefly and a bit ridiculously he realized, that his son had hired a maid. "Uh, is Zack home?" he asked.

"Yes, sir, he is. May I tell him who's calling?"

Now Paul Johnson was genuinely curious. The voice at the other end was refined but with just the trace of an unidentifiable accent. "Ah, tell him it's his father."

"Oh, I'll tell him. He'll be right here," she said, feeling a sudden, vague, but nonetheless powerful dread well up inside her. She knew that Zack's parents as yet knew nothing about her. She walked to the front door and called through the screen. "Zack, it's your father on the phone."

He looked up and tried but failed to conceal his surprise and apprehension. Suzy turned abruptly and disappeared into their bedroom, closing the door behind her.

Zack picked up the phone. "Hi, Dad," he said, far more cheerily than he felt.

"Zack, how ya doin'? We haven't talked in more'n a month. By the way, who's that chick who answered the phone? She sounds like a Mexican or something."

Zack took a deep breath. "Ah, Dad, her name's Suzy, and she's not Mexican exactly."

158

"You're not livin' with her, are you?"

"Ah, well, yeah, we are living together, Dad."

"Well, I guess that shoots this plan all to hell and gone, then. Your mother and I aren't coming to stay for a few days if you're sharing the place with a live-in girlfriend. I mean, hell, I guess I don't mind too much, but your mother'll freak out."

"Well, uh, Dad, I was coming to that. Ah, Suzy's not my girlfriend exactly, I mean she's my friend and all, but…"

"What the hell are you trying to say, son? C'mon, man, just spit it out, willya."

"Ah, we're married, Dad, a little over two weeks ago. I was gonna call you and explain it all…."

"*WHAT?* You got married and didn't even tell us about it?" his father interjected, his voice rising.

"Please, Dad, let me explain, then I'm sure you'll understand." And over the next two minutes, during which his father said nothing, Zack explained the rather odd sequence of events leading up to the Johnson's hasty marriage, lengthening, as he'd planned, the time factor to a more respectable four weeks, and, of course, omitting any reference to the dating service, about which his parents knew nothing. "It just happened too fast for you or anybody else to be here, Dad. She had to leave the next day for China, and we had no way of knowing if we'd ever see each other again."

There was a long silence at the other end while Paul Johnson sorted through this information and tried to formulate the best response. In his mind he couldn't banish the image of the scrawny and much-used bar girls in the ramshackle bars and cathouses of Bien Hoa, which he'd observed firsthand as a paratrooper with the 173rd Airborne Brigade nearly thirty-five years earlier. "Well, son, I guess you're old enough to know what you're doing. At least she seems to speak good English."

"She speaks perfect English, Dad, better'n me. And she's beautiful and a great cook and has a great sense of humor, and she just got a really good job yesterday. I'm really sorry you had to find out this way. I mean, I wanted to tell you and Mom about it, but I just kept putting it off. But now that you know all about it, why don't you come on out for a few days? By the way, where's Mom. Why don't you put her on?"

"Well, that's part of what I was callin' you about, Zack. We didn't say anything 'cause we didn't want to worry you, but she's in the hospital, gettin' an angioplasty. Don't worry," he added hastily, "she's just fine, and she'll be home day after tomorrow, there's no complications or anything, she just had one coronary artery that was about eighty percent blocked, but she's fine now."

"Jesus, Dad, I wish I'd known about it," said Zack, then chuckled. "Well, maybe that makes us even. We both got a little surprise."

"Yeah, I guess, but what we're plannin' to do is take a month off and go to Maui in a coupla weeks. We wanted to stop off and spend a coupla days with you, if that's OK."

"Well, sure, Dad, that'd be great, just tell us when you're comin' and I'll make sure I'm not flyin' a trip."

"Hey, you know, Zack, this is something that's been worrying your mother about our trip, and now you bein' married with someone around every day, do you think you could take care of Lobo for us?" Lobo was his parents' one hundred-ten pound, devilishly black, and frightening doberman pinscher. "Your mother's really worried about leaving him in the kennel for a month, I mean, he's such a big baby, and he gets frantic when we leave him there." Zack knew that Lobo's infantile, slobbering affections did not extend to those outside the family.

"Sure, Dad, I don't know why not. I'll make sure Suzy knows not to cook and eat him."

"Good God, Zack, don't even joke about that around your mother."

"Only kiddin', Dad. Hey, do you want to tell Mom about Suzy? I mean, it might be better if you break it to her, with her just gettin' outta the hospital and all."

"Yeah, it might be better. I'll know she'll want to talk to you as soon as she gets home, though, but I'll tell her before she calls you."

"That'd be great, Dad. And Dad? I love ya."

"You too, Zack," replied his father a little huskily. "Seeya soon, son."

When they'd hung up, Zack went to the bedroom. The door was locked. "Hey, Suzy, open the door, c'mon, everything's fine. I told my Dad all about us. They're coming to see us in a couple of weeks."

In the silence that followed he heard her sobbing. "Go away!" she said brokenly, then resumed crying, more loudly than before.

"C'mon, honey, everything's fine, there's no problem, really!"

"They'll hate me, I know they will."

"They will not hate you. You're being silly, now stop this and open the door."

"If my parents were still alive they'd hate *you*."

"Yeah, well, that's China and I'm not Chinese. This is America, honey. Hell, *everybody* here came from someplace else, even the goddam Indians came from Mongolia or someplace like that. Nobody here cares where you're from, really," said Zack, knowing that it wasn't entirely true but figuring it was more valid in America than anyplace else. "Now open the door, before I break it down and come on in and give you a good spanking."

He heard her half laughing, half crying, then the sound of her shuffling to the door. The lock clicked and the door opened. Her eyes were red and swollen and her nose was running. She grabbed him around the waist and held on fiercely.

Zack would be proven right. His parents *would* love Suzy. Lobo's visit, however, would prove problematic, not so much for the Johnsons, but for a good many others.

* * *

Jack Landry was shown into President Carruthers' office, where he was left standing uncomfortably as Carruthers, reading the latest issue of *Hustler,* pointedly ignored him. Two minutes passed before Carruthers looked up, put down the magazine, and beckoned Landry forward. Landry leaned over Carruthers' desk, hand extended, saying "Good morning, sir," far louder than necessary.

Carruthers was about to take the proffered hand, but then remembered Landry's announcement that he was suffering a bout of diarrhea, and quickly withdrew his own hand. "Sit down, Jack," he commanded rather brusquely. "Do you feel up to handling a highly confidential assignment, one that requires absolute security? You might even say elements of it might be called clandestine, do you get my meaning?"

"I think so, sir," said Landry a bit uncertainly. "Do you mean like maybe illegal if we get caught?"

"Landry, *nothing* my Justice Department ever does could be illegal, do you understand that? Nothing I ever order could be illegal, you understand *that?*" He face was a mask of utter contempt.

"Of course, sir, that would be my position at all times, nothing you could do could ever be illegal, that's absolutely correct," quavered Landry, his voice at least a full octave above normal. His head bobbed up and down furiously by way of emphasis. Landry, Carruthers noticed, was beginning to sweat, both from the tension of his meeting with the president, and also from the sudden desperate need to relieve himself, which itself was being exacerbated by his nervousness. He began squirming uncomfortably as he made a Herculean effort to control his sphincter. "Ah, Mr. President," he squeaked, "could I use the bathroom, please?"

Carruthers looked at him for a long moment, rather enjoying his torture of Jack Landry. He didn't acknowledge Landry's clearly desperate request. "Yes, Jack, I need you to handle an assignment of extreme delicacy. Any compromise of this assignment could prove extremely embarrassing to this administration, to me personally, and of course, fatal to your career in government. Do you understand that, Landry?"

Landry, afraid to even breathe for fear of upsetting his concentration on his sphincter muscle, could only nod jerkily. His face was rapidly turning beet red.

Carruthers, suddenly aware that he was risking a potentially catastrophic bowel explosion in the oval office, which could inconvenience him with a lengthy cleanup, finally relented. "Oh, yes, the bathroom, Landry, out the door, down the hall on the right. Hurry back. We're not through here yet," but Landry had already bolted desperately for the door. Two seconds later Carruthers heard the slam of the bathroom door. He chuckled and re-opened his copy of *Hustler.*

Five minutes later Landry was back, pale and clearly shaken by his near-disaster, near enough in fact that he'd had to discard his shorts in the trash can of the men's room. Carruthers thought he looked like a cholera victim whose fever had just broken. He reminded himself to have Stacy come in and wipe down Landry's leather chair with a disinfectant as soon as he left. "As I was saying," he began, "this assignment involves a matter of national security and must be handled with extreme delicacy. I can tell you that the Chinese are involved and that it concerns a possible plan to assassinate the president."

At this Landry seemed to become a bit more animated. "My God, sir, a plan to assassinate you personally?"

"Well, shit, Landry, do you know of any way to assassinate me *imper*sonally?"

"Well, no sir, what I meant was, how can you take it so, umm, casually I guess is the word."

"It goes with the territory," replied Carruthers in the deepest voice he could manage. "This isn't a job for someone without big balls."

"Oh, I can see that, Mr. President."

"That's why I rely on men like you, Landry, men who aren't afraid to get the job done, whatever they have to do to accomplish their mission, especially when their mission is protecting the life of the most important man in the world." Landry nodded eagerly in agreement. "Now Landry, the job I'm going to give you is to locate a Chinese national who's living in the United States, apparently married to an American. This person was an interpreter working for the state-owned auto manufacturer in China. She was just recently on a tour of the United States for this company when she married this American and disappeared. The affiliate company in the United States for the parent corporation is called the Red Tiger Motor Company. They're located in southern California. Here, you better start writing this down," he said, pushing a pad and pencil across the desk to Hendry. "Your job, Jack, is to locate this individual and determine her current status, like what she's currently doing, is she working, or whatever. I got no name on this person, but you should be able to come up with that from what I've told you. When you find her I want you to report to me immediately for further instructions. Do you understand all that?"

Landry continued scribbling furiously, then looked up as he finished. "You can count on me, Mr. President."

"And remember, Landry, this is to be handled in absolute confidence. This whole thing is Top Secret, Eyes Only, got it?"

"Yessir. Should I use the FBI?"

Carruthers looked at him for a long moment. "No, I want you to go to the cemetery, dig up Jack Lord and hire *him*. OF COURSE I WANT YOU TO USE THE FUCKING FBI, YOU DUMB SHIT! Whaddya think they're for? Now get moving!" Landry leapt to his feet and practically sprinted from the oval office. Carruthers shook his head and went back to his *Hustler*.

* * *

Sid Burnside, acutely aware that he'd somehow have to pull together an organization on very short notice, began once again riffling through the resumes he'd gotten in response to the initial personnel ad in the

Automotive News. He really hadn't defined his requirements very precisely and found himself looking for non-Anglo names as a threshold criterion, reasoning that in the absence of any other qualifying requirements, it might be a good idea to bring in a heavy sampling of protected classes, just to head off any potential future discrimination claims. I'm already covered on the age thing with Maxwell, he told himself. He was flipping through the stack of resumes when his eye hit on Edward White Feather's name once again. Hey, this could be just what I'm lookin' for, he thought, plus he's been a district sales manager and a distribution clerk. Hmm, got some experience in parts, too, hey, this guys sounds pretty well rounded as well as being a friggin' Apache, or whatever. A more critical analysis of White Feather's resume likely would have caused Burnside to note that he seemed to have moved from job to job with a disconcerting frequency. But Burnside wasn't being critical. He was, above all else, in a hurry. He picked up the phone and called the number indicated on White Feather's resume. After four rings an anwering machine picked up, and Burnside left a message for the presumptive Native American.

Just as Burnside hung up, feeling rather good about his display of social responsibility, Suzy Johnson walked in the door, smiling brightly. "Good morning, Sid." She was wearing the same tan poplin suit she'd changed into the day they'd met, with the same Serengeti aviators. She took off the sunglasses and shook her hair into place. Burnside found himself staring at her. Jesus, she makes Tia Carrere look like a six, he thought.

"Hi, Suzy," he greeted her, "let's get all your personnel information, payroll and health insurance started, then we can get to sending off a letter to Zhu. We gotta get him up to speed on all the things we gotta get done before we start sellin' these cars here in the United States."

Forty-five minutes later Burnside was giving her the gist of the letter he wanted to fax to Zhu. She listened until he was finished, making notes. Finally, she looked up from her pad. "How many states have restrictions against, ah, what did you call them, factory stores?"

"Well, I'm not sure, but I think it's a lot, maybe most."

"I think it would be a good idea to be be able to say exactly, Sid, since in companies like this people are always trying to look for inaccuracies or questionable statements. For example, that handout you gave us at your briefing, even though nobody seemed to be paying any attention that day, people back home will be going over it word by word, looking for contradictions and inaccuracies. And if they find any, they'll be demanding explanations, or reading all sorts of hidden meanings into it." Burnside looked her, eyebrows raised. "What I mean is, most people in China spend most of their time checking up on other people. It's the way the system works. They aren't particularly concerned about doing something productive. They're more interested in catching other people not doing *their* jobs. Which I guess is why we don't get too much done in China, at least compared with the people in Taiwan or Japan. What I'm saying is you've got to be very careful about what you say in support of your position or arguments. It doesn't matter if your overall position is right. If they find even the smallest inconsistency in your facts, there are people who'll use it to discredit your entire argument."

Burnside grunted, then observed, "Actually, it sounds pretty much like the rest of the world, only about ten times worse." As Burnside would shortly learn, his estimate of "ten times worse" was fairly accurate.

* * *

Chen Wan Le, chief of powertrain engineering for the Long March People's Cooperative Automotive Manufacturing Company hung up the phone with an almost palpable sense of relief. The news from Lin Cho Hsin, the company president, seemed bizarre but so welcome that Chen hardly wished to question it or prod Lin for more details. Lin had merely informed him that the plan to air ship a total of twenty-two Red Whippet sedans to the US for safety and emission testing was to be put on hold until further notice, that the testing procedures and standards were being waived by something Lin called "executive order." "It would be wise, perhaps," added Lin, "that your department continue working on meeting the standards set by the Americans, but for the moment there appears to be no great urgency. Your priority, Chen, is to ensure that your people can meet the production quotas for engines and transmissions, that is the critical thing. Even the Americans could not be persuaded to buy a car without an engine," he said jovially.

Chen was about to call in his engineering department heads to announce the good news, but then decided that it would be good to keep them under the pressure of a tight schedule. He chuckled, decided to take the rest of the afternoon off, go down to the local farmer's market, and select a succulent young puppy for his wife to prepare for dinner.

As Chen was happily contemplating a sumptuous repast for his evening meal, Lin was looking narrowly at Zhu Fei across his desk. In front of him was a copy of Sid Burnside's briefing report given to members of Zhu's little delegation during their visit to the Chino office. "Tell me, Zhu, what do you know of this man Burnside?"

Zhu appeared to be considering his response thoughtfully. In truth he was a bit alarmed at Lin's sudden and unexpected question, which clearly indicated that Lin knew something about Burnside that he, Zhu, did not, and further, that it was something potentially embarrassing to him, or worse.

Zhu managed to maintain an appearance of calm indifference. "He certainly seemed the best qualified of all the candidates I interviewed, and he was highly recommended by the recruiting firm we used, which was in turn highly regarded in the United States. They had many important large corporate clients." He shrugged. "Why do you ask, Comrade?"

"Have you read this?" asked Lin, picking up the bound briefing report and holding it up for Zhu.

"I have looked it over, but of course I was there for the briefing itself and am familiar with the details." Now Zhu was becoming genuinely alarmed, wondering what clear example of misinformation the report contained.

"You looked it over, you say," said Lin. "You looked it over," he repeated slowly. He put his fingertips together and nodded, then looked at the ceiling.

"Ah, yes, Comrade, I did look it over. Is something amiss?" asked Zhu, trying hard to maintain his appearance of composure.

"Would you say that your colleague Burnside is monumentally ignorant, or simply an idiot, then, Zhu, for there is no alternative assumption. You have hired either an ignoramus or an idiot," Lin said, his voice rising. Then, more softly, "Or, perhaps, a dangerous subversive, who has carelessly tipped his hand!"

"Please, comrade, explain what you are talking about. I simply don't understand. This man Burnside was carefully screened, as best we could screen him. He simply appeared to be an experienced executive from the automobile industry in the United States. Are you saying he is a CIA agent or something like that?"

With a flourish Lin pushed the briefing report across the desk toward Zhu. A phrase had been highlighted in yellow. Zhu's English was not accomplished enough to get the whole meaning of the sentence, though he was able to see the name Reagan, the long-forgotten reference to the Reagan administration's trade policies in the ancient Hyundai market analysis, dusted off and re-submitted by Burnside. He looked up at Lin helplessly. "Comrade, I must apologize, but my English is not so good as to be able to fully understand this. What does it mean?"

"What it means, Zhu, is that you have an affiliate company president who either *thinks* Ronald Reagan is still the president, or *wishes* that he were. Imagine! Ronald Reagan, the most vicious, anti-socialist fascist in the history of the United States! This is either the work of a buffoon or a deliberate provocation! Either way, it is intolerable that this man should be in control of our destiny in the American market! We are proposing to sell the ultimate People's Car to a grateful American public, and you have installed a fascist mad dog to oversee our efforts! Doubtless at this very moment he is plotting the destruction of all our plans and efforts to become a major automotive producer in world markets. And you have abetted him in his subversive efforts, Zhu. Your negligence could be the undoing of us all!"

Zhu sat staring at Lin, momentarily transfixed with shock and horror. He realized instantly that he was being set up for the inevitable failure of the Red Whippet in the American market, ostensibly at the hands of Sid Burnside, who would be surprised to learn that he was at that moment being portrayed as a veritable engine of commercial destruction and ruin. Finally he managed to say, "Certainly, Comrade, there is a logical and innocent explanation for this peculiar reference to a former president, even one so monstrously evil as this man Reagan. Perhaps it is the work of a simple-minded young secretary. As you know, most of the young Americans believe their country was allied with the Japanese in World War II. With their educational system, who could blame a young girl for not knowing the name of their current president?"

"Impossible, Zhu! He is on television twenty-four hours a day, even playing his guitar on a music station, the one all their degenerate youth watch, the one they call MTV. How could anybody in America not know who the president is?"

Zhu realized that further attempts to explain the reference to Ronald Reagan would be futile. Burnside had been identified as the cunning mole, the counter-revolutionary "wrecker," who would bring about the downfall of the Red Whippet in America, should that eventuality develop, as it appeared it would. And he, Zhu Fei, would be held responsible for placing a man of such consummate villainy in such a key position. "What do you think I should do, Comrade?" he asked quietly. His nose, still tender from his altercation with Vera Hawkins, throbbed painfully.

"For the moment, nothing, Zhu. Do nothing. Keep this man under observation, carefully analyze his every communication. Now that we have uncovered his true intentions, I believe he can be neutralized, perhaps even become a priceless asset to us."

Zhu immediately understood that Lin intended to keep Burnside on ice until the failure of the company became obvious to all, then "expose" him as the architect of their destruction. He understood full well that Lin's entire ridiculous hypothesis, which he was sure Lin didn't believe himself, was merely an insurance policy against being sucked down into the vortex of failure that loomed ahead. That it was absurd mattered not at all, any more than equally absurd charges had sufficed to send tens of millions of hapless Chinese citizens to their executions since the revolution. He began to perspire as the realization fully sunk in.

* * *

Sid Burnside sat reading the letter he intended to fax to Zhu. He couldn't see how Zhu or any of the higher ups in Beijing could object to his carefully reasoned position that the introduction of the Red Whippet could not be achieved successfully within the timeframe he'd just been given. He'd skirted the issue of the legality of factory stores in all markets, noting only that there were several states which had statutory restrictions on such operations and that Red Tiger was currently researching the issue to determine whether such states were in a majority and whether, if so, there might be loopholes of which they might be able to avail themselves. Burnside was both highly pleased and surprised that Suzy Johnson was able to organize the letter much better than he himself might have done. "Sid," she had advised him, "at this stage you might want to avoid taking any position from which you can't retreat. I don't know what's going on over there that's caused them to move up their timetable this way. It could be something as simple as Wu demanding a progress report and starting everybody running around trying to outdo themselves to impress him by moving up the introduction date. I just don't know," she shrugged, "but things like this are always happening in China. Somebody demands to know what's being done about something, then there's a big panic for a while before some scapegoat's found and things return to normal. The main thing is to avoid becoming the scapegoat."

Burnside chuckled, then looked at Sherry Maxwell, who'd been casting sidelong glances at the wall clock, which indicated ten after twelve, in the hope that Burnside would take the hint and suggest a lunch break. "Hey, Sherry, whaddya think about being the official Red Tiger scapegoat?" he called out.

Maxwell wasn't sure what Burnside meant but quickly seized on the opportunity it presented. "Well, why don't we talk about it over lunch?" he suggested. "I'm buyin."

Burnside looked at Maxwell, surprised at this extraordinary offer. Bastard must be farther gone than I thought, he told himself, correctly interpreting Maxwell's offer as a sign of his desperation to get to the bar without further delay. "Yeah, it's about that time, I guess. Hey, Suzy, you want to join us? We can finish up our discussion on this letter."

"I'd love to, Sid," she replied, to the acute disappointment of Sherry Maxwell, who was not eager to demonstrate his midday alcohol consumption to Suzy Lin Johnson, whom he suspected of being a spy in their midst. He couldn't quite figure out how the Chinese had cleverly arranged to have her meet Zack Johnson and then marry him, however, since he knew that Burnside had made all such arrangements. They're sneaky bastards, though, he told himself. He watched despondently as Suzy turned off her computer screen, picked up her handbag and headed to the lady's room.

Twenty minutes later they were seated in a local barbecue house, with a black proprietor and practically all black clientele. To Sherry's immense relief, Burnside ordered a pitcher of Coors from the waitress, then motioned to the aging black man behind the counter. "Hey, Sammy, c'mon over and meet our newest employee."

Sammy Lambert, owner of Sammy's Country Barbeque, came over to their table, smiling broadly. "Hey, Sid, howya doin'?" he asked "You ain't gonna get your weight down you keep drinkin' all that beer."

"Ya gotta drink beer with barbecue, man. Hell, I wouldn't drink it at all if I didn't have to come here and get my barbecue fix every coupla days."

"Well, at least you ain't gonna get too much fat from my pork or beef, Sid, so it ain't totally sinful."

"Sammy, this is Suzy Johnson, she just started with us today. She's from China."

Suzy held out her hand. "It's so nice to meet you, Sammy. Sid says the food here is wonderful."

"Well, thanks for that, but where'd you learn to speak English? You lived here a long time?"

"Well, actually, about three weeks. I'm a very fast learner." Sammy looked between her and Burnside. "I was an interpreter for Sid's parent company," she laughed. "I've studied English all my life. I even think in English most of the time."

"Damn, they must have good schools in China, Miss."

"Well, that's true in some ways," she replied.

Sammy excused himself and returned to his station behind the counter. "Sammy's got the best southern barbecue west of the Mississippi," said Sid. "This is one type of American food I'll bet you'll like. I been comin' here for a coupla months now. I could eat this stuff five times a week. Hey, Suzy, whaddya think you'd rather have? Some kind of beef or pork barbeque dish?"

"Well, ah, perhaps I'd like to try the pork."

"That's always a good choice. That sandwich on a roll is really good, and it comes with fries and cole slaw. You wanna try it?"

"Oh, that sounds so good. That's what I'll have." She watched curiously as Sherry filled his glass and drank it down in two long pulls, then refilled it from the pitcher.

He belched quietly, then noticed Suzy watching him. "Ah, barbecue always makes me, uh, really thirsty," he said, taking another long pull at his beer.

"Ah, yes, I see," she responded, "you're taking a sort of, ah, preventive thirst quencher."

"That's it!" cried Maxwell happily. "That's what I'm doing, what you called it. This way I won't get so thirsty when the food gets here."

Burnside rolled his eyes, then sat staring at the table top, massaging his temples with his fingertips. "Why don't we order," he suggested finally, motioning over the waitress. "Hey, Mary, we're ready to order, and you might as well get us another pitcher, too."

Factory Guys

Forty-five minutes later they were finishing their lunch. Maxwell had consumed all but two glasses of the beer from the two pitchers and seemed to have regained a ruddy blush. "Oh, Sid, that was so good," said Suzy. "I've never tasted a flavor like that. Do you think Sammy would tell me some of his recipes, I mean share some of his secrets with me?"

"I don't know Suzy, but I think most cooks are pretty secretive with their recipes and techniques." He shrugged. "No harm in asking him, I guess." He looked up just in time to see Sammy Lambert heading toward their table, having noted that they were finished.

"Everything OK?" he asked, looking particularly at Suzy Johnson.

"Oh, it was wonderful, one of the best things I've ever had. There's nothing like this in Chinese cooking."

"Hey, Sammy," Burnside interrupted, "Suzy was asking me if you could tell her about some of your recipes."

"Aw," he said, looking at his feet with apparent embarrassment, "we people in the restaurant business don' like givin' away our secrets, but what the heck, iffen you ain't gonna open up a barbecue place, I'd be happy to give you some pointers. You like to cook?"

"Oh, I do, it's my hobby. But all I can do are Chinese dishes. I want to learn some really authentic American recipes."

"Well, if you want, you could come in early some Saturday morning and watch us get started, I could show you what we put into our cookin' and such, but you need smokers and stuff like that to do it really right." Normally Sammy would never have acceded to such a request, but he was quite flattered by and taken with the beautiful Suzy Johnson and her almost child-like display of enthusiasm.

"Oh, that would be wonderful. Could I come in this Saturday?"

Sammy nodded his assent, then added, "Sure, we get started at eight thirty. Hey, can you teach me a couple of Chinese dishes? My wife and I both really like Chinese food."

With that, the bargain was sealed, and thus began a pleasant friendship that, in a rather convoluted way, would have quite extraordinary consequences.

* * *

171

That evening, when Suzy Johnson arrived home, Zack greeted her at the door with a big hug. "How's it feel to be the breadwinner, Shan? I felt so good about it I decided to call Continental today and resign so we can spend more time together."

"Well, I'm glad you're not feeling too insecure about me having a job," she smiled. "I think I may be president of Red Tiger before too long."

"Hey, this came for you this morning," he said, picking up a Fed-Ex envelope from the little foyer table and handing it to her. "The return address is somewhere in Maryland. Do you know anybody there?"

"I don't think so," she replied and began opening the envelope. The package contained an unmarked VHS tape, with a short note in Chinese characters.

"What's that say?" asked Zack curiously.

"It says to keep this in a safe place," she said. "That's all." She turned over the cassette, looking for any additional identification.

"Let's play it and see what it is," said Zack, taking the tape from her and walking over to the VCR in the living room. He turned the VCR and the TV on, popped the tape in, and waited. There were a few seconds of hissing snow on the screen, then the tape began with a clearly recognizable President Carruthers reaching over to fondle Suzy Johnson's behind. Zack watched, speechless with anger for several seconds, then exploded, "That sonofabitch! I shoulda stomped him and kicked him in the nuts when he was down!" He stood tight-lipped as the tape continued, but then exclaimed gleefully, "God, what a perfect shot!" as his wife slammed the heel of her hand into Carruthers' nose.

Suzy, watching the Secret Service agent flying through the air to land on the bar, said, "Oh, I hope that man wasn't too badly hurt."

"Yeah, well the bastard pissed me off, jumpin' on you the way he did."

"Oh, look, Zack, there's Mr. Pei," said Suzy, as she watched the PLA security man bring his truncheon down on the Secret Service agent's wrist. "That man had a gun!"

"Jesus, that sonofabitch was gonna shoot you!" shouted Zack. "Those dirty bastards woulda shot you, and maybe me too. I don't believe this!"

They stood and watched the tape several times, Zack clearly enjoying it more with every repetition. "Hey, lemme back up and look at the nose shot again," he said. "I wanna run it in slow motion." He watched, chortling happily, as Carruthers' nose broke once again for their viewing pleasure, this time in slow motion. "I liked that little squawk he gave, God, what a wimp," he said. "Jesus, you nailed him perfectly! I wish this thing had a sound track."

"It was a bit of a lucky blow, but it seemed to have the desired effect," said Suzy, smiling faintly. "You know, Zack, that's the first time I've ever struck another person outside the gymnasium. I'd always considered mastering fighting skills as a sport, nothing more. I never dreamed I'd ever actually use them on anybody."

"Yeah, then the first guy you use them on is the President of the United States." He shook his head. "Christ, the first molester you run into in this country is the goddam president! You know, Suzy, if you tried to make up a story like this about Carruthers, nobody'd believe it. That's how ridiculous this thing is."

"Zack, who do you think sent us this tape?" she asked quietly.

"Well, the tape musta come from the embassy somehow. It looks like it was one of those security camera tapes. I didn't notice any cameras around, but then, I wasn't lookin' for 'em, either. But anybody from in there coulda sent it, I guess."

"The message is in Chinese, so I would assume it came from the Ambassador or one of his people. I think the fact that it wasn't in English means they at least wanted us to know where it came from." She paused, frowning. "Zack, why do you think they sent it to us?"

"I don't know, honey. If they wanted to publicize this whole thing they coulda done it themselves."

"Do you think they were trying to tell us that we may be in danger, and this tape is our insurance policy?"

Zack pulled on his earlobe. "That's an interesting question," he said thoughtfully. "But who would we be in danger from?"

"Well, if it were the Chinese, I can't see why they'd send us this tape. Whoever sent it seems to be trying to protect us, wouldn't you say?"

Zack said nothing for perhaps ten seconds. "Well, the only other interested party would have to be the White House, then. But, I mean, why would they want to bother us? We're out of the picture now, we're not going to tell anybody about that night, so why would the White House want to cause us any problems?"

"The only thing I can think of is simple revenge. Perhaps your president doesn't like having his nose broken by a girl he's fondling. Especially a *gook*."

"A gook?"

"Yes. We can feel it when somebody thinks we're just a bunch of little yellow monkeys, when they patronize us, when what they're really thinking is that we learned everything worth knowing from the white man. Your president oozes it from every pore. Oh, he'd love to fuck me, in fact, he thinks it's his *due* to fuck me, or any Asian woman, at his convenience, and that we should all be properly thankful for the experience." In an instant her features had gone from pleasant and relaxed to a mask of hatred.

"Jesus, Shan, don't get so excited. I think Carruthers thinks its his right to fuck *any* woman, he's not partial to any racial or ethnic group."

Just as quickly her features returned to normal. "Perhaps," she shrugged. "But the fact appears to be that at least *someone* in the Chinese embassy thinks we may be in danger and was willing to risk their own situation enough to send us this tape."

"Nah, I mean Carruthers is a dirt bag, but he's a practical politician. He's not *that* stupid. We couldn't be anything but trouble for him, and he's gotta know that. I mean, what's the bastard gonna do? Send in the IRS to audit us? Get the FAA to jerk my ticket? Have you deported? C'mon."

Despite making light of it for Suzy's benefit, Zack suddenly realized that any of the foregoing possibilities might not be out of character for Carruthers. "You know," he said suddenly, "I'm gonna make three or four copies of this tape and put 'em in different places, maybe even send one to my parents with instructions that they're not to open it. That way we'll always know where we can lay our hands on one if we need it."

"I think that's a sound idea, Zack." Then, "Do you want to eat at home or out tonight?"

"I don't care. Right now I wanna fuck my gook, it's my due."

She stepped close to him and he leaned down to kiss her. In an instant she'd stepped to his right and kicked his legs out from under him with the back of her right calf. A split second later he found himself flat on his back on the living room carpet with Suzy sitting on his stomach, grinning impishly at him. "Your gook, huh?"

"OK, I surrender, you're the Alpha female, you little monster," he laughed, and began unbuttoning her blouse.

* * *

President Carruthers snapped shut the looseleaf-enclosed briefing from the Commerce Department, which called for sanctions against foreign steel producers. He snorted, knowing that the suggestion was politically advisable in the short term, but economically damaging in the long. What the hell, thought Carruthers, in the long term we'll all be dead. He glanced at the wall clock, noting that he was mere minutes from his dreaded appointment with Nate Garmin. Normally Carruthers never called for a meeting with Garmin, there being nothing of import that Garmin could communicate to him, and only grudgingly assented to Garmin's frequently requested (but rarely granted) meetings. But this spelled potential trouble. Christ, that's all I need right now, Carruthers told himself, a big surprise, like getting it stuck up my ass by Garmin's dildo. I gotta get to the bottom of this.

Presently Garmin was escorted into Carruthers' office by his secretary. The two men exchanged pleasantries, then Carruthers decided to get right to the point. I wanna hit him right between the eyes, thought Carruthers, get the truth out of him. "Well, Nate, you wanna tell me about this dildo thing?"

"Huh?" Garmin exclaimed. "How'd you know about that? I didn't want to get you involved just yet, not until I got it straight in my own mind how to announce it. I mean, I'm not sure the public's ready for the idea just yet, I mean you gotta bring these things out gradually, give 'em time to get used to it. I mean, I haven't got it worked out yet how I want to present it. I'm not sure this is the time to go public with it."

"So, I gather you're not quite ready to come out of the closet just yet."

"Hey, that's a great way to put it, Bob, I gotta say, you've got a great way with words," exclaimed Garmin enthusiastically.

Carruthers stared out the window and groaned inwardly. Jesus Christ, I knew it, he told himself, next I'm gonna find out Landry's having an affair with with a frigging chicken, a goddam rooster at that. "Nate, what I wanna know is how the Chinese found out about this thing of yours. Why'd you have to tell *them* about it. I mean, what business is it of theirs, really?"

Garmin looked stricken by Carruthers' tone of disapproval. "Ah, gosh, I'm sorry, Bob, I kinda thought of Ambassador Li as a kind of friend, someone you could share a little secret with. I mean, we have a really good relationship."

"You actually *told* Li about this? I mean, he didn't find out some other way?"

"Well, Bob, I don't think he could have found out any other way. I've been very discreet about it, it's just between the two of us."

"What makes you think so, Nate? How do you know you weren't being recorded during this little confession? Hell, all sorts of people could know about it by now, it'll probably be in the fucking Drudge Report tomorrow, then we'll have to answer all sorts of questions." Garmin seemed to be sinking lower and lower into his chair as he listened to Carruthers, whose voice was rising. "Now, understand, Nate, I don't care what you do on your own time, hell, you know me, I'd fuck a rockpile if I thought there was a snake in it, but you gotta show a little discretion. Now, goddammit, I don't want to hear any more about this dildo thing, not from you or anybody else, and if anybody comes snooping around asking questions, you don't know anything about it, Bootsie doesn't know anything about it, nobody around here knows what the hell anybody's talking about on this thing, you got me? It's just a pure shithouse rumor designed to embarrass this administration, and that's our final position."

Nate Garmin was in a state of numbing shock, both from incurring Carruthers' apparent wrath, but equally from the destruction of what he saw as the highpoint of his career in public office, the Diversified Industrial Liaison and Development Office. He got up slowly and turned toward the door. "I think I understand your position, Bob. That'll be the end of it, I promise," he said softly as he left, ashen-faced and weak-kneed. Later he would spend endless hours speculating as to the meaning of Carruthers' reference to a snake and a rockpile, finally concluding that it was some sort of mystical allegory, quite beyond his ability to decipher.

* * *

Zhu Fei sat down to read the four page fax from Sid Burnside immediately after its return from translation. Burnside had, at Suzy Johnson's suggestion, submitted it in English rather than invite the question of where he got such a capable interpreter. Plus, she feared that someone in Beijing would recognize her Mandarin characters, which were at least as individual as western handwriting.

As he'd feared, Burnside's letter seemed to be raising every possible objection to the Red Whippet's early introduction, objections that would be interpreted as irrefutable proof that Burnside was the "wrecker," doubt-less sent by envious competitors, who intended to destroy Red Tiger's efforts at the outset. That the objections may have had some sound basis was irrelevant, now that scapegoats were being sought. Zhu was especial-ly irked by Burnside's argument that dealers were needed, since selling the cars from the ports of entry potentially violated some sort of stupid laws. The port pickup idea had been Zhu's sole contribution to Red Tiger's mar-keting strategy. Suddenly he found himself wondering if Burnside in fact was some sort of corporate saboteur, or at least a slothful layabout, intent on avoiding the work necessary to get the company up and running in the US. Whatever the situation, Zhu realized that he would be wise to go to Lin with his copy of the translation immediately and demonstrate that he, belatedly, had seen through Burnside's perfidy and was now ready to denounce him with all possible vigor.

Twenty minutes later Zhu, having worked himself into a state of gen-uine and righteous indignation, was sitting before Lin, angrily waving Burnside's letter. "You were right, Comrade," he said sputtering, "this man Burnside has managed to deceive me. He is a wrecker, sent by Detroit, or perhaps by our ancient enemies, the Japanese, or perhaps both! You know how the Americans abetted them in their rape of Nanking," repeating this ancient bit of Chinese Communist propaganda left over from the Korean conflict. "As you read this, Comrade, you can see that his every objection to our schedule is designed to delay the introduction of the Red Whippet indefinitely." He was about to continue, but Lin held up his hand, signal-ing silence.

"Yes, you have erred greatly, Zhu, in selecting this loathesome indi-vidual, but perhaps it could not be helped. You were in a strange environ-ment, without the necessary assets to help you in making your choice, and I've no doubt that this man has been assiduously trained in the arts of deception. Our Japanese and American enemies certainly would not have sent a rank amateur into our midst in order to destroy us. No, they would use a seasoned professional. I should not be surprised if this operative is the very same who exposed our plan to sell counterfeit Cabbage Patch dolls in the US a few years ago. Yes, he is a cunning and very dangerous agent of destruction, of that there can be no doubt."

"Nonetheless, I should not have been fooled by this man, however clever and experienced he is," responded Zhu, knowing that in the People's Republic, self-criticism and confession were not only good for the soul, but quite often beneficial to one's prospects for living to a ripe old age as well. "Yes, had I been more focused on the people's interests, rather than trying to accomplish more than was possible in the allotted timeframe, this would not have happened. I can never erase the stain of this humiliation, Comrade Lin. I ask only that I be allowed to continue in my position in order to be able to make amends from this day forward, and to deal properly with the verminous wrecker Burnside."

"Enough, Zhu, your apology is accepted and will be passed to Comrade Chen and the others whose careers have been affected by your oversight. I am sure that they, like me, will accept your apology, provided that you are more vigilant in the future."

Zhu bowed his head in a gesture of both supplication and profound gratitude. "Thank you, comrade, I shall not fail you again," reflecting fleetingly that had he been a member of the despised and barbaric Japanese race of two generations ago, he'd be kneeling on a *tatami,* preparatory to doing his own abdominal surgery with a razor-keen *tanto.* No doubt such hideous traditions are the main source of their motivation, Zhu told himself.

"For the moment, I wish you to take no action against this man Burnside," said Lin. "Do not alert him in any way to our awareness of his treachery. With luck, we may uncover the entire network of saboteurs and wreckers. It would be naive in the extreme to suppose that this man is acting alone. Doubtless he has confederates who must be stopped also. This man Maxwell, for example. He was selected by Burnside alone, was he not?"

"Yes, Comrade, I thought it best not to interfere with his personnel selection, another grave lapse of judgment, I now see." He hung his head.

"Do not despair, Zhu, as long as we aware of their treachery, their ability to disrupt our plans is limited." Both men were fully aware that their fencing was totally a sham, but each had to maintain the facade to the other of grave concern.

"Yes, Comrade," said Zhu, "as long as we maintain our appearance of ignorance regarding their intentions, they will become careless and their actions easy to interpret. We are in an advantageous position."

"Precisely, Zhu, precisely. We hold all the cards, as the Americans would say."

* * *

Factory Guys

Sammy Lambert pulled into the back employee lot of Sammy's Country Barbecue. At eight o'clock in the morning, he wanted to be early in order to be there before the Chinese girl Suzy Johnson arrived. Sammy found himself, quite inexplicably, looking forward to showing her some of his barbecue techniques. He was flattered by her apparently sincere interest in learning the techniques of that quintessentially American style of cooking, southern barbeque.

He unlocked the front door, disarmed the alarm, went to the dishwasher and began unloading it, piling the plates in precariously high stacks on the counter. Ten minutes later Tom, his cousin and minority partner in the restaurant, came through the door. "Mornin', Sammy, where's that foxy Chinese honey you been sneakin' around with?"

"You watch your dirty mind, Tommy, or I'll be kickin' your lazy ass good. She's just a nice girl tryin' to be a good American, learnin' how to cook for her man proper. And Sid tells me her old man's one big bad dude, boy, the type who'll tear your arms off and use 'em to beat you to death with, you try messin' round with his old lady."

"Hey, it wasn't my idea to bring her in here this mornin', man, hell I'm more scared o' Ellen than *any* dude. She catches me messin' round, it ain't my arm she's gonna be tearin' off." They continued to banter and joke in like manner as they put away the tableware, relaxed and jovial men who clearly enjoyed their work.

They were just finishing up with the silverware when Suzy appeared at the door. She knocked and waved through the glass, then came in. "Good morning, Sammy. Am I too early?"

"Naw, you're just in time, Suzy. Hey, I want you to meet Tommy, he's my cousin and partner in the place here."

She walked over and extended her hand. "I'm so pleased to meet you, Tommy. It's so nice of you to let me watch you work and learn something about barbecue cooking. It was so delicious, I just had to see if I could learn to make it at home."

Tommy looked at her in surprise. "You don't sound like no Chinese lady. How long you been here? I mean, like you speak perfect English, like you been livin' here all your life."

"Well, I was trained in China as an interpreter to speak English like an American, so that's what I do. That, and cook Chinese cuisine. I want to broaden my horizons. That's why I'm here today." She smiled charmingly at Tommy and Sammy.

179

Three hours later Suzy had filled four pages of a notebook with recipes, comments, and equipment requirements for a variety of pork and beef barbecue dishes. By then Sammy, Tommy, and rest of their staff were getting ready for the lunch crowd, one of whom would be Suzy herself. She'd decided to try an order of their baby-back ribs with home fries and a cup of coleslaw. They were, she noted, nothing like any Chinese recipe for ribs, especially in the way the meat fell off the bone. Presently she finished her lunch, then stood up to visit the ladies' room and wash the barbecue sauce off her hands. As she stood before the sink she looked at herself in the mirror for a long moment and reflected on the remarkable series of events that had that had thrust her, only weeks before a girl from mainland China, into a life in which she was married to a strapping and handsome airline pilot, driving her very own sports car, and making nearly $50,000 per year. As they say, she thought, only in America, giving a bemused but appreciative little shake of her head.

Five minutes later she was thanking Sammy and Tommy profusely and insisting that they come to her home for an authentic Chinese dinner in the very near future. "Hey, we'd love to do that," said Sammy, "but you gotta take us one at a time, so's the other one can be here. That's the way we always work it here."

"Then that's what we'll do," said Suzy happily. "We'll have you over one at a time."

And thus was the die cast.

* * *

Chapter 7

US Attorney General Jack Landry smiled as he read the field report on the "Chinese national" the LA-based FBI agents had tracked down through the immigration department. Lin Shan, now Susan Lin Johnson, was married to an airline pilot and living in Pasadena. He wondered about her husband's involvement, if any, in her clandestine activities. Hmm, married in Las Vegas last month, he noted, thinking it would be a convenient way for a foreign agent to enter the United States. Landry had ordered the field office to maintain a distant and discreet surveillance of the Johnson home, and to follow both of them intermittently and see where they went. Mrs. Johnson, the report noted, seemed to be working for the US affiliate company for The Long March People's Cooperative Automotive Manufacturing Company, one Red Tiger Motors, which didn't seem to be doing much of anything, and which seemed to have very few employees. Landry grunted, sure he was on to some kind of shell company, fronting for a Chinese espionage or smuggling operation. Six days had elapsed since the president had given him the assignment. I better notify Carruthers that I got this, he told himself, find out what he wants me to do next.

Forty minutes later, having been directed by Carruthers to drop whatever he was doing and hurry over with the report, Landry was sitting excitedly in the oval office. "I've got 'em under surveillance, Mr. President," he reported proudly to Carruthers.

Carruthers was flipping through the four page report, pleased that the FBI had found them so quickly, and further pleased that the Johnsons owned a home, which suggested permanence. "Umm," he murmured, "good work, Jack. This is just what I wanted. Are you absolutely sure that the field agents have no knowledge of where their orders originated?"

"Absolutely, sir, as far as they're concerned it's a purely routine surveillance. Personally, I think we may be on to something, though. This Red Tiger outfit she's working for looks like some kind of front. One funny thing, though, she went into a little barbecue restaurant in Chino, California early one morning, way before opening time at about eleven thirty, and she stayed for a couple of hours. We couldn't see what was going on. The place is owned by a couple of black guys, I mean African-Americans. We're running a check on them right now."

"OK, Jack, this is what I want you to do for the moment. Keep this lady and her husband under surveillance for the time being, but report immediately to me any change in their status, like if they go on a trip, or move, change jobs, anything, ya got it?" said Carruthers. In truth, he didn't have any firm plans for the Johnsons, only a vague intention to somehow see Mrs. Johnson on a private basis, without her burly and intimidating husband around. He'd been fantasizing about somehow exchanging her freedom for some sort of ongoing sexual liaison. Jesus, it's great to be president, Carruthers thought. What a way to get chicks!

Carruthers jerked his mind back to the meeting. "Ah, that'll be all, Jack, and, ah, sorry I sorta barked at you last time, but this thing's really important to me personally and to the security of the United States. Just keep a lid on the thing for now. It'll all become clear what's goin' on here before too long."

Landry swelled with pride, excused himself, and left. God, it's great to be in a position to serve the president of the United States, he told himself.

* * *

Nate Garmin and Penny Twombly were sharing coffee and Danish in the vice-president's office, discussing Carruthers' executive order to waive the emission and safety standards for the Red Whippet for a period of ten months, after which the cars were to be retrofitted with updated engine and emission components, plus having dual airbags and safety glass installed. "How do you feel about this, Nate?" Penny Twombly asked, licking a bit of sugar frosting off her thumb.

"Well, I guess it's OK, Penny. I don't see a problem. Like Li said, the cars'll pass the current standards OK anyway, and the stuff they've gotta put on later will just make 'em that much better."

"No, what I meant was the PR angle on this thing. I mean, the people in Detroit are gonna go crazy when they realize that we've waived all the government standards for the Chinese, and they still have to go through all that stuff."

"Ah, I wouldn't worry about it too much, Penny. Who are they gonna complain to? *We're* not gonna listen to them, are we? And luckily, the press in this country seems to know that Bob Carruthers knows what's good for the country, even if the people don't. They probably won't even report it, except maybe on page thirty-two, one time only. And if anybody makes a big stink about it, what the heck, we can always send down the IRS, OSHA, or even your people to shut 'em up."

"You know, Nate, it's wonderful to know that we have all this force for good at our disposal, don't you think?"

"Umm, yeah, it is," replied Garmin distractedly.

"What's the matter today, Nate? You really seem down in the dumps. Is Bootsie still mad about that hair dryer and the Atkins Diet book you gave her for her birthday?"

"No, she seems to be over that, but I still don't know what she was so upset about. Nah, I might as well tell you about it." He hesitated, collecting his thoughts, such as they were. "Bob didn't like my idea about the Diversified Industrial Liaison and Development Office. In fact, he sorta freaked out about it, said it'd be an embarrassment to him and the whole administration, and if anybody asked about it, we're supposed to deny any knowledge of the thing. I mean, he really seemed kinda mad at me." He looked at Penny Twombly unhappily.

"Oh, Nate, I know how you must feel," she said, her brow furrowed into a profound expression of abject sympathy. "You put so much time and thought into it." Suddenly she seemed to brighten. "You know, Nate, he's been under a lot of pressure lately, especially with that broken nose thing, I mean the tumor." She smiled at Garmin conspiratorially. "Plus, you know how astute Bob is politically. I know he agreed with your idea, but I'm sure he just didn't feel the timing was right. You know, Nate, timing's everything, in politics and life in general. And nobody has a better sense of timing than Bob Carruthers. I mean, like when he sprung that story about Thomas Jefferson fooling around with his slaves just before the election! He's a political genius, Nate, and sometimes geniuses can be a little short with people. I know he didn't mean to hurt your feelings. If I were you I'd just let it lie until he brings it up again. Bob never forgets anything, you know that, unless he's under oath." She winked knowingly at Garmin. "He'll raise the issue again when he feels the time is right, trust me."

"Boy, I hope so, Penny. This was gonna be my legacy. That's what I really thought."

"It'll *still* be your legacy, Nate, I just know it will."

"Thanks, Penny, I really appreciate that. Hey, I feel lots better already." Why, I'll be remembered for a real turning point in American history, he told himself. It'll be just like Roosevelt's New Deal or Kennedy's New Frontier! Garmin's DILDO! He looked out the window dreamily and grew a little misty.

* * *

It had been two days since Sid Burnside had faxed Zhu the lengthy and detailed letter regarding the need to go a bit slower in exporting the Red Whippet to the US. He as yet had heard no reply, though Suzy Johnson advised him that the management in Beijing would want to analyze his memo in minute detail, then formulate their responses in like detail, before responding. She pointed out that there would be dozens of people whose input would be sought, then granted only after the most careful and cautious consideration. She estimated that it might take a week or more to get a response, despite the impossibly tight time frame in which Red Tiger Motors was working. Burnside as yet knew of nothing of the executive order granting The Long March People's Cooperative Automotive Manufacturing Company a waiver from the normal government standards. Even the *Automotive News* hadn't been made aware of the order, which was certain to raise eyebrows to the vertical throughout the boardrooms of the automotive industry worldwide when it became known outside diplomatic circles.

Burnside did get going and generated a standard letter of intent for interested dealer prospects, once again plagiarized from his Hyundai files, and he'd sent Maxwell off again to do a bit of dealer prospecting in northern California. The letter had taken him the better part of the morning to get onto Red Tiger letterhead, all in all, a tidy day's work, Burnside told himself.

Suzy had spent the morning on the phone, contacting employment prospects preparatory to bringing them in for a personal interviews. She did talk to Edward White Feather, who, it turned out, lived in East LA. After she'd hung up, she thought that he seemed an eager and enthusiastic young man. "Sid, I just talked to this young man, Edward White Feather. What kind of name do you think that is?" she asked curiously.

"Oh, that guy's gotta be a Native American, Suzy, that's what we gotta call 'em now. We used to call 'em Indians."

She looked a little puzzled. "Then what are you, or Zack, for that matter. You were all born here, too."

Burnside seemed to momentarily at a loss for words. "Hmph," he grunted, "that's a good question. I guess I'm a, ah, white European-American, I guess." It was clear that Burnside had never thought of it before. "And you must be a, ah, a Chinese-American, right?"

"I guess so, Sid. Why does everybody have to be put in some category? Why can't I just be an American?"

"Ah, well, Suzy, it's kinda hard to explain, hell, I really don't understand it myself half the time, but the government puts everybody in some sort of classification to see who's entitled to what, I guess that's the idea."

"So what's this man White Feather entitled to, then?"

"Well, I'm not exactly sure what he gets out of the whole thing, but it looks good for us to have him on our staff, shows we're big on diversity and don't have any, ah, prejudices. Then the government stays off our backs."

"So it's good for us to have Indians on our staff?"

"Yeah, that's the idea, something like that. There's a whole list of people who are, ah, I'm tryin' to remember what they call it, a protected class, that's it, who you want to hire if you can."

"What if they're not qualified for the job, are we supposed to hire them anyway?"

"Well, not exactly," said Burnside, "but ya gotta be careful about how you handle it with those people. They got special privileges and protections."

"Am I in a protected class, then, Sid? I mean by that that I'm not white like most Americans, I'm Oriental."

"You? Nah, I'm pretty sure Orientals aren't protected. Hell, you people come here with nothing and within five years you own everything and are drivin' BMWs and Porsches. Hell, *we* need protection from *you*."

Suzy laughed. "Well, I don't think that's quite true, Sid, but it's nice to know that people think we don't need special privileges. Hey, why don't we go over to Sammy's for lunch. I've been thinking about their barbecue all morning."

"Hey, that's a good idea, I was thinkin' the same thing. Lemme just go to the men's room and we'll get going."

Ninety minutes later two thirds of the employees of Red Tiger Motor company were just finishing their lunch in Sammy's Country Barbecue. "Oh, that was so good, Sid. We have to stop coming here so often or I'll get so fat that Zack will run off with another woman."

"Well, you'd have to put on an awful lot of weight before there's any danger of that happening, Suzy." He waved to Sammy for the check.

Sammy approached the table, smiling broadly as he nearly always was. "Everything OK?" he asked, looking between them.

"Oh, I enjoyed it so much," said Suzy of her barbecued beef sandwich on a roll. "I'm going to try cooking ribs for my husband this weekend, Sammy. You know, the recipe you showed me on Saturday."

"Aw, you're gonna do just fine. People who like to eat always like to cook," said Sammy. He reached into the pocket of his apron and produced a VHS tape, which he held out to her. "They got a local cable cooking show here in the western suburbs," said Sammy. "Sometimes they have me and Tommy on for an episode. This here was a good one we did, using one of our favorite recipes. I bet you'll like it," he said, smiling shyly.

"Oh, Sammy, that's so sweet of you. I know what we can do! Why don't you come over to our house next Sunday afternoon, and we can have a big barbecue. Zack will be home for the whole weekend, and we can try this recipe." she said happily, holding the VHS tape aloft.

"I got a better idea," said Sammy. "Why don't you cook us a real Chinese dinner, we kin have barbecue at my house sometime."

"Would you really prefer that?" she asked.

"Well, we both like Chinese cookin', Suzy, and you know how to make the real thing. Just don' be makin' anything too weird, OK?"

"I think I understand, Sammy. I'll stick to the basics, like beef, pork, fish, or chicken. The neighborhood dogs and cats will be spared this time." She was fully aware that many Americans thought that domestic pets were preferred table fare in China. Sammy seemed to recoil, which caused her to laugh heartily. "Don't worry, I won't make anything weird. In the meantime I can watch this tape and get some more pointers."

Burnside dropped fifteen dollars on the table. He and Suzy left chuckling, with Burnside noting, a little wistfully, that he was utterly charmed by this beautiful and witty Chinese girl, who was perhaps twenty-five years his junior.

* * *

"There they are again," said the older of the two men in the black Ford Taurus as Sid and Suzy left Sammy's and walked to Burnside's car in the little parking lot. The two FBI agents were parked nearly sixty yards down the street. "You wanna take any more pictures, Bill?"

"Nah, nothing's changed. You wanna follow 'em or just head back toward their office and see if they show up?"

"Let's just take another route back to the office. So far we haven't seen or heard anything suspicious about the lady or this guy she's with. In fact, the only thing we got is the way she went into the restaurant on Saturday morning. That still makes me wonder, but I guess it could be innocent enough."

"Well, there doesn't seem to be anything going with the two guys that own the place. They got no arrest records, they got families, they're just a coupla workin' stiffs as far as I can see."

"Yeah," said the one called Bill. "I can't see a local barbecue joint being part of some espionage ring, especially being owned by a couple of brothers. I mean, if this were a Chinese restaurant owned by a local branch of the Tong Hatchet Men or some shit like that it might be worth keepin' an eye on, but there's nothing here." He started the car, pulled it into gear, and eased out of the parallel parking spot. "Let's just cruise through the office park and see if they're back there. Then we can head on back to the office and try and pick this lady up and follow her home this afternoon." The other man sighed in agreement. "You hungry?" Bill asked.

"Yeah, whaddya say we stop in a Burger King and get something to eat."

In the four days they'd had the Johnsons under discreet surveillance, the agents hadn't seen anything out of the ordinary, other than the inexplicable visit to the barbeque house before opening time. They hadn't observed any visits from friends or neighbors, and had tailed Zack to the airport twice when he'd flown trips, watching him park his car in the employee lot and then disappear into the terminal, heading toward Continental operations. Neither Suzy nor Zack seemed to exhibit the slightest apprehension about being followed. Nor had the agents' instructions given them a clue about what the Johnsons were suspected of being involved in. Though they were a bit curious initially, the assignment quickly became so uneventful that neither wanted to make the effort to even speculate, preferring to just listen to ballgames or talk radio.

Ten minutes later they were driving slowly by Red Tiger's headquarters, noting that Burnside's Olds Cutlass was parked next to Mrs. Johnson's red Miata once again. "Let's just go and get something to eat," said Fred, the younger of the two men.

"Yeah, let's do that," said Bill. He accelerated back onto the main thoroughfare of the office park, came to the entrance, and wheeled quickly and noisily back out onto the street.

Three hours later they were falling in behind Suzy's red Miata, which, they noticed, she seemed to drive rather tentatively, coming to completely full stops at stop signs and always strictly observing speed limits, to the exasperation of other motorists, including the two FBI agents. They knew the route she took home each night and were about to abandon the tail when she made an unexpected right turn, then turned into a supermarket parking lot. Bill turned in after her and parked about twenty spots from her. They watched as she got out of the Miata and disappeared into the supermarket. "Ah, Jesus," groaned Fred, "she's just going grocery shopping. Let's face it. We're just following around some totally harmless civilian. Look, Bill, I say we go to Bingham and tell him to call this thing off, unless he's got some specifics about what we're supposed to be doing. This is just some Chinese chick who married an American who looks like he does exercise machine infomercials."

"Yeah, well, let's wait until she comes out and see what she's carryin'."

"You wanna lay odds she's gonna be carrying a shopping bag or two? Or maybe you're expecting an AK-47 or a shoulder-fired missile?"

"C'mon, Fred, we got our orders, we're supposed to maintain a discreet surveillance over this lady and her husband until we're told otherwise. Shit, it all counts toward retirement. What do you care how we put the time in?"

"God, now I know what private eyes do all day, working for divorce lawyers, hopin' to catch somebody doin' something they can't explain to the judge." Fred shook his head in disgust.

"Well, look at it this way, you're learning a trade. You'll have a perfect post-retirement opportunity. Private dicks are in great demand, I'm told."

Just then Suzy emerged from the supermarket with a large shopping bag on her hip. "Hey, there she is again." He noted the time of her exit from the supermarket in his little notebook. "I don't believe I'm doing this," he muttered.

Bill started the car and followed her out onto the street again, then stayed with her until she turned into her little concrete driveway. The two watched as her husband came out to greet her, leaning down and giving her a little peck on the lips. "Well, Bill," said Fred, "you wanna come back tonight and peek in the windows and see what they're doing?"

"Shit, yeah, now you're talkin', Fred." Fred looked at his fellow agent and rolled his eyes. As the two agents would eventually learn, their surveillance of the Johnsons, uneventful though it seemed thus far, would figure in some rather bizarre and far reaching consequences.

* * *

As the two FBI agents were listlessly going through the motions of keeping an eye on the Johnsons, Zhu Fei once again found himself sitting across from Lin Cho Hsin, who stared at him rather disconcertingly as he drummed his fingers on his desk. At length, he sighed loudly and began. "Zhu, we have just now received the approval of the US government to begin exporting the Red Whippet to their country. Thus, there are no administrative details requiring further attention. We can begin shipping these cars at once."

"Ah, do you mean immediately, Comrade,?" asked Zhu, clearly showing his alarm.

"Yes, of course, at once, immediately, without further delay! One of our nation's largest cargo vessels is steaming enroute as we speak to pick them up. It has capacity of nearly four thousand cars."

"But Comrade Lin," Zhu sputtered, "we do not have so many cars yet available for shipment. Everything coming from the assembly plants for the next three months is pre-allocated to domestic buyers. We cannot disappoint them by telling them that their cars are being sold to American consumers, and at a lower price yet."

Lin waved his hand dismissively. "The people are accustomed to sacrifice, Zhu, and in any event, they will get their cars in due course. All that is required is a bit more patience on their part."

"But Comrade, why are we again moving up our timetable? We have many matters to attend to in the United States before we can begin shipping cars, matters that cannot be attended to in just a few weeks."

Lin held up his hand for silence. "Zhu, given that we, or perhaps I should say *I*, Lin, exposed the wrecker Burnside, I am astonished at your impertinence in asking why we are moving up our timetable. Could you truly be so great a fool?" he asked, raising his voice. "Or have you been infected by the wrecker himself? Or are you in league with him, Zhu?" he asked more softly. "I wonder."

Zhu's mouth worked but no words came. Finally, he managed to croak, "I do not understand this, Comrade Lin. How can you question my loyalty? I have been deceived by the man, been made a fool perhaps, but he has not infected me with his bacillus. Never!" Then growing a bit more confident, since Lin hadn't interrupted him, "Was it not I who came to you with his latest communication, who saw through his wicked designs in the first place? Would this be the work of a fellow wrecker?"

Lin appeared to be thinking. "Yes, but only if he were very clever, Zhu. On reflection, I do not think you nearly so clever as that."

Zhu felt a nearly palpable relief flow through him at Lin's assurance that he in fact considered him a rather unimaginative simpleton. "Yes, that is true, Comrade, I am loyal and hardworking, but hardly clever. In fact, my wife assures me that I am rather stupid, as do many of my friends, as well!"

"You may, I believe, take them at their word, Zhu. But I believe you were seeking an explanation as to why I am moving up the timetable for conquering the US market." Zhu nodded, feigning rapt attention. "We are in a war, Zhu, a relentless economic war, being waged against us by imperialistic American and Japanese vested economic interests! They know the inevitable result should the economic and competitive might of the People's Republic be brought to bear on them! Disaster! Ruin! And for the Japanese, irretrievable loss of face! Of course, the Americans, being the worst of barbarians, care little about face. Only money and their stomachs concern them. But in war, does one accede to the enemy's timetable, Zhu? Does one?" he demanded.

Zhu, suddenly realizing that the question was not purely rhetorical and that a response was expected, mumbled, "No, of course not, Comrade."

"And you are still wondering why I am moving up our timetable, Zhu? You must be an even greater dullard than I suspected."

"Of course, Comrade, we will strike at our enemies when they least expect it! Now I recognize your genius for what it is! How could I have been so blind?" Zhu briefly considered dropping to the polished tile floor and dashing his forehead against it several times for emphasis but quickly dismissed the contemplated gesture as perhaps a bit overdone. "Yes, we will hit them with the Red Whippet before their beaches are fully defended," hoping that his little military analogy would be appreciated by Lin. "We will take them by surprise, and all the plans of the fascist mad dog Burnside will be foiled at the outset!"

"Precisely, Zhu. Perhaps you are not so stupid as I had assumed."

"I assure you, Comrade Lin, I am at least as stupid as you had thought, perhaps even more so! It took only your keen insights to bring it to light."

"Enough, Zhu," said Lin, finally growing weary of Zhu's fulsome self-degradation. "Be back to me tomorrow morning with a list of all Red Whippet sedans available for immediate export to the US. Include all vehicles scheduled for production in the next ten days. The port workers will be standing by to load the cars as they come off the assembly lines. We will work twenty-four hours a day to load the ship and get them underway."

Zhu hurried from Lin's office, his mind working frantically on a means of escape. If he could only get to the United States on some pretense or another, perhaps he could find Lin Shan. She could hide me, he thought desperately, or perhaps I could seek political asylum. Just as quickly he dismissed the thoughts, realizing that he'd have little chance of arranging a trip to the US anytime in the near future.

* * *

Two pleasant and uneventful days passed at the headquarters for Red Tiger Motor Company before the notification from Beijing that, contrary to Burnside's hopeful assumption, the Red Whippet would be arriving in quantity—four thousand of them to be exact—not in three to four months, but in approximately five weeks.

Burnside was just coming through the door at nine-thirty in the morning when Suzy Johnson wordlessly handed him the fax from Zhu.

Burnside:
    Introduction of Red Whippet by Red Tiger advanced again. Expect four thousand (4,000) vehicles arrive Long Beach in five to six weeks. All certification requirements by US government have been met. You must arrange sell cars immediately upon arrival. Further shipments to follow immediately. Advise if buyers can come to port to buy cars directly.
Zhu Fei

Burnside read the fax, let it drop to his side and stared out the window. "What *is* that place over there? A nut house? It seems like they're trying to make this thing fail over here."

Suzy looked at him thoughtfully. "That may be closer to the truth than you think."

"What's that supposed to mean?"

"Well, this whole thing, the claims we made for the car, the quality problems, the whole thing was a sham from the beginning. Everybody knows the car couldn't be competitive anyplace but the home market, where there is no competition. But nobody can say it, at least if they want to keep their jobs or maybe their heads. So everybody just goes charging ahead maintaining the fantasy that we're going to sell the car in huge numbers over here and that the enterprise will he a huge success and that it will generate a lot of foreign exchange for the People's Republic. And now it seems like somehow their government has gotten your government to waive your exhaust standards. At least I know the car couldn't have passed them a couple of months ago. It couldn't even come close." She had the uncomfortable feeling that she was implicated in the diplomatic agreement to grant the apparent waiver. "So now everything's being rushed like crazy to make sure you won't have time to get your organization ready. I'm kind of thinking out loud right now, Sid, but I think scapegoats are being sought for the inevitable failure, which the party and the company management would rather attribute to a marketing or distribution failure in the US company than to the actual product and any shortcomings it may have. That way their only failure will be personnel

selection and the subsequent failure to get the US company up and running in time. I would guess that Zhu will be in a fair amount of trouble at
this point. And you'll be blamed, though there really isn't anything they
can do to you, other than dismiss you."

Burnside stared at her. "You really think that's what happening?"

"I can't say for sure, but it seems to be the most likely conclusion one
could come to."

"You don't seem too upset about this, Suzy."

"Well, I'm not exactly happy about it, but on the other hand, I'd much
rather be here than getting caught up in the denunciations back home.
Like you, nothing really too tragic can happen to me. Of course, overall,
getting involved in this whole strange situation is certainly the most wonderful thing that's ever happened to me, so I guess I can kind of view it as
a disinterested spectator."

"Yeah, well, I guess I better start getting my resume updated," said
Burnide absently. "It looks like this thing is gonna blow sky-high sometime in the next four or five weeks.

"Well, it's possible there's another version of events, Sid, but I can't
imagine what it could be. I mean, perhaps there's a special export version
of the Red Whippet, build to much higher quality standards that meets
your government requirements, but why they would maintain total secre-
cy over such a thing I don't know."

Burnside looked at her thoughtfully. "Nah, I doubt it, you're probably
exactly right. This thing's gonna crash and burn, and they're setting me up
as the fall guy. Hey, one thing I can do, just like the guys in Detroit, pay
myself a huge bonus out of our payroll account just as the company's goin'
down the tube. Hell, it's the American way!" Suddenly he began to laugh
uproariously. "Me, Sid Burnside, I'm gonna bring down the whole
Chinese automobile industry! I deserve a bonus!"

"Well, seriously, Sid, nobody in this country will hold you reponsible,
everybody over here will know what really happened. The official version
at the home company is really just for internal consumption inside China.
This shouldn't have any real effect on your career in the industry. You'll be
able to get a another job after this. I just feel sorry for Zhu and some of
the people around him. I hope he doesn't end up in a re-education camp."

"Well, if you're right I want to make sure everybody over here really
knows the whole story. And that means we ought to make every effort to
get these cars actually delivered to some dealers and retail customers. In

fact, I'll tell you what, let's send a letter to Zhu this morning, congratulating him on moving up the timetable and asking for five cars to be airfreighted over to give to the automotive press. I know one of the guys over at *Road and Track* and the automotive editor of the LA Times. We'll make sure the world knows about this car."

Suzy said nothing for a long moment. "I think that's a very intelligent move, Sid. Let's send it right away."

Three hours later, while Suzy Johnson and Sid Burnside were enjoying a pleasant lunch at Sammy's Country Barbecue, Zhu was sweatily reading the just translated fax from Red Tiger Motor Company, which congratulated him on so speedily getting the Red Whippet ready for export and requesting the immediate air shipment of five examples for evaluation by the automotive press. The memo concluded by pointing out that favorable press evaluations could have more impact than any amount of money that Red Tiger could spend on advertising and marketing incentives. It further advised him that though they were signing up dealers in California, they were investigating the possibility of getting a California retail license themselves in order to retail the vehicles as they came into the ports of entry. The fax ended with the exhortation, "Send more as quickly as possible!"

This was hardly the response Zhu had expected from the ostensible wrecker Burnside. He couldn't think of how to present this to Lin, but realized that nothing could be gained by delaying his request to see him. He decided to simply acknowledge his puzzlement, pointing out that Burnside clearly was an enemy agent of consummate subtlety and cunning. Likely he was the very one, as Lin had suggested, who had unearthed the Chinese plot to flood the US market with counterfeit Cabbage Patch dolls, thus destroying the entire Taiwanese toy industry—the very mainstay of the Taiwanese economy, in Beijing's view—in one massive, master stroke.

* * *

While the faxes were flitting back and forth across the Pacific in a near-caricature of an Errol Flynn swordfight, Sherry Maxwell was sitting across the table from Jake Dougherty in the country club at which Maxwell had

had his "sudden acceleration" incident in the golf cart. To Dougherty's relief, the cart had not been seriously damaged by its brief immersion in the water hazard, and particularly in view of Dougherty's subtantial outlay of that day for food and drink, the club didn't charge him for the repairs. "So, what're we gonna do, Sherry?" asked Dougherty, finally growing a bit weary of Maxwell's requirement for continual business lunches and dinners. Maxwell took a substantial swallow, then put his martini glass down on the table.

"We're gettin' close, Jake. I'm about ready to issue you our standard letter of intent, assuming we can get together on the timetable for making the facility commitments we're gonna need. Why don't we talk about it over lunch and then maybe play a little golf and finish our business this afternoon?"

Dougherty groaned inwardly, knowing how the afternoon likely would end, with him driving Maxwell back to his hotel, then half walking and half carrying him to his room, to be poured into bed. He resolved to keep Sherry well away from any of the controls for the golf cart this time. "Yeah, what the hell, let's do that, Sherry. Ya got the letter with ya?"

Maxwell reached inside the little leather portfolio he carried and produced a photocopied form letter. "This is it, everybody gets the same letter, Jake. We just fill in the blanks with the specifics of like who you are, the timetables, the planning volumes, and all that stuff."

"You're gonna grant me an exclusive territory, aren't ya? I mean, I'm agreein' to do a lot for you guys, I oughtta get some something for that, make sure you're not gonna put another guy down on the next block with the Red Tiger franchise next month. I think I oughtta get an exclusive deal for all of Sacramento County."

"Well, I don't know about that, Jake, "said Sherry, seizing on the opportunity to extend the negotiations and thereby provide the potential for additional drinking and dining at Dougherty's expense. "I mean, no company I know gives defined exclusive territories for dealers. I can ask the question, Jake, but I don't know how Sid Burnside's gonna react to that. I can give him a call this afternoon if you want."

"Yeah, let's do that, while we're out on the course. Meanwhile, we can fill out the letter of intent right now. Here," he said, pulling the letter in front of him and reaching into his pocket for a pen, "I can fill in the corporate name for ya." Maxwell was a little uneasy about Jake seemingly taking control of the process, not wanting to let it move too quickly, but he could think of no specific objection. Dougherty went to work filling in the appropriate blanks. He finished with the corporate name and his own name and title, then looked up. "Whaddya think we oughtta put in for the planning volume, Sherry?"

"Well, based on your original estimate, four thousand sounds reasonable, doncha think?"

"OK, four thousand it is, Sherry," said Dougherty filling in the number, knowing full well that it was meaningless in terms of any commitments that might be expected of him. "Yeah, what the hell, I'm doin' a thousand new outta the Ford store, and these things only cost a quarter as much, seems like a reasonable volume assumption to me."

"Yeah, I agree with you," said Maxwell, wondering why sales planners always spent so much time making their estimates and juggling all those figures. Hell, this shit's easy, Maxwell told himself.

"Well, I can sign this thing right now," said Dougherty. "I guess you gotta take it back to the office and get Burnside to sign it, then send me my copy. Then I can get busy gettin' the floorplan letters from the bank and gettin' set up so you can start shippin' as soon as the cars arrive. Then you can make me an addendum, granting us an exclusive territory in Sacramento County. Fair enough?"

"Well, I guess so, as long as Sid goes along with it."

Two hours later Sherry Maxwell was dialing Sid Burnside on Jake's cell phone. They were both sitting in the golf cart, Sherry drinking a Tom Collins through a straw. "Hey, Sid, I got Jake Dougherty up here in Sacramento on a letter of intent for a planning volume of four thousand for the first year. He's gonna start on the exclusive facility in the next four months, as soon as they get zoning approval. I got the plans in my desk back in the office. Whaddya think of this exclusive territory thing, though?" Sherry's straw had hit bottom on the Tom Collins, making a loud, static-like slurping sound.

"I got some noise on this phone, Sherry," said Burnside, rapping the phone sharply against his palm. "Are you asking about the exclusive request?"

"Ah, yeah, Sid," carefully moving his glass away from the phone, lest Burnside hear the tell-tale clinking of ice cubes.

"Well, what the hell, Sherry, Saturn's doing pretty much the same thing already. I say we go with it. If this guy's putting up this way, we gotta support him. And how many cars is he gonna take the first go around?"

"Hey, that's great, Sid, and he says he wants maybe a thousand or so."

"Sounds good, Sherry, tell him he's got everything, the exclusive territory, the thousand cars, the whole thing. And we're gonna be doin' the start-up sooner than we thought. I'll fill you in tomorrow when I hear back from Beijing on the details."

"Umm, OK, Sid, I'll tell him", suddenly feeling a certain apprehension at Burnside's words. "I'll call ya tomorrow morning."

After he hung up he looked at Dougherty, then smiled in a congratulatory way. "Well, you got it, Jake, the exclusive, a ton of cars up front, everything you wanted. Let's drink to that." He went to work mixing another Tom Collins, heavy on the gin, and toasted their new enterprise.

* * *

While final arrangements for the initial launch of the Red Whippet in the US market were thus being frenziedly pulled together, Zack Johnson was picking up his parents at LAX, preparatory to a three day visit on their way to Maui. He waited for them to emerge from the baggage claim, as he sat parked alongside the curb. Presently he spotted them coming through the door, pushing a baggage cart and holding onto Lobo, the doberman, who was still wagging his stub of a tail ecstatically at being sprung from his airline travel cage and reunited with his family. Zack opened the door of his Firebird and bounded up to them, hugging his mother, then his father, while Lobo squealed with delight and tried to squeeze himself between the hugging parents and son. "Where's Suzy?" his mother asked a little breathlessly, as she looked at the Firebird and noted that it was empty.

"She's working right now, Ma," Zack answered. "She'll be home between five and six. Then she says she's gonna fix us a terrific dinner."

"Oh, that sounds wonderful, Zack. I can't wait to meet her," his mother replied with apparently sincere enthusiasm. Edith Johnson was, above all else, an eminently practical wife and mother who realized that absolutely nothing good could come of questioning, however subtly, her son's choice of a mate.

"Ah, Ma," Zack began, "Suzy may seem a little nervous when you meet her. She's really worried that you won't like her. But you know, I think within ten minutes you're gonna forget that she wasn't born here, I mean,

197

her English is so good and she's so smart and funny."

"We know you'd never make a bad choice in a woman, Zack," said his mother with a conviction she didn't altogether feel. "And we'll do our best to make her feel at ease."

"I know you will, Ma," said Zack, "and that's one of the reasons I love you both." He pulled his mother over to give her a peck on the cheek, causing Lobo to bark loudly by way of demanding similar attention.

Two hours later they were all relaxing with a drink in Zack's hot tub, discussing the state of the airline business, when they heard Suzy's Miata pull into the little driveway. A moment later they heard the front door slam, then the sound of breaking glass. "Zack?" he heard her call, with more than a note of alarm in her voice.

Abruptly he realized the source of her alarm and climbed out of the hot tub. "Ah, coming, honey, don't worry, he won't do anything," he said, walking rapidly through the kitchen to the foyer, where his bride stood, staring wide-eyed at the huge and evilly black doberman, which was eyeing her narrowly and more than a little disconcertingly. Zack pushed by Lobo and hugged her, ignoring the spreading pool of peach-flavored Snapple at his feet. At this the dog relaxed immediately and began making little mewling noises. "Go ahead and pet him, honey. He just wants to make friends." He looked at the dog. "Lobo, this is Suzy."

She reached down to pet him. "Hello, Lobo, nice dog." She looked at Zack. "I'm sorry, Zack. I just wasn't thinking that he might be here when I walked in. He scared me half to death."

"Yeah, he has that effect on most people. At least we won't have to worry about burglars for the next month while he's with us. Now, c'mon, you've met the dog, let's meet my parents."

She seemed to take a deep breath. "Yes, let's." The incident with Lobo, who was now lapping at the puddle of Snapple, had so unnerved her that she completely forgot her anxiety about meeting his parents. Zack let her precede him out onto the patio, where his parents pretended to be absorbed in conversation.

They stopped abruptly and Zack's father stood up, mouth agape. The image he hadn't been able to help forming in his mind was so at odds with the reality of the five foot six, shapely, and wholesomely beautiful Suzy Johnson that he was momentarily speechless. "Ah, you must be Suzy," he stammered.

She looked puzzled. "Suzy? No, I'm Chris." She looked at Zack accusingly. "Who's this Suzy he's talking about, Zack?"

Now Zack was momentarily speechless. But he recovered quickly and looked at his parents. "I told you she was a cutup," he said, abruptly pulling her to him and giving her a quick noogie on the scalp. She laughed, and then everybody laughed, completely breaking the tension.

Edith Johnson climbed from the hot tub. "Oh, you're right, Zack, she *is* funny, and her English *is* perfect." She looked at Suzy appraisingly, noting with approval and a twinge of envy that her daughter-in-law managed to look quite spectacular with no makeup whatever. "I'm Edith," she said holding out her hand. "I'd give you a big hug, but I'm soaking wet.

Paul Johnson held out his hand also. "I'm Paul," he said, smiling broadly and genuinely. Both of their concerns and apprehensions evaporated in that moment. They might have even understood if Zack told them that they'd married less than twenty-four hours after meeting for the first time.

"Let me just go in for a minute and clean up the mess on the floor, then I'll be right out and join you in the tub," said Suzy, afraid she'd start crying with joy and relief. Ten minutes later she reappeared in her yellow two piece and called from the kitchen door, "Can I get anybody anything before I join you?"

"Yeah, I could use another Coors, honey," said Zack. "I guess everyone else is OK."

She reappeared at the door a few moments later with a can of Coors in each hand, Paul Johnson trying his hardest to keep from ogling her as she walked gracefully over to them and handed one to Zack. Jesus, they must be feeding them better these days, he thought. This lady sure ain't no Bien Hoa bar girl.

She eased herself into the hot tub, took Zack's hand in hers, and smiled dazzlingly at her guests. "What a wonderful way to meet your inlaws, in a hot tub in California!" she said with enthusiasm. "America is so wonderful in so many ways. It's like a dream world."

"Well, you certainly seem to have adapted quickly," said Edith. "Tell me, how in the world did you learn to speak such perfect English?"

"Well, it started when I lost my parents in a mining accident. They were both coal miners and there was a collapse, or something like that. I never did get all the details."

"Oh, you poor thing," said Edith, "how old were you when that happened?"

"I was eight." Edith's mouth dropped open, but before she could speak Suzy continued. "Anyway, I was sent off to an orphanage, which really wasn't so bad. Luckily, the place they sent me was sort of a showplace for the glories of socialism. We were always getting tour groups of foreign dignitaries and high party officials going through. We were very well fed and cared for, and after I was there about a year there they gave all of us a battery of aptitude tests. I scored really high on languages, so I began training to be an English interpreter. It was very intensive, and after a year I was already pretty fluent, at least for a ten year old. We even spent a lot of time watching old American movies to hear the language spoken by Americans and to learn American expressions. But that's about it," she said, shrugging. "I guess I spent a total of over ten years in English studies, in addition to the more routine curricula for a Chinese student."

"That's amazing," said Paul Johnson. "Thirty seconds after you started talking I totally forgot that you're Chinese. I mean, I guess, that you came from China." He shook his head in tribute.

"Really, Paul, if you'd had the same type of immersion in Chinese as I had in English, you'd be able to speak it like a native. It's just that America has never placed a very high priority on learning other languages, since English is so universal."

"Well, I can read and speak German and Spanish," interjected Zack. "I just can't understand them."

Everybody stared at Zack for a moment, then laughed. "Well, husband, after that timely and profound remark, I'd better get started on making dinner."

"Oh, can I watch, Suzy?" asked Edith.

"I'd be delighted to have the company. Plus, I can show you how quick and easy Chinese cooking really is."

"Suzy, good cooks always make it look easy. It just never works out that way when I try it myself."

"Well, I don't know how good I am, but I'm pretty sure I could teach you all I know about Chinese cooking in a three day weekend or less."

Two and a half hours later they were just finishing a delightful meal of thinly sliced pork loin in some sort of a superbly flavored brown sauce, served with an assortment of stir-fried vegetables and perfectly done white rice. The meal had started with an extraordinary hot and sour soup course. "See, I told you this lady can cook," said Zack proudly. "And she's not a one-dish chef, either. Everytime she cooks, she surprises me with something new."

"You know what I'd really like, Edith?" Suzy asked brightly. "I'd like to get the recipes for some of Zack's favorite dishes, the things you used to cook for him when he was growing up."

"Oh, I'd be so happy to share those with you, Suzy. In fact, why don't I cook tomorrow night. We'll go shopping and get some stuff for one of Zack's favorite meals, and we'll do it together."

Later that night as they lay in bed in Zack's guest room, Edith looked at her husband of thirty-one years and asked, "Well, what did you think of Suzy?"

"I dunno," he hedged, "what's your feeling about her."

"I think she's wonderful, the perfect woman for Zack. You've seen how he gets bored with every other girl he's known in two weeks. I don't know what her secret is, but he's obviously absolutely ga-ga over her. I know she's not what I'd envisioned as a wife for Zack, I mean, I always just assumed that she'd be some proper WASPy young lady. Maybe Suzy's better for him."

"Well, now that you mention it," said Paul, hugely relieved that his wife approved, "if she was around all the time I don't think I'd give too much thought to too many nice WASPy girls."

"You know, Paul, I always wondered but was afraid to ask what you were doing with the women of Vietnam."

"Well, let's just say that if I'd met anybody like Suzy in Vietnam we wouldn't be lying her right now having this conversation."

She thumped him on the head with her pillow.

* * *

The following morning President Bob Carruthers was waiting impatiently for Jack Landry to show up and receive further instructions regarding his surveillance of the Johnsons. He'd already advised his secretary that he was not to be interrupted "under any circumstances, short of a nuclear attack, and then only if Washington's targeted," during his meeting with the Attorney General. I'll fix that bitch, he told himself angrily, reaching up once again to feel his still tender nose. Christ, this thing'll never be right again. It even hurts when I put on my reading glasses.

Presently Landry showed up and was ushered into the Oval Office. The president's secretary pulled the door closed behind him. Carruthers motioned for Landry to sit, then began, "Well, Jack, any change on the status of those two people in California?"

"None that we know of, Mr. President. They just seem to go to work, come home, and go out to eat once in a while. They haven't done anything suspicious, if that's what you mean."

"Hmm, interesting, Landry, very interesting," said Carruthers, unable to think of anything more telling with which to impress his attorney general. "Jack, we're coming to the most delicate phase of this operation, one which is so sensitive, so potentially explosive, that if it's not handled right it could destroy us all. We're playing for very high stakes here, Landry, and this thing'll take iron nerve to see it through. Can I count on you?" He stared at Landry with the steeliest gaze he could muster, which a neutral observer might have found downright comical, what with Carruthers' lower lip protruding petulantly and his bulbous nose twitching.

But Landry, ever the cringing sycophant, didn't hestitate. "You can count on me, Mr. President," meeting Carruther's gaze with an equally ridiculous look of squinty-eyed determination, delivered as it was through Landry's incredibly thick glasses, which magnified his rodent-like little eyes disconcertingly.

"That's good, Jack," said Carruthers, glancing left and right as if to assure himself that they were alone. "Because if you can successfully handle this assignment, there may even be a Supreme Court seat available to you. Don't count anything out, Jack. Handle this right and the sky's the limit!"

Landry's mouth gaped. "Me, a Supreme Court Justice, sir? Me?"

"Ah, it's possible, Landry, eminently possible, as long as you don't drop the ball on me."

"You can put that out of your mind, sir. I won't, I *can't*, fumble this assignment," said Landry, his voice quavering with a curious mixture of fear and excitement.

"Good, Landry, because the very fate of our great nation rests on your shoulders." Carruthers cast an involuntary glance at Landry's narrow shoulders, which fit comfortably into a size thirty-two jacket. "Now, Jack, you have to commit this to memory. There can be no written instructions, notes, reminders, anything. Do you understand?" Landry gulped uncomfortably and nodded in the affirmative. "OK, this is what we need done. Sometime in the next three weeks, Jack, I need a team to break into the house belonging to these two subversives. This is gonna have to be handled by DEA, at the very highest levels, and again, there can be no written record of anything relating to this operation. They're gonna have to get people in the drug underground, go to the prison system if they have to to get 'em, get into that house, then plant a large quantity of illegal drugs, preferably something really bad, like heroin, somewhere in the house, but someplace where the inhabitants wouldn't find it in their day to day activities. Someplace discreet." Landry nodded uncomfortably. He was becoming frightened. "Then, the next day if at all possible, I want DEA to raid the place, but it's gotta be when they're both home. Get a search warrant based on some informant's advice that these two are big time drug wholesalers. Remember, the people who pull off the break-in have to be completely reliable, know what the hell they're doing. That's the most critical element of this whole plan. And if somehow they get caught, there can be no way to trace them back to any government agency, or, obviously, to me. Now repeat all of that back to me, Landry."

After Landry complied, Carruthers nodded approvingly. "Good, Jack, you've got the idea. And remember, no notes, no written record of anything, even if it's thrown in the waste basket immediately after use. If you need to ask me anything about this operation, you're to come to this office and speak with me personally, not over the phone, you got that?" Again Landry nodded in the affirmative. "If you have no questions, the next time I want to hear from you is when your people plant the stuff, and after that, when these people are arrested. I'll handle everything from there on out. You can go now."

Landry stood up and said, with far more confidence that he felt, "You can count on me, sir." He strode purposefully out the door.

Jesus, thought Carruthers as he watched Landry leave, that's the downside of appointing shitheads like Landry. I end up with loyal morons. He shook his head in exasperation.

* * *

While Jack Landry was leaving the White House on rubbery knees, Zhu Fei was sitting across the desk from the president of The Long March People's Cooperative Automotive Manufacturing Company, Lin Cho Hsin. He'd briefly explained Burnside's fax, clearly the work of an extremely cunning and subtle counter-revolutionary wrecker, he noted, to feign enthusiasm and support for the accelerated timetable for the Red Whippet's introduction in the US market.

Lin sat silently, pressing his finger tips together as he looked toward the ceiling, his favorite contemplative pose. "Hmm," he repeated several times, apparently lost in deep thought. In truth, Lin was drawing a complete blank in trying to figure out how to best handle Burnside's request for immediate air shipment of the five press cars.

In the end his hand was somewhat forced by Zhu's assertion that, "Surely, Comrade, we could accede to this request. After all, what could be more beneficial to the Red Whippet's success in America than favorable commentary by their automotive press? No doubt Burnside is thinking exactly this, which is why he has cleverly attempted to throw us off the scent of his perfidy with this perfectly logical and reasonable request."

"Hmm, hmm," repeated Lin, still looking at the ceiling.

Zhu immediately realized the dilemma he'd handed Lin, what with possibly giving the world advance notice of the Red Whippet's abysmal quality, total lack of government mandated safety features, and an engine that emitted pre-1960 levels of pollutants. Even between themselves, Zhu knew that it was imperative to maintain the posture that the Red Whippet represented the very pinnacle of automotive technology. To turn the car over to automotive journalists would pop that little bubble, shifting the blame for the coming debacle from Burnside to the parent company. "On the other hand, Comrade, it has just occurred to me that Burnside might have an unhealthy association with the automotive press in America, that for a price they will say anything he wishes them to say. Remember what happened to the last market entry in the United States to come from a progressive socialist state," said Zhu, warming to his argument. "The Yugo was destroyed by wreckers within their press corps, who doubtless were paid handsomely to slander this fine product! While admittedly it was not so fine as the Red Whippet, it nonetheless should have been a market leader. I fear that is where we could be heading should we accede to Burnside's request that we supply the Red Whippet to their press members, who could then defeat all our efforts at the outset." Zhu watched Lin carefully for a reaction, and was gratified to see that his boss seemed to be nodding in the affirmative. "I am sorry, Comrade, I am far too simple to recommend a solution to this dilemma. I must leave it to your wisdom to guide us." He bowed his head in a gesture of respect for Lin's legendary intellect.

"Hmm, hmm," repeated Lin once again. Finally he looked directly at Zhu, and put his hands palm down on the desk. "Either way, it appears that we lose, Zhu. If we supply the requested cars, we run the risk that Burnside has cleverly arranged with members of the press to have them release highly unfavorable test results and comments. If we do not, we forego the opportunity for some extremely favorable advance notice for our products, which as your cunning wrecker Burnside has noted, would be invaluable to our marketing efforts. I am beginning to see how this man managed to deceive you, Zhu. He is very cunning, very subtle. I don't doubt he could fool even a highly intelligent interviewer, let alone you. Perhaps I have been too harsh in my denunciations of your negligence."

"I am grateful for your observations, Comrade. Yes, I believe this man could have tricked even a clever and experienced interrogator, let alone a simple fellow such as I."

"Hmm," said Lin once again, "I shall have give to this some additional thought. I'll summon you when I've made my decision, which should be within the week." He waved his hand dismissively. "You may go now." Zhu left just slowly enough to maintain some modicum of dignity in his departure.

*   *   *

Sid Burnside, having returned once again to his Hyundai files, scanned Hyundai's original bank floorplan commitment letter into his computer, then changed the letterhead, address, and phone number to that of Red Tiger Motor Company, and printed the resulting document. "Hey, Suzy," he called out, "when you get a minute, could you run me about twenty copies o' this letter? What Burnside was referring to was the form letter, which then had to be transcribed onto bank letterhead, committing a dealer's bank to pay the drafts for the cars submitted by Red Tiger Motors to the dealer's bank. Cash drafting, as it was called, had become the standard means of having dealers pay for their cars from the various manufacturers.

Burnside wanted to get one of the sample letters off to Jake Dougherty, along with his letter of intent granting him the Red Tiger franchise. Once they had secured drafting privileges from a dealer's bank, Red Tiger could draft immediately for any amount up to the dealer's credit line commitment. Red Tiger would then remit the agreed upon transfer price per vehicle to the parent company's bank in Hong Kong. Thus could the Long March People's Cooperative Automotive Manufacturing Company be paid for its cars practically the same day as the cars were allocated to the dealers. Well, thought Burnside, at least we'll have one guy in place to ship the things to when they arrive.

Actually, Sherry Maxwell, in his relentless quest for free lunches and dinners, had managed to scare up four more likely prospects, whose applications he had submitted to the Chino office. With luck, thought Burnside, we should be able sign up enough guys to put a reasonable sized dent in the first four thousand cars and keep the Chinese off my back for at least three or four more weeks.

"Hey, Suzy," Burnside called out as she walked over to the copier, "how'd it go with your inlaws? They gone yet?"

"They were wonderful, Sid, just the nicest people. I hope I made a good impression on them. Zack put them on the plane this morning for Hawaii."

"Well, that's nice. And I'm sure you made a great impression on them. I mean, if you weren't already married, I'd try to introduce you to my son."

"Oh, that's so sweet of you, Sid. Is he married yet?"

"Yeah, he was for a while. It didn't last long. Luckily, they didn't have any kids to fight over."

"Well, those things happen sometimes." She decided to change the subject "Sid, do you think we can get enough dealers to take these cars from the initial shipment?"

"Well, we can probably get enough signed up in the next four or five weeks to eat up a lot of 'em. Most of these guys'll try anything, as long as the requirements aren't too steep. I mean, if they can get the franchise without any real investment, they figure what the hell, what's it gonna cost me? So yeah, we can probably work our way through the majority of the first shipment. After that, though, all bets are off." He paused. "Suzy, just how bad are these things. I mean, are they just simple, maybe a little crude, but basically pretty rugged little cars? Or are they really just junk that'll fall apart in a couple of months?"

"Well, Sid, I never really had much experience with cars before, so I maybe don't have much basis of comparison. But if I look at the experience Zack and I have with our cars, I mean, since I've been here nothing's ever gone wrong with either of them, you just turn the key and go, and everything always works the way it's supposed to. Somehow, that's not exactly the ownership experience with the Red Whippet. Everybody who has one always laughs, or maybe cries, about always having to carry around spare parts and tools. They're not like the American or Japanese cars you have here, where you can start out on any trip knowing that you'll get where you're going without a problem."

Burnside stared at her. "That bad, huh?"

"Well, like I said, unless there's some higher quality export version, which I never heard about, even in rumors, yes, they're really supposed to be that bad. I don't think it will go over all that well, to be perfectly frank. But really, Sid, you've known pretty much all along that was the case. You just assumed that it would be years before the cars got here, which I have to admit seemed a reasonable assumption. I even shared it."

"Yeah, well I guess maybe I was clutching at straws."

"Don't worry, Sid, we can find something else after Red Tiger self-destructs. We'll be OK."

"Yeah, maybe," said Sid Burnside glumly, "you're still young and you got marketable skills. I'm just an old has-been, like Maxwell. Wonder what old Sherry'll do," he wondered absently.

"Oh, Sid, I hate to see you worry this way. I think all we can do is just go along and do the best we can with what they give us to work with."

"Yeah, I guess. You know, I still can't imagine why the government would waive its emission requirements, or especially the safety standards. They even got the CARB (California Air Resources Board) to go along with it. Somebody back in China must have a hell of a lot of pull with the people in Washington. I was talking to a buddy over at Honda about it yesterday, and he says their management is totally freaking out, and I imagine the guys in Detroit are doing the same thing. Can you imagine the union bosses at UAW? I mean, that guy Carruthers and his cronies count on their support."

"Well, Sid," said Suzy slowly, "I'm sure we'll find out about it at some point. But you're right, it certainly does seem peculiar. Are you sure they've never done anything like this before? It seems like a big political risk they're taking for not much gain."

"Not that I know of," Burnside replied with a shrug. "Well, I imagine we'll be finding out the story eventually."

Burnside would be proved right, and rather sooner than later.

* * *

Penny Twombly looked at Nate Garmin happily. "Oh, Nate, wasn't it wonderful how Bob handled the CARB with just a couple of quick phone calls. Oh, God, I admire the way that man gets things done, he knows exactly where everybody's hot button is," she gushed. She was referring to the manner in which Carruthers had called the two California senators and at first sought their support gently, but upon sensing a bit of resistance assured them, both members of his own party, that if they balked they'd seen the last of his campaign support for them, especially seeing as his time was limited and that he'd prefer to spend it in the northeast next time around. He then called the governor and offered to send him a sample from his raw FBI file of thirty-two years earlier, which contained an unsubtantiated allegation to the effect that he'd paid for an abortion for a fourteen year old neighbor, at a time when the governor-to-be was twenty-five. Less than forty-eight hours later the governor had issued his own executive order to CARB, waiving the emission standards for the Red Whippet, ostensibly to be reinstated after a period of four months.

"See, Nate, it's all moving along great, the Chinese will begin selling their car here in no time and proving our point about needing a coordinated industrial policy. Once people see the benefits for themselves, it'll be an easy sell. We just have to let Bob handle it. That man is a political genius."

"Yeah, I guess he is," said Garmin without great enthusiasm.

"Oh, Nate, I didn't say that to minimize your contribution. Let's face it. You're the brilliant strategic thinker, the planner. Bob's the salesman. You develop the product, Bob's the guy who goes out and sells it. They're both completely different talents, and both completely necessary. You two are a tremendous team, Nate."

"Gee, d'ya really think so?" asked Nate Garmin, brightening. "I mean, sometimes I get the feeling that Bob thinks I'm, uh, a little slow, you know?"

"Oh, that's silly, Nate, Bob doesn't think you're slow at all. He thinks you're deliberate, that you don't jump to conclusions," said Penny, though not totally believing it. "You never shoot from the hip, Nate. You take careful aim, and then you blow 'em away."

"Yeah, I guess that's true," said Garmin, likening Penny's description of him to that of a gimlet-eyed Texas gunfighter. "Yeah, that's me, taking careful aim, like with my book, EARTH OUT OF BALANCE, and now with the DILDO. Then *POW!*"

Once again Penny wondered about Garmin's strange reference to the "dildo", which she'd first heard uttered by Ambassador Li. She wanted Garmin to explain himself but decided that perhaps it was best not to know the details.

"Ah, that's right, Nate, *POW!* Just like you said."

* * *

Chapter 8

The two FBI agents assigned to the surveillance detail for the Johnsons had made their passes by their house and Red Tiger motors less and less frequent, lest their presence arouse suspicion. They did take the precaution of switching cars occasionally, from Bill's black Taurus to Fred's Buick LeSabre. But overall, the agents found themselves looking in on the Johnsons for only a few seconds at a time, though they still followed Zack to the airport twice, getting themselves stuck in an LA traffic jam coming back both times. Both were completely bored with the assignment, and both realized that eventually they'd be spotted by a suspect alert to the possibility of surveillance. The infrequency of their surveillance caused them to completely miss both the arrival and departure of Zack's mother and father, and, of course, the arrival and non-departure of their outsize doberman pinscher, which had taken to sleeping on the bed next to Suzy when Zack was flying an overnight trip. This she found rather comforting, having quickly been indoctrinated by the six o'clock news with the notion that America in general and LA in particular were exceedingly dangerous places, with muggers, rapists, murderers, carjackers, and kidnappers skulking around every corner and lurking behind every bush. She couldn't quite understand how she hadn't witnessed a single violent crime, or any sort of crime for that matter, since her arrival in the United States, at least if one excluded Vera Hawkins' camera-flogging of Zhu Fei.

Now it was approaching lunchtime as they cruised by the Red Tiger parking lot, noting that Suzy's red Miata was still parked outside. "Whaddya say we get something to eat, Bill?" asked Fred. "I'd like to try that barbecue place, Sammy's. My mouth's been watering for some good barbecue every since that day we followed this Johnson lady there."

"Yeah, what the hell," said Bill. "Why don't we do that? Even if she walks in the place I doubt if she'd recognize us, plus I'd like to see if she could. It'll tell us whether she's alert to being tailed."

Fifteen minutes later they were parking in Sammy's parking lot, looking quite out of place in their jackets and ties, a costume absolutely necessary not so much for proper decorum but rather to provide concealment for their FBI- issue Smith and Wesson .40 caliber automatics. They locked their car and walked into Sammy's, headed for an unoccupied table and sat down. Presently Mary came over to take their order, immediately making both of them as lawmen. "H'lo, there", she said, smiling broadly and whitely. "Can I get you something to drink while you're lookin' at the menu?"

"Well," said Bill, "I think we can order right now." They both ordered barbecued pork on a roll and a large iced tea. They were just being served when Suzy walked through the door with Sid Burnside. "Hey, Fred, don't look around, but that Johnson lady just walked in with that guy she was with last time we were watching this place. Damn, she's a looker! Too bad you can't see her, buddy."

"Hi, Sammy," they heard her call. Bill watched, a bit enviously, as the one called Sammy approached their table, grinning toothily.

"Hey, Suzy, Sid, how ya'll doing today?" he asked. "We got a specially good batch o' barbecued beef we can make you a nice big sandwich with, and some fresh slaw I jus' made this mornin'."

"Oh, that sounds so good, that's what I'll have," said Suzy. Sid nodded also. "And Sammy, you're still coming over Saturday night, right?" she asked.

"Darn right, lady. You better make a lot o' whatever you're gonna make. We both of us like to eat."

"You know, Fred," said Bill quietly, "if that lady's some kind of bad actor, she's managed to short-circuit all of my instincts. She looks about as sweet and innocent as they come. It looks like her and this guy Sammy are some kind of friends. That probably explains why she was in here that morning."

"Doesn't that strike you as a little odd, Bill, a gorgeous chick like that bein' friends with a middle-aged bro?" said Fred, not turning around.

"Hell, I dunno, why's that so weird? She's new here, she probably hasn't had time to develop any prejudices, plus she's a non-white herself." He was beginning to have additional doubts about this rather strange surveillance assignment, suddenly wanting to believe that the beautiful Mrs. Johnson was innocent of any wrongdoing. Abruptly he decided to get up and head to the men's room, just to see if he could get a reaction from her. "I gotta take a leak," he said to his partner, then stood up noisily, glanced at Suzy Johnson, who didn't seem to take any notice of him, and headed for the lavatory.

Two minutes later, as he headed back toward his table, he made brief eye contact with her, got a brief but charming smile in return, but no discernible sense of alarm or recognition. She certainly hadn't avoided his eyes, as had certain other diners, for whom the jackets and ties identified them almost certainly as cops. "Hell," he said as he sat down, "she doesn't even know we're heat. This whole thing is some sort of wild goose chase. I say we go back, make our report, and ask to be taken off this thing. We're not gonna learn any more about this chick and her hubby, cause there ain't nothing to learn, plus we keep hangin' around, they're likely to call the cops on *us*."

And two hours later Fred and Bill were in the office of their supervisor, doing as Bill had suggested, only to be told in no uncertain terms that they were to maintain their surveillance of the Johnsons until told otherwise. "Why?" Fred had asked. "Somebody upstairs got the hots for this chick or something? What the hell, that seems as likely as anything else right now," never dreaming just how close to the truth he was.

* * *

The following Sunday afternoon Sammy and his wife Kate came to the Johnson's for a late afternoon dinner, a ballgame between the Dodgers and San Francsisco, and a bit of relaxation in their hot tub. "You know," said Sammy to his wife, "we gotta get one o' these things." He was sitting with his legs stretched out, examining his toenails, which protruded from the water.

"Yeah, we should," she agreed, "and you wouldn't even have to learn to swim," referring to Sammy's standard objection to putting in a swimming pool in their backyard.

"Yeah, they're really a nice way of relaxing, better'n a pool if you ask me," said Zack, "unless you wanna be able to do laps. And they don't cost an arm and leg. Plus, you can read in it, watch TV, whatever."

"I think I'd better start dinner," Suzy announced, starting to rise. "Does anybody need another beer?"

Sammy and Kate picked up their cans to check the contents. "Naw, Suzy, we're OK for now, but I think I'd like to watch you get dinner, if you don't mind"

"Me, too," echoed Kate.

"No, I'd be delighted," said Suzy, wrapping herself in a towel and handing two more to her guests. "And again, don't worry about Lobo, Kate. He's perfectly harmless." When the Lamberts had arrived at the house, Sammy had displayed no apprehension whatever when confronted with the huge doberman. He'd simply squatted down and invited the dog over to sniff his hand, then petted him vigorously. Kate, however, had to be coaxed out of the foyer, and when she'd left the hot tub to visit the bathroom, she insisted that Zack walk her to the bathroom door.

Ten minutes later everybody was in the kitchen, watching Suzy expertly and quickly bone a chicken. "What's this stuff?" asked Sammy, picking up a bottle of brown liquid and sniffing it.

"Actually, it's not exactly a Chinese invention. It's a sauce made of fermented fish, called *nuoc mam*. It's a Vietnamese concoction that's made its way into a lot of authentic Chinese cooking lately. Our version is a lot milder than the Vietnamese. I think it imparts a very nice flavor to a lot of dishes."

"If you say so," said Sammy a little doubtfully.

"Hey, I promised you, nothing weird," replied Suzy, smiling. "You can see for yourself, this buzzard I'm cutting up is clean and healthy,"

"Oh, God, Suzy, sometimes your sense of humor goes over the line, really," said Zack, feigning putting a finger down his throat. Sammy and Kate, however, laughed uproariously.

Two hours later they were finishing a delicious stir-fried chicken with rice and assorted vegetables dinner, Sammy making the observation that, contrary to popular belief, he wouldn't be able to eat for at least two days. "You see," said Suzy, "there's really nothing easier or quicker than cooking in a wok. The secret's using really high heat and not overdoing anything." With that, they repaired to the Johnson's living room, where Suzy poured each of them a small cordial glass of Johnny Walker Black, straight up. "This will help our digestion," she announced. They sat and talked for a while about life in China, soliciting Suzy's impressions of the United States, and whether she'd be allowed to return to China to visit. At one point Sammy got up and walked over near the TV set and VCR, stretching and patting his stomach. Seeing where he was standing reminded Suzy of the cable TV tape Sammy had done. She got up, walked over to where he was standing, picked it up and handed it to him. "Oh, here, Sammy, that was a wonderful recipe you did on this show. I wrote it all down. Really, you should have your own cooking show."

"Oh, yeah, hey, I'm glad you enjoyed it," he replied, taking the tape in hand, then putting it down on top of the VCR. "I oughtta make a copy of these tapes some time."

They chatted for a while longer, then Sammy and Kate finally stood up and announced that they had to be going. "Next time we get together it'll be at our house," said Kate. Sammy walked over and retrieved his tape, one of several that sat on top of the VCR.

After they'd gone Suzy said, "I hope they really liked their dinner. They're so nice, I really hope we see them often."

"Well, I think most people'd put up with us just to sample your cooking once in a while," said Zack. "I'm sure they'll be back. Hey, let's get naked and go back in the tub!"

* * *

As the Johnsons were bidding farewell to their guests, Zhu Fei was again in the office of Lin Cho Hsin, who'd called him in to announce his decision regarding Sid Burnside's latest request for press cars. "Zhu," he began, "I have given a great deal of thought to this man Burnside's request. I have concluded that the risk in giving the press in the United States advance notice of the Red Whippet's performance is too great. On reflection, I have realized that subjecting the Red Whippet to their usual test procedures may prove so traumatic to them that they almost certainly will attempt to sabotage it themselves, even without the intervention of the wrecker Burnside. Doubtless this man realizes this himself. Their journalists would immediately perceive the threat that the Red Whippet represents to established automakers and to their very economy itself. They will see it as their patriotic duty to do everything they can to denigrate this remarkable product, to keep their public from experiencing it for themselves. After all, we must assume that many of them are fanatical patriots. Just look at the unswerving support they give to the great buffoon, The One Eyed Pink

Python. No, Zhu, these people will do everything in their power to prevent the humiliation of their auto industry in the eyes of the world! We cannot play into their hands! They will get no cars to test until the public has been made aware, through simple word of mouth, of the superiority of the Red Whippet."

"My thoughts, exactly," cried Zhu. "In fact, I was on my way to tell you of my conclusions when you summoned me!"

"Are you saying that you have come to the same conclusion?"

"Well, not exactly," said Zhu, backpedaling. "Ah, what I meant was that the wrecker Burnside would doubtless be planning to corrupt the automotive press, perhaps even with offers of free unlimited use of the Red Whippet for their families. But I confess, it did not occur to me that they already might have been corrupted by their reactionary commitment to capitalism. It took your remarkable wisdom to perceive this much greater threat."

This seemed to mollify Lin. "That is why I am president of this company and you are merely in charge of export sales." He said it as though sales were a minor, even demeaning, function. "No, Zhu, we do not pay you to exercise your meager intellect. You would do well to remember that. Now, you will contact Burnside and advise him only that we can spare no cars for members of the press. Every available car must be sold immediately to the public. You will give no hint that we have seen through his evil designs and those of America's press corps."

"Thank you for showing me the way, Comrade. I will attend to it immediately."

* * *

As Zhu and Lin were plotting to disrupt the sabotage of the Great Reactionary Wrecker Burnside, Huang Lih Sheng, captain of the 98,000 ton container ship Rising Star, waited impatiently for the river pilot to board and guide his vessel up to Tientsin, where he was to take on a cargo of some 3,900 Red Whippet cars from the Long March People's Cooperative Automotive Manufacturing Company for shipment to the United States, specifically to the port of Long Beach in California. The Rising Star could maintain seventeen knots fully loaded, making it approximately three and a half weeks for the crossing.

Captain Huang had never transported motor vehicles before, except individually. Since his vessel was configured for containers and general cargo, the cars would have to be sling-loaded one at a time, a lengthy and tedious task. China possessed no dedicated car carriers, known as RO-RO (roll-on roll-off) ships, such as all the Japanese and European automakers used. Huang had inquired as to why Long March didn't simply strike a lease agreement with Toyota or perhaps Nissan for transport of the vehicles. He was informed that it was vital that the cars arrive under the flag of the People's Republic, in a Chinese ship, and that in any event the Japanese RO-RO ships were fully committed for the foreseeable future. Huang had started to object that the Rising Star had been built in Yokohama, so what difference did it make what flag it was flying? He was brusquely told to stick to commanding his ship and to leave political decisions to those empowered to make them.

Despite his initial reservations, Huang was beginning to enjoy the thought of visiting the United States, especially that most decadent of places, California. He had never been there and wanted to visit Disneyland, plus the visit would afford him the chance to escape his constantly hectoring, complaining, termagant wife, hopefully for at least two months. He was reasonably sure the off-loading in Long Beach would take at least a week, time enough for him to arrange a liaison with a young lady in the Chinese section of Los Angeles, which he was told was quite populous. He was sure his position as captain of one of China's largest ships would impress any young lady.

His fantasies were interrupted abruptly by his first officer. "Pilot's aboard, Captain. He'll be on the bridge with you in couple of minutes."

In maybe a week we'll be underway, Huang told himself. Tientsin direct to Hollywood!

* * *

Sid Burnside went to the went to the fax machine to pick up the paper that had fallen in to the catch basket. It was, as he had hoped, from Zhu. The two paragraph message simply told him that no press cars were to be air-freighted and that the press would be supplied with test units at the appropriate time. Until then, all cars were to be sold only to retail customers, and under no circumstances was Burnside, on his own initiative, to supply cars to members of the press. Burnside stood by the fax machine, re-reading the message. Finally he looked up at Suzy Johnson. "I think you better have a look at this, Suzy."

She walked over to him, eyebrows raised quizzically. She took the fax and read it quickly. "I'd say they don't want anybody making an independent judgment of the cars, at least until they can land a big shipment of them here. They don't want to disrupt the fantasy that the Red Whippet is a world class car. Their version of events over here will be that we failed to adequately prepare our organization, and that's why it failed. But I suppose we'd already surmised that."

"Well, you know what?" said Burnside. "I say we start goin' through the motions of getting this thing up and running. We'll hire some people, like that guy White Feather. In fact, see if you can get him on the phone. Have him come in here as quick as possible, like today if you can arrange it. And I know how we could sign up a bunch of dealers quick, too. We'll get some foxy young chicks to get out there and peddle the franchise for us. Not you, Suzy. I need you here. Plus Zack'd probably wring my neck."

"Yes, I think he might," she said, smiling. "Do you want to respond to Zhu's message today?"

"Yeah, let's send him a fax begging for some press cars. We'll tell him the automotive press is foaming at the mouth for the chance to test the Red Whippet, that our credibility will be suspect if we don't comply with their request." In truth, there had been no press queries at all, save one call from David Versical of the *Automotive News,* simply asking for a best guess as to when the Red Whippet launch might be forthcoming. That had been nearly four weeks earlier, before the drastic acceleration of the timetable. Since the initial announcement of the Red Whippet, with the attendant outlandish claims for its low emission levels and spectacularly low fuel consumption, Red Tiger had simply gone off the radar screens. Even the executive order, granting Red Tiger a temporary exemption from safety and emissions testing, failed to create a lasting stir. This was partly because the mainstream press was not in the habit of broadly covering potentially controversial foreign policy decisions by their favorite president, but also because the order did not name Red Tiger or the Red Whippet specifically but simply referred to the cars as "motor vehicles originating in the People's Republic of China," of which there was currently none. This, of course, implied that the waiver—doubtless a diplomatic gesture of no import—

effectively had no meaning. Even Detroit, preoccupied with resisting the rapidly growing market share of the Japanese, quickly forgot about it.

And so Suzy and Burnside quickly composed the return fax, asking both for more cars to be shipped ASAP, plus requesting reconsideration of the previous request for air shipment of at least five press vehicles to be turned over for immediate testing by the automotive press. The fax concluded with Burnside's remark that, "it will seriously handicap our marketing efforts in the United States if we refuse to cooperate with the automotive press. Indeed, many excellent dealer prospects will base their decision of whether to represent Red Tiger largely on the strength of favorable test results. We *must* comply with these requests."

"Well, that puts the ball back in Zhu's court," said Burnside, actually beginning the enjoy the ridiculous game. "Now, where can we get some good-looking young ladies to get out and sign some guys up for the franchise? I mean, you just can't put an ad in the *Automotive News* or *Los Angeles Times,* specifying "foxes only need apply.""

Suzy chuckled. "Why don't you call the dating service? They certainly did right by me."

"Yeah, I'd like to get that blond chick who busted Zhu's head."

"Are you serious?"

"Well, yeah, I guess so, she's the type I wouldn't mind getting for this particular assignment."

"I know her," said Suzy, quite seriously.

"You mean from that night?"

"No, she's been to our house. She came over one night to ask Zack if he could help her get a job as a flight attendant. We all ended up having dinner and sitting in the hot tub. She works in a pet store in Hollywood. I wouldn't be surprised if she knew some other girls as well. But Sid, are you sure this is a good idea? I mean, she's very nice, I think, but I'm not sure she's got any qualifications for any job we could offer."

"Are you kidding? She fits our requirements to a "T." She's gorgeous, blonde, and probably illiterate. She's every fifty year old car dealer's wet dream. Ah, I mean," said Burnside, stammering.

"I think I know what you mean," said Suzy, smiling faintly.

"Ah, I mean, we could sell out the entire first boatload with her and a couple of others like her on board!"

"No doubt. Well, I guess I could get Zack to get in touch with her, if you really think this is a good idea."

Factory Guys

"Trust me, for our purposes, it's a brilliant idea, a stroke of true genius."

"Well, OK, and you still want me to call this man White Feather?"

"Yeah, sure. We at least oughtta talk to him."

* * *

And so, the following day, at ten o'clock in the morning, a rather strange apparition presented itself to the management staff of Red Tiger Motors in Chino, California. Suzy looked up at the three loud knocks delivered against the door frame to see a rather tall man, bare to the waist and wearing a breechcloth over his buckskin pants, stride into her office. His hair was shoulder-length, his face painted bizarrely, and he wore a brightly colored headband with a large white goosefeather in it. "Ah, you must be Mr. White Feather," she said, managing to maintain a straight face.

"I am. And you are?" the man demanded in a rather deep voice.

"My name's Suzy Johnson, and I'm the personnel director of Red Tiger Motors. I, ah, gather that you're what they call a Native American."

"You have a keen sense of the obvious, Ms. Johnson."

"Well, ah, let's just say the headband with the feather was a dead giveaway."

"Do you see anything inappropriate about my clothing or ceremonial paint?"

With that Suzy Johnson could contain herself no longer. She began to giggle, then broke out uncontrollable laughter. Sid Burnside, who had once attended a sensitivity training seminar during his brief stint with Mitsubishi Motor of America a couple of years earlier, and who had been speechless during the rather odd exchange of greetings, felt a sudden alarm at her laughter. He rushed up to White Feather. "I'm Sid Burnside," he said, offering his hand, which White Feather ignored as he continued to stare at Suzy Johnson. "Don't mind her, she's just arrived from China. She lacks, ah, sensitivity for minorities."

White Feather turned to stare at him imperiously. At length he spoke. "I should say so. I cannot believe that any company would have such an individual in charge of personnel selection. I am going to wait outside while she composes herself. When I return I do not expect to be offended by another of her racial slurs." With that, he turned and strode from the room, went down the hall, out the front door, and took up a station in front of the building, arms folded over his chest and feet spread, as if blocking access to the office.

Suzy finally stopped laughing, then looked out the door and down the hall and saw White Feather standing in front of the building. Her laughter redoubled. "He's still standing out there," she gasped. "Oh, this must be something Zack thought up as a practical joke," she said, though on reflection she couldn't imagine how Zack might have engineered such a strange prank.

In fact, Edward White Feather, who was actually one-eighth American Indian, the rest of his lineage being comprised of Irish, Sicilian, and Hungarian, with a small percentage of his gene pool contributed by an actual DAR member, had made a minor career of actually filing, or threatening to file, EEOC claims against various employers and prospective employers. Most had been unsuccessful, but between a few small settlements coerced from various firms, some unemployment claims, and a bit of public welfare, White Feather, whose original name was Edward Hruska, had managed to keep body and soul comfortably together. He still hoped for the one big hit, the huge settlement of a discrimination claim, that would pave his way to a life of ease and decadent luxury. This had thus far eluded him. He had queried Red Tiger primarily on the basis that it was a new, foreign owned company that might be inexperienced in EEOC matters and thus easy to trip up on some minor interview or application technicality and thus become a potential victim for intimidation.

After perhaps twenty minutes, Sid Burnside, who was genuinely quite concerned about being embroiled by White Feather in some sort of lawsuit, went out to the front door and called out to him. "Mr. White Feather, why don't you come back in and talk with us. You have to realize, Suzy's brand new in this business, she doesn't know all the ins and outs of how we handle minorities in this country."

White Feather maintained his pose, not turning around. He was sure he had just caught Burnside in a potentially lucrative lie. "Do you expect me to believe that this woman is not a native American, ah, I mean, ah, that she wasn't born here." White Feather was momentarily flustered by his temporary misassignment of Suzy Johnson to the wrong group. "How, then, does she speak such perfect English?"

"She trained for ten years as an interpreter, that's what she was when she came here. She speaks better English than we do."

"You're now saying that my English is inadequate, that even a Chinese immigrant is preferable to a Native American?" demanded White Feather, who in truth likely would have been indignantly stoned to death or burned at the stake by real full-blooded members of any of the tribal groups for whom he claimed to speak.

"Oh, Christ, c'mon," said Burnside, finally growing annoyed and realizing that White Feather was merely trying to shake him down. "Hey, look, you can stand out there all day if you want. It gets pretty hot from noon on, though."

"I'll be back at a time of my choosing." He still had not turned around. Burnside shrugged and went back inside.

"He says he'll be back when he feels like it," he announced to Suzy as he walked back into the office.

"Well, he better not make it too long. I have Vera Hawkins coming in shortly. She just got Zack's message and called me."

"Who's that?"

"She's the girl who broke the camera over Zhu's head that night, the one you asked me about yesterday. That's her name, Vera Hawkins."

"Oh," said Burnside absently. "Well, I hope Tonto's gone before she gets here."

A few minutes later White Feather appeared once again in the office. "Are you ready to resume our discussion?" he asked, looking severely at Suzy Johnson.

"Yes, I suppose we are," she said coolly. "And I think you might do well to remember that we are interviewing *you,* not the other way around." White Feather gaped in surprise. He was used to intimidating timorous personnel managers. Before he could form a response she continued, "And would you be so kind as to explain your rather strange costume. It hardly seems appropriate for a job interview."

Again he was taken aback, but sensed that she had raised an issue that could be exploited profitably. "So you're saying that you find traditional Native American garb offensive?" he demanded with as much indignation as he could muster.

"Not offensive," she said, shrugging. "Just ridiculously out of place. I'd think the same thing if you came in here dressed like George Washington. If you insist on walking around that way I suggest that you visit one of the studios in Hollywood. Maybe you could get a small part in a western. By the way, what do you wear when you're not job-hunting?"

Burnside listened to the entire exchange, speechless. While he could-n't help admire Suzy's common sense refusal to be intimidated by the comical Edward White Feather, he felt compelled to at least go through the motions of interviewing him, and without commenting on clothing and war paint. "Now, now, Mr. White Feather," he said soothingly, "we got nothing against your appearance. What the hell, it adds a little color to the place, livens things up around here."

Suzy did have enough "sensitivity" to know not to publicly contradict her boss. "Sid, perhaps you'd like to continue the interview," she said, get-ting up and heading for ladies room, where she sat down to read the *Cosmopolitan* left behind by Burnside's long-departed temp.

White Feather was glad for the opportunity to conduct his interview with Burnside, who, he sensed, was far more likely to fall for his nonsense than the practical and completely unflustered Suzy Johnson. "So, do you have a dress code here, in writing?" demanded White Feather. "I'd like to see your employee handbook, if you don't mind."

"Funny you should ask about that," said Burnside. "It's at the printers right now. I don't have a draft around the office, but I'd be happy to give you a copy as soon as they're printed."

"How can you conduct interviews without being able to share your company policies with the applicants? How can we be expected to make informed decisions about whether we choose to work here?"

"Ah, good point, Mr. White Feather, you're absolutely right. It doesn't make a lot of sense, does it? Tell you what, why don't we postpone the interview until we get the employee handbooks back from the printer. Then I can give you one, heck, I can mail it to you so you won't have to come in here until you've had a chance to read it cover to cover, see if we're, you know, a good fit."

"But I need a job now, Mr. Burnside. Are you telling me that you're advertising for jobs that you're in no position to fill, because you don't even have a policies and procedures manual?"

"Well, I, ah, guess you could put it that way, just a little administrative screw-up is all, kind of getting the cart before the horse, eh?"

"Well, I don't know quite what to do about this, but I think the first thing is to contact my lawyer for some guidance. It's occurred to me that this employee handbook story was contrived to delay my interview until all the positions are filled. It's the sort of tactic I've been subjected to before."

"Hey, c'mon," said Burnside, "that's not it at all." Hell, that's the last thing I need right now, a frigging EEOC action filed by a goddam Indian, he told himself. He was visualizing the jury, listening with rapt attention as White Feather's lawyer related how his great, great grandparents were slaughtered at Wounded Knee. Like most people who'd heard anecdotal horror stories about discrimination claims, Burnside's imagination was running wild. "Hey, I'll tell you what, we'll hold the job open until you've had a chance to read the employee manual. Then if you like what you see, the job's yours, it's in the bag. How's that?"

White Feather was unable to see a potential action arising from Burnside's proposal. Shit, he told himself, all I'm gonna get out of this is a job. "Well, I'm not sure that would bring us to a satisfactory closure of this matter. There is still the question of you allowing a hostile and intimidating work environment, intolerable for any Native American. How can you deny it as long as you have this horrible Chinese woman working for you?"

Suzy had entered the office unnoticed, and was standing inside the doorway. "What horrible Chinese woman, Mr. White Feather?"

Before the startled Edward Hruska could answer, she said quietly, "I think you'd better leave now."

"You're ordering me out?"

"Forthwith."

"What if choose not to go?"

Suzy walked up to within about two feet of the much larger White Feather. "Then I'll make you leave, and much more quickly and perhaps painfully than you'd imagine." Two minutes earlier White Feather would have reacted to such a threat with a snort of derision. But there was something chilling about her sudden change in demeanor. He realized abruptly that it was no idle threat. And while he wasn't totally convinced that he couldn't handle her in a little set-to, he knew that there was no pot of gold at the end of a physical confrontation with a woman whom he outweighed by a good seventy pounds, and worse, an *Asian* woman. Christ, she's probably in a protected class herself. Plus, he told himself, she might just kick my ass. White Feather did have *some* ego to preserve.

"Well, OK," he said, trying to laugh, "if you want to play games." He went out the door, then while walking down the hall regained some measure of bravado. He turned and shouted, "This isn't finished! You'll be hearing from my attorneys shortly! You think you can just come here from

China and take jobs away from Native Americans, huh? We'll see about that. I'll see your ass in court!"

He was still shouting over his shoulder as he turned to shove the door open violently, right into Vera Hawkins, almost knocking her off her feet. "What the hell do you think you're doing, you stupid shit?" yelled Billy Espinoza, who'd given Vera a ride in because her car was in the shop, and who was trying to follow her through the door. "And what the hell kind of outfit is that? You some kinda traveling freak show, or what?"

White Feather, having just been backed down by the much smaller Suzy Johnson, was not about to let himself be backed down by the somewhat smaller Billy Espinoza. "Are you making fun of my clothes?" he demanded.

"Yeah, you look like a complete asshole in that get-up." And with that, White Feather swung a wild roundhouse right at Espinoza, who stepped back and watched as his assailant's momentum caused him to fall, striking his head loudly on the sharp-edged door frame, which Vera Hawkins was still holding open in a pose of wide-eyed shock.

"Oh, shit, oh, man, I cut myself," cried White Feather as blood ran from the deep cut in his forehead. He was sitting on the ground, forehead in his hands in a posture of abject misery.

"Hey, man, like I didn't mean to make fun of your clothes, I was just a little pissed off the way you came through the door without looking," said Billy, suddenly contrite at the sad picture Edward White Feather made sitting in the dust and scraggly brown grass. "Hey, like I'm sorry, man. C'mon, let's go inside and get a bandage for your head. I think you're gonna need stitches." He extended his hand to help the pathetically deflated White Feather to his feet.

They helped him down the hallway, back into Burnside's and Suzy's office, where they deposited him in a folding metal chair before the speechless president and personnel manager of Red Tiger Motors. Finally, Suzy spoke. "Well, Vera, you seem to have a penchant for inflicting scalp wounds. What happened to this one?"

"She didn't do nothing, Suzy," answered Billy. "He busted through the door without looking and almost knocked us over. I called him an asshole and he took a swing at me and fell down and hit his head on the doorframe."

A long silence followed, finally broken by Vera, who asked, "Boy, why in the world you wearin' thet crazy outfit?"

White Feather, not looking up, seemed to gather his thoughts. ""I wear it as I reminder of the oppression that Native Americans have suffered at the hands of the white man."

"Y'all look mighty white to me," observed Vera. "Why you tryin' to pass yourself off like a Injun?"

Before he could answer, Billy interrupted. "What's this oppression shit, man? Me, I'm a wetback, hell, I'm oppressed too, you don' see me runnin' around dressed like Pancho Villa."

"You, oppressed?" asked White Feather derisively, "I and my people are at least *twice* as oppressed as you!"

"That's bullshit, man. We're at least five *times* more oppressed than you!"

"Enough," said Suzy finally, rolling her eyes, "it is agreed. We are *all* oppressed. Me, because I am Asian and a woman, Vera, because she is white and a woman, you, White Feather, because you claim to be a Native American, and you, Billy, because you are of Mexican ancestry. Only Mr. Burnside can claim he is not a victim. Now, with that decided, let's see what we can do to stop Mr. White Feather's bleeding." She quickly went to work with the first aid box from the hallway, first applying a butterfly bandage, then covering that with a large gauze pad, which she taped over. "I think you will need sutures, Mr. White Feather. I suggest you go to a doctor as soon as possible, or you may end up with an ugly scar."

"You really think so?" White Feather asked hopefully. A scar could provide helpful evidence of brutal oppression, plus he thought it might make him look a bit dashing.

"Yes, I believe that it will scar badly if it's not closed with sutures," she said.

"Ah, Mr. White Feather, Ed," interjected Burnside, "I just want to assure you that the job offer still stands." Suzy looked at him and rolled her eyes pointedly.

"Well, I have to think about it, Sid, old buddy." He looked up at Burnside and grinned insolently.

"Mr. White Feather," said Suzy, "you would do well not to overplay your hand."

* * *

Jack Landry read the latest surveillance report from the FBI office in Los Angeles, bringing himself up to date on the activities of the Johnsons. There seemed to be nothing new, except that the Johnsons did have the occasional visitors, all of whom seemed to be there strictly for social purposes. The report did note that the owner of Sammy's Country Barbecue, described as a "middle aged African-American male," had come to the house the previous Sunday with an individual presumed to be his wife. Again, the report indicated that the visit, which included dinner, seemed to be purely social. Landry went back and flipped through the first report again. Two car family, he thought. That means if both cars are gone, nobody's home. He paused briefly to congratulate himself on this astute judgment. Yeah, this should be pretty easy to arrange. He picked up the phone to call Irwin Faulkner, head of DEA, and another of Carruthers' politically reliable toadies.

When his secretary informed him that Faulkner was on the line, Landry picked up and said loudly into the handset, "Hey, Win (as he liked to be called), can you come over here for a secure, face to face meeting, say, late this afternoon?"

"Can you hold, Jack? Lemme just check with my secretary." He punched the hold button, sat back in his chair, and kept Landry waiting exactly forty-five seconds. Finally, he pushed in the blinking button, picked up and said, "Sorry about that, Jack, I had to rearrange a couple of things, but yeah, I can stop in around four-thirty, if that's OK."

"Yeah, that'd be fine, Win. See you then." Landry leaned back in his chair and rehearsed in his mind how he'd present Faulkner's coming assignment to him. In truth, he himself had no idea just what threat Susan Lin Johnson represented to Carruthers. He was more than a little thrilled to be entering what he imagined to be the shadowy espionage labyrinth of mirrored catacombs, in which spies, assassins, counter-spies, and counter-counter-spies plotted the downfall of governments and the destruction of the righteous, such as his boss and mentor (as he thought of the president) Bob Carruthers. I'll take care of those two, he told himself grimly. Think they're going to fuck with the President of the United States on *my* watch, huh? We'll just see about that! He pushed back his chair, went over to his office door and locked it. He returned to his desk, pulled out the bottom drawer, and withdrew the latest issue of *Soldier of Fortune* from it. He opened it, searching for the cover story, then abruptly stood up and went to the door to confirm that it was locked. He returned to the desk, leaned back in his chair, and began to read.

Three hours later Win Faulkner was sitting across from him. After a brief exchange of pleasantries, Landry leaned forward, and said, "Win, what I'm about to tell you comes directly from POTUS." He paused dramatically to let the acronym for the President of the United States to sink in. If Faulkner was impressed he gave no sign. "Ah, and what POTUS wants (pausing again, though not so dramatically this time) is that we maintain utmost security on this operation. POTUS can't be linked in any way with our activities."

"What activities, Jack?"

"I'm coming to that. We have a security threat to the United States and a threat to the life of POTUS himself."

"God, Jack, will you please stop calling him POTUS. It sounds like you're talking about some kind of space alien leader."

"Ah, sorry, that's what we all call him around here, Win," hoping to make it sound like it was a standard term used by the Inner Circle. "But the point is that we've got a national security crisis that has tremendously important diplomatic implications, implications that require that it be handled outside normal police and FBI channels. Way, way outside those channels. You follow me?"

Faulkner looked out the window. "Not really," he said, yawning.

"What I mean is this thing's got to be handled in a clandestine manner. Do you know what that means?"

"Well, I assume that, strictly speaking, it's probably illegal." Faulkner was growing bored with Landry's obvious display of 007 syndrome. And while little more than a posturing bureaucrat himself and not exactly the sharpest knife in the drawer either, he shared the general contempt in which Landry was held by even the most partisan of Carruthers' supporters.

When, twenty minutes later, Landry had explained the plan to Faulkner, closing with the question, "Can you handle this, Win?" Faulkner sat just staring out the window once again, looking exasperatingly unimpressed and disinterested.

"Why don't we just go in and arrange an accident or a fire, or shoot them both and make it look like a botched burglary or something like that? It'd be a lot easier," he said finally.

"That's a good question, Win. POTUS wants, sorry, the president made it clear that both of them must remain alive and unharmed, especially the girl. That's key in this thing, absolutely key."

227

"Well, I guess we could handle something like that. I guess I better get on out to LA and talk it over face to face with Swetford." Lee Swetford was his DEA regional chief in southern California. "How soon you want this handled?"

"As soon as possible. But obviously, that depends on how quickly you can line up the right people and also on the schedules of the alleged perps." Landry enjoyed using cop slang such as perps.

"Well, I guess I better get started then, Jack."

"And remember, above all else, the only thing I want in writing on the whole operation, Win, is the search warrant you're gonna need. Everything else is strictly verbal. There's gotta be no paper trail leading anywhere."

"Boy, I'm glad you made that clear, Jack. I was sure you wanted everything carefully documented."

"No way, Win, no paper trail at all," said Landry once again, not picking up at all on Faulkner's sarcasm.

* * *

That night Suzy Johnson arrived home, fed and walked Lobo, then busied herself with doing laundry and putting it away. Zack, flying a trip to St. Louis, wasn't due in until nearly midnight. As she worked, she wondered how much longer her little sinecure with Red Tiger Motors would last. The whole thing, from the absurd fantasies for the future of the Red Whippet put forth by the parent company, to the bizarre interview with Edward White Feather, then finally to the hiring of Vera Hawkins that afternoon as the Southern California District Manager, had taken on an almost grotesquely surreal quality to her. She would have simply quit upon fully realizing what was happening but felt obligated to Sid Burnside and wanted to help him muddle through the mess as best he could. Plus, her salary of nearly fifty thousand dollars per year was more than generous, especially considering the modest demands being put upon her.

She curled up on the couch to watch TV while she waited for the dryer to finish. Lobo immediately came over, jumped on the couch and put his head in her lap. She petted him absently as his brown eyes watched her adoringly, finally stopping her channel surfing when she came upon

The Simpsons, which both she and Zack found uproariously funny. She divided her attention between the show and thinking about what she would wear for Zack when he arrived home that evening. She finally decided to take a nice long bath, then greet him in the foyer, perfumed, powdered, and softened, wearing nothing but one of his XXL black T-shirts.

Their relationship, far from leveling out, had grown, if anything, more intense. She could barely contain herself in her excitement to see him when he came off an overnight or two day trip. He, to his own amazement and delight, felt likewise. It all seemed almost too intense, too perfect. They'd yet to have a serious argument, let alone anything that could have been construed as a fight. And yet she felt a gnawing insecurity, a fear of the only question they never discussed—the question of children and a family. A dozen times she'd resolved to raise the issue, only to cave in to the fear of disturbing their idyllic romance or even to blighting the joy of the moment. But now, with the future of Red Tiger Motors appearing doubtful at best, she found herself yearning for the purpose and fulfillment of her own family, the creation of which could be granted only by her husband, without the consent or interference of the iron bureaucracy of the People's Republic. She especially feared Zack's reaction to the thought of racially mixed offspring. We have to talk about this, she told herself. We *must*.

Three hours later, exactly in conformity to her script, she met him in the foyer. They kissed and nuzzled. "Oh, Jesus, Shan, I've been looking forward to this moment for the last two days," he said, kissing her neck. He broke away and looked down at her. "Lemme take a quick shower, honey, and why don't you make us a coupla strawberry daiquiries. Then we can get caught up."

"Sounds good, hubby," she said with a provocative smile. "Don't take too long."

Ninety minutes later they lay happily exhausted in bed, with pillows and the bedspread tossed about the little bedroom. Finally Zack propped his head up on his hand, then leaned over and kissed her on the cheek. "Honey, we gotta talk about something."

"Oh, what's that?" she replied, feeling the uneasy apprehension known to at least four hundred generations of spouses on hearing that exact announcement.

He rolled over on his back and stared at the ceiling. "Shan, honey, what are your thoughts about having a family?"

"Well, to tell the truth, I haven't really given it much thought," she lied, despising herself for lacking the courage to tell him the truth. "What were you thinking?"

"Well, I don't know, I just don't want to be an old geezer with little kids, I mean, we aren't exactly old and decrepit, but nobody gets any younger in this life. I mean, I just think we oughtta talk about it, that's all. We don't have to do anything right away, but I think we oughtta start figuring our what we're gonna do eventually."

"Zack, are you saying you think you want to start a family?" she said, hardly daring to believe what she thought she was hearing.

"Well, yeah, at some point we gotta think about it, don't you think?"

Suddenly she buried her face in his chest and put her arms around his neck. He felt her hot tears on his bare skin. "Hey, what's wrong? Is there a problem or something?"

Then she was laughing and crying at the same time. "No, you big, dumb, wonderful bull. These are happy tears, can't you tell?"

"You're happy?"

"Yes, I'm so happy. I've wanted to talk to you about it, but I've been afraid to."

Zack looked at her for a long moment, smiling. "Well, I hope you're never afraid to talk to me about anything, ever again. Do you understand that?"

"Anything?"

"Anything."

"OK, well, did you notice that long scrape on the fender of your Firebird, where I accidentally hit it backing onto the street yesterday?"

"*WHAT?* You hit my *car?*"

"Of course not. I was only checking on your sincerity. You have clearly failed the test," she laughed, wiping away her tears with the back of her hand. "Now, do you think we could practice making a family some more in a little while?"

* * *

Zhu looked at Lin across the desk in Lin's spacious office. "Comrade, Burnside's response to your instruction that he not supply press cars for

5

evaluation proves beyond doubt that the automotive press in the United States is in his employ. He is clearly desperate in his strident demand that we accede to his request to airfreight cars to California for the press. He sees that you have cleverly insured that our fine products cannot be slandered at the outset, making his task of destroying our marketing efforts much more difficult."

"That seems true enough, Zhu," replied Lin. "I seem to have thwarted his evil designs with their press corps for the moment. However, we must assume that this man Burnside is certainly experienced and clever enough to have alternate plans in place to execute his mission of saving the Japanese and American automakers from the competitive ruin they face at our hands. Doubtless he will be much more circumspect in his communications with us in the future. He may act without our knowledge, and we presently have no one in place to keep him under observation, to checkmate his wicked designs. Zhu, has it occurred to you that this man currently holds our fate in his hands, that despite our recognition of his intentions we are largely powerless to stop him? He currently makes all the arrangements for distribution for our product, the financial arrangements to ensure that the people will be paid for their heroic efforts to bring the Red Whippet to the world. He operates largely unsupervised and unimpeded by higher authority." He paused, staring at Zhu.

"But, Comrade, what can we do from here? I could properly supervise him and checkmate his plans were I there, but I am not."

"Precisely, Zhu, precisely. You can do little from here. It is imperative that you travel to California soon to monitor the activities of Burnside and his staff. You must remain in continual contact with me to keep me informed of his plans."

This was the last thing Zhu expected to hear from Lin. He couldn't imagine that he'd be allowed to return to California, or even leave the People's Republic as long as the Damoclean sword of the Red Whippet's impending thud in the US market hung over him. "You want me to travel to the US again, Comrade?" he asked.

"Of course. I need eyes and ears in the headquarters in California. Do you object to this assigment?"

"Of course not, comrade. I will energetically perform whatever duties you assign me, wherever you send me." Zhu's mind was racing with the implications of Lin's announcement. On the one hand, it would position him to possibly defect and claim political asylum, though he wasn't entirely sure that the Carruthers administration would grant it. At the same time it would position Lin to include him among the wreckers, in league with Burnside. Immediately he realized that this was exactly his intent, to prove that he was the victim of a well organized conspiracy, a somewhat more plausible explanation for the failure of the Red Whippet than the plotting of a single individual. Zhu began once again to sweat, as he lately seemed to do whenever in Lin's presence. Maybe he could disappear once in the US, find work as a migrant worker among the hordes of Mexicans he'd heard about, he thought briefly. But all he said quietly was, "When would you like me to leave, Comrade?"

"Fairly soon, Zhu. I shall announce the exact time in due course. But remember, you must surprise Burnside and his staff with your arrival. They should not be allowed to prepare for your visit."

"How long do you think I will be there, Comrade? I fear that my wife will miss me and be concerned. She has heard of the hopeless moral and spiritual depravity of California."

Lin shrugged. "You should be prepared to stay as long as necessary. I see no reason why you should not be able to take her with you."

Abruptly Zhu realized that Lin had given him carte blanche to defect, indicating that he was far more interested in blaming than punishing him. In fact, having Zhu beyond the reach of the Chinese Secret Police would mean that Lin's version of events could not be contradicted by him. Zhu wondered if Lin thought him so stupid as to be unable to figure this out on his own. "That would be very thoughtful of you, Comrade. I am pleased to have you reaffirm your faith in my loyalty."

"I have always thought you loyal, Zhu," said Lin, smiling for the first time. "A simple and rather dull fellow, but loyal."

"I am grateful for your kind observations," said Zhu, bowing his head slightly in acknowledgement of Lin's keen insights.

"Remember, your arrival in California must come as a complete surprise. You must furnish me a report immediately upon arrival. Is that clear?"

"Perfectly, Comrade. I must gather my thoughts in order to best foil the wrecker, Burnside."

* * *

The following day Suzy Johnson seemed so cheerful and bubbly that even Sid Burnside, in a state of some dejection himself, noted the sudden lift in her spirits. "I think we should bring Vera into the office for a couple days of orientation, Sid, then have her go out with Sherry to learn some of the protocols of calling on the dealers."

"Yeah, that might be a good idea," said Burnside, "having her go out with Sherry for a coupla days. At least it'll keep these guys from hitting on her too hard, though she seems to know how to handle herself." He was thinking of how Zhu had looked after his night out with her. Plus, he figured that Maxwell was more interested in keeping his BA at a comfortable level than trying to put the moves on Vera Hawkins himself.

"Do you really want to offer that ridiculous man Edward White Feather a job though, Sid?" asked Suzy. "I think I understand your concerns about lawyers and everything, but there must be limits to what an employer can be expected to tolerate. It's obvious that he was just trying to provoke us, hoping that he can turn it into some sort of lawsuit."

"Yeah, I know that, but this thing has no future anyway. Why spend it fighting a bunch of lawyers trying to make something out of nothing? Most of these cases are just filed for their intimidation value, trying to get people to come up with some money just to avoid the legal fees, which are usually more than what they can settle the whole thing for."

"That seems crazy. It doesn't make any sense. A lot of the things that go on in China must seem crazy to an American, but I can't think of anything they do that equals this. I'm trying to imagine what would happen if a company manager walked into Lin Cho Hsin's office in an outfit like White Feather's. They'd probably march him off to a re-education camp or put him in an insane asylum. And here *we're* the ones who are supposed to be crazy if we don't give him what he wants." She shook her head in disbelief. "Just what do you think we could do with him?"

Burnside seemed to be thinking. "Well, the ad was for a district sales manager." He paused. "Why don't we put him to work as a DSM up in North Dakota or Minnesota? It gets mighty cold up there in the winter. Somehow I don't see this character taking a job like that."

"That might work," said Suzy. "How many more people do you think we ought to bring on board, just to go through the motions of getting this thing up and running? In a way it's not fair to hire someone, knowing that the whole enterprise probably won't last much longer. I mean, some of these people might be passing up other opportunities to come with us."

"Yeah, that's a good point, Suzy. With someone like White Feather it really doesn't matter, but it's not fair to bring others into this thing. Hell, we ought to have enough bodies around right now to go through a few motions. By the way, is that little ad agency down the street finished with coming up with some suggested logos for Red Tiger?"

"Well, they said they'd have the stuff tomorrow. I can call them and see how they're coming."

"Good. See, Mrs. Johnson, just you and me can get this company up and running all by ourselves."

"There is no question, Sid, we make a great team." They both laughed. "Why don't we go over to Sammy's for lunch?"

* * *

As Suzy Johnson and Sid Burnside were walking into Sammy's, hoping to at least have a nice lunch to salvage an otherwise uneventful day, President Carruthers was watching, for the 58th time, the security camera tape in which he was featured in the act of fondling Mrs. Johnson's shapely behind. He had taken to stopping and rewinding the tape at the point at which she started to turn to slap him, not wanting his fantasies interrupted by either his recollection of the stinging slap or the excruciating pain of his breaking nose. He found that if he didn't witness the actual result of his groping, his fantasies became more intense and concrete. He found himself dreaming, at all times of the day or night, of tying Suzy Johnson spread-eagled to a large four poster bed and having his way with her. Jesus Christ, thought Carruthers, what *is* this? I'm not into bondage or S&M or any of that weird shit. He'd rationalized that the object of his fantasies was a specially trained Chinese agent, sent, as he'd told Timothy McGurn, "to fuck up my mind." Carruthers was capable of the most extreme and convoluted rationalizations in defense of his behavior and had finally even convinced himself that ravishing Suzy Johnson, though not too forcibly, would provide for her an experience that would forever shatter her bonds with her communist masters. It's my patriotic, no, my *presidential* duty, he told himself. I gotta fuck her head straight!

He'd yet to work out in his mind by just what mechanism he'd get her out of jail and spirited aboard Air Force One for the anticipated, coast to coast, sea to shining sea, airborne orgy in the private presidential chambers of the 747. Nor had he figured out exactly how to ensure that Heather Carruthers, always on the lookout for a photo-op herself, could be left behind. The personal and logistical absurdity of his overheated fantasies simply did not register with Carruthers. He knew only that he wanted her. Therefore, he would have her. It would all be arranged. Such was the power of the presidency!

Abruptly, he ejected the VHS tape from the VCR, walked over to his desk, and dropped it in the bottom drawer. Jesus, if Heather ever saw this thing, she'd cut off Wee Willie and roast him on a spit. He winced visibly at the thought.

Goddammit, what the hell's going on with this thing, anyway, he wondered angrily. He picked up the phone and almost snarled at his secretary, "Stacy, get ahold of Landry and tell him to get his ass over here right now."

* * *

Chapter 9

Captain Huang Lih Sheng of the Rising Star, docked in Tientsin, stood on the bridge of the huge freighter watching the port workers load his cargo of Red Whippet sedans, one by one, into the cavernous holds of the ship. Even with two of the giant cranes working continuously, the best pace they could maintain was about eighteen cars per hour, and that required perfect and practiced timing from the loading crew, having the cars ready to drive onto the pallet on the dock, men standing by on the ship to guide the pallet over the hatchway, and men standing by to drive the cars to their appointed spots in the holds. That morning Huang had visited the forward first level cargo hold and marvelled at the sight of hundreds of cars, packed nose to tail, door hand to door handle in the forward section of the ship. They were packed so tightly that the drivers had to climb out the windows of the last car in each row. Huang had noticed a slight but clearly discernible odor of both gear oil and gasoline during his brief visit to the hold. He also checked to ensure that the cars were secured in gear, handbrakes on, and wheels chocked. He knew what could happen if just one got loose during rough weather, then knocked loose a couple more, then a couple more. Once aboard, the cars were his responsibility, a fact about which he was not particularly happy, since he'd had no experience in transporting motor vehicles. Nor was his ship the ideal carrier for such a cargo.

On balance, Huang wasn't particularly concerned, given that the size of the Rising Star was such that only really severe weather could cause excessive pitching and rolling, and that with today's weather reporting and satellite imaging, there was simply no way for a modern seafarer to be caught unawares by a hurricane or typhoon. Nonetheless, Huang had the seasoned captain's healthy respect for the vastness of the oceans and just how far one could be from help if something untoward happened.

He was about to turn to go to the officers' mess for the noon meal when a sudden movement caught his eye. A laden pallet was just being eased into the air by the crane, when the car, apparently with neither the handbrake set or the transmission left in gear, began rolling off the front of the pallet. For a long moment its front wheels hung over the front of the pallet. Then the crane operator tried to bring the pallet back over the pier too abruptly, the sudden stop causing the inertia of the car to complete its departure from the pallet. It fell the ten feet to the edge of the dock, glanced off the side of it, then banged into the side of the ship and fell into the water with an impressive splash. Huang left the bridge and strode angrily down to dockside. He was tight-lipped with anger, especially upon being told that the worker who'd moved the car onto the pallet had left immediately thereafter for lunch. He walked over to the side of the dock and looked down into the water. The only remnant of the car was a rapidly widening oil and gasoline slick spreading across the smooth water of the harbor. Huang grunted angrily, then wondered idly how much fuel was in each of the cars. He made his way slowly back up to the officers' mess.

Captain Huang wanted to get underway. He hated the dreary port of Tientsin. Another seven days of loading, he told himself, hoping he'd never have to transport such a cargo again. On the other hand, he could count on perhaps nine or ten days offloading in Long Beach. His spirits brightened at the prospect.

* * *

"OK, where do we stand with this thing, Jack?" Carruthers asked of his attorney general.

"Well, sir, the surveillance is ongoing. But I have to tell you, we haven't been able to pick up on anything unusual with these two. They just seem like a couple of typical newlyweds."

"Well, obviously, Landry, they aren't going to advertise their activities. You were expecting maybe Yasser Arafat and a bunch of PLO guerrillas wearing camouflage uniforms to come to their house? Or a big red star painted on their front door? C'mon, man. These people are pros. That's what makes them so dangerous, for Christ's sake."

"Ah, of course, Mr. President," stammered Landry.

"That's why we're gonna have to get them out of the country, or whatever, any way we can. These people are way too smart and dangerous for your typical FBI field office. Hell, here's the proof," he said, waving the FBI surveillance report at Landry. "They've been watching these people for, what, close to a month, and they haven't come up with anything at all. Nothing, *nada*, zip…." Carruthers paused involuntarily, unable to come up with a couple more synonyms for the word nothing. "Ah, anyway, I think I've made my point, Landry," he finished lamely. "I say it's time to roll this thing up, get these people outta here or in prison, I don't care which. Now, how're you coming on the burglary set-up, I mean planting the stuff in their house?"

"That's all in the planning stage right now, sir. Faulkner over at DEA is on the West Coast right now, getting it all set up. And I made sure he knows everything's strictly verbal on this thing, no paper trail."

"Attaboy, Jack. Keep in mind this Supreme Court thing. Like I said, nothing's out of the question if you handle this right. Bob Carruthers never forgets a friend. Or an enemy. And these people are enemies. Remember what the Comanches always said, I think it was them, anyway: The friend of my friend is my enemy. No, wait a minute. It's the friend of my enemy is my friend. " He paused, seeming to mouth the words. "Ah, fuck it, I'm sure you get the idea, Landry."

"Yes, sir, I do. I think it was the Christians who said that, just before they fed them to the lions."

"Yeah, maybe you're right. But the point is, I want this operation mounted and concluded as soon as possible, like in the next week if you can manage it. Consistent with minimizing the risk, of course."

After Landry had left, Carruthers began plotting how he might best arrange to be on the West Coast for the great raid and subsequent incarceration of the Johnsons. That was the hard part. The details, how he'd make off with Suzy Johnson, would be easy, he told himself. Wonder how long it's been since they've had a good earthquake, he mused. I could go out there for a quick presidential look-see. Or maybe I could tour a military installation. "Hey, Stacy," he called through the door, "c'mere." In a moment her head appeared in the doorway. "I need a list of any military bases in southern California. And find out if they're forecasting any good volcanoes or earthquakes out there in the next coupla weeks.

* * *

As the president was finding out from Stacy that there was no national volcano and earthquake forecast center, two men in their late twenties, named Wilfred Duran and George Sedgely, were sitting in a seedy neighborhood tavern in East LA, talking quietly in a window-side little booth. The two, presently out on bail, awaiting trial for peddling crack near a local high school, had been fingered by a local DEA agent as two likely prospects for the planned breaking and entering operation at the Johnson residence. Between them, the pair had several arrests and a couple of convictions for B&E, as well as for drug related offenses. Their felony records had convinced Lee Swetlock, regional DEA chief, that they were ideal candidates for the job. Swetlock, perhaps taking his cue from the sort of mythology expressed in the movie THE DIRTY DOZEN, clung to the romantic notion that the best possible clandestine operators should be drawn from the criminal class itself. It never occurred to Swetlock to wonder why, if the criminals were so smart and well-schooled, they kept getting caught and recycled through the system. Real cops, of course, knew that most street criminals possessed IQs that rarely exceeded their hat sizes, just as any combat veteran knew that Lee Marvin's dirty dozen would have lasted about twenty seconds against a Wehrmacht or Waffen SS rifle platoon.

But Swetlock wasn't and never had been a real cop. He was primarily a middle level, politically correct bureaucrat, who suddenly found himself being brought along by Win Faulkner, who himself was a purely political appointee. He was generally a comically inept bungler and loved accordingly by the DEA field agents and undercover types who worked for him. So when the word came down to come up with two highly qualified prospects to perform a highly sensitive B&E operation, for which there could be "no paper trail whatsoever," the agent, whose name was Phil Rivera, had gleefully provided the names of Sedgely and Duran for the proposed assignment, noting that he was pretty sure he could get them to go along if the drug charges currently pending against them were

239

dropped. He hoped, of course, that the whole thing somehow would blow up, thereby well and truly biting Swetlock on his hairless ass.

"You really think we can trust this fucker Rivera, George?" asked Wilfred. "Me, I want it in writing before we agree to this fucking thing."

"Well, shit, man, he already told us we ain't gonna get nothing in writing," said George, a tall skinny, sandy-haired man with a receding chin and an acne problem. "But what the fuck, what do we got to lose, man? All we gotta do is break in, then hide this bag o' dope, then get the hell out. How we gonna get caught? We'll be gone before the cops even get the alarm call. And shit, we don't even know if the place *has* an alarm. I say it's worth it. Even if Rivera's full of shit, we're no worse off than before. I don't know about you, man, but I don't need any more hard time."

"Yeah, I guess," said Duran, lifting his Michelob bottle to his lips.

By the time they'd finished their beer, the two "highly skilled professionals" specified for the job by Carruthers had decided to call Rivera and tell him they'd do it.

* * *

While Sedgely and Duran were reaching their decision, Vera Hawkins and Sherry Maxwell were pulling into the customer parking area of Metro Dodge in Fresno, California. They'd made an appointment to see Freddie Newell, owner of Metro, as well as Honda and Toyota dealerships along the same auto row on which the Dodge store was located.

They got out of Sherry's Corsica and went through the showroom door. Vera was wearing a fairly low-cut pale blue dress with matching heels. Her shapely and nicely tanned legs were bare. Though their briefcases and Sherry's suit indicated that they were probably selling something, several salesmen, on getting a quick look at Vera, were on their feet and walking toward them. "Good morning, can I help you?" boomed a fortyish Ted Baxter look-alike, who had sprinted into the lead of the little group of salesmen who were making their way toward Sherry and Vera.

Vera smiled engagingly. Sherry simply asked, "Can you tell Mr. Newell we're here," handing the salesman his business card.

"Ah, yeah, sure," he said. "You got an appointment?" hoping the answer was no, which would allow him to stall them while Newell's schedule was cleared, thus giving him time to get some detail on Vera Hawkins.

"Yeah, we got a ten o'clock appointment with Freddie," said Maxwell with just the slightest edge to his voice. What's this guy think we we are, thought Maxwell indignantly, a couple of stiffs peddling paint sealants? He handed the salesman his card.

Within two minutes Freddie Newell, owner of Metro Dodge, was pumping Maxwell's hand and pretending not to notice Vera Hawkins. Finally, Newell turned to her. "Oh, are you with Sherry?" he asked, taking advantage of his sunglasses to inspect her cleavage.

"Why, yes, Ah am," said Vera, extending her hand to Newell. "Ah just started with Red Tiger, and Mr. Maxwell is just taking me around to meet dealers here in California."

Newell glanced at Sherry, nodding sagely. "That's good, you oughtta listen to this guy. He's been around. What'd you say your name was?"

"Mah name's Vera Hawkins, Mr. Newell," said Vera, giving him a demure smile and thinking that it was downright "disgustin' the way thet ole boy's suckin' up to Sherry here." She'd been around Maxwell long enough to have observed his drinking problem, of which she did not approve. It had seemed to her that someone was always getting cut, stabbed, or shot in her little mountain village of Stone Creek, Tennessee. And almost always because some of the boys had overindulged in the corn squeezin's from Cousin Buford's still. She remembered the incident in which her Aunt Clara had turned Uncle Cletus' twelve gauge on him after he beat her in a drunken rage. "Ya ornery sumbitch," her father'd shouted at Cletus as he lay on the kitchen table, trapdoor down, and moaned as his brother tweezered the birdshot pellets out of his hairy and pungent ass. "Serves ya right, ya varmint," her father had railed as the little number sixes clinked, one by one, into an aluminum pie pan. She shoulda kilt him, he'd muttered for days afterwards, shoulda used buckshot. Vera, as a result, didn't take a benign view of men who drank too much.

"Well," said Newell, "whaddya say we go over the plans I got for your franchise here in Fresno, then we can get some lunch."

"Sounds good to me," said Maxwell, nodding happily. "We gotta get right down to business, 'cause we're shipping cars right now. Got a big boat on the way."

"OK, then we got no time to lose," replied Newell, immediately sensing that the rush would minimize any franchise requirements Red Tiger might attempt to impose. "Just ship me the cars, some tools and parts, and

I'm ready to operate."

"Well, we're still puttin' together the parts package, shouldn't cost more than five grand, six at the most, and you guys provide your own sign. We'll give you the logos and official colors and you make 'em locally."

"Yeah?" said Newell. This was indeed good news. Most manufacturers charged dealers ten to twenty thousand dollars for brand signs that could have been made locally for a fraction of that cost. "Well, we got some guys in Fresno who can do that kind of stuff, do a first class job, too." Hell, he told himself, I can get in on this thing for under ten or twelve grand. If it doesn't work, who gives a shit! What have I got to lose?

Had Newell been a more reflective man, he might have supplied himself a couple of answers to that question that would have given him pause.

Two hours later, after which Sherry and Vera had Freddie Newell provide the requisite cash drafting floorplan letters from his bank and then gave him their standard letter of intent, they were heading out to a pleasant little restaurant favored by Newell. "So, Vera," he asked as he turned to look at her in the back seat, slyly glimpsing a nice expanse of tanned and shapely thigh, "you gonna be our rep, or are you getting another district."

"No, Freddie, Ah'm stayin' right here in your area. We gonna get to know each other real well, Ah should think."

"Well, I'm glad you feel that way, Vera, I always like to think of you factory guys, and girls (chuckling), as my friends and partners. If I make money, you make money, right?" This was a theory that had never quite worked out for Chrysler in the sixties and seventies, Audi in the eighties, or Mazda or Mitsubishi in the nineties, but Newell felt it was just sophistic enough to make sense to Maxwell and Vera.

"Right," said Maxwell, "and if we make money, then you make money, right?"

"Ah, right, Sherry," replied Newell, who actually believed that the factories made money only at the dealers' expense, and would make a lot more if only they listened to their dealers' suggestions on everything, to include marketing, engineering, model mix, and product specification.

"Well, Ah don't' know nothin' 'bout that," piped up Vera, "but Ah cain't see how them Chinese is makin' all thet much money on these li'l ol' cars if they chargin' only five thousand dollars. Ah think they jus' tryin' to undercut ever'body else and git a piece of the action here in the good ol' USA."

"Naw, Vera, I'm pretty sure they aren't just doin' this for their health, ya know," replied Maxwell. "I mean, they got advantages, like coolies workin' for fifty cents a day and a coupla bowls o' rice. That's how they can do it."

"Sherry's right, Vera," said Newell approvingly. "They probably damn near got slave labor makin' these cars. Hell, Detroit could compete with anybody in the world if they'd take all the bums they got in prison an' put 'em to work makin' cars. Hell, any Americans can make a car better'n a bunch o' Chinamen, even a bunch of goddam convicts, am I right, Sherry?"

"Yeah, you gotta point, there, Freddie," said Maxwell, "Americans can do anything better than other people, everybody knows that."

By the end of the long and (for Maxwell) vodka-sodden lunch, Newell had verbally agreed to take "at least" five hundred Red Whippets on the initial allocation. What the hell, he reasoned, what's the worst that can happen? I got the whole rest of the model year to sell 'em, even if they don't take off.

As they returned to the dealership, Vera gave her newly printed business card to Newell, on which she wrote her home phone number. "We really work out of our homes," she explained, "so ya'll kin get me here or leave a message at the office."

"Well, that's good to know," said Newell. "Hey, I get to LA all the time, I even got a season box with the Dodgers, you wanna go to a ballgame sometime."

"Why, that'd be so much fun, Freddie, as long, o' course, as you got a legitimate business purpose," said Vera, smiling coyly. Shoot, she told herself, this'll be better than workin' fer Starlight Escort, an Ah git to pick mah own dates! An' these ol' boys got money!

As they bid farewell to Freddie Newell and were walking to their car, Vera said, "Sherry, Ah think you might want me to drive. You lookin' a bit rough 'roun' the edges, boy."

By the end of the week, they had issued three more letters of intent to dealer candidates, all of whom seemed remarkably alike to Vera. "Hell, I think we got the whole first boatload sold out," observed Sherry happily as they returned to Chino to brief Sid Burnside and Suzy Johnson.

"Jus' whut we gonna do for an encore, Sherry?"

"Hell, I dunno. Maybe it'll be the gravy train for us from now on out," said Sherry, still not having totally abandoned his fantasy of being feted and entertained by eager dealer prospects anxious to acquire the coveted Red Tiger franchise, backed by the supposed economic advantage of unlimited cheap labor.

"Well, Ah jus' hope we won't have to git outta Dodge in a hurry," replied Vera. "They's things about this job Ah'm startin' to enjoy."

* * *

As Vera was wheeling Sherry's car onto the expressway, following Sherry's final five martini lunch of the week, and heading back toward Chino to brief Suzy and Sid Burnside, Suzy Johnson was just concluding a phone conversation with Edward White Feather. Both she and Sid had concluded that it wouldn't be wise to offer White Feather a job in the Dakotas or Minnesota, since their personnel ad had specified southern California and White Feather was certainly cunning enough to figure out what they were trying to engineer. With a sigh, Suzy had simply told Sid, "Well, if all we're trying to do is avoid some sort of lawsuit or government investigation, why don't we just offer him a job in southern California? The way things seem to be heading, this whole thing will come undone in a few weeks anyway. Plus, I wouldn't be surprised if he turned it down. He wants some money just to go away, not a job."

"You know, you're probably right, Suzy," Burnside had replied. "I wouldn't be surprised if he never shows up anyway."

And so Suzy Johnson had called him to announce that after lengthy and careful review of his resume and background, they were willing to offer him the position of District Sales Trainee in southern California. In truth, White Feather had nearly forgotten about Red Tiger Motors and Mrs. Johnson's rather unnerving courage in the face of his attempted intimidation. He was, in fact, currently hoping to arrange some sort of EEOC claim against a small California motorcycle component manufacturer, which was trying to restart production of motorcycles bearing the long-defunct Indian name. White Feather had demanded that the name of the company be changed to the NA (Native American) Motorcycle Company as a condition of his employment, else he would be working in a hostile environment.

So when Suzy Johnson got ahold of him, he rather brusquely

informed her that he'd been forced to seek other opportunities with a company more sensitive to minority concerns. "Yes, Mr. White Feather," she replied. "I'll be sure to work on my sensitivity. I wish you the best of luck."

She looked at Burnside quizzically after she hung up. "Tell me, is this really the way things happen in this country?"

"Nah, not really, this was kind of an extreme case. This guy's act might have worked on some people, though. You just don't scare as easy as he'd hoped." Burnside wondered briefly if her reaction to White Feather was primarily a function of her inexperience or whether she was just as gutsy as she seemed.

It would turn out that they'd never hear about Edward Hruska again, who, after years of trying to intimidate personnel departments with varying degrees of success, managed to pick two unintimidated intended victims in a row, the second one with disastrous results.

It turned out that the little motorcycle components manufacturer had in its employ a CNC milling machine operator named Elroy Wiggins, who spent most of his leisure time with a notorious southern California cycle gang. Wiggins, like most of the company's employees, was outraged that White Feather was, in their view, directly threatening their future prosperity and even their long term employment prospects. And Wiggins, like most members of his tiny sub-strata of American society, saw no reason to waste money and time on lawyers when more direct, immediate, and decisive means of solving disputes were at hand. Accordingly, one night in the parking lot of a local bar, White Feather was accosted by Wiggins and nine members of his gang and chain-whipped, stomped, and beaten within an inch of his life, a personnel solution which his previous victims would have cheered raucously.

Following a week-long hospital stay, he moved to Florida, where he hoped to find a more sympathetic ambient culture.

Suzy decided for the moment to put White Feather out of mind, reasoning that by the time they ever heard from him again, they'd most likely be out of business. She sighed, looked at Burnside, and asked, "Sid, do you think these dealers we're giving these letters of intent to will really take as many cars as they've promised? According to Sherry, we've already got commitments for almost twenty-five hundred of them. That reminds me, by the way, all their banks want to see a copy of our standard dealer sales and service agreements, something about what our buyback provisions are. Do we even have a standard dealer agreement?"

"Well, I can put one together pretty quick," said Burnside, thinking once again about the Hyundai agreement, which he could copy in short order and send out to the banks. "They just want to make sure that if something happens, like a dealer gives up the franchise or goes bankrupt, that Red Tiger will buy back the cars in his inventory. The banks don't wanna get stuck holdin' the bag if everything blows up."

"Isn't that risky, though, giving the banks a commitment like that with everything's that happening.?"

Burnside appeared to be thinking. "Maybe not. We're just going to provide the bank with a copy of a standard dealer agreement. The dealers will be operating with a letter of intent until we actually sign them to an agreement. The letter doesn't have any buy-back provisions in it." He shrugged. "I dunno, whatever happens ultimately ain't gonna be governed by anything it says in our dealer agreement."

"You really think so, Sid?"

"Well, if the parent company pulls the plug on Red Tiger and lets us go into bankruptcy, I don't see how we're gonna have the cash to buy back the cars. What's anybody gonna do? Sue the parent company in China? I wouldn't bet that they'd even respond."

"Perhaps not. Have you looked at the agreements we got from the port handlers, Sid, for the unloading and storage for the cars coming off this ship Rising Star? She's due in a couple of weeks. They wanted a longer term commitment than just the one ship, but I told them we wanted to check out their services before we enter into a longer term agreement."

"Yeah, that's good, I'd try to avoid any long term commitments at this point. Frankly, I don't want to enter into any more agreements, with dealers or anybody else, until we've had a chance to have a look at the product and see what happens with it. I mean, this is the craziest thing I've ever heard of, shipping cars to a market with no testing, no attempt to determine their suitability, anything."

"Well, I think the whole approach was based on the idea that *any* new car that we can sell for five thousand dollars has to be a success."

"Well, I got a feeling we're about to disprove that theory, Suzy. Hey, by the way, when are your in-laws getting back from Hawaii, anyway?"

"They're due in next weekend, Sid. I guess they'll stay for a couple of days and then leave for Kansas."

Factory Guys

"Yeah, maybe I should go with 'em, get a job as a tornado chaser or something like that."

"Oh, Sid, don't worry, everything's going to turn out fine, you'll see."

* * *

Wilfred Duran and George Sedgely sat in the kitchen of Sedgely's little pink and white two bedroom house in East LA. A clutter of empty Shaefer cans and cigarette packs sat on the dirty little formica kitchen table, upon which also sat a clear Zip-Loc bag, filled with nearly five ounces of pure, uncut heroin. "What'd the guy look like who gave you that shit, George?" asked Duran a bit fearfully.

"He was a big dude, man, like six-three and maybe two-fifty, looked like he could break either of us over his knee like a fuckin' twig."

"I mean, you think he was a fuckin' cop, or maybe DEA, man? What was he?"

"I don't know who the hell he was, just a big evil-lookin' dude, and he said if this shit don't end up where he told us to put it, we can both kiss our asses goodbye. And he said it like we're fuckin' *dead,* man."

"How much you figure this shit's worth on the street right now?"

"I got no idea, I don't deal in stuff like this, uncut and pure. I never even seen a bag this big before."

"Jesus, let's get this done," said Wilfred Duran, "I don't wanna be carryin' this shit around or have it on me. This shit's big trouble. I mean, where're we supposed to drop it, huh?"

"There's this couple livin' in Pasadena, and like all we gotta do is break in when they're not home and stash the shit somewhere where they're not likely to find it for a few days."

"What's that supposed to mean? How are we supposed to know where they're gonna look, man?"

"Shit, whaddya think? I wouldn't put it in the refrigerator or leave it on the dining room table. We'll figure something out, hell, there's gotta be a million places in any house people don't look at every day."

"Yeah, I guess," said Wilfred a little doubtfully.

"Plus, once we're in, no matter if the cops come bustin' in right after

247

us, we ditch the stuff someplace and tell 'em we're just a couple o' right-eous burglars tryin' to make ends meet. Who's gonna say otherwise? Hell, we got the rap sheets to prove it. I figure that's the worst can happen. Plus, we'll only be in the place for maybe two minutes, then we're out the door and gone. It's not like we'll be runnin' off with a TV set under each arm."

"How we gonna be sure they're gone, man?" asked Duran.

"The deal is they're both workin', and they have two cars. If both cars are gone, then they can't be home. Shit, if it makes ya feel any better, we can just walk up to the front door and ring the bell. If anybody's home, we just tell 'em we made a mistake and split." Sedgely had finished three beers in the previous hour and was feeling confident. And in truth, mildly buzzed or cold sober, the plan sounded pretty much foolproof to him.

As Duran and Sedgely were making their plans to break into the Johnson's residence, DEA field agent Phil Rivera was sitting in a little tav-ern, also in East LA, doing his best to just be a part of the furniture for the moment. He was growing a bit uneasy about recommending Sedgely and Duran for the break-in operation. Though he still entertained the desire to see Lee Swetlock put into an uncomfortable and embarrassing position, at the time he'd fingered the two petty street hoods for the job, he hadn't known about the plant being such a huge amount of uncut heroin. He had thus surmised that the operation involved something rather serious, the bungling of which could have fairly unpleasant consequences for some-one. On the other hand, he would have agreed with George Sedgely's assessment that it shouldn't be too hard to pull off the plant, barring some almost weirdly bad luck. Rivera shrugged almost imperceptibly, drank down the last of his beer, then stood up and left.

* * *

Captain Huang Lih Sheng sat in his chair on the bridge of the Rising Star, which at that moment was passing seven hundred nautical miles north of the Hawaiian Islands, six days out from Long Beach at the steady seven-teen knots the ship was maintaining. Thus far the weather on the trip had been near-perfect, with calm seas and light westerly winds.

Huang anticipated no problems with weather or anything else for the duration of the trip, though he had a slight apprehension, borne of a snatch of conversation he'd overheard from one of the engine room crew-men. The man, who had worked for a time on a Nissan car carrier, was telling a fellow crewman that they always drained the fuel from the tanks of any cars being transported on the Nissan RO-RO ship. Huang had learned that the Red Whippet sedans, for the most part, had full or near-ly full fuel tanks when loaded aboard at Tientsin. This seemed like an awful lot of work to Huang in order to minimize what seemed to him an incredibly small risk. Plus, to have drained then refueled the vehicles for loading and disembarkation would have delayed departure and length-ened the off-loading at Long Beach. Well, no matter, he told himself. He doubted that the Rising Star would be called upon again to transport cars. He was sure that having made the triumphant socialist statement of hav-ing the first Chinese cars arrive on a Chinese flag carrier, the company would select the more practical expedient of leasing Japanese or Korean car carriers for future shipments.

* * *

Zack Johnson walked into the foyer of his little ranch house, got the standard squealing and yelping Lobo greeting, then put his arms around Suzy and picked her up in a powerful hug. "Umm, you smell nice," he said, noting her perfume. "You wanna relax in the tub for a while and then get dinner?"

"That sounds good. You want to have an all-American dinner tonight, like hamburgers on the grille?"

"Yeah, I think I'd like that." Suddenly he frowned. "What's that racket out there? They got half the street torn up." The jackhammer momentar-ily ceased its hammering.

"I asked them this morning, on the way to work. They said they're replacing the old sewer line, something about it leaking. They said they'd be done on our section in a couple of days. But it *is* loud. I think they should be quitting for the day soon."

"I hope so. We won't be able to hear the TV on the patio with that racket," said Zack, heading for the bedroom to change into his trunks.

Twenty minutes later the road crew stopped for the night. Zack and Suzy sat in the hot tub, talking quietly about the probable future of her job. "How long do you think I should stick it out, Zack?" she asked.

David White

"Well, I dunno, you might as well stick around until it folds, unless another opportunity comes up. I still think there's gotta be a million opportunities for someone who's totally fluent in Chinese and English. I mean, I've heard people who speak both, but I've never heard anyone like you, who could pass for a native in either country. That's gotta be worth something."

"Maybe I could go in with Sammy. Sammy and Suzy's Barbecue and Chinese Restaurant."

He chuckled briefly. "That'd probably work here in LA. It wouldn't be the craziest idea anybody's come up with. But if we're planning to have some little munchkins we probably don't want to be starting a new business right now." He reached over, pulled her to him, and kissed her, which led immediately to fondling and some mutual heavy breathing.

She pulled away abruptly. "Zack, do you think, I mean, do you want me to try to become pregnant?"

"Well, I don't know, but I think it's what both of us want at some point, isn't it?"

"All I have to do is stop taking my pills."

"Did you take one this morning?"

"Of course."

"Well, let's enjoy a little free love while we got the chance," he said, reaching down to slip off her bikini bottom.

* * *

"That's the place right there," said George Sedgely, gliding past the Johnson residence in his fourteen year old silver Cadillac Seville. "Looks like they're both home," he said.

As the two burglars were driving past, Zack was rolling over to kiss Suzy on the neck. "Umm, not now, Zack. I've got to be at work soon and I've still got to feed and walk Lobo. We can try again tonight."

"Hmmph. I guess," he said, getting himself out of bed and heading to the bathroom.

Forty-five minutes later he was kissing her in the doorway. "Seeya tonight, honey. I'll be back from Denver by maybe four-thirty, so figure I'll be home by six."

Suzy finished making the bed and straightened up around the little house, then put Lobo on his leash and walked him around the block. She put him back inside, took a last look around, then left, locking the door behind her. The sewer line crew was just getting started in the early morning haze. She put the top down on her Miata, started the car, then backed down the driveway and out onto the street. The jackhammers had just begun their deafening racket as she turned the corner and accelerated toward the freeway.

She arrived in the Red Tiger office to find Sid Burnside retrieving a small sheaf of papers from the fax machine. He glanced up at her as she came in, smiled, and went back to reading the top letter. "Well, Mrs. Johnson, it looks like the Rising Star is about five days out from Long Beach. We might as well get the transporters lined up, starting today, so we can ship these things within a couple of days. I think we oughtta draft on the dealers' banks the same day the cars leave the port. They'll only be a day or two in transit, and I figure Zhu'll be happy to see all that money flowing into their bank in Hong Kong."

"There's nothing else to attend to, then?" asked Suzy.

"Not really. I checked with customs and all the CARB, EPA, and NHTSA requirements are waived for the moment. I still don't know what to make of that. We just have to pay the normal import duties on our transfer price, then we can ship." He shrugged. "And we better get Vera and Sherry to verify, and I mean in writing, the numbers these guys are taking on their inititial allocation. We can actually break out the allocation by serial number even before the cars get here. So we gotta get those commitments, like this afternoon."

"Well, I'll get on it right away. Where are those two? Aren't they supposed to be here in the office this morning?"

"Uh, yeah, they are," said Burnside, looking around as if to verify that they weren't there. He glanced at the clock, which showed eight fifty-five. "Give 'em another five minutes."

"Well, Mr. Burnside," said Suzy, rolling her eyes, "it looks like this is it. The Red Whippet is about to arrive. Another triumph of socialism. I feel history in the making."

Burnside looked at her and laughed. "Well, I'm glad you haven't lost your sense of humor, Miss Lin."

She smiled a little wistfully. "Nobody's called me that in such a long time, it seems. Yet it was only a few weeks ago that I arrived with Zhu and the others. Sometimes I feel like I've been born again into another world." She paused. "You arranged for the escort service, didn't you, Sid."

He chuckled. "Yeah, I was responsible for that. I don't think Zhu'll ever forget it."

"Well, neither will I, though for very different reasons."

"Yeah, and either will Vera," said Sid, smiling.

Just then she and Sherry Maxwell came through the door to the office. Vera glanced at the clock. "Why, we're heah two minutes *early,* Sherry, there was no need for ya'll to be drivin' like a maniac."

"Yeah, well I needed some coffee, Vera," said Sherry, immediately heading for the Mr. Coffee and pouring himself a large mug.

"When you've got yourselves settled, have a seat over here and we'll go over the commitments we'll need from the dealers on this initial allocation," said Suzy.

Presently Vera and Sherry pulled up chairs in front of her desk and waited for her to begin. "OK, we're going to begin shipping perhaps the day after the ship docks," said Suzy. "And we'll be drafting the dealers banks the same day, so we have to get all the bank agreements finalized this week."

"That soon, huh?" asked Sherry, clearly chagrined at the looming possibility of having to do something more energetic than eating and drinking with dealer prospects. "Do we have the parts kits assembled, and the special tools? And what about all the shop manuals and the technical training for the mechanics, all that stuff?" he went on. These were all highly legitimate questions, Maxwell knew, the answers to which he hoped would be sufficient to stop the distribution process in its tracks for at least a few more weeks.

"I'm afraid we'll have to do all that on the fly, Sherry, so to speak," said Suzy. "Really, the car is simple enough that I don't think the dealers should have too much trouble getting them on the road and keeping them running, at least until we can get the initial parts kits to them. I'm sure they can even cannibalize parts from new cars in stock and replace them later if need be."

"Ooh, this sounds like it could be a big problem," said Maxwell, deciding to make at least one more attempt to derail the impending launch of the Red Whippet.

"I'm sure we'll muddle through somehow," said Suzy, smiling faintly. In truth, she was enjoying a certain sadistic pleasure in forcing Maxwell to face the prospect of a little work.

"Well, Ah'm sure the three dealers Ah done signed up with Sherry'll take a few hunnert cars apiece. They done tol' me so," said Vera proudly, "an' Ah know they wouldn't go back on their word to a lady."

Sherry looked longingly at the wall clock. "Hey, who wants to go to Sammy's for lunch?" he asked suddenly, looking around the office for affirmation.

"C'mon, Sherry, it's only five after nine," said Sid Burnside. "We're three or four hours from lunch."

"Well, hell, I know that Sid, I just wanted everybody to give it some thought, that's all. I could use some barbecue today." In truth, Sherry was trying to plant the idea to ensure that they wouldn't go to the clean little luncheonette three blocks from the office, which served excellent food but no alcoholic beverages.

"Well, I don't know, I was thinking of maybe Emma's today (the little luncheonette)," said Burnside. "Well, we'll see," he concluded, knowing full well the reason for Maxwell's suggestion.

Maxwell turned to Vera and tried to recruit her to the cause. "They got the best southern barbecue in the country," he whispered to her.

Two hours later Vera and Sherry had actually gotten faxed commitments from Jake Dougherty, Freddie Newell, and three other dealer candidates for a total of over twenty-one hundred cars, largely on the strength of their promises not to appoint any other dealers in those trade areas as long as the original five were able to absorb all the vehicles available to them for a period not to exceed five months.

As the little group, forming the entire management staff and workforce of Red Tiger Motors, was making ready to actually take into inventory, then ship and bill for the cars on the Rising Star, George Sedgely and Wilfred Duran were passing by the Johnson residence for the second time that morning. Suzy's Miata and Zack's Firebird were gone, as they had been during their first pass two hours earlier.

"I say we go in right now," said George, turning at the end of the street to go around the block and return to the house.

"Shit, I guess," said Wilfred, cracking his knuckles nervously.

"I'm gonna pull right in their driveway, looks less suspicious, like we're expected, doncha think?" asked George.

"Yeah, I guess so." Wilfred was definitely wound up at this point. "Let's just get in there and get out."

"Don't get antsy on me, man. I'm the one with the bag. I just want you to go to the front window and keep a lookout."

A minute later they were pulling into the Johnson's little concrete driveway. They got out, wincing at the sound of the jackhammers, which had been hammering all morning and were now right in front of the Johnson's house. George headed through the carport toward the back door off the patio, despite his assurance to Wilfred that they could ring the front doorbell and see what happened. He peered into the kitchen, saw nothing, and noted that there had been no alarm notices anywhere on or around the house. He tried opening the door, but it was locked, though not with a deadbolt. Sedgely took off his shoe, looked around the backyard and into the backyards of the neighbors, saw nothing, and broke the pane. The jackhammers kept up their steady racket. He reached around through the broken pane and turned the doorknob. The door opened and Sedgely stepped inside into the kitchen, followed by Duran, who went toward the front of the house to the living room.

Lobo had been in Zack and Suzy's bedroom with his head under the bed, seeking relief from the relentless banging of the jackhammers. The noise hurt his ears and at first had actually frightened him a bit. The metallic hammering had completely masked the sounds of the break-in, even from his acute canine hearing.

Sedgely was just walking past the hall bathroom when he had a sudden inspiration. He removed the Zip-Loc bag of heroin from his safari jacket and laid it on the bathroom counter. He looked at his pimply visage in the mirror and grinned evilly, then reached down to take the lid off the toilet tank.

The plant likely would have succeeded as planned had it not been for what happened next. As Sedgely was lifting the top off the tank a small glass bowl filled with seashells slid off its smooth porcelain surface and crashed to the bathroom floor, sending broken glass and dozens of small seashells skittering across the tile. "Ah, fuck!" muttered Sedgely, and dropped the tank lid loudly on the countertop.

In the bedroom at the end of the hall, Lobo's ears, which had been laid back in pain and discomfort, abruptly shot up as he yanked his head out from under the bed and tore out of the bedroom to investigate. His claws scrabbled on the hardwood floor of the hallway as he charged down toward the bathroom. Sedgely heard nothing of the scratching and rattling claws closing the distance to him as he reached for the bag of heroin, intending to toss it into the tank and replace the top. He had just picked up the bag when movement at the door caught his eye.

George Sedgely looked down into a terrifying black devil-face, surrounding a vicious set of white fangs. In a remarkable display of lightning survival reflex, he spun and tried to dive through the bathroom window, just as the dog was gaining traction. He might have made it out the window had he not gotten hopelessly tangled up in the venetian blinds, leaving himself draped over the window sill, flailing madly in his desperation to escape the demonic black doberman. Just as he was getting a handful of grass with which to pull himself outside, Lobo lunged and fastened his teeth savagely on Sedgely's left buttock. Sedgely screamed and began thrashing wildly with his legs, trying to force the dog to release him, but this only caused the enraged animal to begin throwing Sedgely's lower body from side to side with his powerful neck muscles, as his murderous teeth sawed deeper and deeper into Sedgely's flesh.

Sedgely screamed in pain and terror, and finally managed to flip himself over on the window sill, causing the mouthful of flesh in Lobo's jaws to rip loose and splat wetly onto the bathroom floor. He tried desperately to kick the dog away and did manage for a couple of seconds to hold him at bay with his flailing shoes. But suddenly the dog saw an opening and lunged for the closest and most inviting target, Sedgely's crotch. The powerful jaws clamped shut on Sedgely's genitals, causing him to emit an almost inhumanly loud and high-pitched shriek.

Wilfred Duran stood paralyzed with fear, able to see the dog's hindquarters sticking into the hallway and hearing Sedgely's piercing screams. Abruptly, he steeled himself to charge down the hallway, hoping to make it past the dog, which appeared to be preoccupied with tearing Sedgely to pieces, and get to the kitchen entrance and out the back door. He put his head down and sprinted down the hall, past the dog, which immediately released its hold on Sedgely. He made it through the kitchen entrance and had almost got to the back door when the dog caught him. Lobo slammed into the small of his back at a dead run and knocked him completely through the door and out onto the patio. Duran wisely offered no further resistance and lay on his stomach, trying to cover his face and his head with his hands and arms. Lobo snarled at him briefly, then sniffed at his head. Duran tried to sneak a look at the dog, which immediately bit him on the scalp, causing him to remain completely still, save for his terrified trembling.

Meanwhile, Sedgely lay screaming, almost incoherently, over and over again. *"HEBITMYDICKOFF! HEBITMYDICKOFF! AAAAAaaaa aaaahhhhhh! HEBITMYDICKOFF!"* Actually, Lobo had left Sedgely's dick firmly attached to his body, though his left upper and lower canines had pierced the hapless member completely through. His right testicle had been punctured by one of Lobo's inch and a half long canines as well. Sedgely finally regained the presence of mind and survival instinct to reach forward and close the bathroom door, thus at least protecting himself from the nightmarish doberman pinscher. He flopped back down and just lay there on the bloody floor, moaning.

Unnoticed by either burglar, the sewer line crew had taken a break two minutes earlier, leaving the neighborhood suddenly quiet except for Sedgely's unearthly screams. The foreman looked at one of the pneumatic hammer operators. "Jesus Christ, Jack, there's an axe murder goin' on in that house. I'm callin' the cops." He ran for the cell phone in his truck and dialed the Pasadena PD, as Sedgely let out with further little cries of pain and despair from time to time.

In less than two minutes squad cars began converging from all directions on the Johnson's little house. Cops leapt out with drawn guns pointed at the house and took cover behind the cars. A sergeant finally bellowed into a bullhorn. "This is the police. Come out with your hands in the air. Do not come out with any sort of a weapon or you may be shot. I repeat, this is the police…."

"I can't fuckin' come out," shrieked George Sedgely "Get in here and shoot this fuckin' dog, you dumb motherfuckers. Shoot the fucker! He almost killed me. I'm locked in the fucking bathroom. Help, for Christ sake!"

The cops looked at one another.

"Is this your residence?" said the sergeant into the bullhorn.

"Fuck no, it ain't my house," screamed George. "Now, get in here and shoot this fuckin' dog before he kills all of us!"

"Are you saying there's a dog in there?" asked the sergeant.

"Not in the goddam bathroom with me. I got the door locked. The fucker's outside. Now come in here an get me before I fuckin' bleed to death!"

"Check around back, from the neighbor's yard," said the sergeant, motioning to two of the cops.

Both headed into the neighbor's yard and looked over the fence. Lobo was still standing over Wilfred Duran, who was wimpering and making little keening noises. He saw the cops and ran over to the fence, barking loudly. "Christ, that's the biggest doberman I ever seen," said one of the cops, as he involuntarily backed away from the fence. The other cop ran out into the street to tell the sergeant about the dog.

The sergeant had quickly surmised that the two men on the property were most likely burglars who'd run afoul of the property owner's dog. "OK, let's get the animal control people in here to subdue the friggin' dog, then we can go in there and get those two birds."

"OK, just stay where you are and don't provoke the dog. We're gonna take care of him, then we'll be in to tend to you," said the sergeant through the bullhorn.

Abruptly George Sedgely realized that he'd have to flush the heroin down the toilet. Jesus, thank God I'm in the fucking bathroom, he told himself. He'd examined his dick and found, to his great relief, that he still had one, albeit a rather maimed and battered pink shadow of its former self. He shifted himself into a more upright position and looked around for the packet of heroin. It wasn't on top of the counter. He looked under his legs, then behind himself, and finally peered into the toilet itself. It wasn't behind the commode, nor was it in the tank. Belatedly, Sedgely began to realize that the packet of heroin was lying out in the hall, doubtless kicked there by his wild thrashings as he tried to keep the dog off him. Oh, shit, fuck, he moaned. Jesus H. Christ. He started to open the door to peer out but then heard the furious sound of claws coming up the hallway at him. He slammed the door to the sound of vicious snarling and barking. I'll kill that fucker Rivera, he told himself. That dirty sonofabitch. He wondered briefly what was happening with Duran, then put his hands in his wounded crotch and moaned quietly.

Fifteen minutes later Lobo was contained under a large wire-mesh net, snarling and thrashing. The animal control people injected him with a sedative to knock him out, then carried him off to their van to be deposited in the pound until the owners came home. In short order the cops had Duran handcuffed and treated by a paramedic for minor injuries. They found Sedgely still in the bathroom, but not before they discovered the packet of heroin in the hallway. As the paramedics worked on him, the sergeant put in a call to the narcotics division. "You wanna tell me what you're doin' with this?" he asked Sedgely after they'd read him his rights. He held up the plastic bag with a pair of tongs.

"Hell, I don't know nothin' about that," said Sedgely. "We were just here trying to score some jewelry or other valuables and shit." Sedgely didn't have the good sense to keep his mouth shut, especially in view of his shaken and addled condition. "I found it in the toilet tank when I was lookin' in there for jewelry."

"You were looking in the toilet tank for jewelry?" asked the sergeant.

"Sure, man," said Sedgely, suddenly realizing that he was digging a hole for himself. "Lots o' people hide their best shit in the toilet tank and places like that."

"Is that so," said the sergeant derisively. "How come the bag's completely dry then?"

"Fuck, I dunno, I been layin' here for hours, waitin' to be rescued from that fuckin' dog, man. You guys sure as hell took your time getting here. That's why the fuckin' bag's dry. I coulda bled to death waiting for you guys, what the fuck ya think, sure the bag's dry. I been waitin' here all day."

The sergeant looked at the two other cops and paramedic and shook his head. This made the first time in his career that a burglar had ever complained about the police being too slow to respond.

Four hours later Zack Johnson arrived home, suddenly alarmed by the sight of the two police cruisers still on the scene as he turned onto his street. He raced up the street, screeched to a halt in the driveway, and jumped out of his car. "What's going on here, where's Suzy?" he demanded, looking around worriedly, back and forth between the three cops on the scene.

"There's been a burglary here. It doesn't look like anybody was home, except the dog."

Zack looked at the house. "Where's Lobo, that's the dog's name. He's OK, isn't he?"

"He looked fine when he left for the pound. They gave him a sedative to make him manageable. He tore up one burglar really bad, though, and chewed on the other one a little bit, too. Sir, could I get your name and see some ID?"

Ten minutes later Suzy turned into the driveway. She jumped out of her car and ran up to Zack. "What's going on, Zack?" she asked, badly frightened.

He put his arm around her and held her close. "Everything's OK, honey. Somebody broke into our house, but it looks like Lobo didn't let 'em get away with anything. It looks like we were real lucky."

"Is Lobo all right?" she asked.

"Yeah, we'll go get him in a little while." He shook his head. "That's funny. This is the first burglary I've heard of in this neighborhood." He looked at the cops for confirmation.

"Yeah, we don't get a lot of trouble around here. Can we go inside and do a quick inventory and see if they made off with anything?" asked one of the cops.

Five minutes later they had ascertained that nothing appeared to be missing. "I guess the dog stopped 'em before they could take anything," said Zack.

"There are some guys who are coming down from Narcotics Division to talk to you in a little while, though. One funny thing is that we found a big bag of what looks like pure heroin in the hallway. It looks so far like one of these guys had it with him when they came in, but they're gonna want to talk to you about it anyway."

"Jesus, I don't know what to make of that," said Zack, looking at the cops, then Suzy. "It was in the hallway?"

"Yeah, well, the guy the dog really ripped up said he found it in your toilet tank when he was lookin' for valuables, but it didn't have any water on it."

"He was looking in the toilet tank for goodies?" asked Zack.

"That sounded like a new one on us, too," said the cop. "I don't think you two'll be under any suspicion, but it seems mighty strange that this guy'd be running around with that much pure heroin on him." He shrugged to emphasize his perplexity. "Maybe they'll get the real story from the guy. Hey, I see you're an airline pilot. You fly overseas?"

Zack knew why he was asking the question. "Nah, I'm not that senior. I fly strictly domestic routes."

"Well, nice talkin' to you," said the cop. "Like I said, the narcotics boys'll be here shortly. We'll wait outside until they get here. You guys might want to start cleaning up the place a little."

"Yeah, we better do that," said Zack.

"Oh, Zack," said Suzy as she put her arms around him after they'd walked back inside, "I feel so...*violated.* Those people were in *our* house, going through *our* things. Thank God Lobo was here."

"Yeah, you can say that again. It doesn't look like they tried to take anything, or even got the chance. I wonder why the dog even let them in the house," he said, alluding to the mystery that would never be solved.

Within a few minutes two plainsclothes narcotics detectives rang the doorbell, flashed their badges, and announced themselves. After introductions the pair sat with the Johnsons at the kitchen table. "Well, you got any idea how that bag of heroin got into the house?" asked detective sergeant Vic Murray. The question wasn't asked in an accusatory manner, but nor was it posed in a way that indicated that the detectives automatically ruled out the possibility that the Johnsons were involved in drug trafficking.

"Well," began Zack, "I have to assume it arrived with the two guys who broke in. It wasn't here before."

"The one guy, Sedgely was his name, I think, said he found in the toilet tank."

"Do you believe that?" asked Zack, beginning to grow a little annoyed.

Murray shrugged. "I don't know. It does seem like a funny place for burglars to look for anything, I gotta admit."

"Well, I replaced the flapper valve on that toilet no more than three months ago, and there was nothing in there then. And I haven't looked since."

"Yeah, well, it's probably not exactly good police procedure to tell you this at this point, but the bag was completely dry when we found it on the floor. There wasn't any water around it, either, so in my highly professional opinion, the guy didn't get it out of the toilet tank. One weird thing, though, the top of the tank was off when we came in. Maybe the thing got knocked off when the dog was tearin' this guy up. But it's funny that he came up with the toilet tank story. My guess is that he did take the top off himself, either before or after the dog lit into him, plus, the thing's still layin' on the counter, not on the floor, where it probably woulda landed in a big ruckus. And then maybe he just started shootin' off his mouth without thinking when Zanetta (the uniformed sergeant) asked him about the bag." He paused, then shrugged. "We'll get to the bottom of it eventually, I suppose." Actually, long experience had taught Murray to suppose no such thing, that far more crimes went unsolved than solved. He stood up to leave. "Hey, you fly to any good places, like Europe or Latin America?" nodding at Zack's uniform.

"Nah, just domestic routes. Maybe someday."

The detectives smiled, shook their hands, and left.

After they'd left Suzy and Zack continued to sit at the kitchen table. "There's something weird about this, Shan. I don't know much about that stuff, but a bag that big's gotta be worth a lot of money. What were a couple of low-life burglars doing running around with it in their pockets?"

She stared at the table top for a long time before answering. "I don't know, Zack. It doesn't make a lot of sense, does it. Unless they intended to leave it here, in our house."

They looked at each other, both realizing that it was the most logical conclusion one could reach.

"Ah, well, let's not think about it right now. Let's go get Lobo, then maybe we can go out to get something to eat. You feel like Mexican tonight?"

* * *

As the Johnsons were deciding what to do about dinner, George Sedgely lay on his stomach in the dispensary of the county prison, moaning softly. After the adrenalin rush that had accompanied his mauling and subsequent arrest wore off, he found himself in very considerable pain, especially from his fang-punctured genitalia. "You'll feel a little pin prick from this" said the prison doctor as he injected two syringes of a local anesthetic around the gaping wound in Sedgely's buttock. "Jesus, he tore enough out of your ass to make a pretty good sized meatloaf," the doctor chuckled. "What kind of dog was it?"

"I don't think it was a fucking dog, man, I think it was a fucking sabre-tooth tiger. Goddam, ya gotta gimme something for the fuckin' pain, man. I feel like I been shot in the balls."

The man ignored Sedgely's request for a general anesthetic. "The swelling should go down in your testicle in a couple of days," he said. "You'll be back to normal in a couple of months, able to do anything you could before. That thing should be getting numb by now. Can you feel that?" he asked, touching the edge of the wound with a gauze pad.

"It's pretty numb, I think," said Sedgely. "You really think my balls an' cock are gonna be OK?"

"Yeah, pretty sure," said the doctor, beginning to go to work sewing up the gaping excavation in Sedgely's left buttock. "We gotta keep you pumped up on antibiotics for a coupla weeks, though, make sure nothing gets infected."

He was just finishing up when Vic Murray appeared in the door with his partner. "Can we talk with this guy when you're through with him, doc?" he asked.

"Yeah, I don't know why not. I didn't give him a general or anything, so he should be able to understand your questions. I'll be done in a minute."

Murray waited for the doctor to leave, then walked over to where Sedgely could see him clearly. "How ya feelin', George? Looks like that dog did a number on you. By the way, I'm Vic Murray, and this is my partner, Detective Ruskin."

"I'm so delighted to make your acquaintance," said Sedgely through gritted teeth.

"Better read him rights again, Steve," said Murray. Ruskin complied with a quick monotone recital from his Miranda card. "So, you wanna talk to us, George? You already told the uniformed cops enough to pretty much give us the picture. You wanna tell us what you were doin' runnin' around with that bag o' heroin. We know you didn't find it in that house."

In truth, Sedgely didn't have a clear recollection of just what he had told the cops at the scene, though he remembered the uniformed sergeant's observation that the bag couldn't have been in the toilet tank and come out completely dry. And though he knew that everyone always counseled defendants to keep their mouths shut and to answer only what their lawyers told them to answer, Sedgely had always felt a compulsive need to display his skill at fencing with interrogators. He also believed that he could tell his own story far more convincingly than could any two-bit mouthpiece, especially the sort of asshole you'd find working in the public defenders' office.

Finally he said, "You guys really think I'd be out runnin' around with that much smack in my pocket? It'd be like carryin' a coupla gold bars. Nobody's *that* crazy. You never see that much of that shit in one spot on the street, not here in LA, not in fuckin' Tijuana, not in Mexico City, not anywhere. Let's get real, here, man." He grinned at Murray triumphantly.

Murray had a sudden inspiration, a risky one, but he decided to take the chance. "C'mon, let's knock this shit off, George. Your goddam jacket had traces of heroin in the pocket. We already had it analyzed. And I don't mean just *little* traces either. You were carrying that bag, pal, and we know it. And what's worse for you is we can prove it. So, you wanna play ball and tell us where you got it, or you wanna take the fall all by yourself?"

In truth, had Sedgely actually been carrying the bag for a major dope operation, there would have been no need for deliberation. He'd take the fall, and be damned glad he'd gotten off with his life, which would have been instantly forfeit should he have fingered an actual mob member. Now, however, he began to see a possible way out, plus a way to repay that doublecrossing cocksucker Phil Rivera, who, he reasoned, had to have known about the fucking dog.

He thought for a long moment, which Murray and Ruskin took to be a refusal to talk. They started to leave. "We're gonna go see your buddy Duran, George, see if he's any smarter'n you."

"Wait, I got something to tell you. It's gonna sound really weird, man, but it's the truth. You can check it out with Wilfred. He'll tell you the same story." And so for the next ten minutes Sedgely related the story of how Phil Rivera, whom he identified as "some guy who works for DEA, man, he's a fuckin' fed," had promised him and Duran that all charges on their most recent arrest for crack peddling would be dropped, just disappear, if they stashed the bag of heroin in the Johnson's residence. The two narcotics detectives looked at one another as Sedgely finished, trying to determine whether Sedgely was capable of making up such a story, especially one which could be checked out with Duran.

"You say this guy was a fed?" asked Murray. "How'd you know that?"

"We know the fucker from a way back," said Sedgely. "He busted me an' Wilfred and a bunch of other guys on a cocaine deal a coupla years ago. We were just buyin', though, man, so we only did a year. We just walked into it, it was an accident. But that's how we come to know this guy. He was undercover with 'em then."

"You know this Johnson couple, George?" asked Ruskin.

"Who're they?"

"You know, the ones whose house you broke into."

"Oh, them. No, we didn't know 'em from Adam. This other guy, not Rivera, just gave us their address when he gave us the bag."

"You didn't know this other guy's name, you're sure?"

"Never saw him before or since, and Rivera didn't give us his name. Just told us to meet him in this bar. He was a big, mean-lookin' motherfucker, though, maybe thirty-five or forty. I'd know him if I saw him again."

"Wait a minute, George," said Murray. "You're tellin' us the goddam feds are behind this whole thing, like they gave you this bag o'dope and told you to put in it these people's house?" He shook his head and chuckled. "You really expect us to buy into this thing? What do we look like, a coupla idiots?" In fact, both Murray and Ruskin already found the story, while more than a little strange, at least worthy of further investigation. The existence of Rivera, and Duran's anticipated corroboration would certainly be easy enough to check out. They couldn't see what Sedgely would stand to gain by making up such a story. Plus, as he'd pointed out, just where the hell *would* a penny-ante street hood like Sedgely get five ounces of pure uncut heroin?

"Hey, man, think what you want," said Sedgely. "Just check it out. Go talk to Duran and see if he don't back me up. And track down this sonofabitch Rivera. Someone in one o' the local DEA offices has gotta know who he is."

Murray shrugged. "Yeah, maybe we'll do that. You got anything to add?"

"You guys know everything I know at this point. It ain't much, but it's all true."

"OK, George, you think of anything else, this is where you can find me." He handed Sedgely his card.

Three hours later Murray and Ruskin had verified Sedgely's story with Wilfred Duran, who upon hearing Murray relate Sedgely's agreement with Rivera, simply said, "Yeah, man, that was the deal. George told you that?" He also confirmed Sedgely's meeting with the "big, mean-lookin' motherfucker," and corroborated Sedgely's claim that he never got the man's name. He also stated that he knew nothing of the Johnsons, only that they were to plant the bag of heroin somewhere in their house. And finally, after finishing with Duran, the two detectives confirmed that one Philip Rivera was assigned to the DEA Los Angeles field office.

"Whaddya think, Vic," asked Ruskin, "you wanna look up this guy Rivera and see what he's got to say?"

Murray thought for a long moment. "I don't think it'd be a good idea to do it on our own. We better brief Shannon (their immediate superior) on this. Let him make the call. I got no idea what we got here."

* * *

After they'd retrieved Lobo, Zack and Suzy blocked the broken bathroom window with the remnants of a large cardbox box that had housed Zack's stereo. They'd stopped at the supermarket to pick up a four pound piece of chuck steak with which to reward the dog for his diligent sentry duty of that afternoon. Before they left for dinner, Suzy hugged him around the neck. "That's a good dog, Lobo, we both love you. Now be a good boy while we're gone."

Two minutes later they were leaving in Zack's Firebird. "Well, I guess one thing we don't have to worry about are burglars as long as we got him around. Too bad he's leaving this weekend," he said.

"Yes, that is too bad," said Suzy absently.

Zack glanced at her. "You OK, honey?"

She looked at him and smiled wanly. "Oh, I'm fine. I just can't get used to the idea of those people in our house."

The drove in silence for a while. "What you're really worried about is those guys trying to put that stuff in our house, aren't you?" he asked finally."

She sighed. "Yes, Zack, I am, to be honest with you. In fact, I'm scared to death. This has something to do with that night at the embassy, I just know it does. I can feel it."

Zack stared straight out through the windshield, his lips tight. "I think you're right, honey. I think the idea was to put the stuff in our house then have a big dope raid. We get hauled off to jail and he gets his revenge." Suddenly he hit the wheel with the heel of his hand, causing her to jump. "Goddammit, this shit can't happen in this country!" He seemed to relax for a minute, then laughed. "Well, one thing, they didn't pull it off. Jesus, this is funny when you think about it. First, you break the bastard's nose, then the dog practically tears a couple of his people to shreds." He began to laugh more loudly. "You'd think the dumb shit'd learn not to fuck with the Johnson family, wouldn't you." Suddenly, they were both laughing uncontrollably. "Heather probably busted a lamp over his head when he got home that night," gasped Zack. Their laughter redoubled until Zack finally had to pull over and stop.

Their fear and apprehension had abruptly dissolved into near hysterical laughter. "Oh, God, Zack, I can't breathe," she gasped, hanging on his arm, as tears ran down her face. "We'll fix him! He'll wish he never heard of the Johnson family." They both continued to laugh until they had to stop for breath, finally calming down enough for Zack to put the car in gear again. He was about to pull back onto the road when they looked at each other and it started all over again.

Whatever their own apprehensions, Suzy was right about one thing: POTUS would soon come to wish he'd never heard of the Johnson family.

* * *

Chapter 10

The following morning, at 9:00 AM EST, DEA chief Win Faulkner sat looking at his phone, trying to summon the courage to call Attorney General Jack Landry. He'd spent the last hour getting the details of the botched drug plant at the Johnson residence from a stammering, quavering Lee Swetlock, who, volunteering as little as possible, finally allowed it to be pried out of him that the two "seasoned professionals" entrusted with the job were now residing in the county jail, and further, that one of their own people, Phil Rivera, had been identified by the perpetrators as the DEA contact. "Jesus Christ, Swetlock," Faulkner had demanded upon learning this particular tidbit, "how the fuck did these two guys know his name?"

"Ah, we're trying to determine that right now, Win," replied Swetlock, who in truth didn't know that the answer was simply that Rivera didn't give a shit that Sedgely and Duran knew who and what he was. They were just a couple of petty criminals whom he happened to know through a drug bust and who seemed handy enough for the burglary assignment.

"Well, goddammit, find out and call me back," Faulkner had shouted as he slammed the phone down.

Now he sat trying to think of how to explain all this to Jack Landry, for whom he'd abruptly lost all his haughty disdain. Idiot or not, Landry now held his fate in his hands.

Finally he took a deep breath and dialed the attorney general's direct line. When Landry came on the line, Faulkner tried to sound as commanding as he could. "Jack, we got a problem with that operation out in LA, you know the one I mean."

"What happened? No, you better come right on over and tell me in person." Landry abruptly felt faint. He put the phone down and listened to his heart, which seemed to be thumping inside his skull. Suddenly he calmed down. It's probably nothing, he told himself. Faulkner's just calling me to tell me they couldn't do it on schedule, something like that.

But an hour later Landry truly was on the verge of cardiac arrest, a stroke, or both. "Win, you told me you could handle this," he croaked. "My God, we're ruined, completely ruined." Landry briefly saw himself standing naked in a prison shower, surrounded by huge, leering, tatooed inmates with enormous, quivering erections. He involuntarily tightened his sphincter and emitted a plaintive little squeak.

Seeing Landry's obvious panic, Faulkner pressed the advantage. "I told you this wasn't our kind of operation, Jack. Maybe you shoulda got the CIA or somebody like that to handle this. I mean, I told you, we don't have people trained to do this kind of thing."

Landry just stared at him, wide-eyed with terror. He was too rattled to even remember that he'd received no such objection from Faulkner. "But I thought you could handle it," he quavered. "That's what you told me."

"Like hell I did. I told you the operation was *possible,* not that it was a sure thing. You're the one who told me we had to take the fucking risk. Nobody's gonna pin this thing on me, Jack. I was roped into this."

"But you told me you could do it," repeated Landry a little desperately.

"Bullshit, Jack, that wasn't what I said at all. Now I suggest you get over and tell the president what happened. And remember, don't try to throw *me* under the bus. This thing wasn't my fault. I was against it from the beginning." Faulkner stood up to leave, signaling the end of the meeting and indicating to Landry that he was in the dominant position.

"Wait, don't leave me now, Win," gasped Landry. "You gotta help me."

"There's nothing I can do at this point, Jack. It looks to me like you got yourself into this mess. You're just gonna have to get yourself out. But I wouldn't put off telling Carruthers about it. He needs to know what happened." He walked to the door, opened it with a contemptuous look back at Landry, and left. Well, that coulda gone worse, he told himself, but I better get my resume updated, maybe call in a few markers here and there. I'll be OK.

It took two hours for Landry to compose himself sufficiently to call the White House to request an immediate meeting with the president. He'd popped two Valium tablets in the interim, which did not seem to reduce his sense of panic much but did serve to render him even more incoherent than usual. Plus, his nerve-induced diarrhea had reasserted itself with a particularly savage vengeance. He called Carruthers' direct line. "Hi, Stacy," he said weakly, "Jack Landry here. Is the president available?"

"I'll see, Jack. Can you hold?"

A moment later Carruthers picked up. "You get it done?" he asked without preamble.

"Ah, ah, there's been a little complication, Mr. President. I, ah...."

"Get over here right this minute," Carruthers snapped, then slammed the phone down. Christ, I shoulda known better than to trust that moron with this, he told himself angrily. Carruthers' anger was based entirely on the assumption that his hoped for liaison with Suzy Johnson would now be delayed, that somehow Landry's people just hadn't been able to get the job done as yet. It didn't even occur to him that something untoward might have happened that could have unpleasant consequences. And even if it had, he assumed, there were always plenty of people around to run interference and clean up the messes.

He paced around the office testily, looking at his watch every thirty seconds. Within ten minutes his secretary appeared in the doorway. "Mr. Landry's here, sir," she said.

"Send him in and close the door."

Landry looked pale, and the few hairs covering the top of his head, which he combed over from his left, looked particularly scraggly. "Christ, you look like shit," said Carruthers.

"Thank you, sir," replied Landry. "I mean, ah...."

"Never mind. Now, what's the problem?"

"Ah, yes, the problem," stammered Landry. "The problem," he repeated.

"Yes, that's right, Landry, the fucking problem," Carruthers said, raising his voice. "Let's have it."

"The people we used for the job, Mr. President, they, um, ah, got bit by a dog, or something like that, and the police came and took them away with the drugs from the toilet tank, and then the people came home from work and said they didn't have any drugs in the toilet, and that's when the police left and called up our DEA office in LA and asked about Rivera..."

Carruthers had been listening with growing disbelief to Landry's jumbled narrative. Suddenly he shouted, "Shut up, you fucking idiot! So you're telling me that they got caught, or something like that?"

"Umm, ah, Mr. President, it wasn't our fault, the dog did it, the dog caught them, and then the police came, it was the dog's fault, from what I heard, Mr. President..."

"Will you shut the fuck up, you babbling idiot," screamed Carruthers, causing people outside within earshot to begin disappearing into offices to seek shelter. There was a loud metallic *clank* from the oval office, as Carruthers hurled an empty coffee pitcher at Landry's head.

It missed, but as Landry ducked the tumbling stainless steel missile, the exertion from the sudden movement squirted a runny intestinal discharge into his shorts and down his left leg. "Oh, God, no," gasped Landry, bolting for the door with a stiff-legged gait, hoping to contain any further damage until he could reach the men's room in the hallway.

"Where the hell are you going, you little shit," screamed Carruthers. "Come back here, right now!" Then the smell reached him. He stood wrinkling his nose. Hey, I scared the shit out of him, he mused with a little chuckle. Carruthers relished the ability to inspire fear, even in one so craven as the pathetic Jack Landry. Abruptly, his mind came back to the failure of Landry's people to make the proper arrangements for the incarceration of Suzy Johnson and her husband. He stormed out the door and down the hallway to the men's room. He pushed open the door and saw Landry's wingtips under the door in the toilet stall. "Landry"? he snarled.

"Yes, sir," Landry sobbed.

"Listen to me and listen good, you fucking drone. I want those people arrested on drug charges, and I want it done in the next couple of days, you got me? Just do it, get it done. I gather the cops found the stuff in their house, right? Then have 'em arrested. I don't give a shit about the details." Without waiting for an answer he turned and strode angrily out the door.

Landry sat miserably in the little stall and did his best to clean himself up. Finally, knees still shaking, he got up, pulled up his trousers, struggled into his jacket, and quietly emerged. He looked in the mirror. He was pasty-white, and the hair he normally combed up over his bald head lay in pathetic strings down over his left ear. He drew a deep breath, opened the door, and walked as steadily as he could manage to the exit.

* * *

As Jack Landry was taking his third Valium of the morning, washing it down with distraught little swallows of water, Jake Dougherty and Billy Joe Sisson, his Chevrolet sales manager, were going over the plans for their upcoming Red Tiger introduction sale. "Goddam," said Jake, "I never seen a company move this fast getting cars to market. I think maybe I underestimated this outfit. Yeah, even that guy Maxwell, I mean, I know he likes to hit the sauce a little hard, but he's a lot sharper than you think."

"Yeah, I think you're right," said Billy Joe. "These guys don't mess around. Everybody else always jerks you around forever, it takes 'em forever to approve a franchise application, with all their bullshit. These guys just come right on in and sign ya up."

"Yeah, well a guy like Maxwell, he's been around a long time, he can size up a situation in five minutes better'n most o' these guys in the zone office, sitting around all day analyzing their reports, all your financial statements, all that bullshit." As almost invariably happens in such relationships, Dougherty and Sisson judged factory guys who gave them what they wanted as "good guys," "sharp guys," "a guy who knows his shit," "a guy who knows how to work with ya," etc. Factory guys who insisted on dealers meeting standards or providing documentation were "assholes," "bureaucratic assholes," "paper pushers," or "guys who don't know how to work with ya."

"Yeah, like that foxy chick Vera, I know she comes off like a hayseed, but I'm tellin' ya, that's all an act. I'd bet anything she's an MBA from Stanford or someplace like that," said Sisson, nodding his head sagely. "She told me yesterday that we'll be getting cars the middle of next week, that we should have fifty on the ground the first day. That's what I call havin' it together!"

"Well, that means we wanna be up and running by next weekend. I wanna buy three full pages for Friday, Saturday, and Sunday, and I wanna go on radio with a hundred spots total for the same time period. I wanna hit this thing hard, right up front. We can park the cars on the whole front lawn area. And Billy, get the shop ready to prep these things right off the trucks and give 'em the whole treatment, rust proofing, fabric protection, paint sealant, all the usual, get a coupla extra detailers for the next week if ya need 'em. And call Jimmy when we're through here and get someone down from the agency this afternoon to start pulling together the stuff we're gonna need for the advertising. Shit, I wish we had some brochures, or at least some spec sheets on these things. Hey, what's the warranty on this car?"

Billy Joe shrugged. "Ah, I'm not sure, I gotta ask Sherry or Vera. It'll be competitive, I'm pretty sure."

"Hey, ya know what, Billy Joe? We can make the warranty optional, charge 'em five hundred bucks for it! I mean, shit, as long as we got no brochures or literature, we can sort of make it up as we go along! Boy, this is gonna be great!"

* * *

Late that afternoon Zack was picking up his parents at LAX, on their return from Maui. He and Suzy had decided to say nothing to them about the break-in and their theory about the president being behind it. After they'd settled into the car and were leaving the airport, his mother's radar was set to the high sensitivity mode, sweeping the atmosphere in the car for the tiniest signal of any trouble in his hasty marriage. "So how's Suzy liking her job, Zack?" she asked conversationally.

"I think she likes it OK, Ma, but we just don't know how long the company's gonna last over here. It's my understanding the cars they're importing are pretty uncompetitive. Well, maybe pretty awful'd be a better term. They had to get all sort of special breaks from the government to even let 'em in under our safety and emission rules."

"Well, Suzy's awfully bright, and she's completely bi-lingual, so I'm sure she could get all sorts of great jobs, maybe even teach Chinese at USC or something like that," his mother responded.

"Oh, that's for sure, Ma. Findin' a good paying job for someone like Suzy'd never be a problem." He seemed to hesitate. "But, ah, to tell you the truth, we're kinda thinking of starting a family at some point in the future, and maybe, uh, putting off a career for her until that gets settled." His mother said nothing.

"Son, you must feel pretty good about this relationship if you're thinking of having a family with her," his father said, a bit cautiously.

"Dad, I was never more certain about anything in my life. We clicked the minute we met, and we always will. We're happier every day that goes by."

Suddenly he heard his mother sniffling, then blowing her nose into a tissue. "Oh, Zack, I'm so happy to hear you say that," she said, her voice breaking. "I used to wonder if you'd ever find a girl you'd be happy with. I mean, there always used to be so many of them in and out of your life."

"Well, that was before I met Suzy. She's my life partner."

When they arrived home Lobo greeted them with a five minute sere-
nade of non-stop barking, squealing, and howling, accompanied by running around and around the little house. Both his parents gave Suzy a long
and heartfelt hug, then everybody sat down to talk about Hawaii.

That night they enjoyed one of Sammy's recipes for baby-back ribs,
which astonished Zack's parents. "This is amazing," his father said, "you
just arrived and you're already mastering American cooking." He looked
at Zack. "When's she gonna learn to speak Spanish and start doing
authentic Mexican?"

And by the time they departed Sunday afternoon, Suzy was as firmly a
part of the family as if she'd been there ten years. "Oh, Zack," she said, as
they watched his parents board in the departure lounge, "your parents are
so wonderful, I already love them so much. I can't wait to go to Kansas for
Thanksgiving and meet the rest of your family and all your friends at
home." When they got in their car in the short term parking garage, she
pulled him over and kissed him long and gently. She pulled back and looked
into his eyes. "I think this must be a dream. I don't want to wake up, ever."

* * *

At about the time Zack's parents were boarding their aircraft for home,
Jack Landry, having finally calmed down after spending the weekend
incommunicado and in bed, was meeting Win Faulkner in his office to
discuss what to do next about arresting the Johnsons.

"Let me understand this, Win," said Landry, "right now nobody can
actually *prove* that the drugs that the police found in that house weren't
there before our people arrived, is that correct?"

"Well, Jack, the burglars said they got the stuff through this guy
Rivera, but of course, he'll just deny it, I would assume. So all anybody's
got is the word of the homeowners against the word of the two guys we
used to break in the house. The only problem is that the word of our guys
isn't as credible as the people living there, especially with the testimony of
the cops on the scene, who said there was no way our guys found the bag
in the toilet tank. And we may be able to control the testimony of our own
people, but I don't know about some local cops. Most of them don't much
care for federal agents of any kind, and they might just welcome the

chance to stick it up our ass." Landry winced visibly at Faulkner's last words, his own ass being rather tender and sore from his diarrhea.

"Well, POTUS wants those two arrested, without fail, Win. What the hell, we've done shit like this before with troublemakers, like with that woman who disrupted that campaign stop. Sure, we eventually had to drop the charges, but we kept her in jail for two weeks. We can do the same thing here. I don't see what's different about this."

"Well, Jack, what's different is we didn't try to frame anybody in some of these other cases. We're talkin' about serious charges here, big time drug dealing, not some ridiculous public indecency charge or going after somebody with the IRS, just to give 'em a hard time, and maybe costin' 'em their life savings in legal fees. This is evidence tampering, serious shit."

"POTUS wants it done, Win, and I mean right now. He's got his reasons."

"Yeah, I'm sure he does," said Faulkner.

After he'd left, Faulkner wondered how to handle the arrests. The more he thought about it, the more he doubted that it was a good idea to try to take them down in their home. First, the dog might rip the shit out of somebody in the process, and second, if they killed the goddam dog, they could end up with all sorts of animal lovers freaking out and making a big stink with a human interest sob story. He could see the headline. "K-9 HERO KILLED BY FEDERAL AGENTS." Faulkner rightly assumed that the story of the burglars being foiled by the doberman had made the local news. We'll make the arrests at work, he told himself. That'll be a lot safer, plus there won't be a lot of neighbors standing around to be interviewed, telling everybody what upstanding citizens these two are. Faulkner congratulated himself on avoiding the potential PR problem and told himself that if he'd taken personal charge of the thing from the beginning, none of this bullshit would have happened. I'll have to get rid of that dolt Swetlock eventually, and this Rivera character as well, he thought.

* * *

Zhu Fei and his wife Le were just settling into their seats for the seemingly interminable flight to Los Angeles. Le was delighted to be accompanying her husband on the trip, assuming this very considerable perk to be but a prelude to Zhu's soon-to-announced advancement within the heirarchy of the Long March People's Cooperative Automotive Manufacturing Company. Plus, she looked forward to seeing California, truly, in the minds of most Chinese, the land of milk and honey. As soon as they had buckled themselves in, she took out her little English phrase book and began to study it intently. While Mrs. Zhu entertained certain apprehensions about her personal safety while in the US, occasioned especially by her husband's violent encounter with "hooligans," from which he still bore a scar on his scalp and a slightly bent nose, she planned to carry no handbag on her person when out and about, thereby thwarting purse-snatchers and muggers. And she was realistic enough to know that being forty-eight, rather plain, and a bit overweight made her an unlikely target for rapists. And in any event, there were plenty of places one dared not go in any good-sized city in China, so the personal risk element of America was hardly unique to her.

Mrs. Zhu was totally unaware of any potential marketing difficulties looming with the Red Whippet. She knew nothing of her husband's business activities, beyond the knowledge that he was a fairly high-level executive and that he therefore got to take frequent trips to China's export markets, which were most often to either Chinese "protectorates" such as Tibet, or Third World countries. The company had yet to establish any presence at all in the more advanced nations. She took it as an encouraging sign that they were establishing a beachhead in America, all the more so since her husband announced that she would accompany him on his visit. She hoped for frequent visits to California and other famous spots in America.

Mrs. Zhu thought it a bit odd that her husband had packed much more heavily than he normally did and encouraged her to do the same. Normally, he liked to travel with the bare minimum of luggage. He also instructed her to withdraw most of the money in their savings account and convert it to American Express Travelers Checks, advising her that there would likely be many desirable items to buy in California which they would enjoy at home, particularly the many wonderful kitchen items, such as blenders, excellent quality cutlery, and non-stick cookware.

As they flew east over the coast of the People's Republic, Zhu wondered if he was seeing the land of all his ancestors for the last time. He concluded, rather unhappily, that he probably was. Zhu had no idea what he'd do should he defect and plead for political asylum, though he was not worried about their physical well-being. He had noted during his brief visits to the United States that what was considered abject poverty by the Americans would be regarded as unimaginable luxury in most other countries of the world, even in the People's Republic, which like the former Soviet Union, was largely in a state of near-desperate poverty in practically all areas away from the big cities. He snorted as he recalled the revelation in a *Wall Street Journal* article, shown him by the former Miss Lin, that the average American family below the so-called poverty line owned not one, but two color TV sets.

Zhu was quite sure that whatever happened to him he'd be able to get by. I can manage with just one TV set, he told himself.

As soon as the seatbelt sign was turned off he signaled to a flight attendant and ordered a bottle of beer for each of them.

* * *

Candy Lambert, Sammy and Kate's daughter-in-law, got home from work, picked up the mail, and sorted through it as she went to the refrigerator and poured herself a glass of chablis. She sat down at the kitchen table and kicked off her shoes, going once more through the pile of junk mail to ensure that there was nothing in it of value, then sliding it to the other end of the table into the discard pile. She took a sip of her wine and thought about the little party planned for the following evening with her cooking club. She started to write down a list of all the things she'd need to pick up at the supermarket the following day. She finished and sat mentally checking off all the ingredients she'd need for her father-in-law's recipe. She felt she was missing something but couldn't decide just what it might be. Finally, she sighed and got to her feet, went into the living room, and found the tape of Sammy and Tommy's cooking show. Sammy had given her the tape when she and Roy, Sammy's son, had been to her in-laws' house for Sunday dinner a couple of weeks earlier. She'd planned to run the tape during the little party, duplicating the full sequence and techiques displayed by Sammy and Tommy. She got a paper and pencil with which to write down the complete ingredient list, turned on the TV and VCR sitting atop it, and popped in the tape. The were a few seconds of hissing snow, then the screen filled with the slightly fuzzy but still fully discernible black and white image of the president of the United States, grabbing the behind of some lady standing next to him. There was no sound track. Candy stood transfixed as the groping went on for some seconds, wondering what in the world she was watching. Then she noted the president's hand unmistakably grab hard on the woman's buttocks, shift a bit, then seem to grab even harder. Suddenly the woman turned to face him, giving Candy a good look at her. She was an Oriental woman, she could see, and apparently very attractive. Her eyes widened as she saw the woman slap the president hard enough to snap his head to one side, then another camera angle caught the president's face with an expression of sheer, mindless rage. He tried to hit the woman with his fist, missed, and took a blurringly quick counterblow on the nose from her. He went down, and the woman was immediately dragged down by several men, whom Candy took to be Secret Service agents. It all became very confused after that, with bodies flying through the air, somebody getting hit with a nightstick, and the tape ending perhaps a second or two later. She immediately rewound the tape and watched it again. She couldn't imagine just what it was she was watching. The thought occurred to her that it was some sort of fake, else why wouldn't they have heard something about the incident? And what in heaven's name were Kate and Sammy doing with it? They weren't exactly members of some wacko extremist group, always circulating crackpot tapes and sending demented E-mail messages to each other. She ejected the VHS cassette and looked for a label. There was none, not even a remnant of one somebody might have torn off. And now what had happened to the cooking show tape? Candy was absolutely certain that the tape in her hand was the one Sammy had put in her handbag while she was helping Kate wash the pots and pans. This is really weird, she told herself, shrugging with perplexity. She walked over and looked at her little ingredient list once again. Yeah, I guess I got it all, she thought.

She resolved to show the tape to Roy when he got home. She looked at the kichen wall clock, suddenly wondering where he was. It was nearly six-thirty, well past the time Roy normally got home from his job as a cable TV installer.

Ten minutes later she heard him coming up the steps. "Hey, babe," he shouted through the front screen. "Come on out and see what I brought home!"

"Not another kitten, Roy," she said, looking out the front door.

"Naw, c'mon. They called me this afternoon and told me it came in early," said Roy happily, gesturing toward the new black Mustang GT convertible parked in front of the house.

"Oh, wow, will you look at that," she cried, skipping down the steps. "Take me for a ride this minute, and leave the top down!"

And in the excitement of taking delivery of their new car and the little celebration dinner that followed at Bennigan's, Candy temporarily forgot about the mysterious video tape.

* * *

Win Faulkner, at this point throwing caution to the winds, and knowing that Carruthers' orders were likely to end badly for all concerned eventually, one way or another, simply called Lee Swetlock on an unsecured phone line.

"Well, Lee," he began as Swetlock came on the line, "I managed to convince the president that this whole fuckup wasn't your fault. I made it sound like the FBI surveillance report wasn't correct, especially the part about not knowin' about the friggin' dog. So if you can maintain a low profile for a while and not drop the ball on me again, you may get out of this without any permanent damage to your career."

There was a long silence from the other end. Finally, Swetlock, following a distinctly audible gulp, said, "Thanks, Win, you'll never know how much I appreciate that, especially coming from you."

Faulkner pulled the handset from his ear, rolled his eyes, and shook his head. "Yeah, well, don't worry about it, Lee," he said, "we gotta go forward from here. We can't undo the past, right?"

"Right, Win," said Swetlock, choking with emotion.

And for the next five minutes Faulkner explained that he wanted the Johnsons arrested, not at home, but at their place of work, for the reasons that he'd already worked out in his mind. "And we need it done in the next twenty-four hours, forty-eight at the absolute outside, Lee. That's the timeframe Carruthers has established for us."

"We'll get it done, Win. You can count on me," said Swetlock, voice breaking.

"Attaboy, Lee," said Faulkner, "I know I can. Let's do it." He hung up the phone and looked out the window. Jesus, what a total dipshit, he thought.

* * *

The following morning Suzy and Zack lingered over a leisurely breakfast. Zack was scheduled for an overnight, laying over at Newark Airport, due to be back the following evening. He reached over and took her hand. "You gonna miss me, honey?"

"I miss you all the time when we're not together. It was nice having Lobo here. He was nice company and he made me feel so safe."

"Yeah, we oughtta think about getting a dog at some point. I think they're good for kids, too. And one thing about this job, I'm always gonna have overnights, and when I get enough seniority to start flyin' the big equipment to Europe, I'll be out overnight even more."

"Make sure you call tonight when you get settled." She got up and started clearing the table. Zack stood up and began pulling on his uniform jacket.

"Well, I better get going, honey." He walked over, put his arms around her and pulled her close, then looked into her eyes. "You know, lady, you're the only girl in the world who looks as good first thing in the morning as you did the night before."

"Just remember that. It'll help you stay out of trouble on these layovers." She cocked her head as she looked up at him. "I was just wondering something. Why do they call them layovers?"

"Guess!"

"Forget I asked." She kissed him on the lips. "I'll see you tomorrow night, my love. You can call me at the office if you want."

I"ll do that." He gave her a hug that lifted her off the ground.

* * *

Lee Swetlock was growing excited at the prospect of doing President

Carruthers' bidding, and doing it in such a way that would redeem him from the embarrassment of having his two "seasoned professionals" caught by a dog and the Pasadena PD, and further, letting his agency be potentially incriminated in the whole botched affair. No, he told himself, this time'll be different. His own people would handle it.

Swetlock had assigned the job to five DEA agents from the LA field office. They were to grab the Johnson lady at her place of employment, Red Tiger Motors in Chino. They were to go in at 1100 that morning. Swetlock had calculated that they'd catch her on the premises at that hour, since it was too early to go to lunch, and yet late enough to ensure that she'd have arrived at work. Her husband he planned to arrest in the Continental Airlines employee parking lot. Swetlock had calculated that Mr. Johnson wasn't likely to try to run while wearing an airline crew uni-form, at least not within the airport environment.

He couldn't see anything going awry this time. Nobody kept a dog at the office, he reasoned. This'll go nice and smooth, by the numbers this time, he reassured himself. It'd provide some much needed publicity for himself and the agency as well. Toward that end, Swetlock had notified KABC, the local ABC affiliate in Los Angeles, advising them that they might want to have a news crew available to tape the arrest of a major west coast drug figure, taking place in Chino that morning. From what he'd heard about the comely Mrs. Johnson, he'd be practically assured of getting some prime news airtime. He was trying to imagine Win Faulkner's words of praise at this remarkable display of resourcefulness and imagination. As with any federal agency, future budgets were always a major area of concern at DEA. And public visibility and good PR were paramount in ensuring the continued growth and funding of bureaucratic empires. Well, thought, Swetlock, I'll be doing my part.

At nine-thirty that morning Zack Johnson was just backing his Firebird into a parking spot in the employee lot. He laid his flight and overnight bags on the pavement outside the door, got out of the car and locked it. He reached down to pick up the two bags, then noticed two men in dark suits walking rapidly toward the front of his car. He stood for a moment, looking at them quizzically. Both wore dark glasses but clearly were making eye contact with him.

"Mr. Johnson?" asked the taller of the two, reaching in his breast pock-et for something.

"Yeah, I'm Johnson," he replied.

"Agents Frankel and Jennings," the tall man said, as they both flashed their ID. "You're under arrest for possession of and trafficking in controlled substances." He reached around under his coat, clearly and intentionally revealing a gun in a high ride holster, and pulled out a pair of handcuffs. "Read him his rights," he said, turning to his partner.

Zack instantly made the connection between the two agents and the attempted drug plant in their house. Without giving a second's thought to the possible consequences, he dropped both bags on the pavement, and in one quick but smooth movement grabbed the two agents by their throats, pulled them towards him, and smashed their heads together with appalling force. He held them up and cracked their skulls together twice more. When he dropped them to the pavement, one was bleeding from the ears, the other from his nose. Both were unconscious. Zack stood over them for a long moment, quite seriously debating whether to kill them both. He finally got hold of himself, then reached down and relieved both of them of their guns. He stood indecisively for a moment, looking at them, then ejected the magazines, then the rounds in the chambers, and threw the magazines over the nearby fence into a drainage ditch. He then threw both pistols down on the pavement as hard as he could, picked them up, and repeated the performance. He picked them up and inspected them with satisfaction. The magazine well of one was bent enough to block any attempt to seat a magazine. The other had the muzzle sufficiently deformed to prevent the gun from cycling. "You assholes oughtta take better care of your guns, " he spat, dropped the battered weapons over their prostrate forms, then got back in his car and tore out of the employee lot. His hands were shaking, from both sheer rage and the adrenalin rush of the encounter, but also with abject fear for what they might be doing to Suzy. As he made for the airport exit, he tried to decide whether to head home and see what was going on, or whether to head for the office in Chino. For the first time in his life, Zack cursed his steadfast refusal to get a cell phone. He finally decided that if they had tried to grab him at the airport, they also intended to get Suzy at work. He suddenly realized that they wouldn't want to risk another encounter with Lobo, whom they had no way of knowing was now in Kansas. He quickly calculated the quickest way to the office in Chino and headed for the San Bernadino Freeway.

As Zack was racing to the Red Tiger office in Chino, Sid Burnside was having an impromptu little staff meeting with Vera Hawkins, Suzy, and a badly hung over, nearly somnolent Sherry Maxwell. "OK, guys," he said, "the ship docks day after tomorrow. I figure we can start shipping by the end of the week, maybe right away. The only problem is that we don't know what order they're gonna come off the ship in, so we can't draft the banks today using the vehicle ID numbers. It looks like we're gonna have to ship this week and draft while the cars are in transit. I don't see a problem with that. We got all the floorplan commitment letters, we're ready to go."

"Well, all *mah* dealers are ready to go," said Vera proudly. "They all be expectin' a mighty big shipment fo' the Red Whippet launch."

"Lunch?" said Maxwell, starting to get to his feet a bit unsteadily. "Yeah, let's go to Sammy's. I'm even buyin'."

Suzy put her hand firmly on Maxwell's shoulder and pushed him gently back into his chair. "Vera," she said, "I, umm, think you should choose your words more carefully around Sherry." Maxwell looked momentarily confused, then pushed back his sleeve to look at his watch. He shook it briefly. "Sherry, your watch is right, I'm afraid. It's only nine forty-five," said Suzy.

"Yeah, for a minute I thought I needed a new watch," said Maxwell dejectedly.

"Kin ya'll excuse me?" said Vera, getting up and heading for the ladies' room.

She'd been in the ladies' room for perhaps two minutes when the little group heard the front door open, then close a moment later. They waited expectantly as footsteps came down the hall. And suddenly, there in the doorway to the office, stood Mr. and Mrs. Zhu, luggage in hand.

Burnside stood, momentarily surprised, but then recovered. "Mr. Zhu, how good to see you!" he cried with apparent enthusiasm, coming from around his desk to greet his boss.

"Miss Lin, what are you doing here?" cried Zhu, momentarily ignoring Burnside.

"Who is Miss Lin?" cried Mrs. Zhu, looking at her husband accusingly.

"Zhu, what are you doing here?" cried Suzy Johnson. There was a brief cacophony of Chinese and English expressions of surprise, dismay, and anger.

"It's thet *pervert*," shrieked Vera Hawkins, who'd re-emerged unnoticed from the ladies' room. "It's *him*, the one whut ruined mah Starlight career!" With that, she grabbed a half-full coffee cup from Suzy Johnson's desk and flung it with quite remarkable velocity at Zhu's head. The porcelain projectile, trailing an airborne wake of brown coffee which laced across Mrs. Zsu's beloved suede jacket, smashed against Zhu's forehead in an explosion of white fragments. Zhu crashed back against the doorframe, momentarily stunned but still conscious.

"Git his camera," screamed Vera, quite irrationally she would later realize, thinking that the camera hanging around his neck would still contain the film taken of her *thang*. She charged Zhu, who was sliding slowly down the doorframe to the floor, blood suddenly running down his forehead and into his eyes. He wiped his forehead with the back of his hand, starting when he saw the bright red slash smeared across his knuckles.

"Aaaiiiii!" he screamed, suddenly seeing the maniacal apparition of the she-devil Vera Hawkins, slipping and sliding in her heels as she came across the room, arms outstretched to grab his camera. *"AAAAIIIIIIiiii!"* he shrieked again in pain and terror, grabbing the camera and holding it firmly to his chest with both hands.

"Gimme thet camera, raht now, you li'l shit," she screamed in what seemed an eerie rendition of *deja-vu* to Zhu. She fell on him and grabbed for the camera, and a familiar tug of war began once again. Soon the two were rolling over and over on the polished tile floor, screaming incoherently. Suddenly Mrs. Zhu's eyes rolled upwards in their sockets. She swooned, quite undramatically, and simply collapsed in a heap on the floor.

Mrs. Zhu's faint seemed to bring the others out of their open-mouthed state of shocked disbelief. Suzy moved forward first, trying to separate the combatants. She quickly gave up and jabbed Vera hard with a knuckle, just below her armpit. She seemed to deflate, stunned with the pain inflicted on her by Suzy's perfectly directed blow. "That's enough!" Suzy Johnson said in English, then repeated in Chinese. She reached down and roughly separated the pair. Burnside came forward to help Zhu to his feet. Both Vera and Zhu were spattered with blood from the freely bleeding wound in Zhu's forehead.

"Ah cain't believe ya'll done that to me, Suzy. Ya'll hurt me really bad. I thought you was my friend," moaned Vera.

"I'm sorry, Vera, I didn't want to hurt you, but I had to stop the fighting. I didn't do any damage. The pain will subside shortly. Please, let me help you stand up."

Sherry Maxwell, dimly recalling a resuscitation technique he was sure he'd seen in a western or perhaps a war movie, rushed over to the water cooler, drew a large styrofoam coffee cup of ice water, and dashed it in the face of the still-supine Mrs. Zhu. She jolted into full consciousness, coughing fitfully from the water which had gone into her open mouth. She stopped long enough to get a good look at Zhu, who was trying to get to his feet with Burnside's help. The sight of the blood and Zhu's torn shirt caused her to gasp and faint again.

As everyone dropped what they were doing and tried to revive Mrs. Zhu once again, Melanie Samuels, KABC's rising young on-camera crime reporter, briefly checked her makeup, then nervously watched the five man, camouflage fatigue-clad DEA team position two men to watch the sides and rear of the building, then move up the remaining three to the front of the building, poised to rush through the entrance. Oliver Jamison, a fifty-four year old black camera man and former Marine fire team leader in Vietnam, watched with derision. "Lookit them dudes," he said nodding to the M-16 equipped DEA SWAT team. "One li'l ol' NVA gook with a AK come runnin' out that door, that bunch o' Dial soap, wannabe, whitebread pussies'd shit theyselves bigtime, betcha anything." He spat contemptuously on the pavement.

"Now, Oliver, stop that," laughed Melanie. "It's sexist, calling 'em pussies." Oliver snorted and zoomed in on the three men about to enter the building with his Sony video-cam.

"What the hell's all that yelling and screaming?" asked the group leader. "I sounds like they're killin' each other in there." He felt a sudden clutch of fear. What had sounded like little more than a photo-op for the agency now had an unpredictable element about it. He briefly considered calling for reinforcements, then abruptly concluded that the apparent altercation inside the office might yield priceless evidence, perhaps a major drug transaction gone awry. He had a sudden vision of flour sack sized bags of heroin or perhaps stacked shipping cartons filled with assault rifles. He looked at his two fellow team members, who seemed to be watching him a bit nervously. "OK, we're goin' in," he said with what he hoped was just the right mixture of drama and stoic calm. He pushed the door open with his foot and began advancing down the hall, M-16 at the ready.

He heard Burnside's voice. "We gotta stop the bleeding," he said, referring to Zhu's once again split scalp. The team leader felt his blood run cold. Then he heard Suzy Johnson's voice saying something about trying to keep someone concious and breathing normally. He had a sudden vision of a ghastly neck wound, requiring a tracheotomy. He stopped outside the door to Burnside's office, hesitated, then burst in, screaming

"FREEZE, DROP YOUR WEAPONS! DROP YOUR WEAPONS," he repeated, just beginning to notice that there were no weapons in evidence. His two team members followed him into the room, sweeping the area menacingly with their black M-16s.

Suzy Johnson, looking up from the floor, where she was trying to revive Mrs. Zhu, got over the initial shock first. She looked at each of the DEA men in turn. Finally she said, "Are you quite sure you have the right address? This is the Red Tiger Motor Company. You know, China's distributor for cars in the United States?" She looked at them askance, eyebrows raised, saying it in a way that implied that the G-men were federal versions of the Keystone Kops. "Perhaps you'd like to use the phone book?"

But by now the DEA men had seen enough blood and torn clothes to assume that something not quite kosher had been going on. "OK, everybody, up against the wall, and spread 'em," barked their leader. "And would Susan Johnson identify herself."

Before Suzy could answer, Vera Hawkins, whose blouse was now half-sleeveless, piped up, "Ah didn't do nothing! Ah'm innocent. It was thet li'l pervert over there," she said, pointing at Zhu, who was holding a handkerchief to his forehead. "He was a tryin' t' take pitchers o' mah privates! Ah bet he's into kiddie porn and such!"

"I'm Mrs. Johnson," said Suzy. "Just who are you and what do you want?" It still hadn't occurred to her that the entire scene wasn't just a colossal case of horrifically crossed signals.

* * *

At the exact moment that the DEA agents were speculating that they'd come on a major drug smuggling/kiddie porn ring, Marilyn Summers, one of the many White House interns, was sitting at Stacy's desk, demanding to see President Carruthers. "He called me down just five minutes ago," she whined plaintively. "How can he be busy all of a sudden." She clutched her little leather portfolio, which contained the poem she'd penned for Carruthers the night before, which wailed, on a roughly eighth grade composition level, about a young girl who'd fallen in love with her "teacher." "I have something I just *have* to show him, Stacy. Can't I just go in?"

"I, uh, don't think that'd be a good idea, Marilyn," Stacy replied. "Uh, the First Lady's with him right now. It might be a little awkward."

"I think I get the picture." She got to her feet and snapped her panty thong angrily, just as Heather Carruthers appeared in the doorway, exiting the oval office in what appeared to be a considerable huff. She stopped short, just as Marilyn was getting to her feet with the highly audible *snap*. She stared at the chubby twenty-two year old girl for a long moment, then did an abrupt about-face and marched back through the door, which she slammed violently behind her.

"You miserable *worm*," she snarled at him through clenched teeth. "Little Miss Piggy's out there again. You worthless shit, you told me you weren't seeing that adolescent little twat anymore! Jesus Christ, you could at least carry on with somebody who has a room temperature IQ!" She walked around behind him, as he sat staring straight ahead, afraid to turn to face her. Suddenly, she punched him hard on his right ear, then pulled his head back by the hair with her other hand. "You piece of shit!" she screamed, and begun punching the side of his head repeatedly, as she hung on to him by his hair.

"Oww, Heather, stop it, I won't do it anymore, *ouch*, goddammit, that hurts," Carruthers screeched as the blows rained onto his ear, neck, and cheek. She was about to grab the water pitcher off his desk and begin beating him with that when she abruptly composed herself.

She released his hair, examined her reddened knuckles, and said calmly, "I suppose we're running out of plausible stories to explain your frequently battered condition. Once we're outta here, I don't care what the fuck you do or who the fuck you fuck, you asshole. But if I catch you fucking around again while we're in the White House, I'll burn off your balls and cock with a fucking blowtorch, you got me?"

"You know I wouldn't do anything like that, honey, now, c'mon, nothing like that's gonna happen," he said, wheedling.

The absurd promise almost set her off again. She started to rear back to swing at him, but managed to stop herself. She turned and stormed out of the office, stopping in front of Stacy. "If you ever see that porky little piglet in this building again, you are to call me immediately. Do you fully understand what I'm telling you, Stacy, or would you prefer to spend the remainder of your government career in some typing pool in the basement of the Defense Department?" Heather wasn't connected enough to the activities of the little people to know that there hadn't been a typing pool in the United States in fifteen years.

"I think I get the message, Mrs. Carruthers," she said quietly.

As Heather Carruthers' heels were clicking angrily down the hallway, her husband was in the bathroom of the Oval Office, doing a quick damage assessment in the bathroom mirror. His right ear was slightly swollen and his cheek was bright red. Jesus Christ, she's fucking crazy, he told himself. One of the these days I'm gonna kick her ass good. The thought momentarily soothed the pain in his ear and the stinging in his cheek.

But then he thought of the DEA operation against the Johnson couple in California, and for the first time the near-idiotic recklessness of it fully registered with him. Carruthers had occasional moments of lucid risk analysis, concerning even sex, most frequently when he'd just had the crap beaten out of him by his wife.

Goddam, he thought, I better get ahold of that jackoff Landry and call this thing off. Christ, I think she might actually turn a fucking blowtorch on my cock and balls! Carruthers practically ran back to his desk and ordered Stacy to get Landry on the double.

Less than thirty seconds later he was talking to a thoroughly rattled Jack Landry. "Y-yes, sir, we're right on schedule, we'll have those two people in the bag for you in a little while, sometime in the next half-hour I think."

"What?" screamed Carruthers. "Who gave you the go-ahead on this thing, you idiot?"

"I, I, ah, you, you…." stammered Landry.

"Just stop it in place right now, this fucking instant, do you understand me, you nincompoop?" shrieked Carruthers. "Call it off, stop everything!" He slammed the phone down.

Landry, whose hair had begun falling out in tufts since the break-in had been foiled, picked up the phone and entered Win Faulkner's number. His secretary came on the line, informing him that Mr. Faulkner was currently involved in a "field operation."

"Page him! Find him somehow!" Landry moaned. "I have to talk with him right now, this very instant. It's a matter of the agency's survival."

"I'll have him call you the second I get in touch with him," said the secretary.

A moment later Faulkner, having a late lunch in a favorite diner in Alexandria, took the call from his secretary. He thought about Landry's apparently agonized request, told his secretary he'd comply, shut down his cell-phone, and continued his lunch. He assumed that something else had gone awry in the ongoing saga of the Johnsons. He shrugged. What the hell, at this point I'd be better off not getting involved in any way. That dolt Swetlock can take the fall for whatever happens. He noticed his coffee cup was almost empty. "Hey, waitress, bring me some more coffee," he ordered brusquely.

"Right away, sir, I'll get a fresh pot." The mocha-hued girl stepped out of sight of Faulkner, spit in the pot, and came over, smiling brightly. "Here you are, sir," she said, continuing to smile as she poured. "Just give a holler if you need anything else." Faulkner grunted by way of acknowledgment.

I wonder why those fucking people are always so happy, he asked himself.

* * *

"I said, I am Mrs. Johnson," Suzy repeated for emphasis. "Please be so kind as to identify yourselves, and you might want to stop waving those ridiculous guns around." At that exact moment Mrs. Zhu came around, raised her head, and saw the DEA agents. She gasped, then whimpered softly, and fell back into unconsciousness.

The leader replied, "We're federal drug enforcement agents. You're under arrest for trafficking in controlled substances." He turned to one of the agents behind him. "Read her rights to her."

As the agent droned on from his Miranda card, Suzy Johnson's emotions went from a state of amused annoyance to sheer terror, instantly perceiving exactly what was happening. "Drug trafficking?" she said, putting the back of her hand to her face. "Us?"

There was a stunned silence in the room, finally broken by Vera Hawkins, who said loudly, "Ya'll are plumb crazy! Suzy ain't no drug dealer, she ain't done nothing. Ya'll are jus' a bunch o' goddam, good-fer-nothin' revenooers. Where Ah come from we all know to take care o' varmints like ya'll." She turned to Suzy, who just stood, tears welling up in her eyes. "Don't ya'll worry, honey, Ah'm gonna call my ol' daddy, he an' Uncle Cletus know how to deal with these varmints, they's buried plenty of 'em up on Seminole Mountain." This bit of mountain bravado and folklore was, of course, untrue, but Vera was sure it would make Suzy feel better.

"What the hell are we gonna do with all these people," whispered one of the DEA men to the leader. "There's something going down here, that's obvious, I mean, look at this scene. I say we take 'em all in for questioning. And that broad over there," he said, nodding at Vera, "she's threatening federal agents as far as I'm concerned. To hear her tell it, she's already been involved in knockin' some of our guys off."

Without answering the lead agent barked, "You're under arrest," nodding toward Suzy. "Get her ready to go," meaning put her in handcuffs. "The rest of you are coming along for questioning. If any of you offer any resistance or give us any trouble of any kind, you'll be arrested for interfering with federal law enforcement officers, assault, obstruction of justice, and anything else we can think up on short notice. If you behave yourselves you can remain unrestricted. Any trouble and you'll be in handcuffs, just like your friend."

And so two minutes later Sid Burnside, Mr. and Mrs. Zhu, borne along on a stretcher carried by two para-medics, Vera Hawkins, Sherry Maxwell, and the handcuffed Suzy Johnson were led out into the bright sunlight toward the white government van which would carry them to the Los Angeles County Jail.

Oliver Jamison got an excellent close-up of the tearful but still beautiful Suzy Johnson, then another shot of Vera, looking beautifully angry and defiant, and Zhu, looking battered, bewildered and badly frightened. Sherry Maxwell tried to hold his briefcase over his face as they passed the camera, not because he had anything to hide, but simply because he'd seen the pose often enough in news pictures to assume that it was simply some sort of expected arrest protocol.

Jamison panned on them until they began to climb into the van and continued to tape as the van disappeared down the street. Finally, he lowered the camera and turned to Melanie Samuels. "Where you wanna wrap-up?"

"Oh, right over there, I guess," she replied. "I wanna make sure you can get the corporate sign in the shot, that's the important thing." Melanie had no idea who or what Red Tiger Motor Company was. Nor had Lee Swetlock, when he provided the tip for the story. He'd merely told her it was some kind of Chinese trading company that appeared to be a front for illicit activities, and that there would be an arrest of a major drug kingpin at that location that morning.

In her wrap-up two minutes later, Melanie would say, as she stood in front of the building, with the sign in clear view, "Federal drug enforcement officials indicated that the arrest of Susan Johnson, a former Chinese national married to an American, would likely be the first in a series of arrests and expected indictments involving what appears to be a major Asian drug connection."

Less than five minutes after the news van left the scene, Zack Johnson pulled up in front of the Chino headquarters for Red Tiger. He jumped out and ran down the little sidewalk. The door was still open. He ran down the hallway into Sid Burnside's office, glanced inside, saw no one, and began calling, "Hey, Suzy, where are you, is anybody here?" He ran frantically around the office building, in and out of offices and storerooms, even trying the ladies' room. Finally he went back into Burnside's office and stood looking around, trying to determine where everybody had gone. Suddenly he noticed blood drops at his feet, where Zhu had been sitting, and then he saw more droplets scattered around, along with some smears on the floor where Zhu and Vera had been struggling and rolling around. He sat down in a nearby chair. "Oh, God, no," he choked. His imagination was running wild with what might have happened in the office. Abruptly he realized that whatever had happened probably couldn't have been too tragic, else the place would have been surrounded by hordes of police, gumball-flashing patrol cars, and camera crews from every local and affiliate TV network in Los Angeles. He forced himself to concentrate, and finally concluded that the agents had probably just taken everybody, including Suzy, away with them. He wondered what to do next. Shit, he told himself, there's one thing I better do right now. He went to Suzy's desk, picked up the phone, and dialed his parents' home in Liberal, Kansas. It rang several times before the answering machine picked up. "Ma, or Dad," he said, "whoever hears this first, take that tape I gave you and make several copies of it and make sure some of 'em are in a safe place. I can't explain why right now, just that it's really important. I love ya both." He replaced the handset slowly and again wondered what to do next. It suddenly occurred to him that he'd be safer in the hands of the local police, especially with cops who knew the details of the burglary and attempted drug plant. Even if they turned him over to federal agents, there'd be plenty of witnesses to attest that he'd been restrained and unarmed at the time of the transfer. Zack hung his head briefly, then got to his feet and headed for his car once again.

Five minutes later he was back on the freeway, heading directly for the Pasadena central police station.

* * *

A half hour after the arrest of Suzy Johnson and the departure of the KABC news crew, Jack Landry, nearly incoherent with anxiety, was still waiting for Win Faulkner's confirmation that the DEA operation had been called off. In desperation, he called Faulkner's number once again, once again getting his secretary. "He's not in yet, Mr. Landry," she said. "I did give him your message. Oh, wait! He just came in the door."

Faulkner heard her informing somebody that he'd just arrived. "Who?" he mouthed silently.

"Mr. Landry," she replied, covering the mouthpiece.

"OK. tell him I'll be with him in a minute," he said, rolling his eyes. His secretary tittered. Landry's high-doltage intellect was universally recognized throughout Washington. Finally, he went into his office, after leisurely scanning the mail on his secretary's desk, and picked up. "Hey, Jack, what's up?"

"Didn't you get my message? Why didn't you call right back?"

"Well, I figured it was about this LA thing, and I didn't want to call you on my cell phone. I came right over as quick as I could. I was just walking in the door when you called," said Faulkner in one of his rare truthful statements.

"Never mind all that. What's going on with that thing in LA? Have they made the arrests yet?"

"Well, I don't know, I guess they could have. I didn't ask Swetlock to give me an up to the minute briefing. I mean, arresting a couple of unarmed people can't be that big a deal."

"God, find out what's going on right now, and if they haven't done it, tell them to stop everything right where they are. Do nothing, do you understand, halt them in place, then call me right back." Landry hung up in Faulkner's ear.

Faulkner shrugged and entered Lee Swetlock's number. Swetlock was on within thirty seconds. "Hey, Lee," he began, "did you make the arrests yet?"

"Yeah, we did, about two o'clock your time," said Swetlock proudly. "We bagged six of 'em. It was great. They looked like they were havin' some kind of big fight when we went in. We had no trouble at all, got three US citizens and three Chinese nationals. I think we're onto something really big here, Win, drugs, kiddie porn, there was some loose talk about offing some federal agents, all kinds of shit."

"How'd you arrest 'em all?" asked Faulkner. "We only had a warrant for that Johnson pair."

"Well, actually, we didn't arrest 'em all, just that Chinese lady, Johnson. We took the others in for questioning." He paused. "We did have one problem, Win."

"Yeah?"

"Well, we went to bag the husband at the airport, right in the parking lot, but he got away."

"How'd he do that?"

"We're still trying to piece it together, Win. It sounds like they flashed their badges and he lit into 'em with a tire iron or something like that. One of our guys is still unconscious, the other one's got a fractured skull."

"Wait, you're telling me two armed agents got worked over by a suspect with a goddam tire iron? Where is he now?"

"Well, we're not sure what happened to him. He musta left the parking lot after he worked our guys over. We're lookin' for him, but without getting the local guys involved with an all points, I don't know how we're gonna find him."

"Jesus, don't get the local police involved. This was and is top secret. I don't want anybody knowin' about it, through any source."

Swetlock momentarily felt faint. "Ah, yeah, I got ya, we'll keep it under wraps, Win," he said hollowly. "I'll keep ya posted. Whaddya want me to do with these people, the ones we're just holdin' for questioning?"

"Try and hang on to 'em as long as you can. I'll get back to you on that." Faulkner hung up.

No sooner had he heard the click of the line disconnecting than Swetlock frantically called KABC and asked for Melanie Samuels. He was told she was on a location segment and unavailable. "Can ya give me her cell phone number?" he asked desperately. "It's very important, I mean really important."

"I'll tell you what," the voice came back, "gimme your number and I'll have her call you as soon as she's available."

"Yeah, please make sure she undertands how important this thing is," he said.

"You got it, buddy."

Swetlock noticed he was sweating profusely, despite the dry seventy-two degree temperature in his office.

* * *

While Lee Swetlock was confronting every true bureaucrat's worst nightmare, the loss of facelessness, Zack Johnson was in a small interrogation room with Detectives Murray and Ruskin, relating the events of that morning, as well as his motivation in giving himself up to him.

"Jesus," said Murray as Ruskin watched impassively, "if I get this totally straight, two DEA guys, or at least two guys who said they were DEA, tried to arrest you in the airline parking lot. Then you beat the crap outta of 'em, take away their guns and ruin 'em, then leave. And you go to your wife's office and find her and everybody else gone and blood on the floor. And you're tellin' me that it was these guys who masterminded the break-in at your house last week and tried to plant the bag o' heroin in your bathroom. And you're comin' to us to make sure these same guys can't knock you and your wife off under some kind of suspicious circumstances." He and Ruskin looked at one another. Finally Murray sighed. "C'mon, Zack, this has got to be some kind of weird movie plot. You can't really expect us to buy into this, can you?" In truth, Murray had concluded, based on his conversations with Sedgely and Duran, that Zack Johnson at least believed the story he was telling, just as he felt that the two burglars also believed their story. "C'mon, Zack, what'd be their motivation?"

Zack thought for a long moment. "It's hard to explain." He paused. "Maybe there's something I can show you that'd make it more believable." Suddenly he couldn't see any particular downside to showing the two detectives the video of Carruthers' performance that night. "Can we go to my house? That's where it is."

"Where's that goddam wolf of yours?"

For the first time in the interview Zack chuckled. "He's back in Kansas with my parents. We were just watching him while they were in Hawaii."

"Well, maybe that'll turn out to be the luckiest thing you ever did," said Ruskin, speaking for the first time in the last twenty minutes.

Forty-five minutes later the two detectives were standing in front of the Johnson's VCR as Zack fed in the tape. "Watch this carefully and tell me if you recognize any of the people in the picture." He hit the play button.

"Christ, that's the fucking president, coppin' a feel from that broad," said Murray." Zack looked at him sharply. "Holy shit, that's your wife the bastard's gropin'! Sorry, I didn't recognize her till she turned to face him." He and Ruskin watched the tape run out, speechless. "Let's see that again," said Ruskin.

They watched it several times, both completely convinced that it was authentic, unrehearsed, and unstaged. Finally Murray spoke. "OK, Zack, we seen it. You wanna give us the background to this thing?"

And so for the next twenty minutes Zack explained the seemingly random series of events that led up to him and his new bride being present at the Chinese embassy, which resulted in Carruthers' outrageous behavior. "She busted his nose good, you could hear it crack all over the ballroom. Too bad there's no sound track on this security tape. That's why he was wearing that bandage across his nose a coupla months ago. That whole tumor story was just a smokescreen. There was nothing wrong with that bastard's nose before he tried to grope my wife and then took a swing at her. And this whole goddam thing about the drug plant and the DEA guys tryin' to drag us off all came from that sonofabitch. He was just pissed that Suzy broke his nose and made him look like the asshole he is."

Nobody said anything more for several moments. Finally Murray looked at Zack. "You got any more of these tapes?"

"Yeah, I got a number of 'em in safe places."

"I'm glad for that, Zack, for both of you," said Murray quietly. "You know, me and my partner here been cops a long time, more'n twenty years. We heard it all, and we gotta pretty good sense for the truth. And I don't mind telling you I think what you're telling me is the truth, at least as far as you know it. There's too many things that fit together here."

"Maybe you oughtta keep that thing for safe-keeping," said Zack. "I got others, but it might be nice to know there's one locally in safe hands if anything weird happens. Now, how can I find out about my wife?"

Murray shrugged. "I guess we can call the DEA field office and ask about her. We can tell 'em we got you in custody."

"You think that's a good idea?" asked Zack. "They'll want to come over and get me right away, I'd think."

"Yeah, well that doesn't mean we're gonna give you up that easy. We'll tell 'em to get a court order remanding you into their custody, that'll probably take a few hours, maybe a day. There's something really weird about this thing. If you really stomped these two guys like you said, you'd think they'd have an all points out on you, havin' every cop, sheriff, and meter maid in southern California out lookin' for you."

"You really think so?"

"Hell, yeah. These feds get really upset about some suspect resisting arrest, especially beating up a couple of their people in the process."

"What would you do with me, then?"

"I dunno, take you back to the station, let you cool your heels there for a while. I wanna talk about it with the chief, and maybe show him this tape if you don't mind."

"You know, I'd really rather you didn't show it to him. You can let him know that you saw it, but I'd really rather just leave it here. The fewer people who see it the better for the moment. It may give us the leverage to get this dirtbag to leave us alone, but if it gets to be public property, his motivation to back off may be gone."

Murray seemed to think about this for a moment. "Yeah, you may be right. OK, I'll just tell him we saw it and left it here for the time being."

When they got back to the police station in mid-afternoon, Zack simply lounged around Murray's office, reading magazines. At four-thirty Murray came in. "They got your wife down in the LA county jail, Zack," he said. "They're holding the rest of them for questioning. Everybody's OK. I told 'em to let her know we got you in custody over here and you're fine, too."

"God, I wonder what she's thinking," said Zack. "She comes to this country and the first thing that happens is the president tries to feel her up, she lets him have it, and now the bastard's got the whole federal government after her." Actually, Zack was remarkably unconcerned about Suzy's state of mind, knowing with certainty that she was mentally as tough and resilient as a samurai blade. He chuckled as he thought of her probable reaction to being likened to anything of Japanese martial origin.

* * *

As Zack was reflecting on just what might happen next, a thoroughly rattled Lee Swetlock was finally talking with Melanie Samuels. "Ms. Samuels, I gotta ask you a big favor," he said. "It's a matter of national security, with major diplomatic overtones."

"What can I do?" she replied, suddenly excited at the prospect of being onto a story with major international implications.

"Ms. Samuels, I gotta ask you not to run that story tonight, or ever maybe. It's gonna be a major embarrassment for this administration, which is in the middle of some very delicate negotiations with the Chinese right now."

"Well, can you be a little more specific, Lee? I can't just spike a story unless I have enough detailed reasons to go to my producer with. I mean, you invited us out there. You told me that there was some kind of big Asian drug connection involved. And frankly, the whole thing struck me as pretty interesting on the face of it. You got this big office building, almost empty, and just five or six people in there. You got these two really good looking ladies, one American and one Chinese, I mean, the story's gotta lot of good eyeball, Lee. I'm gonna need a really good reason not to air it."

"Please, Ms. Samuels, Melanie, I'm asking you not to air this thing. I can give you a lot of good future stories, but only if you pass on this one."

That turned out to be the wrong thing to say to Melanie Samuels, who, while only twenty-six, been around long enough to know that the promise of future scoops in return for not doing something adverse to one's interests was a hollow promise. "I'm sorry, Lee," she said coolly, "if you can't come up with some specifics regarding this big diplomatic problem, I gotta let it run. Call if you come up with anything." And she hung up. Melanie figured there was something already potentially big to be making Swetlock as panicked as he clearly was. And if he came across with more facts, the story could get bigger still. I can't lose either way, she told herself happily.

* * *

As Melanie Samuels was hopefully speculating that she was on to something really big, Jack Landry was hurrying to the White House to personally inform Carruthers that the arrest of Mrs. Johnson had already taken place, and that her husband had already turned himself in to local police. His knees were actually knocking when he stood still, and he had to force himself to walk the last thirty feet to Stacy's desk outside the Oval Office. She looked up and smiled as he approached. "He's expecting you, Mr. Landry. Just go on in."

Landry looked in and saw a weary-looking Bob Carruthers, who appeared to be reading the op-ed page of the *Washington Post*. He looked up and motioned for Landry to enter. "Have a seat, Jack, and give me an update," he said distractedly.

This was the first display of civil behavior that Landry had seen from Carruthers in some time. He relaxed just a bit and proceeded cautiously. "Well, Mr. President, by the time we talked, they'd already arrested Mrs. Johnson, the Chinese girl. The husband's turned himself in to the local police. They picked up a number of others for questioning." Carruthers showed no reaction. Landry watched him carefully. Finally, he said, "What are your instructions, sir?"

"My instructions, Landry?" He shrugged. "Just let them all go. This whole thing was just a big fuckup from the beginning. I just want to forget about the whole thing."

"Ah, yes sir, I'll see that it's handled right away, the minute I leave. Ah, sir, there was one thing the Los Angeles DEA guy, a man named Lee Swetlock, wanted to report. I don't know exactly what it means."

"Well, what is it?" asked Carruthers with obvious irritation, as though Landry had clearly overstayed his welcome.

"Well, ah, I don't know what this means, but this Susan Johnson, who seems to speak perfect English from what I'm told, she, ah, said for them to give you a message. She insisted that you personally hear it."

"Yeah?" said Carruthers, immediately feeling a stirring in his groin. I don't believe this, he told himself excitedly, she's gonna come crawling! "What'd she say exactly?" he asked, suddenly becoming more animated that he'd been since Landry had entered the room.

"Well, this is third hand, Mr. President, but I'm pretty sure I got it right. She said to ask you if you enjoyed the tape of the evening at the Chinese embassy and if you'd like to be able to see it on national television." Landry noted with alarm that the color had drained out of Carruthers' face. "I, ah, don't understand it, but she said that you would."

"OHHHhhhhh!" said Carruthers. "OHHhhh, shit. Shit, piss, and corruption."

"What is it, sir, what's she talking about?"

"Oh, shit, I knew this was a fucking setup. She's in on it. She's got the fucking tape. We gotta get it back, whatever it takes. Quick, Landry, I want you to get back to them, through this guy of ours out there, whatshis-name…?"

"Swetlock, sir."

"Yeah, Swetlock, have him tell her, I mean in the next five minutes, we'll withdraw all charges and issue a press release saying it was all a big mistake, a case of mistaken identity. Tell her we'll do all that if she gives us the tape. Do all that right this second, Landry, get it done. I want all those people released as soon as they come across with the tape. Tell her they'll never hear from us again. Just don't let that tape out of their possession." Landry just sat staring at Carruthers, trying to fathom what was going on. "Goddammit, *MOVE*, you stupid shit! Use the phone in there," he said, pointing to the room off the Oval Office.

Landry ran into the next room, thinking he'd gotten off remarkably lightly, at least as compared to his previous meetings with the president. He dialed Faulkner's number, eager to bring the whole bizarre episode to some kind of closure. Faulkner came on the line immediately. "Win, I'm with POTUS right now," said Landry, his voice expressing a modicum of confi-dence for the first time since the surveillance operation began, "and he wants you to contact Swetlock personally and see that the group we arrest-ed this morning is released with all due apologies. Say it was a case of mis-taken identity, ah, an unreliable informer, whatever, make up something good. You're good at that sort of thing." He listened to Faulkner's grunted acknowledgment. "Now this is the most important part, Win. He's got to go to the Chinese woman, this Susan Johnson, and ask her for all copies of the tape in return for us cutting her loose and dropping all charges."

"Jesus," said Faulkner, "I wonder what's on that fucking tape that Carruthers wants it so much. But, Jack, what are we supposed to do if she tells us to fuck off, and how'd we know that we have all the copies, any-way?"

Landry thought for a long minute. "That's a good question, Win. I don't know. Lemme put you on hold and I'll ask POTUS." He went back into the Oval Office and stood in front of the president's desk, waiting to be acknowledged.

"Well?" Carruthers asked with obvious annoyance.

"Ah, sir, Faulkner wants to know what we should do if she refuses to give us the tapes. Or if she gives them to us, how do we know that we have all the copies?"

Carruthers jumped to his feet, about to shout, "Just get it handled, you idiot!" That was always his first impulse when confronted with a vexing problem. But the exertion of jumping to his feet suddenly caused his ear to throb painfully where Heather Carruthers had tried to use the side of his head for a punching bag. The jolt of spousal inflicted pain brought him back to reality as perhaps nothing else could have. "Ah, shit," he muttered softly. "Yeah, that could be a problem. Christ, if we don't turn her loose, they give the tapes to the media. And if we turn her loose, she may do it anyway. What can we do, Landry?" he asked almost plaintively.

Landry was practically bursting with curiosity regarding the content of the tapes in question but was afraid to ask Carruthers about them. "I don't know, sir. Maybe we should just drop the charges against her and take it on faith that she won't take any further action, official or otherwise. That's possible, I suppose, don't you think?"

Carruthers seemed to be thinking, and in fact was coming to the realization that he had no options at all other than what Landry was suggesting. He didn't even know whether the Chinese were behind the whole thing. "OK, Jack," he said with more decisiveness than he really felt, "have Faulkner personally call this woman and personally, with no involvement by anybody else, tell her that he's speaking for the president of the United States, and this whole thing's been a terrible mistake, I mean, don't get into any details, just tell her it's been a terrible mistake, and that we'll drop all charges if she just gives us the tape. I think that's the best we can do right now. You got all that?" Landry nodded. "OK, tell that to Faulkner exactly, and tell him I want him in contact with this lady immediately, not in an hour, not in five minutes, but immediately." Landry rushed from the office to comply.

Exactly six minutes later Suzy Johnson, sitting on a bare wooden bench in the holding tank, saw the jailer coming towards the cell. "Mrs. Johnson, you got a phone call." He opened the cell door and glanced at the huge and ugly female biker, who displayed a badly swollen lower lip as she looked back at him sullenly from the other side of the cell. Further examination later that afternoon would reveal a broken jaw as well. "What happened to her?" he asked.

"We had words," Suzy replied, shrugging. "Who's calling?" hoping almost desperately to hear Zack's voice, but also knowing that it would almost surely mean that he was in custody as well.

"I dunno, lady, I was just told to bring you upstairs to the phone. Follow me."

He brought her upstairs to a little office. "I'll be right outside," he said, leaving her wondering why they were leaving her alone to take a phone call, then decided that the phone was tapped anyway. She picked up and pushed in the blinking button.

"Zack?" she said involuntarily.

"Ah, Mrs. Johnson," said Win Faulkner, "I'm calling directly on behalf of the president of the United States. He wants me…"

"Where's my husband," she demanded, cutting him off.

"He's, ah, he, ah, turned himself in to the Pasadena police. They've got him at the moment."

She immediately understood her Zack's motivation in going to the local police. There was a pause while she processed this information, feeling hugely relieved. "All right, who are you and what do you want?" Her demeanor and tone were not at all what Faulkner had expected from a cowed and terrified female prisoner undergoing her first incarceration experience.

"Well, like I said, I'm calling directly on behalf of the president."

"I'd assumed as much. Why can't he call himself?"

"Please, Mrs. Johnson, let me finish," said Faulkner, immediately assuming that Suzy Johnson was one of the president's jilted cast-offs, who happened to have an incriminating video tape of them in some sort of compromising situation. Christ, the dumb shit probably set up the camera himself, he thought. "Mrs. Johnson, my name's Win Faulkner, and I'm head of the federal Drug Enforcement Administration. And the president wants me to assure you that this whole unfortunate episode was a terrible mistake, it never should have happened, it was a problem that started with an informer who turned out to be less than reliable and truthful."

"Really, now," said Suzy. "I should have thought he'd have come up with something more imaginative than that. After all, he's such an accomplished liar."

"Ah, you're certainly right about that," Faulkner blurted involuntarily. "I mean, well, anyway, he wants me to tell you that if you'll just surrender the, ah, tapes that we'll drop all charges, and, umm, you'll never hear from us again."

Without hesitation Suzy replied, "I don't think so, Mr. Faulkner. You'll drop all charges and release me and my husband immediately, and I'll give you absolutely nothing." She paused to let this sink in with Faulkner. "Except this: If we hear nothing from Mr. Carruthers or any of his people or agencies ever again, those tapes will never see the light of day. But they'll be ours, now and forever. And if I ever get the merest suspicion that he's using the government to persecute me or any member of my family, those tapes will become public domain. Do you understand me?"

Jesus, I'd hate to meet *her* in a dark alley, thought Faulkner, never suspecting how literally the sentiment could be construed. "OK, I understand, Mrs. Johnson. I'll explain your position to POTUS."

"Who?"

"Ah, that's an acronym for the president of the United States."

"Oh, for a minute there I thought you were talking about some ridiculous Hollywood space alien. And one more thing, Mr. Faulkner. I'd better be out of this disgusting place and reunited with my husband within the next half hour. And he'd better look just as good as he did this morning when he left the house. Be advised, this is not a negotiating posture. Do we understand each other?"

"Ah, yes, Mrs. Johnson," Faulkner said. "I should be back to you very shortly."

Two minutes later Faulkner found himself talking directly with the president, who'd quickly brushed Landry aside as the go-between. Faulkner, during the next couple of minutes, explained Suzy Johnson's position and demands, concluding with the observation that, "she sounds like one tough cookie, Mr. President." Carruthers involuntarily reached up and felt his nose. "I mean, whoever she is, she doesn't seem the least bit intimidated by being in jail, or anything else for that matter."

"Do you think we can trust her?" asked Carruthers, immediately realizing how stupid the question was.

"Well, I, ah, just can't say, sir. But I think she may have us over a barrel. I don't see what we have to gain by calling her bluff. Ah, what I mean is I don't get the feeling at all that she's bluffing."

Carruthers sat and thought for a long moment. "All right, Faulkner, call her back and tell her we'll go along with her demands. Make sure she's out of jail right away, and get the local cops to release her hubby and put them back together, and do it right now. I don't want this crazy bitch freaking out if she has to stay in jail two seconds over her deadline."

After he'd hung up, Carruthers felt a cold, focused rage growing within him. Vicious bitch! OK, bitch, that's rounds one and two to you. But

301

Bob Carruthers has a long memory. He started. Jesus Christ, I'm even starting to talk about myself in the third person, like that idiot, Viagraman. He shook his head to clear it. This thing's not over, he told himself with a murderous sense of self-righteousness.

At least Carruthers was right about one thing. It wasn't over.

* * *

Chapter 11

Melanie Samuels sat at her desk and looked through her messages. There were four from Lee Swetlock, coming at roughly forty-five minute intervals. She threw them all in the waste basket under her desk. She'd planned to talk to her producer about possibly holding the Red Tiger story, but then decided to say nothing, finding herself more than a little annoyed that he thought her so stupid as to fall for the promise of future fat and juicy stories. The segment was scheduled to run at 6:18 PM, then again during the eleven o'clock news broadcast. She looked at the wall clock, noting that she had time to step out for a quick sandwich at the corner deli before coming back in to watch the segment on the monitor in her office.

Lee Swetlock, at the same time, was heading for Palm Springs for a short and unannounced little vacation, intending to make himself not only invisible but totally incommunicado as well. He simply assumed that his government career was over, though in fact his mediocrity would stand him in good stead. In the confusion and panic of what happened in the next few days, Swetlock would never be positively fingered as the one who, idiotically, had involved the media in the whole affair.

While the clock was ticking down to the airing of the Red Tiger DEA raid segment, the Johnson's were being re-united in Detective Murray's little office in the Pasadena police station. Both were clutching each other fiercely and both were alternately crying and laughing. "God, let's just go home, Zack. This has been like a nightmare. I need a bath from being in that horrible place." She didn't mention her altercation with the female biker and didn't plan to. Nor did her husband get a hint of how she'd handled Faulkner, the tale of which she'd relate that evening without bravado or fanfare.

He finally released her and held her at arms length, looking at her for any sign of trauma or physical injury. There was none. "Honey, how would you like to spend the night in a hotel with your old man? I'm told it can do wonders for a lifeless marriage. Imagine what it'd do for ours."

"I think I'd like that, Zack. Maybe we should just go home, get a change of clothes, and disappear for a day or two. I want to call Sid and tell him what's going on, but I really wouldn't mind not going in tomorrow. And somehow I'm a little nervous about being in the house tonight with everything that's been happening."

"I'm thinkin' the same thing, honey. Let's just go home and let me get out of my uniform and grab an overnight bag, then we'll get outta here. I gotta call Continental and talk to 'em, let 'em know what's going on." He walked over to the door, stuck his head out, and called out to Detective Murray. "Hey, Vic, we want to thank you for everything, I mean, for listenin' to the whole crazy story and all and keepin' me safe here."

Murray smiled. "Well, it was kind of an adventure, I guess. Here's your tape back. Guard it carefully. And good luck to you both."

"Hey, you got any kids, I mean like younger ones who'd like to see an airliner cockpit?" asked Zack suddenly.

"Well, Billy, my eleven year old's always playing all those aviation video games. I guess he'd get a big kick out of it."

"Hey, great, I'll get both of you on board an MD-80 one day when you're off and let him sit in the pilot's seat. Just lemme know when you want to do it."

"Hey, count on it, Zack, that'd be great," said Vic Murray enthusiastically.

Ninety minutes later Suzy and Zack were checking into the Beverly Wilshire for the night, intending to get cleaned up, then have dinner in one of the hotel restaurants. "I'm dying for a bath," said Suzy, kicking off her shoes and pulling off her cotton sweater, then starting to wriggle out of her jeans.

Zack stopped sliding open the closet door and stood staring at her lithe, smoothly muscled and incredibly enticing body. He crossed the room in four long strides, picked her up and tossed her on the bed. "You're clean enough for me, lady," he said thickly as he pulled off his clothes and tossed them aside.

They didn't get out of the room for another two and a half hours, after which they went downstairs and enjoyed a pleasant seafood dinner and a bottle of a nice Napa Valley Chardonnay. Between their lovemaking and the dinner they blissfully missed the six o'clock news and Melissa Samuels' coverage of the Great Red Tiger Raid.

* * *

As the Johnsons were enjoying an after dinner brandy and holding hands across the table, Candy Lambert was restlessly trying to read a *Ladies Home Journal*. She was feeling the maddening frustration of trying to place a face with a name or event and coming up blank. Finally she turned to Roy, who was talking with a friend in New Jersey via the Internet. "Do you ever see someone you're sure you've seen before, you just can't remember where?"

He looked up from his keyboard. "Sure, babe, all the time. I think I got Alzheimer's."

"No, I'm serious. This is driving me crazy."

"Who?"

"Well, there was this girl, she was Chinese or Japanese, or something like that, who was on the six o'clock news. I could swear I've seen her before. I just can't think of where. She was getting arrested for drug dealing or something, I didn't really get the details."

"Well, you can watch it again at eleven, if you want. Maybe it'll register. But hell, there's a few billion Chinese out there. I kinda doubt if this is the same person you're thinking of."

"Yeah, maybe you're right," she said doubtfully. And then something clicked. "Holy-Moly!" she said, loudly enough to startle her husband. She ignored his questioning look and rushed over to the VCR, rummaged through the four or five VHS cassettes stacked on top, pulled out the unmarked one, and popped it in. "Hey, c'mere, look at this. You won't believe it."

He got up and walked over. His eyes widened in surprise as he watched the president begin to grope a woman standing next to him. When the woman turned to face Carruthers, Candy let out with a shout, "That's her, that's the girl on the news tonight, I swear it."

Then her husband shouted, "Holy shit, I know that girl!" They fell silent and stood, transfixed, as the tape played out. "Play it again!" Roy commanded. "Jesus, that's, oh, shit, what's her name, Suzy something-or-other, that's it. She comes in the place a couple times a week. She's good friends with Ma and Pop. They even been to her house for dinner. They told me she's a fantastic cook."

They watched the tape twice more. Finally Roy said, "Where'd you get this thing, honey?"

"That's the really weird part, Roy. Your daddy gave it to me. He put it in my purse the other night when we were cleaning up after dinner. It was supposed to be the tape of that cooking show they did for the cable company, you know, the one on baby-back ribs. I actually saw him do it, I mean I was looking right at him when he dropped it in my purse."

He shook his head. "Do you believe this guy Carruthers? No, you know what, Candy? At this point I'd believe *anything* somebody told me about that man. Nothing'd be too weird to believe about this guy."

"You don't think this tape's a fake?"

"Hell, I dunno, it could be, I guess. But like I told you, if somebody told me Carruthers was getting it on with a friggin' horseshoe crab, I wouldn't necessarily call him a liar. Hey, you know, I wanna call Ma and Pop and have them watch the eleven o'clock news, just tell 'em to watch it and call us if they see anyone in the news they recognize, and if they do, call us right away."

And so ninety minutes later, Sammy and Kate Lambert, up well past their normal bedtime, turned on the KABC eleven o'clock news. Both were totally nonplussed. "Wonder what that boy's talkin' about," said Sammy, as he propped himself up in bed and clicked on the TV set. And eighteen minutes later they were watching Suzy Johnson, Sid Burnside, Sherry Maxwell, Vera Hawkins, an east Asian man they didn't recognize, and an east Asian woman on a stretcher they'd never seen before either, being herded down the sidewalk of Red Tigers Motors headquarters by a group of fatigue-clad, M16-toting men.

Both gaped in disbelief. "God, that's not a drug place, it's a goddam car company," shouted Sammy. "They're just a bunch of, what's Sid call 'em, factory guys!" He reached across Kate to reach the phone on the night table and dialed Roy and Candy.

Twenty minutes later Sammy and Kate sat wondering about the

strange tape described to them by Candy and Roy. Sammy finally made the connection between the evening at the Johnson's house and probably getting his cooking show tape confused with something far different. "Hey, Kate, you still got Zack and Suzy's number around here, doncha?" A moment later she'd come up with it from her little kitchen cardex. Sammy dialed their number and let it ring until the answering machine picked up. He started to leave a message, but then didn't know quite what to say and hung up the phone slowly. "Nobody's home. Jesus, they probably got both of 'em in jail someplace," he said unhappily.

Had Kate and Sammy discovered the contents of the mysterious videotape they'd simply have returned it to their friends and not shared the contents with anybody, not even other friends. Unfortunately, Roy and Kate, knowing Zack and Suzy only indirectly and peripherally, had no sense of innate loyalty toward them or even any real appreciation of the problems it might cause them if they shared the contents of the tape with outsiders. And in fact, they quickly concluded that exposure of the tape could help them out of whatever present difficulties they might be in. "We should do something about this," Candy said to Roy solemnly as they turned out the lights and went to bed.

* * *

And in fact, something was already being done about "this." Within minutes after airing, Melanie Samuels' Red Tiger segment was known to the government of the People's Republic, the management of the Long March People's Cooperative Automotive Manufacturing Company, and, particularly, Ambassador Li.

Promptly at eight-thirty the following morning the ambassador, with no appointment or advance notice of any kind, was angrily demanding to see the president of the United States. In his briefcase was a copy of the news segment from KABC in Los Angeles. "I'm sorry, Mr. Ambassador," Stacy told him, "the president's in a breakfast meeting with the Joint Chiefs at the Pentagon this morning."

"I must speak to him immediately," repeated Li, as though he hadn't heard her at all. "The premier wishes to hear your president's explanation of this outrageous behavior by your federal drug agency. Unless this situation is defused there will be the most serious consequences," said Li, fixing her with his most imperious gaze.

"Ah, Mr. Li, I can see if the Vice-President's available, if you'd like to explain your problem to him."

Li seemed to hesitate, then realized that he could make Nate Garmin an ally, albeit a dubious one, in soliciting some sort of concession from the administration in response to this latest diplomatic flap.

He nodded approvingly. "Very well, I should like to see Mr. Garmin, if you would be so kind as to arrange it."

Moments later Li was being ushered into Garmin's White House office by Stacy. "Hey, how ya doin', Mr. Ambassador?" exclaimed Garmin happily. "What a pleasant surprise!"

Li suddenly realized that Garmin, guileless soul that he was, had no clue of the reason for his visit. "Mr. Vice-President," he began, "I wish I could say that this were a pleasant social call, but it is not."

"Uh, it's not?" asked Garmin. "Gee, what's wrong?"

"You know nothing, I take it, of your government's actions against the personnel of our Red Tiger Motor Company in California?" Garmin's face registered confusion. "The affiliate company, Mr. Vice-President, which will distribute our remarkable new car, the Red Whippet, in the United States."

"Oh, yeah, I understand now. What happened? Are you having a problem with the immigration people or something?"

Li looked at Garmin for a long moment. "A picture, or perhaps in this modern age I should say a video tape, is worth a thousand words." He reached in his briefcase for the VHS tape, pulled it out, and gestured toward the VCR in Garmin's office. "May I?"

Li said nothing as the tape, which ran for a total of ninety seconds, played. "Would you like to see it again, Mr. Vice-President?" Garmin just stood with his mouth open. "We thought it most interesting that the girl being led away in handcuffs was the very same who suffered a sexual assault at the hands of your president. It is curious, is it not? I would have thought that your president was not quite so reckless that, whatever his bizarre sexual behavior, he would wantonly provoke an economic giant and nuclear power such as the People's Republic! To do this at one of our corporate headquarters! Then to invite members of your sensationalist press corps! These are unthinkable provocations! Our, ah, self-es*teem* requires that all appropriate apologies be tendered and that redress for this terrible insult be offered forthwith! We have been slandered in the eyes of the world as the lowest of all capitalist vermin, *drug dealers!*"

Nate Garmin's mouth worked, but no sound emerged. Finally he managed to say, "Why, this is terrible, Mr. Ambassador, just, just, really bad, I mean, like awful. I don't what to say, except I'm really, really, sorry."

"I should hope your president is so sorry as you, Mr. Vice-President. I can readily see that you are a sorry man indeed, certainly the sorriest I have ever met." Garmin nodded in sad agreement. "But however sorry you may be, that solves nothing. All the progress between our two great nations is at risk! Our trade agreements, our cultural exchanges, the mutually beneficial technology transfers, all could be lost! Why, think of the blow to your personal political ambitions with the loss of the DILDO!"

"My God, you're right," Garmin gasped. "My legacy, destroyed." His head hung in despair.

"I will wait here to speak with President Carruthers," announced Li, seating himself in front of Garmin's desk. At length, after watching Garmin's agonized hand-wringing, Li offered him some solace. "Please, Mr. Vice-President, I am sure that you knew nothing of this appalling incident." He felt the need to maintain at least some sort of bridge with Garmin, knowing that the People's Republic considered it in their interests to see that he succeeded Carruthers. He mused on what appeared to be the rather minimal likelihood of Garmin actually being elected. But then he thought of Carruthers, shook his head, and gave a little shrug.

Two hours later, Carruthers, having been warned by Stacy that Ambassador Li was lying in wait for him in Garmin's office, managed to sneak into his own office without Li spotting him. He told his secretary to tell Garmin to come see him and not let Li know that he was back.

A few minutes later Garmin appeared, looking distracted, even a bit haggard. "Christ, what's the matter with you, Nate?" Carruthers asked. "You look like your frigging goldfish croaked."

"I think it may be even worse than that, Bob," said Garmin with apparent sincerity. "Li came to see me. He showed me this tape from California, some kind of news broadcast where some drug guys were arresting a bunch of people at their company headquarters, and that girl who broke your nose at the embassy was there, they were dragging her away in handcuffs, and the ambassador was really mad about us calling them drug dealers or something like that…"

"Nate, *Nate!* Will you please slow down and explain what you're talking about.

"Well, I think you get the idea, Bob, and then he told me my political future was tied to the DILDO and that I could be finished."

"Goddammit, Nate, I do *not* get the idea, for Christ's sake. What the hell are you talking about, and what's this about this dildo thing again? I said I didn't want to hear about it, ever. Is there some sort of tape involving *that?*"

"No, not that, hey, why don't I just get the ambassador and have him show you the tape. It's easier than having me try to explain it."

"Yeah, why don't you go get him," growled Carruthers, thinking that practically anything would be easier than having Garmin try to explain himself on any topic.

Moments later Ambassador Li entered, went straight to the VCR in Carruthers' office, inserted the tape, and hit the play button. "I hope you can offer a reasonable explanation for this, Mr. President," said Li, unsmiling.

Carruthers bridled at Li's tone. Fucking little gook, who's he think he is, he asked himself. Carruthers watched the tape with interest but without understanding until he caught sight of Suzy Johnson being led away. His jaw dropped, as two conflicting thoughts ran through his head. Jesus, she's even better looking than I remembered, juxtaposed with "I'm gonna kill that cocksucker Landry!" The stirrings of tumescence began, then deflated just as quickly as the two thoughts collided, then stirred again as Carruthers got a quick look at Suzy Johnson's shapely denim-clad behind as she climbed into the DEA van. There was another instant deflation as the scene cut to Melanie Samuels' wrap-up, with the Red Tiger corporate sign prominently displayed and Melanie intoning that the arrests were expected to be just the beginning in what was the breaking up of a major Asian drug cartel.

Carruthers was nothing if not a quick study. "My God, Ambassador Li," he began, "I don't know what this could be about, but by God, I'm going to get to the bottom of it!"

"You don't recognize the girl?" asked Li.

"Which girl is that, Mr. Ambassador?" asked Carruthers with extraordinarily convincing puzzlement.

"Please, Mr. President, I am quite sure you have watched the tape I gave you, many more times than once. How is it that this same girl is now being arrested for drug trafficking? It is an extraordinary coincidence, even given the persistent rumors of drug related campaign contributions to your last presidential bid. All groundless rumors, I am sure, Mr. President, but what a terribly suspicious matter to be publicly aired, nonetheless." Carruthers groaned inwardly as he instantly perceived the potential for further blackmail from the Chinese, now coming from a completely new direction, yet still all arising from the groping incident.

"Mr. Ambassador, the girl and all the others were freed last night. It was all an unfortunate incident brought about by a treacherous and unreliable informer. I didn't know until now that the incident was covered by the media in California. Does anybody know if it's been picked up nationally by any of the networks?"

"It does not appear that it has been, at least yet," said Li. "But then, it is still early. It may make the national coverage this evening. But allow me to congratulate you, Mr. President," Li continued. "It is remarkable, truly remarkable that you would be so informed on the details of what is certainly a minor local law enforcement matter in California, even knowing that the girl and the others were released last night. You are clearly closely in touch with the, how do you say it, the pulse of things. Well, I must go and report the details of our discussion with our leadership in Beijing. They are eager to hear of your explanations, I am sure. And they will want to know what you propose in order to set things right between the American and Chinese people once again. Perhaps you may wish to think about this yourself while I am communicating with our leaders, yes?"

"Uh, yes, I will think about it, Mr. Ambassador. And one thing you and your people might want to keep in mind, too. If this thing doesn't get picked up nationally as a big story, and I don't think it will, any public discussion of it, whether originating from here or Beijing, will only turn a spotlight on it. As you know, the memory of the American people is very short, Mr. Ambassador. Seeing the charges repeated, however false they may be, will do neither of us any good, any good at all."

Li stared at him. "That is true," he said finally. "True enough," thinking that Carruthers, scoundrel that he was, had remarkable grace under pressure.

After the door had closed on Li's semi-charitable thought, Carruthers shrieked, "I'm gonna kill that cocksucker Landry!" He jerked the phone off its cradle. "Stacy, get me Landry this instant!" He looked up at Garmin.

"You can go, Nate." He waved him away. "And I don't want to hear about this dildo business right now, I ain't got the time to worry about it at the moment." Garmin slunk from the Oval Office, unspeakably thankful that he wasn't on the receiving end of Carruthers' wrath.

* * *

As Li and Carruthers were parting, both smugly assuming that they alone controlled the ultimate circulation of Melanie Samuels' story, Candy and Roy Lambert were having breakfast, discussing what to do with the strange little tape they'd inadvertently gotten from Sammy. "I dunno, Candy," said Roy, chewing on an English muffin, "I think the thing to do would just be to call this lady Melanie Samuels over at KABC and tell her you got something she oughtta see, let her take it from there."

"Do you think she'd come to the phone?"

"Sure, I guess so. She's always lookin' for a story, and you got an interesting one. At least it looks interesting. And it's a further development of what she did yesterday. I'm pretty sure she'd want to talk to you. *I* would if I were in her position."

After Roy had left for work Candy sat at the kitchen table, looking a bit indecisively at the tape. Finally, she pulled the phone toward her, called information, and asked for the number for KABC television. To her pleasant surprise, she found herself talking to Melanie within less than a minute.

"Melanie Samuels," she picked up.

"Oh, hi," said Candy. "Oh, it's so nice to get to talk to you. I see you all the time on the news, Miss Samuels."

"Well, I'm glad to hear that. Melanie will do nicely. What's your name?" Melanie was actually a rather sweet and good-natured young lady, who always made it a point to be kind and patient with callers, time permitting. It often paid off with interesting leads, as well.

"I'm Candy Lambert, and I've got something I think you should see, Melanie. It's about that story you did yesterday about those drug arrests in Chino."

"Is it an article or a copy of a newscast, something like that?"

"Well, not really, it's a video-tape involving the president and that Chinese or Japanese girl they arrested yesterday, and a whole bunch of other Chinese looking people. It's kinda hard to explain, I think it'd be better if I just showed it to you. It's really weird, like."

"You say it involves the president, like you mean Bob Carruthers, and that Chinese girl, the real pretty one?"

"Yes, you can see 'em both plain as day on the tape."

"Candy, ah, can you tell me what they're doing?" she asked, immediately assuming that it was some kind of weird sexual encounter.

"Well, actually, it looks like they're fighting, I mean she slapped him really hard, then he tried to hit her, then she hit him in the face and knocked him down, like some sort of karate move. I mean, it was a real nasty shot by someone who looked like she knew what she was doing."

By now Melanie was becoming genuinely interested. "Are you telling me you actually have a copy of this tape, I mean, right in your possession?"

"I'm holding it in my hand, looking at it."

"I wouldn't want to impose, Candy, but if you don't live too far from here, do you think I could come over to your house right now and have you show me this tape?"

"Well, I, I, guess, Melanie. I don't think I want to be on TV, I mean, I'd have to talk it over with Roy, he's my husband."

"Candy, I give you my promise, I won't ask you to do anything you don't want to do. But I'd be lying if I said I didn't want to see that tape."

"Well, I live in West Covino. I guess you could come over now if you'd like. I can call in and tell 'em I'll be a few minutes late for work."

"I can be there in thirty minutes. Can I have your address?"

And thirty two minutes later Melanie was pulling up in front of the Lambert's little house in the KABC van with Oliver Jamison. Candy met them on the porch. "Hi, I'm Candy," she said, holding out her hand.

"I'm Melanie, and this is Oliver. He's my number one cameraman." Oliver nodded.

"Well, c'mon in, and I'll run this thing. I think maybe it asks more questions than it answers," said Candy.

They went into the living room and watched Candy pop the tape into the VCR.

They watched it twice before Melanie commented on it. "God, this is too much. If thing's real, it's, it's, I don't know *what* it is. But we've got to get to the bottom of it. Oliver, just what kind of a tape do you think this is?"

"Looks like some kind of security camera tape to me. That's why it's in black and white and don't have no sound track. But it looks real enough. And that girl who nailed him, she's definitely the one we taped yesterday, no doubt in my mind. One thing I know *ain't* true. All those Chinese people definitely do *not* look alike. Cause if they all looked like this chick, I'd be livin' there myself."

"Calm yourself, Oliver," laughed Melanie. "Candy, could you let me have this tape. I promise you I'll return it to you, you have my word on that. But I want to have our edit guys look at it and make sure it's not some kind of fake."

"Well, that'd be OK, I guess. But could I have a copy to keep here?"

"Sure. Oliver can make one right in the truck. It'll take a few seconds." She handed the cassette to Oliver, who headed out the door with it.

"How did you get this thing, Candy?"

"Well, my parents know this girl, they've been to her house for dinner. She goes to my father in law's barbecue place for lunch all the time, along with some of the other people from her office. Sammy and Kate, those are my inlaws, they really like her. They say she's really sweet. In fact, they're in shock over this drug thing, they say it's ridiculous. I don't what they're doing with this tape. I got it from them, accidentally, I think. Sammy was giving me a cable TV tape he did on one of his recipes for baby-back ribs, and I think he somehow got it mixed up with this thing. I almost fainted when I put it on. Here I thought I was getting a recipe for ribs, and suddenly there's the president groping this girl, and then she smacks him, and he tries to hit her, and next thing you know there's a big riot goin' on."

Oliver came back in and handed Candy a copy of the tape. "Let's run it on your VCR, make sure it's good," he suggested, which they did.

"Candy, I'm going to go back to the ABC studio and give this to our edit people, first thing. If they think this thing's authentic, we have to talk some more. And obviously, I want to talk to this girl. In fact, the next thing I'm going to do is call the LA County jail and find out if she's still in there. Candy, I really appreciate your calling me on this. Can I ask you a big favor?"

"Sure, I guess."

"Can you keep this between us until I break the story? I guess what I'm asking for is an exclusive."

"Well, sure, it was your story in the first place. I'm not calling anybody else."

"That's wonderful, Candy. I'll try to return the favor some day. I really mean that."

* * *

As Melanie Samuels was running back to the studio to have the tape looked at by their edit technicians, Sid Burnside was was being reassured by Suzy Johnson that she'd be back the following day. Only Vera and Sherry were with him at the moment, Zhu and his wife having locked themselves in their hotel room, while Zhu maintained a lively telephone exchange with Lin. Both, of course, concluded that the fascist mad-dog Burnside had finally, irrevocably tipped his hand in arranging the drug raid and involving the press to publicize the whole ghastly affair. They were discussing only the question of how to best present their irrefutable evidence of Burnside's fascist perfidy, and were energetically poring over his every communication of the past two months, searching for any hint, however subtle, of the wrecker's treachery.

Finally, Burnside concluded his conversation with Suzy and hung up. "Well," he announced, "Suzy'll be back with us tomorrow. She's fine, just a little shook up over the whole thing." He rubbed his hands together. "Well, we gotta get ready, boys and girls. They're gonna start takin' 'em off the Rising Star by late this afternoon, and we're gonna be shipping as soon as they hit the dock and clear customs. That means the first of 'em roll tomorrow! I'm goin' down to the port late this afternoon to see the first of 'em comin' off the ship, so if any of you want to go along for the great occasion, you're welcome to come."

"They oughten to have some news people down there to record the whole thang. Mayhap it'll make people fergit about them crazy revenooers whut come in here yesterday," said Vera, looking from face to face for affirmation.

"That's good thinking, Vera," said Sid. "You got a good head for marketing and PR. I already called two of the networks about it this morning. They said they can get somebody down tomorrow or the next day. Hell, the viewers can't tell if they're lookin' at the first car comin' off or the five hundredth."

The resultant timing would ensure that the media would be on hand for what would turn out to be quite a sensational news event.

* * *

Suzy Johnson replaced the handset after speaking with Burnside and flopped back down on her pillow. Zack had disappeared into the bathroom. She could hear the shower begin as she reached over on the night table for the remote and turned on the TV, finally landing on The Weather Channel and watching the local radar summary. Amazing, she thought. In America one can turn on the TV and see what the weather's going to be right over your house in the next hour. She began channel surfing looking for local news, fearful that the drug arrest story was still being carried. She hadn't seen the tape herself but knew that it had aired the previous night at six and eleven, having gotten this information from Burnside only moments before. Her relief at being reunited with Zack and being released, with all charges dropped, was being supplanted by anger that the entire episode, masterminded by Carruthers, had occurred at all. At the moment she felt no fear, either of him or any of his people, only a slowly forming rage at what they'd tried to do her and the man she loved. Her thoughts were abruptly interrupted by Zack's voice. "Oh, Mrs. Johnson," he called musically.

"Yes, hubby?"

"Mrs. Johnson, could you wash my back for me."

"What about your front?"

"That too, if you'd be so kind."

She chuckled, got out of bed, ran her fingers through her long black hair, and opened the bathroom door. "Oh, it's so slippery in here," she said, getting into the shower with him. "Can I hold on to this for support?"

Two hours later they were finally checking out of the hotel and trying to decide what to do with the rest of the day. Neither really wanted to return home.

As the Johnsons were walking to their car, discussing the potential activities of the day, Melanie Samuels was looking over the shoulder of the senior edit technician as he rewound the embassy tape once again. "Well, Greg, whaddya think?" she asked.

He shrugged. "Well, this isn't exactly the FBI crime lab, but it looks totally real to me. I can't see any evidence at all of any manipulation. There's one splice, right here, just after she turns to face him. That was shot from another angle, using a different camera, like you'd have with a surveillance setup. My guess is they made the splice just to make sure the viewer got a good look at all the faces involved. I looked at it frame by frame, especially the part where this lady hits Carruthers in the nose. There's no way that was faked. His whole face is distorted with the impact. Look." He stopped the action to show Carruthers' upper lip pulled up over his teeth by the impact, his left cheek puffed out, and his hair standing out as his head snapped back. "Unless they got somebody who looks just like Carruthers to volunteer to get his nose flattened, this thing looks real to me. I mean, there's plenty of old stills of fighters' faces right at the moment somebody lands a real haymaker. That's what he looks like right here."

"Do you think she broke his nose?" asked Melanie.

"Yeah, I'd say she did. I mean, that sort of blow is intended to do that, do maximum damage without hurting yourself in the process. This lady knows something about fighting skills. I mean, she's been trained."

"Kinda makes you wonder about that nose tumor story a coupla months ago, doesn't it," said Melanie. "I've got to talk to this Johnson girl right away." She'd already learned that Suzy Johnson had been released late the previous afternoon. She'd gotten her phone number from a contact inside the LA County jail and had tried repeatedly to call her at home. She'd also tried to track her down at the office, but was told by Sherry Maxwell that, "Mrs. Johnson won't be in today." She'd left her number in the hope that Suzy would call her, but felt it unlikely she would do so, assuming she got the message. After all, she wasn't likely to be in a very charitable mood toward KABC in general and Melanie Samuels in particular, she told herself.

"There's nothing on this tape with a date on it, is there?" Melanie finally asked. "I'd really like to know when this happened."

"There's nothing I can see on it," said Greg. "It musta been fairly recent, though."

"What makes you think so?"

"Look at his hair. It's gone from just salt and pepper to gray again, like it does everytime he's trying to look more presidential," Greg replied.

"You know, you're right. He was a lot darker no more than four or five months ago. And he doesn't look as overweight as he did a year ago, either. You know, I bet this happened recently, like a couple of months ago." Melanie said. "And I'll bet anything, *anything,* that the nose tumor story was nothing but a coverup for what this lady did to his nose. You know, Greg, I want to meet this girl, just to make her acquaintance. She sounds really neat."

"Yeah, just don't do anything to piss her off. If she's willing bust the president's nose, Christ knows what she'd do to a reporter who's buggin' her."

"Damn," said Melanie, "this is making me crazy, not being able to talk to her. There's something really big here, I can feel it. That dummy Swetlock over at the DEA office was completely panicked about us running the thing. He was talking about national security, some kind of diplomatic disaster, stuff like that if we ran the segment." She stood up, biting her knuckle. "Where's Oliver? I'm going back out to that Red Tiger place right now. I've gotta talk to somebody out there, find out what they're doing." She headed down toward the switchboard. "If a Susan Johnson or anybody connected with some company called Red Tiger Motors calls for me, give 'em my mobile number and tell 'em to call me immediately," she told the receptionist. "You better write that down."

* * *

Strangely, none of the dealers, of whom there were five currently, heard anything about the drug raid at Red Tiger headquarters. Freddie Newell's sales manager had actually seen the episode but merely assumed that it was about some shell company with a similar name, never having met Burnside or Suzy and getting only the most fleeting glimpse of Vera, and, of course, seeing Maxwell only as a man holding a briefcase over his face. He'd forgotten completely about it the following day. Jake Dougherty up in Sacramento was outside the LA-based KABC broadcast area and never saw it, either.

Now, just as Melanie Samuels was heading out toward Chino in the frustrated hope of running into Suzy Johnson or at least getting some specific information about Red Tiger, Jake Dougherty was practically

318

hugging himself with delight over the response to his radio and newspaper blitz. The phones were ringing and people were stopping in continuously to see and drive the Red Whippet, marvelling at the price of $4995. Even allowing for the inevitable curiosity seekers, Jake was estimating that they might sell between fifty and a hundred of the Chinese *wundercars* on Friday and over the weekend, at least based on the level of traffic they were getting. He was pumped. Billy Joe Sisson, the new car sales manager, was pumped. The salesmen were pumped. And finally, the finance and insurance managers, salivating at the prospect of selling the warranty as an option, plus all the usual rust-proofing, paint sealants, and fabric protection, were double-pumped. Jake had arranged to have the first buyer photographed with his new car, with the promise of getting his picture in the local paper as the first American to buy a car from mainland China. The picture would be taken as many times as necessary, with Jake calculating that all the buyers who didn't make it into the paper could be handled with the explanation that, as things turned out, there was actually another buyer on the other side of the showroom, unknown to Jake, who'd closed his deal a split-second earlier.

Unfortunately, or perhaps fortunately for Jake Dougherty, he would get only twenty-four cars from Red Tiger for the weekend, before events intervened. But for the moment, he was a happy man. He watched with satisfaction as the promotional company he'd hired for the weekend began inflating the forty foot-long blimp which was to fly, tethered a hundred feet over the dealership, for two days and nights with a large red star featured on its flanks. Jake had been assured by the owner of the promotional company, a rather eccentric old man, that the star would readily lend instant identity to the franchise. Jake, ever displaying a perhaps healthy indifference to politics, seemed to think it was a good idea.

Yeah, Jake told himself, that guy Maxwell's a lot sharper than he seems at first. Goddam, I'm gonna make a ton of money with this thing!

* * *

As Jake Dougherty was enjoying his last days of automotive optimism and charitable goodwill toward all things Chinese, Captain Huang Lih Sheng of the Rising Star was noting that the offloading of the Red Whippet sedans was going decidedly more quickly than had the loading operation back in Tientsin. He frowned as he watched from the bridge of the huge freighter. He had hoped for a few extra days of riotous carousing in what he imagined to be the fleshpots of LA's Chinatown. He had fantasized that the Chinese community in California was merely a transplanted version of the old Shanghai of song and fable.

The only real holdups had been caused by the large number of cars which simply refused to start, usually due to dead batteries, which then had to be jumped from the portable battery carts the port handler had on hand for such purposes. There were, however, a few which suffered from maladies other than battery problems. These had to be pushed onto the pallets, then pushed off when they reached the pier. Huang had been observing a Nissan ro-ro ship a couple of berths down, which disgorged what seemed to be several thousand cars in less than a day. He shook his head. How does one compete with people such as these, he asked himself.

As Captain Huang was musing about the advisability of trying to compete head-on with the Japanese, Engine Room Oiler Chou Sen watched with interest as the American dockworkers kept up a steady, non-stop motion, coming down below decks, starting the Red Whippets, then driving them onto the pallets, going with them topside, then returning for another. He had never seen Americans before and was fascinated by their size, especially that of the black Americans, many of whom seemed to possess remarkable physiques. He kept opening doors for them, lifting the hoods of those Red Whippets which would not start, smiling at them until his face ached, generally trying to appear friendly and helpful. Chou watched with interest as they attached the jumper cables to the batteries, then started the cars. He'd wait until they pulled off the cables, then lowered the hoods. What is this American word "shitbox," he asked himself, which he kept hearing from the generally unsmiling American dockworkers as they kept going back for the battery carts. Finally he tried it himself, smiling at a large black American and pointing to a Red Whippet sitting with its hood open. "Shitbox, shitbox," he said, grinning as he pointed to the car.

"Fuckin' A, brother, that's what it is for sure, a little shitbox if I ever seen one." Chou grinned even more broadly, pleased that he and the American appeared to have established some common ground of opinion.

Chou wished he could communicate more fully with the Americans. He was sure they would like each other.

* * *

Melanie Samuels walked slowly up the sidewalk from the Red Tiger office, now more confused and doubtful than ever. She had talked, largely conversationally, with Sid Burnside for the better part of an hour, starting with a sincere apology for any untoward publicity KABC might have caused them. "I'm sorry, I was just tipped off by a DEA official that there'd be a big drug bust going down here, and I'm, well, in the news business."

Burnside had held up his hand. "No apology necessary, Melanie. It wasn't your fault at all. But I do hope you'll believe me that Mrs. Johnson has nothing to do with any business but Red Tiger Motors, she's a really wonderful lady with a nice guy for a husband. It's kind of a Hollywood love story between those two, it looks like to me. This is just a distribution company for the state-owned automaker from China. I assume you've heard about the cars, about how they're super low emissions with fantastic fuel economy."

"Yes, I have," she replied. "I'm sorry, I just didn't make the association. You're the people responsible for bringing them in?" Burnside nodded. "When will they start coming in?"

"Well," said Burnside, looking at his watch, "they offloaded the first ones about three hours ago. You might want to bring a camera crew and get some footage later this afternoon or maybe tomorrow. I mean, there's no big drama or anything like that, but they're the first cars to come to this country from China. It's the beginning of a new era, you might say."

"You know, Sid, I think I'll do that, or at least arrange for one of our reporters to cover it if I'm tied up on a crime story, which is really my beat." She seemed to hesitate. "Sid, do you think Mrs. Johnson and her husband would speak to me, I mean, after what happened yesterday and all. I don't mean an interview necessarily, just to talk to me. There's something really weird about that DEA raid in here yesterday, I don't mean weird about you or your people, I mean about the whole thing, why they even came in here like that, like a bunch of Green Berets. They're saying it was all a big mistake, something about crossed signals with an informer or something like that. Frankly, I don't buy it. I think it was planned, and that Mrs. Johnson was actually the target, but then something didn't turn out the way they expected and they had to let her go." She didn't plan to enlighten Burnside about the existence of the tape and her own near-conclusion as to what was really going on.

"Are you saying somebody was trying to make it *look* like she was involved in drug dealing?"

"Yeah, frankly I do think it was something like that. I just don't know why."

"Well, I don't know what Suzy'd think about talking to the press at this point. You can certainly ask her, but if I were her I'd be a little gun-shy after yesterday."

"Well, I'd still really like to meet her, if only to apologize for what happened. By the way, is her English fairly adequate? It can be really tough to get someone's trust if you're struggling to communicate."

Burnside chuckled. "Adequate? My guess is she'd score in the high seven hundreds on the verbal SAT. Her English is perfect, better'n mine. She barely has any trace of an accent. If I know her, she'll have you figured out in about two seconds, so I wouldn't worry about communicating with her."

"Well, that's good," said Melanie a little uncertainly. Now she was really interested in meeting Mrs. Johnson, who was beginning to sound like a rather fascinating character, as well as being the focal point for a potentially huge story.

She and Oliver got in the van and drove slowly out of the office park. Melanie picked up her cell phone and entered the Johnson's number. She was surprised when it picked up at the first ring. "Hello," said a deep male voice.

"Mr. Johnson?"

"Speaking."

"My name's Melanie Samuels, Mr. Johnson. I'm the reporter who did the arrest story about your wife for KABC, and I'd like to apologize for any trouble I've caused you." Before Zack could respond or hang up she rushed on, "I was just told by a DEA official that there'd be a big arrest there that morning. I had no idea that the whole thing would later be called a big mistake by them." She heard Zack's non-commital grunt. "I was wondering if I could talk to both of you, I mean, without cameras or anything like that for the time being."

"What's there to talk about, if the whole thing was just a big mistake?"

"Well, I don't think it was just a big mistake, Mr. Johnson. I mean, I don't think it had anything to do with your wife being involved in drug trafficking, but I have reason to believe that it was planned for other reasons. It was no mistake."

"Oh? What makes you think that?"

Melanie took a deep breath. "Mr. Johnson, I got a very strange videotape of an incident involving your wife and the president, I mean the president of the United States. I'm sure it's her, as are some other people who know her well." She paused to let that sink in with Zack.

"Where'd you get it?"

"Let's just say it fell into my hands in a strange, almost accidental way. The people who had it didn't even know what it was. Do you know the tape I'm talking about?"

She heard Zack sigh audibly. "There's only one I know of. Describe it to me."

"It's a tape of the president groping your wife and then getting slapped by her, and, well, I imagine you know the rest."

Zack grunted. "Yeah, that's the tape, and yeah, it's authentic. So what do you want to ask Suzy?"

"Well, obviously, I'd like to find out what it's all about. I mean, this is potentially serious stuff."

"No shit," Zack growled. "It's potentially really serious for us, lady. First this bastard gropes my wife and tries to punch her, then she decks him, and then he sends the whole federal government after us. So yeah, it's serious all right. I just want to let it lie. I don't think Suzy wants to end up in every tabloid in the country, like that stupid bimbo Marilyn Summers."

"Do you think she'd come to the phone for me?"

"I'll have to ask her. I don't make her decisions for her." Zack had immediately figured out that their promise to Faulkner was invalidated, now that they couldn't control the distribution of the tape. He wondered how Melanie had gotten a copy of it. The only thing that made sense to him was that she'd gotten it from the same unnamed source who'd supplied their copy. "Why don't you give me your number. If she wants to talk to you, she'll call you back."

Ten minutes later the Johnsons were sitting at their kitchen table, unhappily sorting out their options. "Zack, I'd bet anything Sammy and Kate picked it up by mistake that night." She jumped up and went over to the VCR, picked up a tape and popped it in. A few seconds later she called, "That's got to be it, Zack. The cooking show tape's still here. He picked up the wrong one." She went to the phone and dialed the restaurant. Sammy picked up after four rings. "Sammy, this is Suzy, I want you to know I'm not mad at you, but did you discover that tape of Carruthers and me?"

"Ah, no, it wasn't Kate an' me, Suzy. We gave it to Roy and Candy by mistake, and they watched it after they saw that thing on the news and called the reporter. They thought they were helpin' you out. They thought you were still in jail. I'm real sorry, Suzy. I woulda just gave it back to you."

"Well, I'm glad to know that this reporter is the only who's seen the tape. Maybe I can work with her. I don't think she'll call the other networks. I mean they'll want to keep it to themselves. Sammy, please just make sure Roy and Candy don't give it to anybody else, that's really important."

After she'd hung up with Sammy, Suzy looked at Zack unhappily. "Let's talk about moving to Kansas. I've got a feeling we're about to become famous, if not rich. I guess this whole thing is my fault. I should have never left that copy sitting on top of the VCR. I'm sure that's where it got mixed up with Sammy's cooking tape." She paused to gather her thoughts. "The only control we have at this point is keeping the story restricted to one reporter, this girl you just talked to. It's not much, but we can at least try to get the right story out, one that Carruthers' people can't twist too badly."

Zack listened with growing admiration. She hadn't become hysterical, irrational, or panicked. And she'd quickly zeroed in on the best alternative. "God, you're smart. Sometimes I love you for that more than your fabulous body."

"How comforting to know that we'll still have a relationship after my body's not so fabulous. I might as well call this lady. Give me the number."

Melanie Samuels could scarcely believe her ears. Suzy simply told her that she'd talk to her only on the condition that Melanie was the only one who'd discuss the matter with her, at least as long as the story was told as fully as Suzy wanted it told, and as long as there was no disclosure of their personal lives, or the lives of any other non-public figures involved. "In other words, you'll have the story exclusively, as long as I'm satisfied with the caliber and content of your reporting. If you'd like to come over right now, you may. But don't come in a press vehicle of any kind, come alone, and don't expect to record any of what we discuss today."

"Those conditions are fine, Mrs. Johnson. I can be there within the hour." She hung up, thinking that Mrs. Johnson did indeed speak perfect English and that she was extremely bright and articulate. "Oliver, you better take me back to the studio, so I can get my own car. She doesn't want me showing up in a newsvan. And I gotta go alone."

"You wanna be wired?"

"No, the lady said no recorders, and I don't want to break faith with her. I got a feeling she's a straight shooter."

An hour later Melanie was pulling her BMW Z-3 into the Johnson's driveway. She got out, picked up her handbag, then decided to leave it in the car, figuring it might arouse the suspicion that it contained a tape recorder. She rang the bell and was greeted by Zack Johnson. "Hi," he said, "I've seen you on channel seven. I'm Zack." He held out his hand. "And this is Suzy," gesturing towards her. "C'mon in."

God, what a hunk, Melanie thought immediately, and turned to Suzy. "I'm Melanie," she said, smiling her brightest and most sincere smile, and almost failing to hide her disappointment at being sworn to not reveal personal details of their lives, seeing a sensational human interest element heavily stoked by the almost too-beautiful couple.

"Please come in and have a seat," said Suzy, walking into the living room. "You can ask the questions and we'll answer the ones we feel are appropriate."

"OK, can you tell me how and you and Zack met?"

"No. That's personal."

"Oh, I thought, well, I'm sorry, let's try again. Where did the incident on the tape occur?"

Suzy looked at Zack, who shrugged. "It was at the Chinese embassy in Washington, a little over two months ago."

"Can you tell me what you were doing there?"

"I guess so." And so Suzy related how she worked for the Long March People's Cooperative Automotive Manufacturing Company as an interpreter and had been invited, along with a group of about twenty executives, accountants, and engineers, to a dinner at the embassy, at which the president and vice-president showed up.

"And can you tell me what happened between you and President Carruthers?"

"I met him in a receiving line for about ten seconds, and, well, I gather you've seen the security camera tape."

"You didn't know him before that?"

"I'd only ever seen him on newscasts in China."

"What happened after the, ah, little altercation?"

"They took Zack and me away and kept us in a little office for perhaps an hour, then they just let us go, sent us back to our hotel in one of the embassy's limousines. Ambassador Li even gave us a bottle of champagne."

"Do you think you broke the president's nose?"

"I'm fairly sure I did. It certainly sounded like it. I really wasn't trying to hurt him, but it was just an instinctive move. He swung at me, then was all out of position, and I countered."

"What happened next?"

"Well, nothing, really. We just came back home and settled into our lives. I left the home company and joined Red Tiger as the personnel director. We didn't even give the incident any further thought."

"How did you know about the tape, Mrs. Johnson," asked Melanie, suddenly changing the subject.

Suzy glanced at Zack once again, then said, "Somebody sent it to us, a couple of weeks after the incident."

"Do you know who?"

"Not for sure, but it had a message in Chinese characters on a note that came with it. It said something to the effect that we should keep it in a safe place. It was mailed from someplace in Maryland."

"Could I see the note?"

"I don't see what's gained by showing it to you, and it might be traced back to the sender in some way. I would assume it was from somebody who was trying to help us."

"Then they just arrested you, that's what happened next?"

The Johnsons looked at each other.

"No, that's not what happened at all. Last week two men came here and tried to plant a large bag of heroin in our bathroom. But my in-laws' doberman pinscher was staying with us while they were in Hawaii. The dog stopped them, in fact he left one of them with some quite serious injuries. I suppose they've still got them in jail."

"That was your house?" asked Melanie, suddenly remembering the story of the heroic dog foiling what had been described as a burglary. "I don't remember anything about them planting a bag of heroin here."

"It wasn't reported that way," said Zack, speaking for the first time. "The story was just that they'd found a bag of heroin on one of 'em and that they were just here trying to commit a simple burglary. But the plant part is true. The burglars told two detectives in the Pasadena police department that some DEA guy had promised 'em that he'd arrange to get some other drug charges against 'em dropped if they managed to plant the stuff in our house."

Melanie's mouth fell open. This had to be the connection. "Wait a minute. Could you explain that again?"

When Zack had done so, he added, "The two Pasadena cops, two guys named Murray and Ruskin, told me about it when I was holed up with 'em the day they arrested Suzy. I turned myself in to them. I figured I'd be safe with 'em since they knew the deal with the burglary."

"Do you know the name of the DEA agent?"

"I don't think Ruskin or Murray ever mentioned it to me, just said it was a DEA guy. I guess you could talk to 'em yourself if you want the name. They're both pretty decent guys. And they both saw the tape, right here, the other day after I went to the police station to turn myself in. I figured I had to show it to 'em to help explain what was goin' on with this whole arrest thing."

"What do you think *is* going on?"

"I know it sounds crazy," Zack said, "but I think this guy Carruthers is just tryin' to get even with us for Suzy breakin' his nose in public. And she definitely broke his nose. You could hear it all over the room. That whole nose tumor story he went on TV with was just a big smokescreen."

Melanie Samuels' head was spinning. The whole thing just seemed to be too ridiculously crazy to be true. But then she knew that practically nothing was impossible where Carruthers' personal behavior was concerned. And she simply couldn't think of any conceivable alternative theory to explain the events of the past two days.

"Does Carruthers know about this tape?" she asked finally.

"He certainly does now," said Suzy. "While they had me in jail, I told the DEA people, it was a man named Swetlock, to personally communicate with the president, asking him if he'd seen the tape of the events of that night in the embassy, and would he perhaps like to see it on national TV. But actually, I'm quite sure he'd seen the tape already, or at least knew from the embassy that they had one."

"What happened then."

"A man, who said he was speaking directly for Carruthers, a man called Faulkner, called me in jail and offered to release all of us immediately if I'd give him all copies of the tape. I told him to release us and I'd keep all copies, but that as long as they didn't bother us, we'd never make them public."

"What happened?"

"We were released immediately, within twenty minutes. And now, unfortunately, Zack and I no longer control the tapes. I don't suppose you'd consider just forgetting about this whole thing, would you?"

"I, I can't, Mrs. Johnson. I'm a reporter. This is a big story, a monster story. Assuming it checks out, and I'm pretty sure it will, it has to be told. I just want to tell it in a way that you and Zack don't get hurt and so that Carruthers' spin doctors can't turn it around and make him the victim, which he's very good at doing."

"So I've noticed. What are you planning to do next?"

"Well, I think I'd like to talk to the two detectives and then interview the guys who broke into your house last week. And finally, I want to track down the DEA guy who put the thieves up to it. If I can do all that it should put a hard lock on the story. At some point I'd almost have to interview you and Zack on camera."

"I'd have to think long and hard about that, Melanie. Zack and I want many things from life. Fame is not one of them."

"Maybe we could do it a way that your privacy would be protected."

"If you can think of a way, let us know. But I have to tell you, we're not particularly enthused about the idea."

* * *

As Melanie was concluding her interview with the Johnsons, KABC and KNBC were down at dockside getting some footage of the Red Whippets coming off the ship. Thus far a total of three hundred sixty of the cars had accumulated in the port handlers' storage area. The newspeople walked around them curiously, looking in windows and occasionally raising a hood. "Jesus, these things look like something out of the fifties or sixties," said one cameraman.

"Yeah," said another gray haired technician, "it kinda reminds me of the original Renault, except it's front engine."

While the news crews were getting a bit of footage, Engine Room Oiler Chou watched as a dockworker tried to start one of the Red

Whippets. The starter motor groaned feebly, then stopped altogether. The stevedore cursed, started to get out, but then saw Chou energetically dragging the battery cart over to the car. He opened the hood, and Chou immediately, as he'd seen the stevedores do, connected the booster battery cables to the terminals on the Red Whippet's tiny battery. He grinned and shouted "Shitbox," to the man in the car, who turned the key. Nothing happened. He cursed and jumped out, leaving the key in the start position. "Fuck it, I'm goin' to lunch," the man said angrily, and walked off.

Chou watched him go, disappointed that he hadn't been able to help. He peered under the hood, unable to discern the cause of the problem, then walked slowly away, his first attempt to overcome an automotive malfunction clearly a failure.

Unknown to Chou, he had connected the booster to the car battery backwards, and now current from the eighty amp booster battery was flowing in reverse through the Red Whippet's primitive electrical system. It's main wiring harness began to smoke, then insulation began to burn. Within perhaps two minutes flames appeared under the hood, small at first, then larger and brighter. Soon the underhood wiring, belts, and hoses were burning. Within seconds the underhood and firewall insulation were burning also, then the dash area in the interior of the car. Suddenly there were shouts of alarm in Chinese and English as crewmen frantically looked for a fire extinguisher. By now the vinyl upholstery was blazing and acrid black smoke was filling the hold. In a remarkably short time the entire car was in flames. The fuel tank of the blazing car began to swell with the radiant heat of the fire. It was cooled temporarily by the ten gallons of low octane gasoline that nearly filled it, but then a seam ruptured. Fuel spewed from the tank, landed on the deck, then ignited. The flowing fuel fire quickly communicated itself to other cars in the immediate vicinity, and within three minutes the Rising Star's number three cargo hold was a raging inferno, completely out of control and unstoppable, as fuel tank after fuel tank erupted.

Men boiled out of the ship and down the gangways, as the fire spread with incredible speed. Miraculously, no one was lost. Thick black smoke boiled into the air over the harbor, and soon flames were visible topside, as the contents of the upper deck holds ignited. Fifteen minutes after the fire began, flames were leaping over one hundred feet into the air. The gasoline-fueled fire had begun to ignite everything even remotely flammable within the ship itself. The heat was too intense for the harbor tugs, which the harbor-master had hoped could push the Rising Star from its berth and out away from the pier and other ships. LA fire department fire-fighters and harbor fire fighting vessels finally arrived and kept the fire from communicating itself to the other ships, but it was too late to save the pride of China's merchant fleet. Within two hours the Rising Star had burned almost to the waterline.

Captain Huang Lih Sheng, returning from a pleasant afternoon with a beautiful Chinese call girl, stood aghast, certain at first that he was looking at the hulk of another ship, much as a burglary victim momentarily wonders if he's at the right house upon seeing everything upended. The comment from the Chinese seaman about draining the fuel from cars before transport played in his head. Huang was in civilian clothes. He turned and walked away slowly, too stunned to think clearly. He headed back toward a Chinese restaurant he knew.

* * *

Of course, the news of the loss of nearly all of China's first shipment of new cars to the United States would be greeted by Lin Cho Hsin, Long March's president, as final proof of industrial sabotage, proving beyond doubt that the Americans and Japanese would stop at nothing, including destroying Chinese merchant vessels, to resist market entries from the People's Republic. Lin, obviously, believed no such theory, and in fact welcomed news of the disaster as proof of the magnitude of what they were up against in the US market. Who could have guessed that they'd be facing such treachery! He felt quite confident that he was now safely out of the line of fire in explaining the failure of the Red Whippet. He was actually disappointed that nearly four hundred of the cars had made it off the ship before it burned. Doubtless their perfomance and reliability has been affected by their exposure to the intense heat and fumes from the fire, he told himself, already thinking of a plausible response to the inevitable consumer reaction to the four hundred vehicles that made it safely ashore.

He hoped to persuade the party leadership that further shipments of the Red Whippet be postponed until the Red Tiger organization could be purged of Burnside and other wreckers and until adequate measures could be put in place to ensure security for China's priceless exports. He planned to propose that their merchant ships be escorted by naval vessels, thus reinforcing his apparent conviction that all problems associated with the Red Whippet were external and required the sternest (and most costly) measures to deal with.

As Lin was calculating how to best present his industrial sabotage theories, Melanie Samuels was meeting with Detectives Murray and Ruskin at police headquarters. She was alone once again, with no tape recorder in evidence. Neither detective seemed to show any reticence whatever about talking with her. Within thirty minutes they had confirmed in detail what the Johnsons had already told her, and further, they gave her the name Phil Rivera, the DEA agent who had set up the burglary in return for supposedly getting the previous drug charges dropped against Duran and Sedgely. "Those two oughtta still be in the LA County jail," said Murray. "They'd never make bail after getting caught with that much smack on 'em. You maybe oughtta talk to them, too." Murray paused. "This thing's all true, you know, Melanie. I'd bet my badge and pension on it."

"I'm afraid you're right, Vic," she said a little sadly. "In fact, at this point I know you're right."

* * *

The news that the Rising Star was a smoking hulk, with practically all its cargo charred and melted junk, was greeted with a mixed reaction by the government of the People's Republic. On the one hand, nobody took seriously the hypothesis that the ship had been sabotaged. The annals of the industries, transportation systems, and distribution channels of the People's Republic were filled with plenty of examples of various disasters brought about by indifference, incompetence, and low expectations. On the other hand, given the timing of Carruthers' DEA operation and the media invitation thoughtfully extended by Lee Swetlock, the party leadership felt quite confident that a major diplomatic incident could be plausibly created over the affair.

Ambassador Li had been in communication with Beijing the better part of the day, trying to formulate an appropriate sounding protest regarding the loss of the Rising Star, one which would include a demand for Chinese investigators to be allowed free access to CIA and FBI files, which doubtless would contain information on terrorists and subversives. Li also assumed that the tape, which he believed to be safe in his hands and of course those of the former Lin Shan, would be doubly explosive if revealed after Carruthers' incredible attempt to have the girl and her husband falsely arrested. Li reflected that though Carruthers had shown a remarkable facility for extricating himself from embarrassing situations, he also possessed an equally remarkable propensity for compounding his own difficulties.

Two hours later Li had in hand the communique he was to hand to Carruthers, which demanded a full investigation of both the DEA operation directed against Red Tiger Motors and the "obvious sabotage" of the Rising Star, with the investigations to be conducted jointly by Chinese and US security agencies. Li called the Oval Office to ensure that Carruthers was available, demanded an immediate appointment with him, and summoned his car and driver to head over to the White House.

Meanwhile, Carruthers had locked himself in the Oval Office after hearing the news of the Rising Star burning. He'd watched the newcasts, which showed the huge freighter burning, throwing off incredible clouds of thick black smoke into the already less than sparkling-clear LA air. Wonder what that stupid twit Penny Twombly'd think of that, he chuckled.

His musings were interrupted by the buzz of the intercom. "Ambassador Li's here to see you, Mr. President," Stacy informed him.

Carruthers sighed. "Send him right in, please."

Li entered and marched smartly to within two feet of Carruthers' desk, almost in a military reporting manner. Without smiling, he announced, "I have with me the non-negotiable demands of the People's Republic of China in regard to the sabotage of the Rising Star, as well as the deliberate provocation of arresting and then slandering our trade representatives in California." He lay a brown manila envelope on Carruthers' desk, then turned as if to go.

"Oh, c'mon, Li, knock this shit off," snarled Carruthers. Li seemed momentarily shocked by Carruthers' language and demeanor. "Nobody sabotaged that boat of yours, and we already discussed that goddam DEA deal out there. If you're smart, you people'll just keep your mouths shut about the whole thing. There's enough people poking around the campaign financing rumors already without getting your name connected with big-time drug dealing in this country. Christ, everybody already knows you're the frigging armory for the Crips and Bloods out in LA. This thing's not just *my* problem, Li. It's yours, too. So don't come in here rattling your goddam saber. Now, let's talk reasonably."

Li nodded, almost imperceptibly. "So we shall, Mr. President, so we shall," he replied, seating himself in front of Carruthers' desk. "But you would do well to remember that all your presidential pressures and problems will be but an unpleasant memory should certain events which occurred in our embassy some two months ago come to light. Events which inevitably would reveal certain highly irregular concessions that various of your government agencies made to us in regard to exporting our cars to the United States. And finally, you should be further aware that the leadership of the People's Republic would not view it as too tragic or altogether inimical to our interests were Mr. Garmin to succeed you."

Though Carruthers had assumed as much, it rattled him that Li clearly had been authorized to tell him so. "OK, just what is it your leadership wants?" he asked guardedly.

"It is all in here, in writing," Li shrugged, gesturing toward the manila envelope. "But it is simple enough in principle. To be able to successfully root out these terrorists and saboteurs, we must have unfettered access to certain government files, among them certain FBI, CIA, and NSA files. Of course, we would not be so unreasonable as to expect you to allow us private access. Stopping international terrorism must be a united effort, do you not agree?"

Carruthers just sat and stared at him. He started to speak, then stopped, and just continued to look at Li. "Do not be too upset, Mr. President. View our relationship as a business. It is now time for you to make good on your contractual obligations. You are simply a, ah, how do you put it, a vendor, yes, a vendor to us. We gave you money, prepaid it in fact. It is now time for you to provide the services we require."

"That's it, then?" Carruthers asked. "You want to rummage around in our top secret files?"

"And, of course, you will be turning over any FBI files on members of Congress you may possess. I should add, files which you possess illegally."

"Is that all?" Carruthers asked, his voice rising.

"Not quite, Mr. President. There is still the matter of your outrageous, libelous behavior toward our hardworking trade personnel, whose careers likely will never recover from this injury. Doubtless it is too late to redress the wrong done to these loyal citizens (all four of whom, unknown to Li, were Americans), but perhaps we could be in time to rescue the fortunes of certain other hard working Chinese, our poor swineherds, who are suffering terrible hardship as world prices for pork plummet. We ask only that the United States Department of Agriculture buys two million metric tons of unprocessed swine products per year at a floor price not below $1.50 per pound, for a period of two years."

"Are you crazy?" Carruthers exploded. "We got a goddam collapse in hog prices in this country right now. The pig farmers'll be marching on Washington with their goddam pitchforks!"

"Holding high public office requires the ability to make the often difficult choice between two unpleasant but nonetheless clearly distinguishable alternatives, Mr. President. The choice is yours." Then he softened his tone. "Surely managing this little problem is well within the province of your legendary political skills. Perhaps you could mandate vastly increased pork consumption in the armed services and the federal prison system, or perhaps the school lunch program. No doubt your Food and Drug Administration could herald the many health benefits of pork fat, which, as you know, are widely unappreciated. You could make use, as you have before, of the simple mechanism of executive order, as for example, I, ah, believe that you did in waiving all the government mandated standards for our superb new car."

Carruthers seemed to deflate, shrinking back into his chair. "That's it, then?" he asked hollowly. "The files and the pork deal?"

Li had been given latitude to press for one more concession if he deemed it advisable. "Well, actually, Mr. President, there is one more small matter, at least a small matter to a country of such great power and wealth as the United States." He paused as if selecting his words carefully. "There is in China another long-suffering group, which, through no fault of theirs, has come on hard times. I speak, of course, of the employees of the state-owned electric eel aquatic farms. It seems that, ah, however sophisticated our socialist central planning becomes, some small mis-estimates are always being made, much as with your hog farmers, yes?" Li smiled and shook his head self-deprecatingly. "Alas, it would seem that the demand for these remarkable energy sources was not what we had hoped,

Mr. President, despite their value as a source of high quality protein once their energy output wanes. It is much as if one were able to devour a flashlight battery when it is exhausted. We were hoping that you might see your way to ensure the purchase of perhaps ten million pounds of these remarkable creatures, at, ah, only one dollar per pound, certainly a mere pittance when one considers the value received. Ah, as a one time gesture only, Mr. President, to relieve the sufferings of these poor state fishery workers."

"Huh? You want me to buy ten millions pounds of electric eels? How do you even transport the goddam things? In rubber tanks? Those things are dangerous as hell, aren't they?"

"Well, ah, actually no, Mr. President. These particular specimens are, unfortunately all, umm, dead, due to some sort of fresh water parasite. They are quite harmless at this point. But all were properly processed and pickled soon after their unfortunate demise," Li added hastily. "They are quite tasty and nutritious, I am told. Surely, the vice-president would lend his support to such an initiative. Though the eels can no longer function as an energy source, Mr. Garmin is a strong advocate of positive symbolism, is he not? Perhaps he could eat some at every campaign appearance, even demonstrate his compassion by publicly distributing them to hungry minorities or senior citizens," he added sympathetically.

Carruthers stared at a spot on the wall over Li's head, momentarily seeing Nate Garmin flinging long, snake-like eels into a cheering crowd. Jesus Christ, first this dildo thing, now the new electric eel diet. I can't believe Heather picked that idiot. "OK, Li, is that finally it?" he asked dejectedly.

"I should not be so impertinent as to speak for the party leadership, Mr. President, but yes, for the moment, I believe, that is it, as you put it." He stood to leave. "We shall be in touch within the week to discuss the details of our required access to your security files. I shall report that you have been most cooperative, Mr. President. And, of course, Premier Wu sends his warmest personal regards, as always." Li stopped before reaching the door and turned to face Carruthers once again. "But Mr. President, the leadership was not pleased with your clumsy persecution of the girl, who did nothing more than defend herself against your disgusting advances. I believe we discussed this before. I can tell you that if we hear of any further such attempts to harm this American of Chinese ancestry, the interest due on your obligations will increase." He paused, and struggling to

keep himself from laughing, added, "For example, there are alarming sur-
pluses in need of foreign markets with our sea-slug farms. Need I say
more?" As before, the sentiment was Li's alone, who, like any reasonably
gallant male, did not to like to see any beautiful young woman abused.

After he'd left, Carruthers put his head down on his folded arms and
whimpered softly. "Jesus Christ," he sobbed, "my fucking legacy, being
rolled in hogshit and buried under ten million pounds of dead fish." Then
he abruptly pulled himself together. He straightened up quickly. I've
toughed out worse than this, he told himself. Nobody can touch me as
long as I'm holding the Garmin card! Carruthers made a mental note to
double the vice-president's Secret Service detail.

* * *

Chapter 12

As President Carruthers was contemplating his legacy, Melanie Samuels was just finishing her interview of George Sedgely and Wilfred Duran. She'd gotten the interview as a favor from a county jail official, who got her in under the auspices of being Duran's and Sedgely's attorney. She wasn't surprised when everything the pair told her supported everything she'd heard from Ruskin and Murray, including the name of Phil Rivera. "What office does this guy Rivera work out of?" she asked them.

"Hell, I don't know," said Sedgely. "I never been there. I only seen this guy on the street and right here in the lockup. He busted us on a possession rap for coke a while back. He don't really seem like a bad guy, like some of these federal guys, real assholes, if you know what I mean. He's more like one o' the local guys, kinda like Murray. He ain't a bad guy, either."

"Did he ever tell you how he was going to get the charges dropped on the crack arrest?" she asked.

"Well, he never went into any details. He just led us to believe he could get it done. Personally, I think he coulda handled it, but then the whole thing blew up when we ran into the goddam dog. Nobody figured on the dog. I figured the guys who thought up this thing were just stupid, but then Murray told me the dog didn't belong to the people in the house, he was like just visiting. Just our fucking luck, eh Wilfred?" He glanced at his erstwhile partner.

"And you didn't know the people who lived there?"

"Like I told the others, I never seen 'em, never heard of 'em, didn't know nothin' about 'em. I just figured they musta mattered to somebody. We didn't have nothing against 'em."

"Have you heard from this man Rivera since your arrests?"

"What are you, crazy? You think he's gonna come around here askin' us how we like the food or something? He's gonna say he don't know

337

nothing about us or any crazy dope planting operation he put us up to. So now we're just a coupla burglars with a huge bag of heroin on us, lookin' at a big time dealin' rap."

"Yeah, you guys have a problem," she said, not unsympathetically.

"Hey, look, miss, just think about this for a minute. What would a coupla small timers like me and Wilfred be doin' with that much smack? It's worth a small fortune. If we'd stolen it from someone we'd already be dead, even in here. Or maybe I should say, *especially* in here. And say we just, say, found it and didn't give it back to the right party, we'd still be dead meat. Nobody's botherin' us, nobody's tellin' us we can kiss our asses goodbye. 'Cause that dope came from some DEA stash they got somewhere. It don't belong to *nobody* on the outside." Wilfred nodded his agreement. "Tell me, you tried to talk to this guy Rivera yet?"

"I've put calls in to him. He hasn't called back yet."

"Yeah, I wouldn't hold your breath, miss. They probably got this guy assigned to the field office in Cody, Wyoming right now."

"Well, he still has a voice-mail."

"Lotsa luck, lady. He left us holdin' the bag on this one, big time, and my guess is he ain't about to return your calls."

Fortunately, Melanie was a fairly resourceful young lady, with a fair number of helpful friends. Nor had she felt any compunction whatever, as she had with the Johnsons, about recording the conversation in its entirety

* * *

Sid Burnside, Vera Hawkins, a bleary-eyed Sherry Maxwell, and Suzy Johnson sat around Burnside's desk, amid the scattered remnants of a hasty McDonald's breakfast. "Well," Sid began, "we got just shy of four hundred of these things off the ship before the fire. I take it they're OK?" he asked, looking at Maxwell.

"Near as I could tell, Sid," Sherry replied. "I mean, there's a lot of ash and soot on 'em, but they seem OK other than that. There wasn't any fire damage." Fortunately, most of the cars had been parked with their windows fully closed, so at least the oily black soot hadn't hopelessly blackened the interiors.

"Well, kids, like they say, life goes on," said Burnside. "Let's at least get these cars divvied up and shipped today and tomorrow. We got enough to show the flag at least. Just make sure we manually record all the vehicle ID numbers on those that survived, or we'll never be able to match up the certificates of origin with the right cars. Sherry, you and Vera'll have to go out and get that done. You might want to go home and change into some old clothes or jeans to keep from getting soot all over yourselves. Suzy and I'll stay here and coordinate with the dealers, tell 'em what they can expect in the next couple of days."

After they'd left Suzy looked at Sid for a long moment. "How long do you think we should maintain this farce, Sid? I mean, it's no longer just in the realm of the abstract. Now people are actually going to be asked to spend their money on the Red Whippet. Dealers are actually going to be stocking these things. You know, we really ought to go down to the docks, get in one and drive it around. It could give us some sense of perspective on this whole thing. I mean, Sid, this thing has been like a big joke until now. All of a sudden, it doesn't seem quite so funny. People could get hurt here, maybe in more ways than one. These cars don't have any of the safety equipment your government requires. Somehow that all got waived."

"Yeah, I been worried about that too, Suzy. And I still can't figure out how all that emission and safety stuff got waived, I mean not only by EPA and NHTSA, but by California, too. I've never heard of anything like this in my life, not since I've been in this business anyway."

"Sid, I'll leave this strictly up to you. It's just a thought, well, actually, it's more on the lines of a suggestion, one that I've got very mixed emotions about making. I mean, the company's still paying us, so they have a right to expect a certain level of loyalty."

"What are you getting at, Suzy?"

"Well, I just think if these requirements were waived, the public has a right to know about it. I'm sure it was all done legitimately, ah, but assuming it was, there couldn't be any harm in seeing that the public's informed, could there?"

Burnside laughed. He looked at her affectionately and said, "C'mon, you know as well I do that there's something not totally kosher goin' on here. So what are you suggesting?"

"You're right. I'm rationalizing, and you're right about something not being right about this thing. I say we call that girl Melanie Samuels and just tell her that the requirements have been waived. It would be a sort of public service."

"I could do that," said Burnside thoughtfully. "We seemed to have a pretty good rapport when she was in here the other day."

"Do you think we should do it, then?" she asked.

He looked at her thoughtfully for a long moment. "Yeah, I guess I do."

"Then let me do it. I know this woman myself, probably a lot better than you do, Sid. And having me tell her the story ties in with something else we've already discussed, I'm pretty sure."

"I'm not following this at all, Suzy. What're you talking about?"

"I think I'd better, ah, as you might say, take the heat on this. For reasons I can't explain, I'm better positioned to present the story to Miss Samuels. And I think I can do it in a way that she never really has to disclose her source at all. I think I may have some leverage with her, Sid. You see, or I'm afraid you don't at this point, I'm in a position to give her something, unrelated to Red Tiger, that she badly wants."

"Well, I can't say this makes a whole lot of sense to me, but if you think it's the best way to handle it, I'll defer to your judgment. Just one thing, though. Please let me know if I'm gonna suddenly get called by her or somebody else."

"Of course, I'll do that, but I think after the story breaks all kinds of people might be calling to verify what they've heard. I'm sure all the other networks will want to speak with you." Suddenly she chuckled. "We could give them Zhu's number at the hotel, I suppose. I could offer to translate for him." Both laughed heartily. Neither Mr. or Mrs. Zhu had been seen in the office since the day of the DEA raid. Suddenly, she became serious. "You know, Sid, I feel terrible about not taking Mrs. Zhu out shopping or something like that. The poor thing's locked up in that hotel, afraid to come out for anything. Can you imagine, an hour after your arrival in the United States you're staring into the muzzle of a machine gun, then being dragged off to jail." Abruptly, she reached for her phone and dialed the hotel number, hoping to be able to invite Mrs. Zhu out for a shopping trip and just give her somebody beside her husband to talk with.

* * *

Factory Guys

That night when Zack arrived home he was surprised to see Melanie's BMW Z-3 in the driveway. He pulled his Firebird into the carport, went in through the kitchen, saw nobody in the house, and then walked out onto the patio, where he saw, to his surprise, Melanie and Suzy relaxing in the hot tub, laughing and chatting like old friends. "Well, this is cozy," he said. "Hi, Melanie. At least I can see you're not wired."

"Suzy's pretty smart. I think that's what she was thinking when she invited me over and told me to bring my suit. I notice we didn't get into anything interesting until we were in the tub. You gonna join us?" she asked, hoping to get a look at Zack in swimming trunks.

"Yeah, you know, it's funny, Suzy and me get into all sorts of interesting things in that tub."

"Melanie's joining us for dinner," said Suzy, reddening and hoping to change the subject abruptly. "Ah, Zack, why don't you make us a batch of strawberry daquiries and join us?"

"Be back in just a minute," he said, turning to go inside.

Melanie watched as he disappeared into the kitchen. "C'mon, you've got to tell me how you two met, not for the record, I mean, I just wanna know."

Suzy smiled. "Maybe sometime later, when I feel I can count you among my friends, and I hope I'll be able to."

"I do too, Suzy," said Melanie seriously. She was already finding Suzy Johnson an utterly fascinating character, astonished, as were most Americans, by her total bi-lingual fluency in two such disparate languages. She'd already learned about her childhood and training.

A moment later Zack walked back onto the patio, carrying a small plastic pitcher of frozen daquiries and three plastic cocktail glasses. Melanie inspected him surreptitiously through her sunglasses. He *is* a hunk, she told herself. Zack poured each of them a glass, then lowered himself into the tub.

He leaned over and kissed Suzy lightly on the lips. "OK, babe, what's going on here. You selling out to *The National Enquirer,* or what?"

"Please, Zack, Melanie works for KABC, not *The National Enquirer.* That wasn't nice," she laughed.

"Only kidding."

"Really, she tells me that she's talked to the two burglars who broke into our house and that their stories confiirm everything that we've heard from the two detectives, that some drug enforcement agent put them up

341

to planting that bag of heroin. He was named Rivera, and there is such an agent here in Los Angeles, but he won't return her phone calls."

"I'm not surprised at that," said Zack. "They probably got him assigned to poppy field surveillance in Burma or someplace like that."

Melanie chuckled. "That's almost exactly what one of the burglars said. Don't worry, I'll probably get to him, one way or another. He may refuse to say anything, but that's just about as meaningful as having him spill the whole story, maybe worse, because it makes people's imaginations run wild. I just want to be able to truthfully say that I tried to talk to him. If he says something to the effect of 'no comment,' or refuses to come to the phone, so much the better."

Zack smiled. "I see you have an instinct for this. An instinct for the jugular."

Abruptly, Melanie changed the subject. "Do you think you'd ever consent to be interviewed on camera?"

Suzy and Zack looked at each other. "I, I don't see how we could, Melanie," said Suzy. "I don't want people staring at me wherever we go, getting hounded by newsmen and photographers and ending up on the cover of the *The National Enquirer.*"

"Isn't there some other way, Melanie?" asked Zack. "I mean, couldn't you just tape us, or do one of those interviews where you block our faces?"

"I've thought about that," she said. "There's only one problem, which I'm sorry to say I caused. We've already got some really good footage of Suzy the day they arrested her. ABC in New York will want that tape, whatever we do from now on out. And throughout southern California, there's bound to be somebody who inadvertently video-taped the segment, and who'll be offered a big reward by other networks or the paparazzi from the tabloids to get it from them. I'm afraid that cat's outta the bag at this point." Suzy and Zack looked at each other, clearly dismayed. "Suzy, Zack," said Melanie gently, "I know this isn't easy for you, but I'll share an observation I've made over the years in this business. Most people who end up being the center of attention for an extended time period actively cultivate it. They want it, like Marilyn Summers. She craves the attention and does everything she can to get it, and there are always people willing to buy stories like hers. But people like you, who haven't done anything wrong and who don't want to stay in the spotlight aren't interesting to the public for very long. Look, I'm not going to lie to you. You two are interesting to the extent that you're a beautiful Chinese girl who's married a studly example of American manhood. I mean, you're the ultimate photogenic couple, and there'll be a certain interest level for a short time in your private lives, but that won't last. What's there to find out? You're a couple of family-oriented people with mainstream values, who live quietly and don't bother anybody. I mean, from a news standpoint, you're pretty boring."

There was a long silence. Finally Zack chuckled. "That's a hell of a note. Now we're boring, honey."

Melanie laughed. "Only from a news standpoint, Zack. Frankly, were you not married to this gorgeous lady, I'd be putting the moves on you rather shamelessly. I never get to meet guys like you in the news business. In fact, do you know any nice, single airline pilots?"

"I promise to keep an eye out," Zack said, smiling.

"Seriously, Zack, I promise you that if we can do an interview, it will be done in a way that your credibility absolutely can't be challenged. I'll make sure that your side of the story is nailed down tight."

"I wonder whether you can deliver on that promise," said Zack. "What if somebody higher up decides he doesn't like the way you did the story? Or wants to edit it in a way that destroys our credibility. There's no question that Carruthers has a lot of friends in the press who run interference for him and trash anybody who threatens him."

Melanie thought for a long moment before speaking. "There's more than a little truth in what you're saying, Zack. But there are two things offsetting that possibility here. One, this thing's on tape, and there's a lot of corroborating testimony here, from those detectives, plus those two guys they've got in jail. Who, incidentally, I *did* tape. There isn't a whole lot of wiggle room for Carruthers' spin doctors to work with on this one. The second thing is if anybody in our organization tries to edit or minimize this story, I'm going to scream bloody murder, publicly. And I'll make a copy of all the interviews for my own personal use, which I'll then supply to everybody from Rush Limbaugh to Fox News. And I'm not kidding. But really, I don't think there's any chance of that happening. The press's love affair with this character is wearing a little thin at this point. I mean, how long can people keep looking the other way?"

"Well, I'm glad you feel that way," said Suzy. "Because I've got another little piece of news that I think bears on this whole story, one that you and a lot of other people will find quite interesting."

"Oh, what's that?"

"You're aware, of course, that the US government has exhaust emission and safety standards for cars sold in this country."

"Sure. That's been true for at least thirty years, maybe a little longer."

"And are you aware that if you don't meet those standards, you can't sell cars here?"

"Well, I don't now the details of how the enforcement works, but yes, I suppose if the cars don't meet the standards, they can't be sold here, or something like that."

"The Red Whippets we're bringing in don't meet your standards."

"How's that possible?"

"I haven't the slightest idea. All I know is that all the standards were waived completely. Not just your federal government standards, but the California standards as well."

"Have you ever heard of such a thing before?"

"Well, I'm new here, but my boss, Sid Burnside, has been in the business a long time, and he says he's never heard of anything like it. Sid says the EPA won't bend the rules for anybody, not Ford, not GM, or anybody."

"What do you think's happening here?"

Suzy shrugged. "I think the timing's interesting. We really hadn't planned on bringing the cars in here for some time, probably years. The biggest single problem was getting them to pass your emission standards. We weren't even close to being able to do it, at least on a production basis. Then shortly after the incident in the embassy, everybody's running around, getting ready to ship the cars in quantity to the US. We couldn't figure out what was going on, then finally we were told that all the government standards had been waived."

"Are you suggesting that the Chinese government used the embassy incident, or I should say the tape of the incident, to blackmail the administration?"

"Well, it's certainly a thought. The timing's a bit of a coincidence," said Suzy.

Melanie's mind was racing. She was wondering whether to pursue the waiver herself or whether to assign it to their science editor, let him track it down. Suddenly she decided to at least get started on the story, call CARB and find out why the emission standards had been waived in California, then call EPA in Washington and ask the same thing. And I better get one of the cars to test at one of our state inspection stations, she told herself. "Suzy, could I borrow one of the cars, I mean, just to see and drive it and maybe run it through one of the state inspection stations?"

"I can ask Sid. I don't think he'd object. Frankly, I don't know how anybody could reasonably turn down a request like that."

* * *

The Johnsons and Melanie Samuels were just sitting down to one of Suzy's dinners when the trucks rolled up to Jake Dougherty's Sacramento Chevy store. There were three, each carrying eight Red Whippet sedans in various colors. Everybody ran outside excitedly, from lot boys to mechanics to salesmen, to look at the new merchandise. Jake himself quickly concluded a phone call he was on to rush out to get a look. "Hey, Billy Joe," he called out, "make sure sure the detail guys and a coupla mechanics stay late to get at least ten o' these prepped for tomorrow. The dowdy appearance of the little cars didn't fully register with anybody, since vehicle styling is often difficult to judge from the elevation of a car carrier. "C'mon," Jake called to the driver, "Let's get these things off the truck. I wanna drive one."

"You're sure about that, huh?" asked the driver, not smiling. He began pulling down the ramps on the trailer.

Twenty minutes later the assembled multitudes were watching Jake and Billy Joe Sisson drive off the lot, squeezed tightly in the front seats of a smurf-blue Red Whippet. They started off down the street, engine buzzing anemically, and trailing a faint stream of grey oil smoke. There was an audible crunch from the transmission as Jake upshifted to second. Thirty minutes later the crowd was starting to disperse, wondering where Jake and Billy Joe were. Finally, the receptionist ran out the front door and announced, "Jake's down at the Burger King on Elkhorn. He thinks they ran outta gas." One of the detail men went inside to get a gas can, then looked around wearily for a car with a dealer plate on it.

"Don't say nothing, Billy Joe," said Jake as they stood looking hopelessly inside the Red Whippet's engine bay. "I mean, this thing ain't that bad. It's a perfect commuter car, just the thing for around town. It was OK before it stopped runnin', doncha think?"

"Ah, well, it wasn't too bad, Jake, I mean it's probably really sturdy and built to last, so ya can't expect everything for five grand, can ya?"

And in fact the now lifeless but "sturdy and built to last" Red Whippet

345

before them had suffered an oil pump failure as the pump drive gear fractured. The oil-starved engine had seized solidly. The detail man finally arrived and dutifully began pouring fuel in the tank, then stepped back as the filler neck overflowed. "It's fulla gas, boss," he said. He went around and tried to start the car. The starter engaged, but of course wouldn't turn the solidly locked engine. "I can hear the starter clickin', but she won't turn over. Must have a dead battery," he announced, somehow overlooking the fact that the car had started on the lot and made it as far as the Burger King.

"Well, wait here, and we'll send someone back with a battery," said Jake, climbing in the other car with Billy Joe.

"Hey, the thing really runs good," he announced as he arrived back at the dealership. "I think it's got a bad battery, that's all. Ah, don't run any miles on any o' the others, guys," he added, lowering his voice, "and let's keep the demo rides to a minimum. Let's just get 'em cleaned up, prepped, and ready for sale for the weekend. There's gonna be people all over the place tryna buy these things in another twelve hours. And guys, we wanna hold some gross on these things, don't be givin' 'em away. After that ship burned up, I don't how many o' these things we're gonna get for the next coupla weeks."

Jake went into his office, sat down, and pulled out the bottle of Cutty Sark he kept in his desk. He poured himself two fingers into a clean coffee cup, tossed it off, then poured another. In a moment he felt better. Hey, that thing wasn't that bad, he told himself. I'm just used to drivin' Hondas and Acuras. They weren't all that great their first year, either, thought Jake, unwilling to make the recollection that they were indeed very good their first year.

* * *

The following morning Melanie Samuels was getting the keys to a Red Whippet sedan that Sid Burnside had brought our from the marshalling area at the dock. "I think the controls are pretty self-explanatory, Melanie. I put a manufacturer's plate on the back for you, and it's all gassed up."

"Thanks, Sid, I'll bring it back soon," she said, looking at the frumpy little car rather doubtfully. All she planned to do with it was to drive it straight to the CARB emissions inspection station over near Hollywood and have them run it through the test regimen. Five minutes later she was wondering who would buy such a car. It was frighteningly underpowered, the brakes on her particular example pulled sharply to the left, and it had the fit and finish of a piece of aluminum lawn furniture. She was going as fast as she dared on the freeway, which was barely forty-five miles per hour. Angry motorists stuck behind her finally pulled out to pass, staring at her balefully as they went by. Finally, after a rather traumatic ride, she pulled into the inspection station. She stopped in the employee parking area, went inside, found the supervisor, and announced herself. "I'd like to get this Chinese car tested for emissions if I could. It's supposed to run super-clean, and I'd like to see if it's up to the claims." She smiled winningly at the supervisor.

"Well, sure, I guess we could do that. You say you're from KABC? Hey, I know you, I've seen you on the news. Are you going to have a news crew down here?"

"We might, if there's a story here."

Thirty minutes later the man came into the waiting area, holding some kind of a printout. "Ms. Samuels? I gather this isn't your car, is it?"

"No. The company just lent it to me to test."

"Well, this is pretty strange. We ran the car through the test twice, because we wondered if there was something wrong with our equipment the first time."

"It was *that* clean?"

"Well, not exactly. This particular car, and maybe there's something wrong with it, but this car emits like sixty times the California limits for hydrocarbons, twenty-eight times the limit for nitrous oxides, and thirty-eight times the limits for carbon monoxide. I mean, this thing wouldn't meet the emission limits for the first year, 1968. In other words, this car's about like an old Model T Ford or something like that in terms of exhaust emissions."

"Are you sure of what you're saying?" Melanie asked.

"Yeah, here's the printout," he said, handing it towards her. "I mean, maybe there's something really wrong with this particular car, but I don't know what it could be. And in fact, when there is something wrong with these things, usually only one emission value is affected, like nitrous oxides, or maybe hydrocarbons, because they're affected by different factors and variables. But I've never seen a car where they're *all* screwed up."

"Thanks," said Melanie a bit absently. She could scarcely credit what she was hearing. Plus, she now had to face the drive back to the port in the feeble but highly poisonous Red Whippet.

An hour later she was reporting her findings to Sid Burnside, who just sat with his mouth open. "I don't believe this," he said. "I mean, they can't get away with something like this. Even here, we always assumed that the cars had to pass the existing standards. I always had my doubts about the claims they made for it, but I figured they could pass whatever standards are in place now. Jesus, I'm gonna take another one of 'em down to the inspection station this afternoon," he said, shaking his head.

Burnside's test example proved even worse than Melanie's car, and compounded its humiliation by overheating and blowing a head gasket just as it reached the port on the return trip. Christ, I'm goin' home for the day, said Burnside to himself. And he did.

Melanie spent the rest of the afternoon in a maddeningly frustrating effort to verify the emissions waiver by both the CARB and EPA. She was bounced from one department to the other in both agencies, put on hold indefinitely several times, spoke with a number of minor functionaries, but could gain no information on the question of a waiver. Finally, in exasperation, she demanded to speak with Penny Twombly and was told rather curtly that "Ms. Twombly is not available."

"Well, then you'd better tell Ms. Twombly that there's a story that's going to run on ABC tomorrow that's going to raise major questions of corruption inside the EPA, directly involving Ms. Twombly and other members of the present administration. Do you understand me? Now take my name and number, and you'd be well advised to tell her that *she'd* be well advised to call me and give me her side of the story before I run with what I've got, which is pretty ugly."

And these people wonder why everybody hates the government, she fumed, as she waited for the call back. And I'm a *reporter,* she told herself. God knows what some poor slob with a problem has to go through.

Remarkably, within the hour Penny Twombly's secretary called back, announcing that "Ms. Twombly will speak with you now."

"How good of her," Melanie said.

Penny Twombly came on the line. "Ms. Samuels," she said imperiously, "I don't like to hear talk of corruption in my agency. This had better be good."

"It's nice to have got your attention. Can you confirm that your

348

agency has waived the emission requirements for China's new car, this so-called Red Whippet?"

"Well, we didn't waive them, exactly."

"What's that supposed to mean?"

"The cars pass all our existing standards, but they may not all meet the emission limits the Chinese have claimed for them until they get some new parts, or something like that."

"How do you know that? Have you tested the cars?"

"Well, ah, not exactly, I don't think we have."

"Isn't that highly irregular?"

"Well, the Chinese gave us firm assurances that the cars meet the standards. Otherwise the president would never have issued the executive order granting the waiver. That's what I meant when I said EPA didn't really grant the waiver."

"Let me understand this, Ms. Twombly. You're saying that you just took the word of the Chinese that the cars met our standards, and on that basis, issued a waiver by executive order?"

"Ah, yes, of course, I mean, we have very cordial relations with the Chinese."

"Have you ever exempted anybody else from the testing regimen?"

"I, I'll have to check. I'm not sure."

"I take that as a no, correct?" Before the stammering Penny Twombly could respond, Melanie continued. "I just personally had one of these cars tested at a CARB emission facility in Los Angeles this morning. It emits more pollutants than a whole fleet of normal cars, like up to sixty times the allowable limits. Can you explain that?"

"I, ah, I can't explain that, no, but, ah, I'm sure there's an explanation for it."

"There's an explanation for everything, Ms. Twombly, but not all explanations are very satisfactory. But let me confirm just one more thing, Ms. Twombly. You're saying that Bob Carruthers issued the executive order granting the waiver?"

"Ah, yes, he did, I was there when he signed it."

"When was that, exactly, if you remember, and what number was it?"

"Well, I'm not sure, I don't have it in front of me right now."

Melanie bored ahead. "Well, was it before or after he got his nose broken?"

"Oh, it was definitely after, like a couple of weeks maybe," said the slow-witted Penny Twombly, momentarily glad to be able to answer what she thought was a harmless and irrelevant question. "I was there when it happened."

"Oh, good, then I can call you for an eyewitness account of what happened that night. Thanks so much for your help. I'll be in touch." She hung up, leaving Penny Twombly staring at the phone and fighting down a rising sense of panic

Penny Twombly took several deep breaths, then entered Nate Garmin's direct line. She was badly shaken by the news that the Red Whippet didn't meet any current standards at all. The idea that the Chinese, the *Chinese,* would lie to her and Nate Garmin, was simply unthinkable. They're just like us, she choked. They couldn't do something like this. Presently Nate Garmin came on the line. "Hey, Penny," he exclaimed happily. "Bob was telling me about this unbelievable thing today. It's another great Chinese idea. They got these electric eels that you can use for lighting and stuff like that, and when they're all worn out, you can eat 'em! They're gonna be coming in before too long and Bob wants me to take this thing, you know, kinda under my wing. Whaddya think of that?" Carruthers had figured it might keep Garmin harmlessly occupied for a while.

"Oh, that's wonderful," said Penny, though wondering if Carruthers wasn't pulling Garmin's leg, as he was occasionally wont to do. "It sounds like a great idea," trying to imagine an eel-filled aquarium with a flourescent tube glowing on top. "But, ah, Nate, I got a strange phone call from a reporter in Los Angeles a few minutes ago. She said the Red Whippet from China doesn't meet any of our emission standards. She said she had one tested at an emission inspection station in California this morning and it was really terrible, worse than anything. I mean, like it made like sixty times the allowable limits, or something like that."

"Well, maybe the car needed a tuneup, or something like that," said Garmin. "I mean, Ambassador Li promised us that the cars met all our standards, didn't he? That's why Bob issued the executive order, to help 'em speed things along. I mean, if there's a problem, and I'm sure there's not, it's on the Chinese. Hey, they just gotta fix it, right?"

"Ah, Nate, she asked me a funny question when I had her on the phone. She asked me if Bob granted the waiver before or after that girl broke his nose. What do you think that means?"

"Gosh, I dunno. I think maybe he just felt kinda bad about that big ruckus in the embassy that night and was maybe kinda trying to make it up to them. You know how Bob's always taking responsibility for everything, even if it wasn't his fault. I mean, like the economy and peace in the world. I think that may be why he gave the executive order for Li, cause he felt bad about that Chinese girl comin' on to him that way."

"You know, Nate, I'll bet you hit it right on the head. Bob was just trying to make it up to the Chinese for the embassy thing, and he figured it was a harmless little gesture that doesn't cost us anything and really helps the Chinese get into the market here with an environmentally safe car. And I'm sure you're right. The car just needed a tune-up, that's all. You know, I'm tempted to call that reporter back and give her a piece of my mind."

"I think you oughtta do that, Penny. Boy, the more I think about this the more it burns me up." After he'd hung up Garmin reflected on the clear hostility of the Los Angeles press toward the Carruthers administration. They're trying to wreck everything, he told himself. The environment, our foreign policy, and now they're taking shots at the DILDO. That's my legacy they're messing with!

* * *

Suzy and Zack were finishing dinner in their little kitchen. They had talked at length about Melanie's request that they grant her an on-camera interview and were reaching the unsettling conclusion that their interests were best served by doing so. "You know, honey," Zack said putting his arms around her and looking into her upturned face, "Melanie's probably right. The whole thing probably won't last long. And one o' the guys I fly with lives on a ranch a coupla hours north of Denver. We could hole up there for a few days when the thing airs. There's no way anybody'd find us up there. He keeps buggin' me to come out there and spend a few days. It's just him and his wife and their horses."

"That would be a godsend, Zack, as long as they didn't find us out there. I'd hate to think of a bunch of reporters invading somebody's property."

"This guy's five miles off the main road, and it's private property. Anybody comes out there, he can call the sheriff and have 'em thrown in jail. A press card doesn't impress people out there near as much as a badge and a six-gun. You wanna call Melanie and ask her to spell out what she's gonna ask us, and also who else she's gonna include in the story?"

She sighed. "I guess so. At least I feel comfortable with her. And I believe her when she says she'll do her best to protect our interests."

"Yeah, so do I."

* * *

Two hours after Melanie Samuels had spoken with Penny Twombly, PhD (Elem.Ed.), she was in the office of her producer, Bill Daniels, excitedly trying to explain the story she was working on. She was becoming so overwhelmed with the sheer enormity of it that she was stumbling over her presentation to Daniels. "Hey, take it easy, Melanie, slow down. Just start at the beginning again, with when you did that segment on the dope raid, or whatever it was, that day out in Chino."

She took a deep breath. "I'm sorry, Bill, but the more I get into this thing, the bigger and bigger it gets. It's so hard to swallow I'm choking on it. The only problem is it's true, I'd bet my life on it."

And so for the next thirty minutes she explained to Daniels the story of how it all started with a heads-up from Lee Swetlock, then how she came on the strange tape from Candy and Roy Lambert, then the interviews with the two detectives, the taped discussion with Sedgely and Duran, then the long afternoon with the Johnsons, then finally the revelation of the executive order exempting the Red Whippet from the EPA standards. She finished with her own description of what had happened at the CARB test station, and at last the conversation with Penny Twombly.

Daniels just stared at her. "That's just about the weirdest thing I've ever heard, Melanie. I mean, it's too bizarre to make up."

"Well, obviously, if it was just a fantasy, there were a hell of a lot of participants whose stories all fit and who are all having the same fantasy. And there was a fantasy tape. And the fantasy arrest of Suzy Johnson, and the fantasy dropping of all the charges later that day after she has a conversation with this DEA guy Faulkner. And a fantasy executive order, and Carruthers' fantasy nose problem. And the biggest fantasy of all, told to me by that ridiculous EPA woman, Penny Twombly, that the car meets all

352

our emission standards comfortably, which she knows for a fact because the Chinese told her so."

"Melanie, we gotta kick this thing upstairs. This is a big story. This is home office material. You better turn over everything you got to Winslow (the station general manager)."

"Like hell, Bill. This is my story and mine alone. It came to me and I developed it. Nobody's gonna take it from me. I'm the only one Suzy and Zack Johnson'll trust. I can guarantee they won't grant interviews to anybody else, and I doubt that those two guys Duran and Sedgey will, either. I got the tape of our conversation, and without it to grease the skids, I wouldn't bet that those two'll talk to anybody on camera. And I'm keeping that tape all to myself. And if the network doesn't like it and wants to fire me, I can find employment in about two or three hours with CNN or Fox News. The story, all the material, and all the contacts go with me, too. You can keep the great DEA raid tape if you want. It's pretty old news."

"C'mon, nobody's talkin' about firing you, Melanie. Calm down. You're one of the rising stars around here."

"Well, I'm sorry if I got a little excited, but this is my story, not just because I found it, but because I'm the only one who can get it right. And that's particularly important, Bill. These people, the Johnsons, are counting on me to protect them with the completeness of the story. I'm not going to see them get trashed with an incomplete story that leaves a lot open to speculation or gives Carruthers' spinmeisters anything to work with. This thing is bad, I mean *really* bad, the most disgusting thing I've personally ever heard of. I want every facet of the story nailed down tight, which it can be if everybody in it gets to tell their tale."

Daniels sighed wearily. "I'll run it by Winslow right now. You wanna come and tell him what you've told me?"

"Yeah, I guess I might as well. And we might as well get this show on the road."

And so two hours later Melanie had secured Dennis Winslow's support in letting her handle the story. "Why the hell not?" he'd asked Daniels. "Melanie's as good as anybody else for this sort of thing. I mean, this is gonna be a factual investigation, not Barbara Walters askin' some bubble-head like Marilyn Summers, 'But how do you *feel* about that?' God, I'm so sick of smarmy shit like that I have to drink Pepto Bismol before watchin' it."

Winslow, who was only three months from retirement and didn't much care about the home office reaction to the segment, then made another decision. "We're gonna run this thing as local news. What the hell, most of the players are local Californians. That way, it'll keep the rumors about it down in New York, which'll likely keep the White House from findin' out about it in time to try and stop it. After the fact, everybody in New York and Washington's gonna go berserk, but by then it'll be too late. We'll have our story out there and nobody's gonna be able to spike it or water it down. But that means we gotta run this thing real quick, like day after tomorrow. Make sure you can get all the interviews done and this thing organized by then, Melanie." He rubbed his hands together. "I can't wait to see it."

And so, shortly thereafter, Melanie was on the phone with Suzy Johnson, setting up a time the following day to come over and conduct their interview, which, she estimated, with setup and everything, would take about three hours. Suzy simply asked that Melanie transport her crew in an unmarked van of some sort, to avoid arousing the curiosity of the neighbors.

* * *

The following morning Jake Dougherty, now soberly contemplating the probable market appeal of the Red Whippet, was watching prospects, of whom there were many, taking short demo rides through the local streets. With few exceptions, they got out of the Red Whippets and went directly to their cars and left. Those who didn't generally wandered over to Jake's used car lot or browsed around the new car area, peering into windows and reading window stickers. He grabbed Billy Joe Sisson, who was hurrying past carrying a buyer's order on a new Chevy pickup. "Hey, Billy, we write any of these Chinese things yet?"

"Not that I know of, Jake. We're givin' a lot of rides, though. Something's bound to stick. Hey, I gotta give this deal to finance." He rushed off, leaving Jake standing alone on the lot. Holy shit, thought Jake suddenly. I wonder if those bastards drafted the bank on these little shit-boxes yet. Jake quickly made up his mind to call the bank first thing Monday morning and tell them to pay none of Red Tiger's drafts if they hadn't sold any of the cars by then. Jesus Christ, he thought, they can have the goddam franchise back if we don't do any of these things by then.

Jake was getting himself in a state of considerable agitation, wondering whether the Red Tiger drafts had hit his bank yet. Once the bastards got my money, it's gonna be a lot harder to get out of this thing, he thought nervously. Suddenly, he spotted Alan Sachs, his controller, walking into the showroom. He ran over. "Hey, Alan, I'm glad to see you," he said.

"Yeah, I just came in to make the month-end adjustments. You should have the statement by Monday afternoon."

"Hey, great. Ah, Alan, did Red Tiger draft on these cars yet?"

"Well, yeah, they did, late yesterday afternoon. I called the bank to get our floorplan total about four o'clock. They hit the bank with drafts totaling, ah, just shy of ninety-eight thousand, if I remember right. Why?"

"Ooohh, shit. Oh, shit. I got a bad feeling about this franchise, Alan, I'm havin' second thoughts. Nobody's buyin' the things yet, and we musta showed about twenty people the thing this morning alone."

"Well, I gotta admit, Jake, I was lookin' at one close yesterday afternoon, and maybe it's an early production one and all, but the thing kinda looked like something a bunch o' Chinamen got together and built in a field or something. I mean, it was pretty crude."

"You really think it was that bad?"

"Well, maybe I've seen worse, but I can't remember exactly when."

Jake just stood and watched another couple get out of the Red Whippet and practically run for their car. Goddam, I wonder where I can find that bastard Maxwell on a Saturday, he asked himself.

* * *

"Mrs. Johnson, would you swear that you and your husband are the people seen in the tape we just viewed?"

"Yes."

"And was it the president who was grabbing you and whom you then slapped?"

"Yes."

"And was he trying to hit you with his fist before you struck him in the nose?"

"That's certainly was what he appeared to be doing. In fact, I'd have to say yes, there's no question that's what he was trying to do."

"Do you think you broke his nose?"

"It felt and sounded like it. I really wasn't trying to, but I believe that's what happened

The interview went on in like vein for over an hour, in minute detail, to include the arrest in Chino, the discussion with Win Faulkner, and finally, their release from confinement. Then it turned to the question of the waivers given for the Red Whippet by executive order from the president himself.

"Are you aware that shortly after the incident in the Chinese embassy the president of the United States issued an executive order exempting the Red Whippet cars from American emission and safety standards?"

"None of us in the office out here in California knew about any executive order or exactly when it was issued. We just found out sometime later that the requirements had been waived and that the cars could go on sale shortly."

"Did that seem unusual to you?"

"Well, I had no experience in this area, but my boss thought it was rather strange."

"Do you think the issuance of the waiver was a response to diplomatic pressure from the Chinese government on the administration, threatening to publicize the embassy incident if the special waivers were not granted?"

"I wouldn't have any way of knowing, although the timing of the whole affair is curious. I guess it's possible.

"Were you aware that the Red Whippet, the car that's been allowed by the EPA and NHTSA to go on sale in this country, is the worst polluting new car ever tested by the California Air Resources Board?"

"Not until you told me. We never tested it. In fact, the first of them just arrived a few days ago."

"Mrs. Johnson, are you now or have you ever been an agent of the government of the People's Republic of China?"

"I am not nor was I ever."

After they'd finished Suzy looked a little wanly at Melanie. "I feel worn out, just drained."

"You were very good, Suzy. Very good. You just answered the questions without a lot of unnecessary detail or elaboration. People who are fabricating a story usually add a lot of superfluous detail. They think it makes them more credible. You answered my questions just as I hoped you would." She paused. "What are you going to do for the next few days?"

"Zack and I are getting out of town for a while. Continental gave him a few days off, and he's not flying for a few more anyway, so we'll be able to get out of here long enough for things to quiet down, I hope."

"I think that's a good idea. Could you let me know where you can be reached?"

Suzy looked at Zack. "Yeah, Melanie," said Zack, "I'll give you a number where we can be reached. It's a cell phone, which I'll leave on while we're gone. You won't know where we are, but you'll be able to contact us if you feel it's really important."

Melanie spent the rest of that day interviewing George Sedgely and Wilfred Duran at the LA County jail. The only condition the pair had attached to the interview was that their faces be blanked and their names not be revealed. Melanie readily acceded to their demand and was rewarded with a virtual duplicate of their first statements to her. She made her fifth and final phone call in search of Phil Rivera, finally identifying herself as a reporter for KABC news, and was told that Rivera was "not available."

"Is Lee Swetlock available, then," she asked the operator.

To her surprise, Swetlock came to the phone. "I'm afraid I can't help you any with further information about anything regarding DEA operations in this district, Ms. Samuels. I mean, you wouldn't play ball with me, so we don't have to talk to the press, right?"

"Whatever you say, Lee. I really didn't want to talk to you anyway, though. I'm looking for Phil Rivera, you know, your undercover guy. Nobody seems to know where he is."

"Huh? Why do you wanna talk to him?" Swetlock had no idea that Melanie had discovered the connection between the Johnson break-in, the attempted heroin plant, and Sedgely, Duran, and Rivera.

"Somebody told me he's good in bed. I'm dying to meet him. So where can I find him?"

"He, ah, he's out of town, backpacking somewhere in the Sierra Nevadas. I wouldn't have any idea how to get hold of him."

"OK. I take it I can quote you on that, right?" She hung up.

Swetlock sat, momentarily transfixed with fright. He began sweating as he picked up the phone to try to locate Rivera and order him out of town, to "the fucking Sierra Nevadas for a week, or maybe a camping trip in the Dakota Badlands. Just go, now!"

Melanie spent the next fourteen hours straight with Bill Daniels and the edit technicians putting the segment together for airing the following night at six and eleven. When they were finished the segment ran for thirteen minutes, several times the length of a normal local news segment. She was finally satisfied with it, sure it was tightly wrapped, convincing, and powerful. They said goodnight at nearly 3:00 AM and went home.

* * *

Chapter 13

Carruthers was wrestling, thus far without notable success, to come up with a reasonable-sounding rationale for the coming announcement of the joint investigation by the Chinese state security police and American security personnel, ostensibly rooting out terrorists and destroying their infrastructures, and which would involve giving the Chinese access to sensitive and often top-secret files. Carruthers figured that the flap over the obvious security breaches would blow over fairly quickly, since the aggrieved parties, the FBI, CIA, and NSA were not an organized political constituency. *All I gotta do is get it in when nobody's looking,* he told himself. *Maybe I could get Marilyn to give another interview. And hey, if it gets really rough there's always some third world tinpot dictator out there I can bomb.*

The swine products deal with FDA worried him more. Though it represented no actual risk to national security, the farmers were a group Carruthers was loath to offend. Carruthers mentally tried to calculate the total number of federal employees and military personnel who ate in mess halls and government cafeterias, plus the total population of the federal prison system, hoping to see whether he could dispose of the surplus Chinese pork by mandating daily pork on the menus of these institutions. He quickly gave up trying to come up with an estimate and decided to give it to McGurn, his chief of staff, to assign for analysis. *Shit, we could probably dump a few million tons on the North Koreans, too,* he told himself. *The bastards are always whining about not having enough to eat. Hey, maybe we could even strike a deal with 'em: Pigs for peace! I like it!*

Hell, the eel problem's just a drop in the bucket, ten million bucks for ten million pounds of Li's slimy eels. We can turn 'em into fertilizer if we have to.

Carruthers was starting to feel a bit more upbeat again. Everything'll be OK. I just gotta space these little fuckups out a little, time 'em right. Damn, I wonder what that Chink broad's doing. I gotta get a copy of that tape out in California. She's even foxier than I remembered. He decided to call Win Faulkner and order him to procure a copy somehow.

* * *

As Carruthers was enjoying his last few hours of tranquility, Zack and Suzy were driving north from Denver to visit one of Zack's friends, Hugh Jackson, a Continental captain with whom he flew and who'd become a good friend during the past couple of years. He was always badgering Zack to bring a girlfriend up to his ranch for a long weekend. Two hours after leaving the outskirts of Denver they were turning down the little dirt road that led to the ranch house, some five miles away. The sign over the gate identified the property as the Bar-Nine Ranch, a fair size spread on which Jackson raised cattle and pumped a little oil. "Oh, Zack," Suzy said, sighing, "I just can't get over this country, how big everything is. I didn't know there was this much space in the whole world! And we're not even near the ranch house, yet?" Zack nodded. "Your friend must be very rich."

"Hugh? I don't think so. This ranch has been in the family for generations. He's just a workin' stiff like me. Or at least he lives like one." Presently the ranch house came into view, a small and unimposing little two story brick house. Suzy glanced at him but said nothing. "You were expecting maybe a castle?"

She turned to him and smiled. "Well, given the size of the property I'd, well, assumed that it would have a big house."

"It'll be plenty for us, honey. And nobody'll find us here, that's for sure, not unless we want them to."

The pulled up in front of the house as a tall, gray-haired man with a rugged and weathered countenance and a tall, still blond, fortyish and very pretty woman came out. "Welcome to the Bar-Nine," the man announced as they stepped out of their rental car.

"Jack, Hazel, meet Suzy," said Zack shaking hands with Hugh. "I gotta tell ya right up front. She's beautiful but she's bad news." Suzy scowled and punched his arm. "She's got us into all kinds of trouble, so we have to hole up here for a few days."

"Well, you've come to right place, honey," said Hazel. "Welcome to the Wild West."

During the next thirty minutes, spent over coffee at the kitchen table, Zack filled in Hugh and Hazel on the events of the past several months. "It's not like we're fugitives from the law or anything like that. It's more like fugitives from the press. Nobody but my parents knows we're here. I gave this Samuels girl a cell phone number, but she's got no way of knowing where we are. The area code's just an LA area code, so I don't think you'll have to worry about reporters crashing all over your property."

"Well, the hell with all that, Zack. Tell us how you met this beautiful lady," said Hazel, placing her chin in her hand and looking at Zack expectantly, eyebrows raised.

* * *

Zack and Suzy Johnson, far from the maelstrom they'd been so instrumental in creating, happily enjoyed the company of their friends as Melanie Samuels counted down the hours, then the minutes, to the airing of her blockbuster segment. Starting with the drive time KABC radio programming at four o'clock, the network started running teaser promos for her upcoming segment, asking such questions as "can we trust Federal drug enforcement officials not to falsify evidence? Find out on News at Six." Or, "has the president's sex life influenced foreign policy decisions? Find out on News at Six."

It was clear to Lee Swetlock, driving home in his car that afternoon, that something was up when he heard the promos. "Oh, shit, oh, shit, oh, shit" he muttered as he drove. He'd been speculating that his conversation with Melanie Samuels the previous afternoon was merely a fishing expedition, but then finally realized that if she knew about Rivera at all, it was no fishing trip. He considered calling Win Faulkner to give him a heads up that something big was about to break but then decided that his present low profile seemed to be standing him in good stead. After all, he still had his job and hadn't yet been transferred to the Georgetown, Guyana DEA liaison office

Sid Burnside, Sherry Maxwell, and Vera Hawkins, all ignoring Jake Dougherty's anguished cries and Freddie Newell's death threats left on the voice-mail, sat quietly in Burnside's office waiting for Melanie Samuels' segment to air. Suzy had told them when it was due to run, advising them to watch it, that it would "explain a lot," as she put it. Burnside had brought in some munchies, two six packs of Coors, a bottle of vodka, and a couple bottles of bitter lemon. "Well, kids," he said, "we might as well have a little party. I don't know if we'll be open tomorrow."

Sherry sat morosely, staring at the vodka bottle, and hoping that someone would make the first move. To his immense relief, Vera reached over and tore off a Coors. "Might as well have a cool one," she announced, popping it open and raising it to her fellow employees of Red Tiger Motor Company. "Shoot, ah feel like we're all in thet movie whure thet big rock done hit the earth, all of us just awaitin' fer it. This ain't that bad, not by a long shot." She took a long pull at her beer and watched Sherry put ice and four fingers of vodka in a plastic tumbler, then splash in a bit of bitter lemon. He waited a decent four seconds for the beverage to chill, then took a long swallow.

"Shit, this was my last chance," said Sherry, looking at his glass reflectively. "This was what I been waiting for all my life, then this happens."

"What happens, Sherry?" asked Burnside, chuckling. "The product was never any good to start with, we just been peddlin' a dream here. We just didn't know it until now. Hell, we're lucky the ship burned and took almost all of 'em with it. I'm just glad none of us were part of this whole scam to get the requirements waived. I guess the Chinese were behind all that, but I wouldn't be surprised to see us have to testify when they start investigating it." He reached over and opened a beer for himself. "Maybe we'll find out what really happened here, how the timing got moved up, the cars got all the requirements waived, all that stuff. I just don't know why this Samuels girl is getting involved with a story like this."

"Ah don' know nothin' 'bout none o' that," said Vera. "Ah still think anybody'd buy a car like that must be plumb crazy. They the worst li'l ol' piece o' crap Ah ever seen, and that's no lie." She took another pull on her beer.

Burnside looked at his watch, reached over, and turned on the TV set. "It probably won't run until last. They always save the good stories until then." He got up and walked around the little office, disconnecting the phones. "I hate being interrupted when I'm havin' a party," he said.

And exactly fourteen minutes later Los Angeles area television viewers were watching Melanie Samuels, very attractive, cool, calm, and matter-of-fact, begin her segment with the observation that "this is perhaps the most disturbing story I and my colleagues at KABC have ever report-ed. It involves a sexual assault at the very highest level of our federal gov-ernment, blackmail of the current administration by a foreign power using recorded images of gross personal misconduct by the president, an attempt by drug enforcement officials, at the specific direction of the pres-ident, to frame and prosecute innocent citizens of this country, and final-ly, the suspension of our automotive environmental and safety regulations to allow the Chinese to compete illegally in the United States with an unsafe and environmentally hazardous product."

And during the next thirteen perfectly timed and edited minutes, Melanie Samuels told her story, with the embassy tape running at normal speed twice, then once in slow motion, then once more with the frame frozen where Carruthers' nose was being crunched by the heel of Suzy Johnson's right hand, leaving no possible doubt whatever as to the identi-ty of the person having his nose broken for trying to punch her. "This is the tape the president was trying to recover from Mrs. Johnson when he ordered her released and all charges dropped after her false arrest on drug charges," Melanie added at the end of tape. She also made it clear that the source of the tape hadn't been the Johnsons, though without specifiying how it came into her possession.

The attempted drug plant story was nailed down tight by the testi-mony of Sedgely and Duran, along with Melanie's statement that not only did Phil Rivera exist as an LA office DEA agent, but that he had refused to return her many phone calls, in which she'd identified herself as a crime reporter for KABC.

Five minutes before the segment even concluded, Freddie Newell was frenziedly entering the Red Tiger number, only to be told that the phone was temporarily out of order, as were callers from the other networks and radio stations in Los Angeles and the surrounding area.

"Well, what the hell," said Sherry Maxwell, "that coulda been worse. She didn't say they're bad cars or anything like that. I mean, I don't think people care about the emissions, d'you guys?" He looked around the little office for affirmation.

Burnside rolled his eyes and poured himself a vodka and bitter lemon. "Well, guys, why don't we have a few more snorts then we can all go out to dinner somewhere. How's Mexican sound tonight?" He'd seen enough and wasn't watching anymore.

As the staff of Red Tiger Motors talked quietly and disconsolately, the segment finally closed out with Melanie standing in front of a forlorn-looking Red Whippet, noting that "this vehicle, tested this morning by CARB, emitted over sixty times the allowable limits for tailpipe pollutants. KABC is currently investigating the issuance of the executive order by President Carruthers which allowed these vehicles entry to not only the United States but the state of California as well. We are presently attempting to confirm a report that the governor issued the executive order exempting these vehicles in California."

"Pore Suzy an' Zack," said Vera unhappily, dropping her now-empty beer can into a nearby waste basket. "They oughtta geld that worthless varmint Carruthers. Hey," she said, brightening, "I wonder if Suzy'd teach me some o' that kung-fu stuff."

"God, I hope not," replied Burnside. "You're already too dangerous as it is."

It took less than ten minutes after the airing for ABC in New York to hear about the broadcast and demand that the tape be transmitted to them immediately. Twenty minutes after that reporters were on the phone to the White House press office demanding a full explanation of the LA broadcast. And finally, two hours after that ABC had supplied the White House with a complete copy of the broadcast tape for their own review and comment.

President Carruthers, Timothy McGurn, his chief of staff, and Ernie Schaaf, his press secretary, stood in Carruthers' office, wordlessly watching the ABC broadcast for the second time. Carruthers finally spoke as Melanie Samuels was wrapping up. "What the hell, this coulda been worse. So I was coppin' a little feel. What's that got to do with my stand on the issues? With all the shit that's happened, I can't see people getting all that excited about this. I mean, it's not like I raped her."

McGurn looked at him in disbelief. "Are you crazy? The difference here is that this is on *tape,* you're standing there feelin' this lady up, then you try to belt her. Even Pat Ireland and those other feminist loonies are gonna have a hard time swallowing this one." He paused, shaking his head. "And what about this waiver you gave the Chinese for their cars? Every environmental group in the country is gonna go crazy if what that reporter says is true. It sounds like every one of those cars could create a smog alert all by itself."

"You really think we got a problem, huh?" asked Carruthers. "All right," he said grimly. "The first thing I want is a meeting with the

Chairman of the Joint Chiefs. Some sonofabitch out there's gotta be askin' for it. I need a target, I don't give a shit what. Just get me a building with a roof on it, someplace where somebody *could* be makin' germ weapons or some shit like that. We'll work out the details later. And we need someplace with no real air defenses. The last thing I need right now is a pilot being paraded through the streets of Lagos or some shithole like that. Just don't pick someplace *too* goddam defenseless. I don't want an F-18 comin' back with a friggin' spear stickin' in the wing. That's bad PR, usin' laser bombs on a bunch o' bare-assed tribesmen. And I don't need another Somalia deal, like that day we killed half the goddam civilian population of Mogadishu."

"Well, that may take the heat off for a few days," McGurn conceded, "but we gotta address the question of you grabbin' this lady's ass then trying to punch her. And what about the goddam executive order waiving all our safety and emission requirements?"

"Yeah, you're right," said Carruthers, nodding vigorously. He stood thinking for a long moment. "All right, here's what we do first. We're gonna announce that the executive order was based on Twombly and Garmin's assurances that the Chinese cars met all our standards. Wait a minute! Keep Garmin's name outta this thing. I can't let anything happen to him right now. That dumb broad Twombly's gotta take the fall for this. We'll say that she, ah, got taken in by the Chinese and accepted their assurances that the cars were OK, then briefed me without letting me know the details. I want her resignation first thing tomorrow morning, and I want her out of her office immediately. Wait, I don't even want her going in to EPA tomorrow at all. I don't want the press talkin' to her. Just see that she disappears for a few days, promise her anything, just get her outta town. And Christ, don't let anyone talk to Garmin. Lock the dumb shit in the basement if you have to, just keep him outta sight. And if he starts in with this thing about wantin' his dildo, just get the goddam thing for him. I gotta keep him happy and occupied for the moment."

McGurn and Schaaf glanced at each other but said nothing.

"We'll gonna get out of this OK. We just got to do a little damage control. We've pulled it off before. Hey, I got it! I know how I can explain grabbin' that chick's ass. It's a little weak, maybe, but I can sell it. It'll give us that crack we need to drive a wedge into this story. My supporters'll believe anything I tell 'em, and most of the rest of the people out there don't give a shit enough to worry about it. Tim, I want a press conference scheduled for noon tomorrow, on the White House lawn. We might as hit this story head-on. And right now, this minute, I want that executive order rescinded and all those Chinese cars impounded by customs, EPA, the FBI, whatever. We gotta be seen taking strong action on this thing."

"Ah, Mr. President, do you want Heather to be at the press conference, too?" asked Schaaf.

"Umm, lemme think about it." We'll be OK, he told himself. And someday I'm *still* gonna fuck that Chink broad, fuck her till her nose bleeds!

* * *

From nine o'clock on that night the local press maintained a steady vigil outside the Johnsons' house in Pasadena. For a while they went door to door, hoping to learn something about the Johnsons and their where-abouts from the neighbors, only two of whom had seen the broadcast. They did, however, quickly track down Phil Rivera at his little garden apartment in the eastern suburbs. Rivera quickly calculated that he'd be better off simply confirming the whole story rather than trying to lie about it. He could truthfully say that he didn't know any of the ultimate objectives of the plan, only that it allegedly involved a matter of national security. "That's what I was told by my supervisor," he said simply. "I thought it was some sort of plan to get some foreign intelligence types outta the country. But yeah, it was a drug plant in that house. Whatever these people were doin', it wasn't involved in any way with drugs, as far as I know. Hey, maybe I shoulda questioned it a little more, but they made it sound like this thing was so top secret, so sensitive, that nobody was going to share any information on it with a peon like me. Hey, if you really want to get the lowdown on this thing, maybe you oughtta talk to my boss, Lee Swetlock. Here, I'll give you his direct line." Rivera's interview, given in his living room to an NBC crew, was, like Suzy Johnson's, completely convincing.

As Phil Rivera was finally getting in his final licks against his boss, the crew of Red Tiger Motors was enjoying a somewhat raucous Mexican din-ner not far from the office. All three were at least slightly drunk on mar-garitas, beer, and whatever they'd drunk before arriving at the restaurant.

"Ah say we should buy all them li'l ol' shitboxes ourselves," said Vera. "They all gonna be instant collectors items. Why, mah Uncle Cletus got himself a collection o' more'n three hunnert different kinds o' beer cans. He says they worth near ten thousand dollars, and he didn't pay nothin' for 'em."

"I don' know about that, Vera," said Sid. "I mean, these cars may not have too much collectors appeal. You ever see them guys in the parks in the city, those old guys sweepin' dog turds into them little, like, dustpans? Ain't nobody makin' a collection o' dogshit, though."

Everybody broke into hooting laughter at the rather disconnected remark, especially Vera, the drunkest of the three, who finally quieted down enough to say, "Oh, Sid, you are the *funniest* man Ah ever met. Ya'll are jus' plumb crazy. Nobody collectin' jus' any ol' dogshit," she said, then broke into laughter again.

The three of them stayed until midnight, long after the other diners had left. "Well, I guess we better get going," said Burnside.

"Ya'll are too drunk to drive. Ah'm gonna take Sherry back to the hotel, then Ah'm gonna bring you home, Sid. Cain't be a-havin' you endin' up in the pokey."

"What about you? You're drunker'n me, Vera."

"Why, Sidney, ain't no nice young po-liceman gonna give li'l ol' me a ticket." She batted her eyes at Burnside and Sherry.

"Yeah, you gotta point," grunted Burnside, fishing in his pocket for his keys. "Let's go."

Forty-five minutes later they were pulling into Burnside's driveway. "Hey, thanks for the ride, Vera. I really appreciate it. Can you stop by for me in the morning?"

"Why, o' course, Sidney, you sweet ol' teddybear. But first I gotta make sure you're safely tucked in beddy-bye."

She took his arm and walked him to the front door. "Gimme the key," she said.

She opened the door, then steered Burnside into his living room. "Which way?" she asked.

"Hey, you gotta go now," said Burnside. She was marching him down the hallway to the bedroom. "Hey, Vera, you can't stay here. I'm fine, I really am."

"Now, Sid, ya'll wouldn't turn out a lady in the middle o' the night, would you?" She pulled his jacket off, then undid his tie and started to unbutton his shirt.

"Hey, Vera, c'mon, you gotta go," said Burnside, though not very forcefully. She stepped back and pulled off her blouse, then undid her bra and tossed it aside. "Jesus Christ, Vera, I'm old enough to be your father."

"That never woulda stopped *mah* ol' daddy," she said, giggling. "Sidney, ya'll are jus' the sweetest ol' teddybear. How come ya'll never come on to me? Doncha think Ah'm pretty enough?" She pirouetted for him.

"Well, I guess you could lay down here and take a little nap. But then you gotta go." Jesus Christ, thought Burnside, this Red Tiger thing's making us all crazy. He fell into bed, then turned out the light just as Vera snuggled up to him.

* * *

As Sid Burnside was wondering how he'd ended up in bed with a beautiful young lady almost thirty years his junior, Suzy and Zack were finally getting to bed after a sumptuous steak dinner, followed by hours of chatting and playing Trivial Pursuits. To everybody's amazement, while Suzy practically zeroed out on entertainment and sports, she cleaned everybody's clock on everything else, from geography, to world history, and science, making her and Zack the overall winners for the evening. He watched her admiringly as she brushed her teeth, then joined him in bed. "God, you're bright. I just hope the kids get your brains."

"I'm not smarter than you, Zack. I just had a much more rigorous education, without a lot of distractions. You know a million things that I'll never know. I don't think I'd do too well flying an airliner, for example, or trying to work on my car."

"Hell, you're even smart in the way you don't bruise my ego."

"That's one of the things I love most about you. You don't seem to have an ego, or at least an unhealthy one." Suddenly, she asked, "Zack, do you think Melanie's right about people just forgetting about us pretty soon?"

He thought for a long moment. "Yeah, I think she probably is. We're really not all that interesting to the public. I mean, they want sensational stories, people who are always goin' to the right spots, makin' the right friends. Who are *our* friends? There's my pilot buddies, people like Kate and Sammy, maybe someday Vic Murray, they're all people pretty much

368

like us. There's no story here. Maybe someday we'll be featured in one of those "Where are they now?" stories you see once in a while. We'll be a little older, with a coupla kids and a dog, still boring to the outside world."

"I don't find *you* boring," she said, running her fingertips lightly up his inner thigh.

"Nor I you, my sweet, and so to hell with everybody else."

* * *

At eight o'clock Pacific time the following morning, two car-loads of federal marshals descended on Jake Dougherty's Chevy-Red Tiger store, gathered the keys to all the Red Whippets, and informed Jake's service manager that the vehicles were not to be started nor driven, under pain of a $50,000 fine per count, and that arrangements were being made to return the cars to the port of entry and thence to China. Similar scenes were repeated in the four other Red Tiger dealerships that morning, as well as in the port, where some three hundred fifteen Red Whippets still awaited shipment. "I don't give a shit what you do with the goddam things," Jake's service manager told the leader of the group. "And I doubt that Jake does, either," not knowing that Jake's bank had already been drafted for the cars.

When Jake arrived two hours later and was told the news, he stood fuming silently for several minutes, while Billy Joe Sisson and the service manager watched him cautiously. "The fuckers stuck it up my ass again!" he shouted suddenly, as though all non-Japanese Asians were engaged in some monstrous conspiracy to bankrupt him. Dougherty ran into his office, reached into his bottom drawer for the Colt Python .357 Magnum he kept there, laid it on the desk top with a solid metallic thud, then dialed Air West's number to get the next plane to Los Angeles. Speaking to the reservationist was enough to remind Jake that he couldn't carry a gun on the plane. "Uh, ah, never mind," he said apologetically, then slowly hung up. Shit, everything's a goddam pushup in this fucking business, he told himself. Goddammit, I hate these lyin' factory guys. By now he'd calmed himself enough to dial Sid Burnside's number in Chino and ask him what was going on.

As Jake Dougherty was trying to get in touch with Sid Burnside, who was at that moment waiting for Vera to change clothes back in her little apartment, the president and the first lady were having a heated discussion in their bedroom. "Goddammit, you got a lot to lose, too, Heather. You gotta help me sell this thing. You gotta *be* there for everybody to buy it. Nobody's got the balls to call *you* a liar. This'll fly, but only with your help. C'mon," he wheedled.

"All right, you slimy worm. What do *I* get out of this thing? Just being the first lady is nothing more than an embarrassment now. I want something of my own, like head of something really important, maybe director of the CIA, or head of Department of Transportation, or maybe a seat on the Supreme Court." She paused, her eyes narrowing. "That's it! *That's* what I want! You just better make it happen, Bob. Next time one of those old farts croaks or retires, you're gonna nominate *me*. That's the deal. Otherwise, you can do your little soft shoe routine out there all alone, you got me?"

"You got it, Heather. That's a great idea, you a Supreme Court Justice. Hey, that'd be good for both of us! You got it, lady. Now, let's go over this thing one more time."

* * *

There was a knock on the door. Then Suzy and Zack heard Hazel Jackson's voice. "Hey, guys, if you're awake, Carruthers is holding a press conference in about a half hour. You might want to see it."

They looked at each other. "Sure, we'll be out in a few minutes," said Zack. "C'mon, honey, you wanna see who we're bombing today?"

She stretched and smiled. "I guess so. It's so nice to know we're influential in politics. Who says one person can't make a difference?"

"God, don't tell me you're gonna start liking all this celebrity status."

"Only kidding. Can I get in the shower first?"

And so at precisely ten o'clock Rocky Mountain time, the Jacksons and the Johnsons were sitting at the kitchen table, having scrambled eggs and bacon, when Bob Carruthers appeared behind a podium on the White House lawn, with Heather standing a step behind and a few feet to his right, smiling and nodding. When the group quieted down, Carruthers began. "I've called this press conference to announce a serious security threat to the United States, originating in the African republic of Chad." An audible groan went through the assembled reporters, who looked at each other with rolling eyes and shaking heads. Carruthers ignored the clear expressions of doubt before him. "Our intelligence analysts have provided irrefutable proof of something we've suspected for some time in that country, which has known ties to Middle Eastern terrorist groups. We discovered only four days ago that what outwardly appears to be a lawn fertilizer processing plant is in fact a chemical and biological weapons production facility." Somewhere among the reporters someone was heard to mutter something about there being no golf courses or tended lawns in Chad. "Accordingly, after consultation with the Joint Chiefs last night, I have ordered the weapons plant destroyed by Seventh Fleet naval airpower and cruise missiles. These attacks were launched approximately two hours ago and will reach their targets shortly. Let us all pray that these brave naval aviators all return safely to their waiting carriers. I'll entertain your questions now."

A female reporter from CBS leapt to her feet in the front row. "Mr. President, what is your response to the allegations in the story originating in Los Angeles last night?" she practically shouted.

"I'm sorry, but I was hoping to answer questions regarding this morning's military action in Chad." He turned to another reporter, ignoring the woman.

"Mr. President," shouted a reporter from NBC, "is it true, then, that this military action in Chad was initiated to divert attention from the story my colleague from CBS was referring to?"

"That's an outrageous allegation," said Carruthers, managing to look quite convincingly outraged by the outrageous but true allegation.

He looked at Sam Donaldson, who was gesturing at him. "Yeah, Sam, go ahead."

"Mr. President, with all due respect, would you please get serious. Nobody's interested in one of your live-fire exercises against a bunch of helpless Africans. We want to know about these charges of corruption, sexual assault, illegal arrests of innocent parties, you know, all that good stuff." He fixed Carruthers with an accusatory stare.

Finally Carruthers shrugged. "I'd have hoped for a more sober and mature attitude from members of the press at the onset of a military operation, where the lives of our brave military professionals are at risk, but all right, I'll take questions now regarding the broadcast in Los Angeles last night." If Carruthers had hoped to put them on the defensive with his remarks, it didn't seem to be working. There wasn't a kindly or even neutral face among the reporters.

Donaldson continued. "Well, thanks for that, Mr. President. Now, would you please explain the groping incident in the Chinese embassy a couple of months ago. First, do you deny that it was you on the video tape?"

"No, Sam, I don't deny that at all. It was me all right." He turned to face the First Lady. "Honey, could you come up and join me for a minute?" Heather Carruthers came forward, smiling and looking at her husband adoringly. She moved close to him and took his arm in her hand. He returned the look, then turned once again to the reporters seated on the lawn. "The night of the incident followed a long day of strategy sessions with the Joint Chiefs. I'm not a military man, and it takes a tremendous amount of concentration to absorb the information I need to render command decisions in my role as commander in chief. I don't mind confessing that these sessions leave me physically and mentally exhausted, just drained, especially knowing that American lives depend on the quality of my decisions." He could see, even sense, the reporters relaxing. It's working, they're gonna buy it, he told himself. "The night that incident occurred was one of those late evenings where all I wanted to do was just get home to my wife and go to bed." Several female reporters smiled. It's gonna fly! They're going for it, he told himself. He looked down into Heather's eyes, who returned the look. "As most of you know, Heather and I have a very, how do I put it, a very close, very physical relationship. I mean, sometimes we just can't keep our hands off each other, even in public." Heather held him in her adoring gaze. "That night I was just so tired, and it's always Heather at my side, that I just reached over to give her a friendly little, ah, caress. I mean, the girl next to me was about her size, and she was just in my peripheral vision." They're going for it! He reached around and placed his hand on Heather's broad behind. She looked pleasantly shocked, and gave him a look of good natured exasperation. The reporters tittered. "I just didn't know who I was touching for a minute, though the lady in question sure straightened me out on that in a hurry." He chuckled self-deprecatingly, as Heather gently but pointedly removed his hand, giving her head a good-natured little shake. The reporters guffawed. I did it, he told himself. They bought it!

I don't believe this, thought Sam Donaldson disgustedly, then stood abruptly once again, his cobra-like head exuding menace, hood distended for the strike. "Wait a *minute*, Mr. President, are you also saying you thought that you were trying to *punch* your wife that night?" he practically shouted.

Carruthers was thrown badly off balance by the question, and the sudden change in demeanor he saw in the faces of the reporters. He tried to recover with a display of humor. "What, me mistake Heather for *that* girl? I said I was tired, not blind drunk!"

There was a stony silence, during which nobody smiled, tittered, giggled, or laughed. "I mean, once I got a good look at her, there was, uh, no confusion, and, ah, uhh," he finished in a small voice, suddenly realizing that he was digging himself in deeper. "Ah, that'll be all, no more questions, this is, umm, old news, the ah, American people want to move on, I have to get back to work for the American people," he trailed off, turning hastily to leave. He looked into his wife's face, which had gone white with fury.

And at that moment, Heather Carruthers, who had endured the ongoing humiliation of hundreds of extramarital dalliances from her husband, the dozens of public accusations from sexually assaulted, abused, discarded, and exploited women of all ages, and his thousands of broken promises, simply went over the edge. "You piece of shit!" she screamed. "You were nothing without me! *NOTHING!*" And with that, she snatched the mike off the podium and began beating it against his skull, the sound cracking loudly through every live TV speaker in the land. He fell to the ground, trying to protect himself with his hands, and squealed with pain and terror as the heavy stainless steel microphone thudded against his head, face, chest, and shoulders.

Finally he rolled over into a fetal position, covering his head and screaming. "Stop it, Heather, you're gonna put Garmin in the White House, don't do this, not Garmin and his dildo. *STOP IT!*" he shrieked.

The reporters and everybody else present sat transfixed with shock and horror as Heather Carruthers continued to flail away with the microphone, each blow echoing throughout the world through the still-functioning mike. Finally, the president's Secret Service detail recovered sufficiently to rush to Carruthers' aid and pull the berserk Heather off of him. He continued to lay curled up for long moments after she'd been dragged away, whimpering. There was a total silence from the gathered reporters, who sat stunned at the incredible display of marital violence. The only sound was Carruthers' gasping voice. "No, not that, not Garmin! I bet he's playing with his dildo right now! He can't be president, he can't," he

David White

whimpered. His gasping and sobbing words went out clearly to 36,844,632 households throughout America and over eighty-five million more world-wide. Mercifully, a member of the White House staff hurriedly walked up to the still-fetal Carruthers and unplugged the mike. Ernie Schaaf took the podium and announced, "Ah, just a little spat, folks, nothing to be alarmed about, happens all the time with people everywhere." He tried to smile, but managed only a grim rictus, showing large, yellow, and rather crooked teeth.

"Hey, Ernie," shouted a reporter from the *Washington Times*, "what's this dildo thing in connection with the Vice-President?"

"Ah, no comment," said Ernie, "I'm not sure what that's all about. I'm not even sure if that's what the president was saying."

Garmin would, in due course, be called upon to explain the reference to the dildo, which he attempted to do by rather incoherently describing his proposed Diversified Industrial Liaison and Development Office. The public and press had, unfortunately, been cynically conditioned by Bob Carruthers' outlandish lies and prevarications. Alas, nobody bought Garmin's explanation of the alleged acronym, except Ambassador Li, who, like the innocent and hapless Nate Garmin himself, had no idea what a dildo was. The more general reaction, from the most extreme left to the most rabid right, was to the effect that, "I wonder how long it took that dumb shit to come up with that one," accompanied with a snort of derision. Poor Nate Garmin, simple and innocent *naif* that he was, was merely assumed to be just one more kinky deviate within the Carruthers administration.

Perhaps the most nonplussed group of all regarding the bizarre episode were the citizens of Chad, at least those lucky enough to possess TV sets. They were able to watch the president of the United States being beaten nearly senseless by his wife, while US Navy jets roared over their heads to blow an empty and defunct pre-fab housing plant to smithereens.

Two thousand miles away from Carruthers' Washington press conference, Zack, Suzy, Hazel, and Hugh sat watching in disbelief. Finally, Zack asked, "What's this thing about a dildo?"

"What's a dildo?" asked Suzy.

"Ah, I'll explain it sometime, honey," said Zack. "You shouldn't be in need of one for a few years." This brought forth snorts and guffaws from Hazel and Hugh.

374

"Boy, you weren't kidding about her being bad news, Zack," said Hugh, looking at Suzy wonderingly. "She's bringin' down the president and his whole administration."

"I didn't do anything wrong," said Suzy a little uncertainly. "This whole thing was forced on Zack and me. I didn't want to bring down anybody." She glanced out the window. "I wonder what what's going to happen to Sid and Vera and Sherry, and all the people at the home company. Nothing like this ever happens in China without someone being blamed and having to pay."

"I gotta think that the payments are gonna come from the people at the top, though, honey, since all these problems really started with them. It wasn't anybody's fault here that the cars were so bad. They were just trying to set up an organization to sell and service 'em. Nobody here even knew how bad the situation was."

And in fact the whole debacle eventually played out in China pretty much as a potentially brilliant diplomatic initiative gone awry, due to circumstances that really could not have been foreseen, though the general manager and president of the Long March People's Cooperative Automotive Manufacturing Company, Lin Cho Hsin, was in a certain amount of hot water for his failure to properly develop an adequate export version of the Red Whippet before beginning to the ship the cars. Lin pointed out, however, that he had been assured that the standards had been waived through the efforts of the Chinese diplomatic mission to the United States, and that he was merely seizing upon what appeared to be a heaven sent opportunity. The whole disaster was finally attributed, in the main, to the treachery of the Carruthers administration and its hireling, the arch-fascist wrecker, Sidney Burnside, who would thereafter have a file maintained on his whereabouts and activities by the Chinese intelligence services.

Zhu was brought back to China by Lin, along with his wife, in order to support the story of their alert but belated recognition of Burnside's perfidy, whose sabotage was directly attributed to Carruthers and his henchpersons, among whom Penny Twombly and Nate Garmin were counted. Finally, Ambassador Li supported the view that they had all been doublecrossed by the Carruthers administration, which had gone back on its word to grant the Chinese certain very reasonable allowances in getting started in the US market. He continued to insist, however, that the president be held to his promise of having USDA buy a huge quantity of swine products, plus the ten million pounds of dead eels. Li felt that these initiatives were among his greatest personal triumphs and did not wish to see them abandoned.

The attempted narcotics plant in the Johnson residence and Suzy's subsequent arrest and questioning of the rest of Red Tiger's employees were vaguely explained away as an "improper DEA operation, unfortunately sanctioned by several Los Angeles area DEA officials who clearly exceeded their authority." Both Win Faulkner's and Jack Landry's resignations were "regretfully" accepted. Landry would eventually hang out a shingle in Valdosta, Georgia, advertising himself as a personal injury lawyer, while Faulkner would accept a GS-18 make-work position in the Justice Department.

Jake Dougherty's demands that his bank's draft payments be returned forthwith fell on deaf ears. Red Tiger Motors had no assets, aside from its payroll account, which was closed out by the home company the day of the president's news conference, before, unfortunately, Burnside was able to draw their final paychecks on it. Dougherty spent nearly an hour sitting on the curb in front of his showroom, staring morosely out over the new car storage lot. They fucked me, he told himself. They fucked me and got away with it again. It wasn't that Dougherty couldn't afford to take the nearly $100,000 hit. It was the idea that a couple of lying factory guys had stuck it to him again. He began sobbing softly.

Abruptly, however, Jake Dougherty, ever the alert entrepreneurial auto dealer, looked up over the new car lot. That's it! he told himself. Collectors' items! That's what they are! I can get a waiver to sell the little shitboxes as off-road vehicles, for display and off-road use only! Hell, these things are no more ridiculous than a Bricklin or DeLorean. Own a part of history! His mind was racing with the possibilities. He wondered briefly if he should call the Franklin Mint and offer them the whole inventory. Call it the East Meets West One World International Brotherhood Commemorative Edition. And there will only be twenty-four produced! Tender your deposit of only $2,495.00 today to assure your own special place in history. Balance of $7,495 due on delivery!

Just as quickly he dismissed the idea of enlisting the Franklin Mint in the scheme. What the hell, I can do this myself. Who needs those guys? Hot damn, this is gonna be great!

A continent away, at the exact moment that Big Jake Dougherty was forming his plans to capitalize on the Red Whippet disaster, Supreme

Court Justice William Geoffrey Parkham, sitting wearily in his chambers, gazed loathingly at the brief on his desk. He picked it up and scanned the document, which argued that the plaintiff, one Gerald J. Gillway, age sixty-one, had been illegally denied employment as a running back for the Miami Dolphins (a life-long ambition, the brief noted), because he was a paraplegic, having broken his back in the structural collapse of one of the rental properties he owned. The brief specified that under the terms of The Americans With Disabilities Act, the Dolphins were required to assign as many players as necessary to carry Gillway during offensive play.

Parkham tossed the brief back onto his desk, then slowly took off his reading glasses and wiped them on a handkerchief. He shook his head sadly. I can't take any more of this, he muttered to himself. He pulled over a yellow legal pad, and in his precise hand began drafting his letter of resignation.

* * *

It took a few days for the fallout from the bizarre and sensational news conference, featuring Heather Carruthers' first round TKO of her husband, to truly begin settling. As Ambassador Li had once speculated that he might, President Carruthers actually went on Oprah Winfrey to blubber that upon finishing his term, "I'm going to devote my life fully to God and my family," and to "beg the American people for their forgiveness." The latter seemed to be at least partially granted, since after the broadcast the president's job approval rating jumped from thirteen to a more respectable thirty-six percent.

Despite widespread cries for immediate impeachment proceedings, more sober heads prevailed. Not even Carruthers' most partisan and vitriolic enemies within the Congress could stomach the idea, however politically irresistible it at first seemed, of the so-called leader of the Free World being an acknowledged nitwit who was getting it on with a female sex toy. Watching the whole affair play out, Carruthers was, one again, forced to acknowledge that "she pulled my nuts out of the fire on this one, no doubt about it," grudgingly admiring her political savvy in insisting on Nate Garmin as his running mate.

And so when Justice Parkham's surprise retirement was announced, Carruthers' wasted no time in nominating Heather as his successor. A few opposition senators mounted a timorous and feeble objection, pointing out that Heather, contrary to her public persona as "the greatest lawyer in the United States," in fact had been involved in only two minor litigations in her entire career, both of which were fat, juicy, slow-pitch softballs tossed her way by the firm's partners, and both of which she botched. So despite nationwide gasps of disbelief over the nomination, her appointment would sail through the Congress by a comfortable margin, supported entirely by polls clearly demonstrating that mainstream women voters overwhelmingly found her a cruelly abused and sympathetic figure, while feminists approved strongly of the way she beat the snot out of her "lying, cheating, exploitive husband" on world-wide television.

As for the former employees of Red Tiger Motor Company, Sid Burnside, to his pleasant surprise and considerable relief, found himself a job as general manager of a huge used car mega-store in Los Angeles. And also, to his even more pleasant surprise and eternal bafflement, Vera Hawkins insisted on moving in with him. Burnside would never understand that his appeal to Vera was simply that he was practically the only straight male of any age who treated her nicely without the sole motivation of getting into her superbly filled pants.

Sherry Maxwell went back to the Florida Keys only long enough to pack his few belongings, then returned to southern California, where he took the civil service exam and finally secured a position for himself as a drug and alcohol counselor. This he managed largely on the strength of the civil service points he got for his ten percent disabled veteran status, acquired in 1963, when he had fallen out the back of an Army deuce and a half and badly broken his arm while returning to Fort Campbell, Kentucky in a drunken stupor. "I *been* there, I know what it's like," Sherry became fond of pointing out to both his supervisors and his charges, careful to avoid mentioning that he was, indeed, *still* there.

And finally, as for the heroine and hero of our story, if this grim tale could truly be said to have any, Suzy and Zack would move to Kansas, to be close to his family and to provide what they quite correctly assumed to be a healthy environment for their children. Within the year Suzy would give birth to a spectacularly beautiful pair of little girls, who immediately became the epicenter of not only their lives, but those of Edith and Paul Johnson as well.

Zack would continue successfully with his airline career, while Suzy eventually would establish a perpetually backlogged personal Chinese language tutoring service, which offered an eight week total immersion course of instruction to mainly West Coast corporate clients, at $25,000 a pop.

And at last, as Melanie Samuels had confidently predicted, the Johnsons would quickly fade into obscurity, proving beyond doubt, as they'd hoped, that they were indeed pretty boring people.

kak•is•toc•ra•cy (kak′i stok′rə sē),   *n., pl.*   **-cies.**
government by the worst men in the state.   [< Gk
kákisto(s), superl. of *kakós* bad + -CRACY] **—ka•kis•to•**
crat•i•cal (ke kis′tə krat′i kəl), *adj.*

The New Oxford Dictionary